SPACE IN LANGUAGE AND COGNITION
Explorations in Cognitive Diversity

Languages differ in how they describe space, and such differences between languages can be used to explore the relation between language and thought. This book shows that even in a core cognitive domain, such as spatial thinking, language influences how people think, memorize and reason about spatial relations and directions. After outlining a typology of spatial coordinate systems in language and cognition, it is shown that not all languages use all types, and that non-linguistic cognition mirrors the systems available in the local language. The book reports on collaborative, interdisciplinary research, involving anthropologists, linguists and psychologists, conducted in many languages and cultures around the world, which establishes this robust correlation. The overall results suggest that most current thinking in the cognitive sciences underestimates the transformative power of language on thinking. The book will appeal to all researchers interested in the relation of language to other areas of cognition – linguists, psychologists, anthropologists, philosophers – and especially to students of spacial cognition.

STEPHEN C. LEVINSON is Director of the Max Planck Institute for Psycholinguistics and Professor of Comparative Linguistics at the University of Nijmegen. His publications include *Pragmatics* (Cambridge, 1983), *Politeness* (co-author, Cambridge, 1987), *Rethinking linguistic relativity* (co-editor, Cambridge, 1996), *Language acquisition and conceptual development* (co-editor, Cambridge, 2001), and *Presumptive meanings* (2001).

Language, culture and cognition

Editor
STEPHEN C. LEVINSON
Max Planck Institute for Psycholinguistics, Nijmegen

This new series looks at the role of language in human cognition – language in both its universal, psychological aspects and its variable, cultural aspects. Studies will focus on the relation between semantic and conceptual categories and processes, especially as these are illuminated by cross-linguistic and cross-cultural studies, the study of language acquisition and conceptual development, and the study of the relation of speech production and comprehension to other kinds of behaviour in cultural context. Books come principally, though not exclusively, from research associated with the Max Planck Institute for Psycholinguistics in Nijmegen, and in particular the Language and Cognition Group.

1 Jan Nuyts and Eric Pederson (eds.) *Language and Conceptualization*
2 David McNeill (ed.) *Language and Gesture*
3 Melissa Bowerman and Stephen C. Levinson (eds.) *Language Acquisition and Conceptual Development*
4 Gunter Senft (ed.) *Systems of Nominal Classification*
5 Stephen C. Levinson *Space in Language and Cognition*

SPACE IN LANGUAGE AND COGNITION

Explorations in Cognitive Diversity

STEPHEN C. LEVINSON

Max Planck Institute for Psycholinguistics

CAMBRIDGE
UNIVERSITY PRESS

PUBLISHED BY THE PRESS SYNDICATE OF THE UNIVERSITY OF CAMBRIDGE
The Pitt Building, Trumpington Street, Cambridge CB2 1RP, United Kingdom

CAMBRIDGE UNIVERSITY PRESS
The Edinburgh Building, Cambridge, CB2 2RU, UK
40 West 20th Street, New York, NY 10011-4211, USA
477 Williamstown Road, Port Melbourne, VIC 3207, Australia
Ruiz de Alarcón 13, 28014 Madrid, Spain
Dock House, The Waterfront, Cape Town 8001, South Africa

http://www.cambridge.org

© Stephen C. Levinson 2003

First published 2003

Printed in the United Kingdom at the University Press, Cambridge

Typeface Baskerville No 2. 11/12.5 pt   *System* LATEX 2_ε [TB]

A catalogue record for this book is available from the British Library

Library of Congress Cataloguing in Publication data
Levinson, Stephen C.
Space in language and cognition: explorations in cognitive diversity / Stephen C.
Levinson (Max Planck Institute for Psycholinguistics).
p.   cm. – (Language, culture and cognition; 5)
Includes bibliographical references and index.
ISBN 0 521 81262 3 (hb) – ISBN 0 521 01196 5 (pb)
1. Space and time in language.   2. Psycholinguistics.   3. Cognition.   I. Max Planck
Institut für Psycholinguistik (Nijmegen, Netherlands)   II. Title.   III. Series.
P37.5.S65 L48   2002   401′.9 – dc21   2002067212

ISBN 0 521 81262 3 hardback
ISBN 0 521 01196 5 paperback

For CARG and the Gang of Five

Contents

Figures

xi

Tables

Preface

This book is about the relation between language and spatial cognition. Spatial cognition is at the heart of our thinking. It has long been noted that spatial thinking provides us with analogies and tools for understanding other domains, as shown by the efficacy of diagrams, the pervasive spatial metaphors of everyday language, the evocativeness of place in memory, and the special role that geometry, astronomy and cartography have played in the development of science and technology. Spatial cognition probably plays this central role because it seems to be the evolutionarily earliest domain of systematic cross-modal cognition: any animal needs to relate what its eyes, ears and limbs tell it about the immediate structure of the world around it – foraging, avoiding predators and finding home-base require this. Yet many species operate with restricted abilities to pool this information freely, and human higher-level cognition and consciousness may have evolutionary origins in a special, freer exchange of information across all the modalities that contribute to spatial knowledge and awareness.

This book is especially concerned with just one aspect of spatial cognition, namely **frames of reference** as expressed in spatial language and everyday thinking. Consider a sentence like: *The cat is behind the truck.* It is ambiguous (or general) over two kinds of scenes: one in which the cat is at the truck's rear-end, and another in which it is by one side of the truck, but the truck is between the speaker and the cat. In the first interpretation, *behind* is taken to mean at the intrinsic facet (of the truck) that we would call a *back*, and in the other interpretation, it is the speaker's location that determines what is going to count as *behind*. These are different frames of reference (sometimes called the 'intrinsic' and the 'deictic') – based on the truck and the speaker respectively – and this book is about this kind of difference in the way in which we can construe spatial relations. This kind of distinction is by no means a shallow linguistic difference, a semantic nuance as it were. Consider the following extraordinary symptoms of damage to the right parietal area of the cortex, damage which is well known to produce in some patients a 'neglect' of the left visual field. Bisiach and Luzzatti (1978) asked a group of such patients to imagine the cathedral square in their native city, Milan: when told to imagine they were standing on the cathedral steps they could describe the right side of the square but not the left, but when told to imagine standing at the other end of the square facing the cathedral, they could now describe the other side (again to their right), but not the prior one. Clearly, the patients had a complete mental model of the square independent of their imagined position in it (otherwise they could not have described both sides), but the projection as it were of a mental image from a particular vantage point is always obscured for them on the left side. The complete memory of the square is said to be in an *allocentric* frame of reference, while the visual imagery is in an *egocentric* frame of reference, and the two clearly are processed in different areas of the brain (most likely the hippocampus and the right parietal respectively). Thus spatial representation is a complex, multi-layered phenomenon, and distinct frames of reference implicate distinct mental systems.

This book has two main goals. First, it should serve as an introduction to an important subject – spatial coordinate systems in language and cognition – which has not generally been treated in a unified way, but rather conceptualized differently in different disciplines. All of the different senses, vision, audition, touch and smell, generate spatial representations, and in many ways these seem necessarily divergent. But since we can talk about what we see, or image a description, some convergence must be possible, but how much? Secondly, the book uses this particular domain of spatial coordinates to ask searching questions about the general nature of the relation between language and thought, or linguistic coding and non-linguistic categories. For it turns out that there are very substantial differences between languages in the semantic parameters utilized in spatial description, and that makes it natural to ask how these parameters correlate with non-linguistic cognition. The major discovery that is documented in the book is that these linguistic differences correlate with, and seem to induce, major differences in spatial cognition across human groups. This is an unexpected finding, and it has major implications for how we should think about the language–cognition interface.

These two lines of enquiry converge in general questions about what may, somewhat grandiloquently, be described as the 'architecture of the mind'. Some real insight into this structure can be derived from cross-linguistic and cross-cultural observations. An analogy may be telling: just as we may be able to trace the course of an underground river system by dumping dye into a river before it goes underground, so by focussing on language-specific semantic parameters and seeing where they turn up in 'inner space' – the conceptual system – we can perhaps discover something about our inner languages or representations and how they connect to one another.

In this book, I have followed a construal and typology of systems that has emerged out of the work of the Language and Cognition (previously Cognitive Anthropology Research) Group at the Max Planck Institute for Psycholinguistics, work with many colleagues that is based on in-depth field analysis of over forty, mostly unwritten languages spoken in small-scale, traditional societies. This we feel gives us a much better grip on human diversity in spatial language and cognition than has hitherto been available. Most of the literature on spatial language is predominantly based on familiar European languages, and the corresponding psychology and neurophysiology on that of Western subjects. Theories and typologies that have come from this narrower base often diverge from the picture I present here – even though I have of course drawn on all this scholarly background (see especially Miller and Johnson-Laird 1976, Herskovits 1986, Svorou 1994, Talmy 1983, 2000, Vandeloise 1991).

What will emerge from the studies that are reviewed in this book are a number of major surprises, raising fundamental questions about the nature of human spatial cognition. The surprises include:

Different human groups use different spatial frameworks, often with distinctive sets of coordinate systems in both language and cognition.

The diversity of frame-of-reference systems can be organized in a universal typology that distinguishes just three major types, from which languages and cultures draw a subset.

There are robust correlations between frames of reference used in language and frames of reference used in non-linguistic memory and reasoning, suggesting a major 'Whorfian' effect of language on cognition.

Consonant with selected frames of reference, different human groups seem to use different types of 'mental map', with consequent differences in many aspects of behaviour, communication and culture.

These discoveries pose a number of far-reaching questions: Why should human cognition in this central area be so variable, and apparently so much under linguistic and cultural control? How could such a central area of cognition – which is in many species indubitably hard-wired – come to be so much a matter of cultural 'software' in our own species? The answer suggested is that this constitutes central evidence for a co-evolutionary perspective on human cognition, wherein culture and the biological foundations for cognition have co-evolved and mutually adapted.

Acknowledgements

What I know about spatial language and cognition I have acquired in collaboration with many scholars, particularly those who have worked in or been attached to the Max Planck Institute for Psycholinguistics. Working with these scholars on this subject has been the best intellectual adventure of my academic life. I cannot list them all here, but some I must. First, Pim Levelt and Wolfgang Klein had run a project on spatial and temporal reference at the Institute for years before I arrived in 1991, and their path-breaking conceptual work (see, e.g., Levelt 1984, 1996, Jarvella and Klein 1982) made our later work possible. Other senior scholars at the Institute, including especially Melissa Bowerman, have been continuous guides.

The work reported on here – especially in Chapter 5, but throughout this book as well – was undertaken in a collaborative way with many other scholars. From 1991, there worked in my research group the following scholars, each of whom contributed in many ways to both the data and theory here described, as often reflected in reference to their own work: Martha Alibali, Felix Ameka, E. Annamalai, Giovanni Bennardo, Balthasar Bickel, Jürgen Bohnemeyer, John Bowden, Penelope Brown, Eve Danziger, Sue Duncan, Michael Dunn, James Essegbey, Nick Evans, Deborah Hill, Bill Foley, Suzanne Gaskins, Marianne Gullberg, Raquel Guirardello, Daniel Haun, John Haviland, Ingjerd Hoëm, Elizabeth Keating, Adam Kendon, Anna Keusen, Sotaro Kita, Kyoko Inoue, Hedda Lausberg, Lourdes de León, Paulette Levy, Kristine Jensen de Lopez, John Lucy, Bill McGregor, Sergio Meira, Laszlo Nagy, David Nash, Sabine Neumann, Asli Özyürek, Eric Pederson, Björn Rasch, Bernadette Schmitt, Eva Schultze-Berndt, Annie Senghas, Gunter Senft, Chris Sinha, Jane Simpson, Aaron Sonnenschein, Miriam van Staden, Sabine Stoll, Christel Stolz, Jürg Wassmann, Thomas Widlok, David Wilkins, Roberto Zavala. This book owes a fundamental debt to all of them – they have contributed data and ideas in abundance to the programme on which this book reports. However, this book is my particular take or overview of the collective results, and they will not necessarily agree with every detail of theory, data or analysis.

I should single out a few colleagues who were especially engaged in the space project, and have played a crucial role in thrashing out the theoretical framework and methods in many a brain-storming session: Balthasar Bickel, Penelope Brown, Melissa Bowerman, Eve Danziger, Suzanne Gaskins, John Haviland, Sotaro Kita, Lourdes de León, John Lucy, Eric Pederson, Bernadette Schmitt, Gunter Senft, Thomas Widlok, David Wilkins. In this case, because they care passionately, they will each disagree intensely with some of my analyses below – but, OK folks, your turn! Also crucial at various points was advice from Pierre Dasen, Paul Kay, Wolfgang Klein, Ewald Lang, Pim Levelt, David McNeill and Dan Slobin. I should mention a special debt to Laszlo Nagy, who crunched the statistical data in Chapter 5 on my behalf, and helped draft a paper that never appeared (on which the chapter is based), because it was dependent on another that suffered a similar fate. In addition, our research group has been blessed by the most extraordinarily capable PhD students, who have contributed to the space project over the years, and whose names are mentioned above. I also owe thanks to many students and assistants who have helped in the preparation of field kits, experiments, field equipment, diagrams, drawings and analyses of data – especially Gertie de Groen and Bernadette Schmitt.

There is another fundamental kind of debt that I owe, this time to the people of OolappaaLaiyam in Tamilnadu, the people of Hopevale (in far north Queensland), the people of Majosik' (Tenejapa, Chiapas, Mexico), and the people of Rossel Island (Milne Bay Province, Papua New Guinea). These are the people who really opened my eyes to the diversity of human language and cognition. I would like to thank particularly those who patiently worked alongside me and tried to teach me the ways of their communities: O.K. Sundurum, Roger Hart, the late Tulo Gordo and the late Jack Bambi, Antun Gusman Osil, Xun Gusman Chijk', Isidore Yidika. They have all helped me, an outsider helpless in their complex social and physical environments, at some risk to their own local standing. They helped me, I think, because they could sense they had something important to tell the wider world. Some reward perhaps is that it will be their voices that, preserved in the Max Planck archives, will talk to their descendants at a time when they participate fully in the world of scientific knowledge.

Anyone who has done fieldwork beyond the end of the normal lines of communication will know only too well the logistic, political, diplomatic and emotional travails that are entailed. I have been fortunate to have been helped by many colleagues and local authorities, and to have shared some of the burdens with my wife, Penelope Brown, whose expertise on Tzeltal is reflected in many of the pages below.

For much help in the preparation of a complex manuscript, I am grateful as ever to my indefatigable secretary and assistant, Edith Sjoerdsma. A number of scholars read the manuscript and gave me written comments – my thanks to Jürgen Bohnemeyer, Penny Brown, Nick Enfield, Pim Levelt, Gunter Senft and two anonymous referees. Finally, I have drawn on a number of articles that I have published earlier, and I am grateful to the American Anthropology Association, Cambridge University Press, MIT Press and Annual Reviews Inc., for permission to reuse material and republish various paragraphs, as indicated in footnotes.

COMPANION BOOKS

There are two other books in this series that have emerged from the same large collaborative project. One of these, *Grammars of space* (ed. Levinson and Wilkins), provides a great deal more information about linguistic description in a number of the crucial languages under discussion, written by experts in each of the languages and their cultural settings. That book also gives a good idea of the linguistic methods employed for the classification of languages according to the typology of frames of reference. A second book, *Tilted worlds* (Brown and Levinson), provides an in-depth look at one cultural group where absolute and intrinsic frames of reference are dominant. Here we were able to study in depth all aspects of the language and cognition, including language acquisition and gesture, in a Highland Mayan community. This last book will give the reader a sense of the rich texture that is inevitably lost in a wide survey of the kind represented by this book.

CHAPTER I

The intellectual background: two millennia of Western ideas about spatial thinking

Spatial thinking is crucial to almost every aspect of our lives. We consult our spatial memories constantly as we find our way across town, give route directions, search for lost keys, try to find a passage in a book, grope our way to the bathroom in the night, and so on. The intricacy and importance of all this becomes apparent when it goes wrong. I recently saw a man reduced to near insanity because he had 'lost' his car in a huge airport parking lot (really, of course, he had lost himself). The Balinese, whose system of spatial description requires compass-like orientation, consider loss of cardinal orientation a sign of madness ('Not to know "where north is" is to be crazy', Geertz 1972: 446, cited in Wassmann and Dasen 1998: 693). The neuroscience literature is replete with exotic syndromes, where lesions in specific areas of the brain induce specific spatial inabilities, as in the following description of a patient with topographical amnesia:

> Whenever he left his room in the hospital, he had trouble finding his way back, because at any chosen point of the route he did not know whether to go right, left, downstairs or upstairs... when he eventually arrived in front of his own room, he did not recognize it unless he chanced to see some distinguishing feature, such as the black beard of his roommate...   (de Renzi 1982: 213)

Spatial competence involves many different abilities, from shape recognition to a sense of where the parts of our body are with respect to one another, from navigation to control of the arm in reaching for something, and so on. The evidence from human brain lesions and from animal studies is that these abilities are based on a myriad of distinct neurophysiological systems, all of which converge to give us a coherent subjective sense of space.[1] Our conscious apprehension of space can also be dissected analytically into component parts – for example, the characteristic shapes of objects, their spatial relation to our bodies as we point to them, the sense of where we are with respect to our larger surroundings, and so forth. No single book could do justice to all we now know about this fundamental domain of human experience.

This book takes up just one strand of this complex cloth, albeit a subject that has a central importance for spatial abilities, namely the coordinate systems that underlie spatial memory and classification. For example, when I think that I must have left my glasses in front of the TV, I am using a different kind of coordinate system than when I think I must have lost my keys in the grass to the left of the tree over there. The first makes crucial use of the sidedness of objects like television sets, while the second makes essential use of my bodily coordinates. Understanding the difference between such ways of specifying where things are is one of the central tasks of this book. Another major aim is understanding the similarity and difference between *thinking* 'I must have lost my keys in the grass to the left of that tree' and *saying* it. Put that way, it seems that the thought and the sentence meaning must be identical. But for all sorts of reasons that cannot be right – there is a metric precision and visual detail in our thoughts that is not present in language. In addition, and here is a startling fact, in many languages there is no way to express *that* specific thought at all! For many languages do not provide the linguistic means to express an egocentric coordinate system of the sort implied by the English expression *left of*. Speakers of languages without such a coordinate system must either have different thoughts, or thinking and language must be dissociated and thus potentially work on different lines. It turns out – and much of this book is devoted to showing this – that in fact language and thought closely parallel one another, and thus linguistic diversity is reflected in cognitive diversity. Cross-linguistic variation therefore provides us with new empirical insights into old philosophical conundrums about the relationship between language and thought.

Why is this rather specific theme – coordinate systems or frames of reference in language and thought – of general interest? First, it concerns the very heart of complex spatial thinking. There are simple spatial notions, like the proposition that object X is at named place Y, which do not directly invoke anything as complex as a coordinate system. But as soon as object X and landmark Y are substantially separated in space, it becomes important to think about X as *in some specific direction* from Y – some kind of angular specification becomes relevant, and a coordinate system is necessary to provide that.[2] Coordinate systems or frames of reference thus play a crucial role in many kinds of human thought and activity, from navigation to the design of our cultural environment, from moving our eyes or limbs to scientific models of the universe. A better understanding of naïve spatial thought – the kind reflected in everyday language or action – can contribute fundamentally to all the sciences concerned with our use of space, from archaeology or geography to neuroscience.

A second major source of interest is that there are significant cross-linguistic differences in this domain. Much of this book revolves around the difference between languages with predominant 'relative' frames of reference, versus those with predominant 'absolute' frames of reference. The first is familiar enough – it is the kind involved in the earlier-mentioned reading of *The cat is behind the truck* as 'The truck is between the speaker and the cat' (this is often, erroneously, called the 'deictic' frame of reference). The second is less familiar – on the horizontal plane it can be illustrated with a sentence of the form *The cat is north of the truck*. Interestingly, there are languages where this is the main or only form of coordinate system in spatial language. Since such systems are exotic, examples are described in some detail in the chapters below. This opposition between language types turns out to have quite deep cognitive consequences for users of the two types of language. This is shown below in a series of experiments, and in observational studies of wayfinding and gesturing. The end result is a clear and quite surprising finding: the choice of a predominant frame of reference in language correlates with, and probably determines, many other aspects of cognition, from memory, to inference, to navigation, to gesture and beyond.

Some of the reasons why this finding is so unexpected lie in a web of preconceptions about the nature of naïve human spatial conception which has been woven into two millennia of Western thinking. Many of these preconceptions have arisen in the history of Western philosophy, from which many of our scientific concepts of space have been borrowed. Later some of these speculations passed into the new discipline of psychology, and, more recently, into the wider circle of the cognitive sciences. This chapter sketches just a little of this background, focussing on concepts important for appreciating the findings described later in the book – naturally it cannot pretend to do justice to a domain as important to the history of physics as it is to psychology. Let us first begin with a glimpse of the new facts that will prove problematic for the preconceptions about naïve human spatial conception that have such a long ancestry in our intellectual tradition.

This book focusses on variation in spatial language and cognition that our long Western tradition about human spatial thinking has led some researchers to think unlikely or impossible. The following anecdotes may help to convey the sense of surprise. Scientific research is not about anecdotes, but small, wayward observations can often be where it all starts. Some, often chance, experience has to alert the researcher that there is something wrong with the existing paradigms. This book is an attempt to at least shift the paradigm of the study of human spatial thinking a little, and although many scholars have contributed to this new perspective, here are some of the small experiences that drove home to me personally the simple message that human spatial cognition is not fixed, but culturally variable:

1. Old Tulo, Guugu Yimithirr poet and painter, whom I am trying to film telling a traditional myth in Cape York, Australia, tells me to stop and look out for that big army ant just north of my foot.

2. Slus, a Mayan speaker of the language Tzeltal, says to her husband, facing an unfamiliar contraption: 'Is the hot water in the uphill tap?' It is night, and we have just arrived at an alien hotel in a distant, unfamiliar city out of the hills. What does she mean? She means, it turns out, 'Is the hot water in the tap that would lie in the uphill (southerly) direction if I were at home?'

3. Roger, another Guugu Yimithirr speaker (and last speaker of Barrow Point language), tells me that I am wrong – in a store 45 km away there are indeed frozen fish, and it's here, 'on this side' he says, gesturing to his right with two flicks of the hand. What does he mean – not it turns out what I thought, namely that standing at the entrance to the store, it would be to my right. No, what he means is that it would be to my left. So how to explain the gesture? He gestured north-east, and he expected me to remember that, and look in the north-east corner of the store. This makes me realize just how much information I am missing each time he says anything.

4. Xpet, a Tzeltal-speaking teenager, is looking at two photos that are identical except that they depict mirror-image arrangements. My wife Penny has put them in her hands, because Xpet has failed to distinguish them in a communication task, and Penny is asking her what the difference is between the two photos. Xpet stares, looking first at the

one, then the other. Her brow furrows. 'They're the same' she says, adding 'but this one has a dirty finger-print on it'. Nothing can shake her out of the apparent conviction that they are two tokens of the same photo.

5. We've been searching for ancient cave paintings deep in the bush, following instructions from various old hands. Dan, a Guugu Yimithirr speaker, is thrilled to find them after a day-long bush trip through dense and difficult forest. We are sitting in the cave entrance, and disoriented myself, I ask him to point back to base. He does so without hesitation, right through the hillside we are sitting on. I check with an accurate prismatic compass, and ask him for other locations. Checking later on maps, it turns out that he is spot on – absolutely dead accurate, as far as my compass can discriminate.

6. Jack Bambi, Guugu Yimithirr master story-teller, talking about a man who used to live nearby points directly at himself – no, there's no connection to himself, he's pointing south-east, to where the man used to live, through his body as if it was invisible. Years later, I have the same immediate misinterpretations looking at Tzeltal speakers, and realize this is the same phenomenon: in some striking way, the ego has been reduced to an abstract point in space.

7. I film this same Jack Bambi telling the story about how he was shipwrecked and swam miles to shore through the sharks. Watching my film, John Haviland realizes that he filmed Jack telling the same story two years before, and he goes and compares the films frame by frame. Despite the fact that Jack is facing west on the first telling and north on the second, the linguistic and gestural details of how the boat turned over, who jumped out where, where the big shark was and so on, match exactly in cardinal directions, not egocentric ones – the events are directionally anchored in all their detail in Jack's memory.[3]

By the time this book comes to an end, I promise some scientific evidence that shows that these anecdotes are symptoms of systematic differences between human groups, differences that specialists in spatial language and cognition never thought could exist. But the reason why we did not expect them needs a little exposition, because they lie deep in the history of the field. This chapter tries to provide a sketch of this background, concentrating on frames of reference in the history of ideas and in recent theory in the cognitive sciences.

1.2.1 Place and space, absolute and relative, in Western philosophy

I do not define time, space, place and motion, as being well known to all.
                                  Isaac Newton (in the Scholium to the *Principia*, 1687)

Many commentators have pointed out how slowly and laboriously an abstract notion of space was evolved in Western thought. It is worth reviewing some of this history, because the developing ideas have been built on naïve concepts, often enshrined in language. Early Greek thought was preoccupied with discussions about whether space should be thought of materially (as in the school of Parmenides and Melissus) or as a void (as argued by the Epicurean atomists) – the one school arguing that it was impossible for nothing to have extent, and the other that, however big the extent of space was, it was always possible to throw a javelin beyond it, requiring an empty infinity (Jammer 1954: Chapter 1, Sorabji 1988: Chapter 8). Plato held a material view of space (viewing air as a substance with geometrical properties), so allowing a general identification of tridimensionality and matter that was to play a central role in medieval thought, and indeed in Descartes' ideas (Sorabji 1988: 38, Casey 1997: Chapter 7). (This view has played some role in recent linguistic theorizing about the nature of naïve spatial thought, where it has been supposed that dimensional expressions in language might form the heart of spatial cognition – see Lang 1989, Bierwisch and Lang 1989).

A material view of place was easily ridiculed by Zeno – if everything is in a place, and place is something, place itself is in something, but what? Aristotle's solution was to view place, not as the displacement volume of, e.g., air by a body, but as the adjacent or inner boundary of the matter containing the object. Aristotle therefore viewed space as a nested series of places, up to the outer sphere containing the universe. This reduction of space to place, and the denial of empty space or the possibility of a vacuum, sets Aristotle outside the slow but triumphant emancipation of a space concept in line with the development of physics. But the emphasis on place remains close to naïve reasoning – most languages probably have locutions for 'place' (i.e. the location where things are or belong), but few have expressions for 'space'.[4] Aristotle tried to stay close to the phenomenology, and he came to worry about what we today call 'frames of reference'. First, if a boat is moored in a flowing river, is the place always changing, since the containing fluid is? If we take the water as reference point, the answer seems to be counter-intuitively 'yes', so Aristotle chose the banks of the river, arguing that its place is the nearest containing surface that is immobile (for the millennia of puzzlement this caused, see Sorabji 1988: 188–92, Jammer 1954: 68–72). These ideas introduce the notion of a reference point, landmark or 'ground', which plays an important part in naïve spatial language. Secondly, Aristotle held that space/place had six phenomenological dimensions:

These are the parts and kinds of place: above, below, and the rest of the six dimensions. These are not just relative to us, they – above, below, left, right – are not always the same, but come to be in relation to our position, according as we turn ourselves about, which is why, often, right and left are the same, and above and below, and ahead and behind. But in nature each is distinct and separate. (*Physics*, book 4, cited in Casey 1997: 53)

The directions 'up' and 'down' in particular he viewed as special, and part of nature, 'up' anchored to the celestial spheres and 'down' to the centre of the earth (Casey 1997: 360, n. 14). The discussion implies that Aristotle recognized that directions can be set both relatively, in terms of the orientation of the human frame, and absolutely, in terms of the cosmos.

Classical Greek thought left behind certain inconsistencies – Euclid's geometry of the plane, Aristotle's concept of place, Ptolemy's celestial projections – that seem to have inhibited the development of a rectangular coordinate system right up until the seventeenth century. Much of the medieval discussion of space revolved around the incoherencies in Aristotelian dogma (Duhem 1985). It was not until the Renaissance, with the rediscovery of the ancient atomists, and connection to the Arabic, Jewish and late classical traditions, that space began to be thought about again as an infinite three-dimensional void, as in the work of Patritius, Bruno or Gassendi (Jammer 1954: 83–92). Newton built on this tradition in his celebrated distinction between relative and absolute space: 'Absolute space in its own nature, without relation to anything external, remains similar and immovable. Relative space is some moveable dimension or measure of the absolute spaces' (*Principiae*, quoted in Jammer 1954: 97). Newton (ibid.) goes on to explain that because we cannot sense absolute space, therefore 'from the positions and distances of things from any body considered as immovable, we define all places . . . And so instead of absolute places and motions, we use relative ones; and that without any inconvenience in common affairs.'

Leibniz, in his correspondence with Newton's champion Clark, attacked the Newtonian concept of absolute space as unnecessary metaphysics: space is no more than the relative locations of things – a mere network of places, and when we ascribe motion to one body rather than its reference point, this is an arbitrary convenience. This relational quality of locations – as things located with respect to other things – is fundamentally reflected in much ordinary spatial language, as we shall see. Leibniz was thus on the threshold of a theory of relativity, but Newton's concept of absolute space was to rule up till the end of the nineteenth century. By 1769, Kant thought he had found incontestable proof of the reality of Newton's absolute space in the distinction between **enantiomorphs**, or three-dimensional objects that differ in handedness, like a left vs. a right shoe (he called them 'incongruent counterparts'). Suppose, he said, the universe consisted of a giant hand – it would have to be a right hand or a left hand, and yet that would not be determinable from the set of internal relations between its parts – the thumb would remain a set distance from the fingers in either hand. Only in a yet larger spatial framework, absolute space, could the handedness be determined (see Van Cleve and Frederick 1991 for modern discussion). Kant had found what was missing in Leibnizian space – namely direction (about which, more will be said below). In later work, Kant attributed absolute space to intuition, an *a priori* conceptual form that organizes our perception of space – it is thus an intuition utterly independent of the ensemble of concrete relations that Leibniz thought space could be reduced to. Kant's nativist ideas, his psychologizing of space, played an important role in the early history of psychology, for example in Helmholtz's psychophysics (Hatfield 1990), and similar ideas pervade modern American psychology in the nativist tradition. Incidentally, the terms 'absolute' vs. 'relative', as applied to frames of reference, will come to have a slightly different meaning in this book, but one sanctioned by the history of thought (see Chapter 2).

This brief review cannot do justice to what has proved one of the most central themes of philosophical and scientific discourse. Such an outline only gives us the line of thought that proved congenial to classical mechanics, but there were many other currents, many of them theological (indeed Newton's absolute space was partly motivated as further evidence of the divine). But enough has been said to give us some conceptual pegs, and to illustrate a number of important themes that will recur below: naïve human spatial reasoning tends to be couched in terms of place rather than space, in terms of relative locations to other objects rather than to abstract location in a spatial envelope, and yet seems to presuppose larger spatial schemas of the kind indicated by Aristotle's six directions or Kant's intuitions about space.

1.2.2 The anthropocentric bias

'Man is the measure of all things'   Protagoras (481–411 BC)

Spatial cognition has been intensively studied in the twentieth century by sciences as diverse as ethology, cognitive and behaviourist psychology, child development, neurology and the brain sciences generally. There is, for example, a wondrous literature on animal wayfinding and orientation (Schöne 1984, Waterman 1989, see also Chapter 6 below); and it is striking how much less is known about human (and more generally primate) spatial cognition and behaviour in the wild. Nevertheless, the information on human spatial abilities and their neurophysiological basis is enormous, and quite beyond review in a book of this scope.

But there is one element of this modern work that is contradicted by the findings in this book, and thus needs documentation and discussion in this section. This element is a consistent emphasis on the exclusive centrality of egocentric, anthropomorphic, relativistic spatial concepts and abilities, as opposed to allocentric, abstract, absolute spatial information. The attitude is summed up by Poincaré (1946: 257): 'Absolute space is nonsense, and it is necessary for us to begin by referring space to a system of axes invariably bound to the body.'[5]

Take as an example the study of how spatial information is handled in the primate brain. The picture that emerges is one of great complexity, with multiple systems of egocentric coordinates for each sensory mode (Paillard 1991). Thus, when we pick up a coffee cup, the visual system processes the two-dimensional retinal arrays to extract, partly by stereopsis, partly by the analysis of properties of the array itself, a model that includes partial depth information from a particular viewpoint (Marr 1982). Next we abstract and recognize three-dimensional objects, perhaps by matching them with an inventory of three-dimensional models, thus recognizing the cup and its orientation and placement in depth from the retina. This information then drives the reaching mechanism, first through shoulder-centred coordinates, and then (through different neural pathways) the hand-based coordinates that achieve a grasp on the object seen (Jeannerod 1997). How the retinal coordinates are translated into shoulder- and hand-based ones remains a matter of contention: perhaps information is translated into a general spatial model and then out again, or perhaps specialized dedicated translation processes are involved (Stein 1992). There seem to be two independent neural pathways involved in the perception of space, called the 'what' and 'where' systems, the one controlling, for example, our perception of what things are and the other their location in egocentric space (McCarthy 1993, Ungerleider and Mishkin 1982). Findings like this are potentially highly relevant to our topic of the language of space: Landau and Jackendoff (1993) have speculated that the what/where distinction shows up directly as a universal of language, giving us object-names specialized for shape on the one hand, and closed-class spatial morphemes (like our spatial prepositions) on the other (a view challenged below).[6] This general emphasis on egocentric, relativistic concepts of space has rarely been challenged – but most effectively by O'Keefe and Nadel (1978) who claim that absolute spatial concepts, mental maps of terrain, are encoded in the hippocampus (see also O'Keefe 1991, 1993, Burgess *et al.* 1999, Maguire *et al.* 2000).

Although the notion of 'mental maps' in psychology is half a century old (Tolman 1948), the same bias towards the study of egocentric spatial information and coordination is also to be found in psychology. Thus, for example, in the study of children's spatial abilities, it is suspected that allocentric behaviour is actually generated by operations on egocentric information (for a review, see Pick 1993). In the psychology of language, it has been repeatedly asserted that human spatial language is a direct reflection of our egocentric, anthropomorphic and relativistic spatial concepts (Clark 1973, Miller and Johnson-Laird 1976). Rooted in this tradition is the prediction that all languages use the planes through the human body to give us, as Kant (1991 [1768]) put it, our first grounds for intuitions about space, in terms of 'up' and 'down', 'left' and 'right', 'back' and 'front'. This prediction turns out to be false, as we shall see, and raises the possibility that this entire tradition partly reflects the linguistic prejudices of the Indo-European tongues.

Despite the large amount of work on the neuropsychology of human spatial cognition, when we come to language and conscious spatial thinking most of what we know comes from introspection and the inspection of our own European languages. This phenomenology has a long tradition, and it has repeatedly harped on a limited number of themes, among which are the following.

1. Human spatial thinking is always *relative* in character, not absolute (Miller and Johnson-Laird 1976).

2. Human spatial thinking is primarily *egocentric* in character (Piaget and Inhelder 1956, Clark 1973, Miller and Johnson-Laird 1976, Lyons 1977).

3. Human spatial thinking is *anthropomorphic*: spatial coordinates are derived from the planes through our body, giving left and right, front and back, up and down as the primary planes (Kant 1991 [1768], Clark 1973, Miller and Johnson-Laird 1976, Lyons 1977: 690–1).

Much of this can be traced back to Kant's influential paper of 1768, which was an attack on Leibniz's relative theory of space as described above. Kant argued for an absolute conception of space, but he conceded that our apprehension of it was based on an egocentric and anthropomorphic model:

In physical space, on account of its three dimensions, we can conceive three planes which intersect one another at right angles. Since through the senses we know what is outside us only in so far as it stands in relation to ourselves, it is not surprising that we find in the relationship of these intersecting planes to our body the first ground from which to derive the concept of regions in space . . .

One of these vertical planes divides the body into two outwardly similar parts and supplies the ground for the distinction between right and left; the other, which is perpendicular to it, makes it possible for us to have the concept before and behind. In a written page, for instance, we have first to note the difference between front and back and to distinguish the top from the bottom of the writing; only then can we proceed to determine the position of the characters from right to left or conversely.   (Kant 1991 [1768]: 28–9)

Kant went on to argue that left and right are irreducible concepts. One might think, he argues, that one could dispense with right/left concepts by substituting maps of the stars or of the terrain. But Kant points out that these devices in turn rest upon an orientation of the map in one's hands, and a relation between one's sides and the regions projected from them. Nor can one even appeal to the apparent absolute nature of cardinal points; for the compass only assigns north, and we must fix the rest of the points by directed rotation, for example by the clockwise order N-E-S-W. But a moment's reflection reveals that the notion of handedness and clockwiseness are one and the same:

Since the different feeling of right and left side is of such necessity to the judgement of regions, Nature has directly connected it with the mechanical arrangement of the human body, whereby one side, the right, has indubitable advantage in dexterity and perhaps also in strength.   (Kant 1991 [1768]: 30)

Most modern thought parts company with Kant on the psychological relevance of absolute space (but see O'Keefe and Nadel 1978), insisting on the primacy of relativistic concepts:

Ordinary languages are designed to deal with relativistic space; with space relative to objects that occupy it. Relativistic space provides three orthogonal coordinates, just as Newtonian space does, but no fixed units of angle or distance are involved, nor is there any need for coordinates to extend without limit in any direction   (Miller and Johnson-Laird 1976: 380).

But Kant's arguments for the centrality of the egocentric and anthropomorphic nature of spatial apprehension are echoed two centuries later by psychologists:

The conceptual core of space probably originates, as Cassirer (1923) and others have maintained, with the body concept – with what is at, in, or on our own bodies. The first spatial relatum we learn to use is ego ... Piaget and Inhelder (1948) claim that escape from this egocentric space requires considerable cognitive development ... The ability to decentre does not displace the egocentric conception of space, but it supplements it ... Egocentric use of the space concept places ego at the centre of the universe. From this point of origin ego can lay out a three-dimensional co-ordinate system that depends on his own orientation. With respect to this landmark other objects can be located as above or below (ego), in front or in back (of ego), to the left or to the right (of ego).
(Miller and Johnson-Laird 1976: 394–5)

And the same view is held by many linguists:

Looked at from one point of view, man is merely a middle-sized physical object. But in man's world – the world as man sees it and describes it in everyday language – he is, in the most literal sense, the measure of all things. Anthropocentricism and anthropomorphism are woven into the very fabric of his language: it reflects his biological make-up, his natural terrestrial habitat, his mode of locomotion, and even the shape and properties of his body.   (Lyons 1977: 690)

The presumption of the universal basis of this egocentric and anthropomorphic conception of space can be found throughout the branches of the sciences of mind. For example, in the study of language acquisition, it is commonly held that

The child acquires English expressions for space and time by learning how to apply these expressions to the *a priori* knowledge he has about space and time. This *a priori* knowledge is separate from language itself and not so mysterious ... The child is born into a flat world with gravity, and he himself is endowed with eyes, ears, an upright posture, and other biological structures. These structures alone lead him to develop a perceptual space, a P-space, with very specific properties . . . the child cannot apply some term correctly if he does not already have the appropriate concept in his P-space. Since this is so the concept of space underlying the English spatial terms, to be called L-space, should coincide with P-space.   (Clark 1973: 28)

Even anthropologists, who might have had sufficient experience of other cultures to know better, have suggested that bodily experience is universally the basis for spatial thinking, and further that this spatial thinking is mapped onto the social world too, to make an embodied cosmos. Thus Hertz, using many ethnographic examples, argued eloquently for the Kantian position that the cosmos is seen as a mapping of the body to space:

The relation uniting the right to the east or south and the left to the north or west is even more constant and direct, to the extent that in many languages the same words denote the sides of the body and the cardinal points. The axis which divides the world into two halves, the one radiant and the other dark, also cuts through the human body and divides it between the empire of light and that of darkness. Right and left extend beyond the limits of our body to embrace the universe.   (Hertz 1960: 102 [1909])

These views have been reiterated by modern anthropologists like Needham (1973), who views the notions of left and right as the primordial source of binary oppositions in culture and cognition.

It will become clear below that there are languages and cultures where these generalizations seem quite out of place (and an inkling has already been given in the anecdotes above) – indeed I will argue that they are simply false. The problem is that, as in so many other aspects of psychology and linguistics, we are heavily biased by our own Western cultural traditions and languages. This tradition has, since Aristotle's six directions, generally placed the human body at the centre of our spatial notions.

This view receives a new kind of emphasis in cognitive linguistics, where the experiential and bodily basis of human categories are presupposed: our apprehension of the body in space gives rise to a set of image schemas that lie behind the extended uses of the spatial prepositions, and that are the source of numerous spatial metaphors (see Ungerer and Schmid 1996). Some important cross-linguistic work done within this framework (Svorou 1994, Heine 1997) shows that terms for human body-parts are indeed amongst the most frequent diachronic sources for abstract spatial expressions (as in *behind*) – however it also makes quite clear that there are other frequent models, in particular landscape, celestial, meteorological and animal-body sources for grammaticalized spatial expressions. This work unfortunately fails to clearly differentiate uses of such expressions in different frames of reference – details that cannot easily be gleaned from grammars – and is thus of limited utility to the issues central to this book.

There are many deep insights into the nature of spatial language (see, e.g., Miller and Johnson-Laird 1976, Bloom *et al.* 1996, Talmy 2000), and reference will be made to these especially in Chapter 3 below. However, the argument will be that in the matter of frames of reference, the tradition in which the human body is the source of all our notions of orientation and direction is a major ethnocentric error. It is not only that there are languages that do not use the bodily coordinates to construct a relative frame of reference, but there are also many other aspects of such languages, and of the interaction and cognition of their speakers, that point to a fundamental demoting of the body as a source of spatial concepts. These are points taken up especially in Chapters 4 and 6 (see also Levinson and Brown 1994).

1.2.3 Nativism and linguistic diversity

Kantian ideas are echoed in the nativist tradition associated with the cognitive science movement. For many theorists, natural language semantics reflects universal categories directly (following Fodor 1975, Fodor *et al.* 1975), so that language can be viewed as the immediate projection of innate concepts:

> Knowing a language, then is knowing how to translate mentalese into strings of words and vice versa. People without a language would still have mentalese, and babies and many nonhuman animals presumably have simpler dialects.
>
> (Pinker 1994: 82)

Learning a language is thus simply a question of mapping local words onto antecedent concepts:

> [T]he child acquires English expressions for space and time by learning how to apply these expressions to the *a priori* knowledge he has about space and time ... The exact form of this knowledge, then, is dependent on man's biological endowment – that he has two eyes, ears, etc., that he stands upright, and so on – and in this sense it is innate. (Clark 1973: 28)

In a similar vein, Jackendoff (1983: 210) therefore holds that the inspection of spatial language (and English alone will do) will give us a direct window on conceptual structure, the central system of concepts used in thinking about space. Landau and Jackendoff (1993) further explore the idea that the universal properties of spatial language reflect underlying neural pathways, specifically the distinct streams of information involved in the 'what'/'where' systems of Ungerleider and Mishkin (1982). And, most pertinently for us, Li and Gleitman (1999, 2002) have argued specifically that frames of reference are universally available in thought, and universally projected in language.

I believe these views reflect some deep confusions. First, language has very specific semantic properties that are due to its role as a learned, public, broadcast system, and which cannot be properties of the corresponding non-linguistic, purely internal, conceptual structure (see Levinson 1997b, and the discussion in Chapter 7 below). Linguistic semantics is not conceptual structure (as Fodor, Jackendoff, Langacker and others have supposed) – it is a mere pale shadow of the underlying mental systems that drive it. Take, for example, the metric precision involved in seeing a cup before me, judging its distance from me, and reaching for it – there is nothing like this metric precision in ordinary language locative descriptions. Indeed there is no one internal mental representation, but a myriad of internal representations of space each appropriate to its own sensory inputs or motor outputs. Thus a direct one-to-one mapping between non-linguistic concepts and the semantics of linguistic expressions seems most improbable.

Second, the view that semantic structure and conceptual structure are one and the same thing is not informed by knowledge of linguistic, and specifically semantic, variation in the spatial domain. The fact is, as documented in this book and the companion volume (Levinson and Wilkins in preparation), there are linguistic expressions based on incompatible, rival ways of construing spatial scenes – for example, there are many languages in which *The boy is to the left of the tree* is simply untranslatable (although functional equivalents with different logical and spatial properties can be found). The consequence is simple but profound: we cannot hold both to the thesis of the congruency of thought and language and to the thesis of the universality of conceptual categories. We can either retain the thesis of the congruency of language and thought and give up universality, or give up the thesis of congruency and retain the 'psychic unity of mankind'. These are issues we return to at the end of this book.

The picture that will emerge from the facts presented in this book is that there is considerable linguistic diversity in the expression of this, one of the most fundamental domains of human cognition. The diversity is not just a matter of different forms of expression – the very underlying ideas are distinct. These different semantic notions correlate with different non-linguistic codings of spatial scenes. In all probability, these correlations reflect the power of language, in making a communicational community, to construct a community of like thought. Thus we are brought back to the old ideas of linguistic relativity and linguistic determinism (see Gumperz and Levinson 1996, Bowerman and Levinson 2001), which remain anathema to many current strands of thought, but for reasons that are ill thought out. The implications of this linguistic and cognitive diversity for current theory in the cognitive sciences – for the status of 'innate ideas', and for theories about conceptual development in the child – are explored in depth in the final chapter of this book, after we have reviewed in the body of the book many facts about diversity in spatial language and cognition.

1.2.4 The centrality of spatial thinking in human psychology

From classical times to the present, the centrality of spatial thinking in human cognition has been fundamentally presupposed. This is an element in the long history of Western thought about spatial concepts that I shall certainly not dispute. We are indeed clearly so good at thinking spatially that converting non-spatial problems into spatial ones seems to be one of the fundamental tricks of human cognition. Casting problems into a spatial mode of thinking is reflected in all the diagrams, sketches and graphs that we use as aids to thinking. Our graphical tradition is not unique, of course, but even cultures that traditionally lacked maps have elaborate spatial schemata (as in the dream-time landscapes of Aboriginal Australia) which are used to encode myth, religion and cosmology (see Chapter 6, and the references in Levinson 1996a). Another wide cross-cultural source of evidence for the primacy of spatial thinking is the prevalence of spatial metaphor across many other domains, notably time (where spatial expressions like *before* quite normally double up for temporal specification), but also kinship (as in 'close' and 'distant kin', or the vertical metaphor of 'descent' in kinship), and social structure more generally (as in 'high' and 'low status'), music ('high' and 'low tones'), mathematics ('high' and 'low numbers', 'narrow intervals', 'lower bounds', 'open' and 'closed sets', etc.), emotions ('high' spirits, 'deep' depressions) and much more ('broad learning', 'a wide circle of friends', 'the place for respect', and so on). Just as maps stand in an abstract spatial relation to real spatial terrain, so spatial arrangements can give us symbolic 'maps' to other domains. Spatializations can even give us maps of the mind, as exploited in the classical and medieval art of memory (Yates 1966), in which the orator was taught to remember themes through the visualization of a tour through a building.[7] Spatial models of the mind are recurrent themes in the history of psychology, from phrenology to modern theories of localization of functions in the brain.

Linguists from time to time have argued that spatial notions lie behind most grammatical constructions (the doctrine of 'localism', reiterated in modern cognitive linguistics): locative constructions often provide the template for not only temporal and aspectual constructions, but also existential, change-of-state and causal constructions (see Lyons 1977: 282, 718–24, Langacker 1991). Psychologists have suggested that these 'localist' tendencies may reflect the evolution of language out of spatial cognition (O'Keefe 1996).

There is direct psychological evidence for spatialization in human thinking. For example, in the most basic cases of logical inference, subjects seem to translate the problem into spatial terms (Huttenlocher 1968). More generally, visual imagery has been shown to be a representational system with specific spatial properties, so that, for example, manipulation of a mental image of a shape has analogue properties similar to real spatial transformations (e.g. the further the rotation, the longer it takes, see Shephard and Metzler 1971, also Kosslyn 1980), although the role of visual imagery in inference remains controversial (Tye 1991).

What exactly is the cognitive advantage of using spatial models for thinking? It may be, as some philosophers have argued, that 'it is quite impossible to think abstractly about relations' (Reichenbach 1958: 107), thus making visualization and spatialization inevitable. Some recent psychological work suggests that the advantages may be computational – for example proving a valid inference in a deductive system is a complex business (and there is no decision procedure at all for predicate logic), but building a mental spatial model, checking that it is the only one that fits the premises, and then deriving the conclusion is a relatively simple way to check validity. If humans do in fact convert problems into spatial models for this reason, then we can readily see the efficacy of diagrams, graphs, tables and the like: a picture can be worth a thousand words because a spatially presented problem can be more readily translated into spatial thinking – it is already as it were in the right format (Johnson-Laird 1996).

But whatever explains the efficacy of spatial models, there is little doubt we use them widely, and one reason may simply have to do with evolution's tendency to work with what there is at hand. As we shall see in Chapter 6, navigation is probably the most complex computational problem that every higher animal faces – so neural mechanisms for spatial computation are going to be highly developed in almost every species. Evolution is *bricolage* – creative use of historical junk. It is likely that in the human brain these ancient brain structures have been put to new and more general uses in the extended symbolic world that human beings inhabit – and, as the data in Chapter 6 suggest, we have probably lost our navigational hardware in the process. But before proceeding further, it will be helpful to have some idea of the overall storyline in this book.

1.3 SYNOPSIS

The story that will emerge from this book can be explained quite simply. I will advance the thesis that human spatial thinking is quite heavily influenced by culture, and more specifically by language; when languages differ in crucial respects, so does the corresponding conceptualization of spatial relations. This can be thought about, if one likes, as a limited kind of 'Whorfianism' – Benjamin Lee Whorf, together with Edward Sapir, being credited with the thesis of 'linguistic relativity' whereby 'users of different grammars are pointed by their grammars toward different types of observations and different evaluations of externally similar acts of observation, and hence are not equivalent as observers but must arrive at somewhat different views of the world' (Whorf 1956: 221). This thesis fell out of favour with the rise of the cognitive sciences in the 1960s (more historical background is provided below), so in a modern context any evidence for even a restricted version of it will naturally be treated with a great deal of suspicion, and will need to be accumulated in both quantity and quality.

Now the area of spatial cognition is one of the very *least likely* places where we would expect to find Whorfian effects. This is because knowledge and reasoning about space is a central adaptive necessity for any species that has a home base or has any strategy for optimal foraging. On first principles, then, spatial cognition is likely to be enshrined in an ancient, modular, innate system. We can even point to some ancient brain structures like the hippocampus, where certain kinds of spatial knowledge are laid down right across the vertebrate orders, from birds to primates. And there are other special neural pathways subserving spatial cognition, all of which makes the whole thing appear to be 'hard-wired' in humans just as it is in beasts. Moreover, the scientific literature contains many putative universals of human spatial cognition and spatial language, which we will review below. This literature suggests that spatial language is simply a direct projection of innate spatial concepts. In short, spatial cognition does not look like happy hunting grounds for the would-be neo-Whorfian. Indeed, Whorf himself was commendably cautious here:

> Probably the apprehension of space is given in substantially the same form by experience irrespective of language . . . but the **concept of space** will vary somewhat with language. (Whorf 1956: 158, emphasis original)

However, it turns out that we have drastically underestimated the potential for human language difference in this area. Languages just do turn out to use fundamentally different semantic parameters in their categorization of spatial relations – different coordinate systems, different principles for constructing such coordinate systems, yielding different categorizations of 'same' and 'different' across spatial scenes. I describe this in earnest in Chapter 3. This much is indubitable fact, and forces a revision of the idea that spatial language is just a projection of a single, underlying innate set of spatial categories – it cannot be that simple, because there are many different kinds of spatial description enshrined in different languages.

But this book is especially concerned not with establishing this fact about language difference (see, for example, the companion volume, Levinson and Wilkins in preparation), but looking at its consequences. The claim explored here in detail is that such linguistic differences have surprisingly far-reaching cognitive effects. How can one show this? The strategy that we, myself and many colleagues, have used is similar to one already employed with important results by John Lucy (1992b). In recipe form it is just this:

1. Pick a domain (in this case, space).
2. Look at the *linguistic* coding of the domain in languages; sort languages into types A, B etc., on the basis of differences in the coding of the domain.
3. Look independently at the *non-linguistic* coding of the domain in non-linguistic cognition in speakers of language type A and B etc.

The second step is not trivial – it requires an analysis of the semantics of a language at a depth which is never available from grammar books. Special methods need to be devised – for example, communication tasks between native speakers which will reveal the linguistic resources available for use in the chosen domain. These techniques are briefly described in Chapter 3, but in more detail in the companion volume Levinson and Wilkins in preparation. But the hard part of the recipe is step 3: one has to invent methods for exploring the structure and content of *non-linguistic representations* of the domain. This requires some ingenuity, because the techniques have to be developed. And this step is by no means easy to execute, because one needs to run artificial or natural experiments across cultures of quite different kinds from our own, while maintaining comparability in the essentials. The difficulties – methodological, ethical, cultural and political – are substantial, which is one reason why such little work of this kind has been done.

Step 3 also presents two substantial kinds of difficulties. The first sort are conceptual – each of the disciplines that has a stake in non-linguistic cognition, from ethology to cognitive psychology, neurophysiology to philosophy, has its own apparently incommensurate frameworks of analysis. But in one crucial area, the coordinate systems underlying spatial cognition, a lot of existing analyses can in fact be brought into correspondence. This I show in Chapter 2, which provides the conceptual underpinnings for the book. The second major kind of problem facing the analysis of non-linguistic conceptual categories is methodological: how can one show what they are? The way we have chosen to implement step 3 in the sequence above is to develop a simple paradigm ('the rotation paradigm') which distinguishes between two distinct types of conceptual categorization of spatial scenes without the use of language. That is to say, we have developed non-verbal tasks that – without anything being said – reveal the underlying spatial coordinate systems utilized in memory and inference about spatial arrays. Under this paradigm, a great many tasks can be developed, which test different aspects of psychological ability: for example, the kind of memory used in recognition, versus the memory involved in active reconstruction of a spatial array, or the mental transformation of a motion path into a route map, or the inference about where some unseen object ought to lie.

The evidence from this line of work, summarized in Chapter 5, suggests very strongly that people who speak a language that favours one specific frame of reference will tend to *think* in similar terms, that is, they use a coordinate system of the same underlying type in language and non-verbal cognition. The significance of all this is explored in Chapter 7.

But there are other ways to pursue these issues. One line of enquiry is ethnographic – some glimpse of this is provided in Chapter 4, where the role of special styles of spatial thinking in two cultures distinct from our tradition is sketched in a bit more detail. What such ethnographic enquiries reveal is that many aspects of everyday life revolve around a specific 'cognitive style' that can be attributed in part to the language. But for reasons of space they cannot be pursued here – see especially the companion volume Brown and Levinson in preparation, and the many references in Levinson 1996a. This rich detail may help to persuade those who are inclined to doubt the experimental findings in this book that human cognitive diversity is a brute reality that can be explored from many different angles.

Another avenue of research is also described in this book. This involves a more abstract line of prediction. Suppose that we have shown that for a specific domain (here spatial coordinate systems), two languages A and B utilize fundamentally different semantic parameters (call them A' and B'). Now, suppose we can demonstrate on first principles that, *in order to use* semantic parameters of the type in A', individuals would have to carry out various mental calculations that users of B' would not require (or not at least by virtue of B'). Let us call this mental calculator α. Now we can set out to try and find if speakers of A have α, while speakers of B do not. This line of argumentation is followed in Chapter 6. There I argue that speakers of languages that utilize cardinal directions (like 'north'), where we would use coordinates based on our body schema (like 'left' or 'front'), would have to be not only good at knowing where (e.g.) north is, but would also have to maintain accurate mental maps and constantly update their position and orientation on them. It is simple enough to test this prediction, by transporting people to new locations and getting them to point to old ones. But there is also a more subtle way to test this: by observing people's unselfconscious gesturing while speaking. This brings us back to an ethnographic perspective and the many things that can be learned from it.

Finally, in Chapter 7 I try to pull this all together. The end result of all the investigations detailed in the body of the book is a clear and quite surprising finding: the choice of a predominant frame of reference in language determines many other aspects of cognition, from memory, to inference, to navigation, to gesture and beyond. The consequences of this surprising finding are then worked out. The finding argues against a strongly nativist line on the universal nature of basic human concepts. Still, there is a limited typology and a strong set of universals in this domain. This prompts a reconsideration of a number of fundamental assumptions. What exactly is the relation between linguistic categories and the concepts we do most of our thinking in? How many different types of internal representation are actually necessary to support language? How are we to think of universal overarching types of complex concepts which nevertheless accommodate much linguistic diversity? If we discard strong 'nativism', how are we to account for patterns of variation in human concepts that show both strong universal trends and cultural specificities? The data described in the book throw important light on the questions, and an attempt is made to answer them, adopting carefully considered positions on lexical meaning, its relation to non-linguistic concepts, human conceptual development, and cognition in an evolutionary perspective.

The overall picture that emerges is that our species is not cognitively uniform – there is diversity in cognition just as there is diversity in language, clothing, hairstyle, kinship practices, modes of subsistence, ritual and religion. Some readers, anthropologists perhaps, will think this platitudinous. Others, cognitive scientists no doubt, will react more strongly to this threat to the 'psychic unity of mankind'. I believe that this horror reaction stems from an oversimple view of human epistemology and I will try to lay this demon to rest. Essentially, the point will be that humans have co-evolved with culture, and that culture has one great virtue over other kinds of adaptation, namely the speed with which it can change in response to new conditions. That is why our species dominates almost every niche upon the planet. Because language is both an external representation used for communication, and an internal one intimately connected to other internal representations, cultural changes in language will have repercussions in cognitive style. Linguistic and cognitive diversity is there because it has proved highly adaptive.

1.4 CONCLUSIONS

In this chapter a range of background issues have been reviewed, mostly by way of historical synopsis, which are highly pertinent to the interpretation of the data that will be presented through this book:

• What are the 'natural', pre-linguistic or innate, spatial concepts in human cognition? How abstract are they?
• Why does spatial thinking have a centrality in human cognition?
• What is the role of bodily axes and coordinates in spatial cognition?
• What is the nature of the relation between linguistic categories and non-linguistic concepts, both in general and in the spatial domain? Are

there a multiplicity of underlying representations, or one multimodal representation of space? If the latter, what is its relation to spatial semantics?

- How much linguistic diversity is there in this domain, not only in expressive form, but underlying semantic parameters? Given that there is diversity, what linguistic universals can be stated in this area?
- Given semantic diversity, what happens to the underlying cognition? Does it remain a universal constant, translated into various restricted linguistic concepts, or does it adapt to the language it must locally support?
- What are the general implications from the spatial domain for the relation between language and human thinking?

These questions and issues recur throughout this book, and are certainly illuminated if not fully resolved by the detailed findings to be presented.

CHAPTER 2

Frames of reference

2.1 THE CONCEPT OF A SPATIAL FRAME OF REFERENCE

The notion of 'frames of reference' is crucial to the study of spatial cognition across all the modalities and all the disciplines that study them. The idea is as old as the hills: medieval theories of space, for example, were deeply preoccupied by the puzzle raised by Aristotle and mentioned in Chapter 1, the case of the boat moored in the river. If we think about the location of objects as places that they occupy, and places as containing the objects, then the puzzle is that if we adopt the river as frame of reference the boat is moving, but if we adopt the bank as frame, then it is stationary (see Sorabji 1988: 187ff.).

But the phrase 'frame of reference' and its modern interpretation originate, like so much else worthwhile, from Gestalt theories of perception in the 1920s. How, for example, do we account for illusions of motion, as when the moon skims across the clouds, except by invoking a notion of a constant perceptual window against which motion (or the perceived vertical etc.) is to be judged? The Gestalt notion can be summarized as 'a unit or organization of units that collectively serve to identify a **coordinate system** with respect to which certain properties of objects, including the phenomenal self, are gauged' (Rock 1992: 404, my emphasis).[1]

In what follows, I will emphasize that distinctions between frames of reference are essentially distinctions between underlying coordinate systems and not, for example, between the objects that may invoke them. Not all will agree.[2] In a recent review, Brewer and Pears (1993), ranging over the philosophical and psychological literature, conclude that frames of reference come down to the selection of reference objects: take the glasses on my nose – when I go from one room to another, do they change their location or not? It depends on the 'frame of reference' – nose or room.[3] This emphasis on the ground or relatum or reference

24

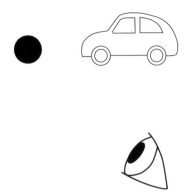

Figure 2.1. Scene allowing descriptions in multiple frames of reference

object[4] severely underplays the importance of coordinate systems in distinguishing frames of reference, as I shall show below.[5] Humans use multiple frames of reference: I can happily say of the same assemblage (ego looking at a car from the side, with the car's front to ego's left as in Figure 2.1): "The ball is in front of the car" and "The ball is to the left of the car", without thinking that the ball has changed its place. In fact, much of the psychological literature is concerned with ambiguities of this kind. I will therefore insist on the emphasis on coordinate systems rather than on the objects or 'units' on which such coordinates may have their origin.

2.2 'FRAMES OF REFERENCE' ACROSS MODALITIES AND THE DISCIPLINES THAT STUDY THEM[6]

In this book, we shall be very much concerned with the partial isomorphisms across spatial representations in different modalities – in vision, in touch and gesture – in our sense of where we are in a wider world, as well as in language. If there were no such isomorphisms we could not reach to what we see, or talk about what we feel with our hands, or give route descriptions in language and gesture. On the other hand, the spatial representations specialized to the different sensory modalities each have their own native frames of reference, vision operating fundamentally in a viewer-centred frame, touch and grasp for example requiring an object-centred frame. This raises questions about the translatability of spatial information from one frame to another, which will also prove an important issue. Nevertheless, despite these differences, there are

Table 2.1. *Spatial frames of reference: some distinctions in the literature*

'relative' vs. 'absolute':
(philosophy, brain sciences, linguistics)
(a) space as relations between objects vs. abstract void
(b) egocentric vs. allocentric
(c) directions: relations between objects vs. fixed bearings

'egocentric' vs. 'allocentric'
(developmental and behavioural psychology, brain sciences)
(a) body-centred vs. environment-centred (Note many egocentres: retina, shoulder, etc.)
(b) subjective (subject-centred) vs. objective

'viewer-centred' vs. 'object-centred' or
'2.5D sketch' vs. '3D models'
(vision theory, imagery debate in psychology)

'orientation-bound vs. orientation-free'
(visual perception, imagery debate in psychology)

'deictic' vs. 'intrinsic'
(linguistics)
(a) speaker-centric vs. non-speaker-centric
(b) centred on speaker or addressee vs. thing
(c) ternary vs. binary spatial relations

'viewer-centred' vs. 'object-centred' vs. 'environment-centred'
(psycholinguistics)
(a) 'gaze-tour' vs. 'body-tour' perspectives
(b) 'survey perspective' vs. 'route perspective'

---

important alignments across modalities that allow us to talk about the same or similar frames of reference shared by some of them.

If we are to make sense of the notion 'same frame of reference' across different modalities, or inner representation systems, it will be essential to see how the various distinctions between such frames that have been proposed in different disciplines can be ultimately brought into line. This is no trivial undertaking, because there are a host of such distinctions, and each of them has been variously construed, both within and across the many disciplines (such as philosophy, the brain sciences, psychology and linguistics) that explicitly employ the notion of 'frames of reference'. A serious review of these different conceptions would take us very far afield. But some sketch is essential, and I will briefly survey the various distinctions in Table 2.1, with some different construals distinguished by the letters (a), (b), (c).[7]

First, then, **relative vs. absolute** space. Newton's distinction between absolute and relative space has played an important role in ideas about frames of reference, in part through the celebrated correspondence between his champion Clarke on the one hand and Leibniz on the other, the latter holding a strictly relative view.[8] For Newton, absolute space is an abstract infinite immovable three-dimensional box with origin at the centre of the universe, while relative space is conceived of as specified by relations between objects: psychologically, he claimed, we are inclined to relative notions (to repeat in part an earlier quotation): 'Relative space is some moveable dimension or measure of the absolute spaces, which our senses determine by its position to bodies...and so instead of absolute places and motions, we use relative ones' (quoted in Jammer 1954: 97–8). Despite fundamental differences in philosophical position, most succeeding thinkers in philosophy and psychology have assumed the *psychological* primacy of relative space – space anchored to the places occupied by physical objects and their relations to one another. A notable exception is Kant, who came to believe that notions of absolute space are a fundamental intuition, although grounded in our experience through the use of our body to define the egocentric coordinates through which we deal with it (Kant 1991; see also Van Cleve and Frederick 1991). O'Keefe and Nadel (1978; see also O'Keefe 1993, 1996) have tried to preserve this Kantian view as essential to the understanding of the neural implementation of our spatial capacities, but by and large psychologists have considered notions of 'absolute' space irrelevant to theories about the naïve spatial reasoning underlying language (see Clark 1973, Miller and Johnson-Laird 1976: 380). (Absolute notions of space may though be related to cognitive maps of the environment – discussed under the rubric of 'allocentric' frames of reference below.)

The distinction between relative and absolute space early on acquired certain additional associations: for example, relative space became associated with egocentric coordinate systems, and absolute space with non-egocentric ones (despite Kant 1991),[9] so that this distinction is often confused with the egocentric vs. allocentric distinction (discussed below). Another interpretation of the 'relative' vs. 'absolute' distinction, in relating relativistic space to egocentric space, goes on to emphasize the difference in the way coordinate systems are constructed in absolute vs. relative spatial conceptions:

Ordinary languages are designed to deal with relativistic space; with space relative to the objects that occupy it. Relativistic space provides three orthogonal coordinates, just as Newtonian space does, but *no fixed units of angle or distance are involved, nor is there any need for coordinates to extend without limit in any direction*.

(Miller and Johnson-Laird 1976: 380, my emphasis)

Thus a system of fixed bearings, or cardinal directions, is opposed to the relativistic 'space concept', whether egocentric or object-centred, which Miller and Johnson-Laird (and many other authors, like Clark 1973, Herskovits 1986, Svorou 1994: 213) have assumed to constitute the conceptual core of human spatial thinking (Miller and Johnson-Laird 1976: 395). But since, as we shall see, some languages use as a conceptual basis coordinate systems with fixed angles (and coordinates of indefinite extent), we need to recognize that some languages utilize what may be appropriately called absolute coordinate systems. Hence in this book I have opposed absolute vs. relative frames of reference in language.

Let us turn to the next distinction in Table 2.1, viz. **egocentric vs. allocentric**. The distinction is of course between coordinate systems with origins within the subjective body frame of the organism, versus co-ordinate systems centred elsewhere (often unspecified). The distinction is often invoked in the brain sciences, where there is a large literature concerning 'frames of reference' (see, e.g., Paillard 1991, Burgess *et al.* 1999). This emphasizes the plethora of different egocentric coordinate systems required to drive all the different motor systems from saccades to arm-movements (see, e.g., Stein 1992), or the control of the head as a platform for our inertial guidance and visual systems (again see papers in Paillard 1991). In addition, there is a general acceptance (Paillard 1991: 471) of the need for a distinction (following Tolman 1948, and O'Keefe and Nadel 1978) between egocentric vs. allocentric systems. O'Keefe and Nadel's demonstration that *something* like Tolman's mental maps are to be found in the hippocampal cells is well known.[10] O'Keefe's recent work is an attempt to relate a particular mapping system to the neuronal structures and processes (O'Keefe 1993). The claim is that the rat can use egocentric measurements of distance and direction towards a set of landmarks to compute a non-egocentric abstract central origin (the 'centroid') and a fixed angle or 'slope'. Then it can keep track of its position in terms of distance from centroid and direction from slope. This is a 'mental map' constructed through the rat's exploration of the environment, which gives it fixed bearings (the slope) *but just for this environment*. Whether this strictly meets the criteria for an objective, 'absolute' allocentric system has been questioned (Campbell 1993: 76–82).[11] We certainly need to be able to distinguish mental maps of different sorts: egocentric 'strip-maps' (Tolman 1948), allocentric landmark-based maps with relative angles and distances between landmarks (more Leibnizian), and allocentric maps based on fixed bearings (more Newtonian) – matters dealt with in Chapters 4 and 6.[12] But in any case, this is the sort of thing neuroscientists have in mind when they oppose 'egocentric' and 'allocentric' frames of reference.[13]

Another area of work where the opposition between egocentric and allocentric frames has been used is in the study of human conceptual development. For example, Acredolo (1988) shows that, as Piaget argued, infants have only egocentric frames of reference in which to record early spatial memories; but contrary to Piaget, this phase lasts only for perhaps the first six months. Thereafter, infants acquire the ability to compensate for their own rotation, so that by sixteen months, if placed in a room with two identical windows on opposite walls, they can identify one of them (say to their left) as the same location even when entering the room from the other side (when the relevant window is now to their right). This can be thought of as the acquisition of a non-egocentric, 'absolute' or 'geographic' orientation or frame of reference.[14] Pick (1993: 35) points out, however, that such apparently allocentric behaviour can be mimicked by egocentric mental operations, and indeed this is suggested by Acredolo's (1988: 165) observation that children learn to do such tasks via adopting the visual strategy 'if you want to find it, keep your eyes on it (as you move)'.

These lines of work identify the egocentric vs. allocentric distinction with the opposition between body-centred vs. environment-centred frames of reference. But as philosophers point out (see, e.g., Campbell 1993), ego is not just any old body, and there is indeed another way to construe the distinction as one between subjective vs. objective frames of reference. The egocentric frame of reference would then bind together various body-centred coordinate systems with an agentive subjective being, complete with body-schema and distinct zones of spatial interaction (reach, peripheral vs. central vision etc.). For example, phenomena like 'phantom limbs' or proprioceptive illusions argue for the essentially subjective nature of egocentric coordinate systems.

The next distinction on our list, **viewer-centred vs. object-centred**, comes from the theory of vision, as reconstructed by Marr (1982). In Marr's well-known conceptualization, a theory of vision should take us from retinal image to visual object-recognition, and that, he claimed, entails a transfer from a viewer-centred frame of reference, with incremental processing up to what he called the 2.5D sketch, to an object-centred frame of reference, a true 3D model or structural description.[15]

Since we can recognize an object even when foreshortened or viewed in differing lighting conditions, or in silhouette, we must extract some abstract representation of it in terms of its volumetric properties to match this token to our mental inventory of such types. Although recent developments have challenged the role of the 3D model within a modular theory of vision,[16] there can be little doubt that at some conceptual level such an object-centred frame of reference exists. This is further demonstrated by work on visual imagery, which seems to show that presented with a viewer-centred perspective view of a novel object, we can mentally rotate it to obtain different perspectival 'views' of it, for example to compare it to a prototype (Shepard and Metzler 1971, Kosslyn 1980, Tye 1991: 83–6). Thus, at some level, the visual or imagistic systems seem to employ two distinct reference frames, viewer-centred and object-centred.

This distinction between viewer-centred and object-centred frames of reference relates rather clearly to the linguistic distinction between deictic and intrinsic perspectives discussed below: the deictic perspective is viewer-centred, while the intrinsic perspective seems to use (at least partially) the same axial extraction that would be needed to compute the volumetric properties of objects for visual recognition (see Landau and Jackendoff 1993, Jackendoff 1996, also Levinson 1994). This parallel will be further reinforced by the reformation of the linguistic distinctions suggested in the section below.

This brings us to the distinction between **orientation-bound vs. orientation-free** frames of reference.[17] The visual imagery and mental rotation literature might be thought to have little to say about frames of reference. After all, visual imagery would seem to be necessarily at most 2.5D and thus necessarily in a viewer-centred frame of reference (even if mental rotations indicate access to a 3D structural description). But recently there have been attempts to understand the relation between two kinds of shape recognition: the process where shapes can be recognized without regard to orientation (thus with no response-curve latency related to angular displacement from a familiar related stimulus), and another process where shapes are recognized by apparent analogue rotation to the familiar related stimulus. The Shepard and Metzler paradigm suggested that only where handedness information is present (as where *enantiomorphs*[18] have to be discriminated) would mental rotation be involved, which implicitly amounts to some distinction between object-centred and viewer-centred frames of reference: discrimination of enantiomorphs depends on an orientation-bound perspective, while the recognition of simpler shapes may be orientation-free.[19] But some recent controversies seem to show that things are not as simple as this (Tarr and Pinker 1989, Cohen and Kubovy 1993). Just and Carpenter (1985) argue that rotation tasks in fact can be solved using four different strategies, some orientation-bound and some orientation-free.[20] Similarly, Takano (1989) insists that only orientation-bound forms should require mental rotation for recognition. However, Cohen and Kubovy (1993) claim that all this makes the wrong predictions since handedness-identification can be achieved without the mental-rotation latency curves in special cases. In fact, I believe that, despite these recent controversies, the original assumption – that only objects lacking handedness can be recognized without mental rotation – must be basically correct for logical reasons that have been clear for centuries.[21] In any case, it is clear from this literature that the study of visual recognition and mental rotation utilizes distinctions in frames of reference that can be put into correspondence with those that emerge from, for example, the study of language: absolute and relative frames of reference in language (to be firmed up below) are both orientation-bound, while the intrinsic frame is orientation-free (Danziger 1996).

Linguists have long distinguished **'deictic'** vs. **'intrinsic'** frames of reference, because of the rather obvious ambiguities of a sentence like *The boy is in front of the house* – the boy can be at the house's front, or the boy can be between the speaker and any side of the house (see, e.g., Leech 1969: 168, Fillmore 1971, Clark 1973). It has also been known for a while that linguistic acquisition of these two readings of terms like *in front*, *behind*, *to the side of* is in the reverse direction from the developmental sequence 'egocentric' to 'allocentric' (Pick 1993): 'intrinsic' notions come resolutely earlier than 'deictic' ones (Johnston and Slobin 1979). Sometimes a third term **'extrinsic'** is opposed, to denote, for example, the contribution of gravity to the interpretation of words like *above* or *on*. But unfortunately the crucial term 'deictic' breeds confusions. In fact there have been at least three distinct interpretations of the 'deictic' vs. 'intrinsic' contrast, as listed in Table 2.1: (a) speaker-centric vs. non-speaker-centric (Levelt 1989), (b) centred on any of the speech participants vs. not so centred (Levinson 1983), (c) ternary vs. binary spatial relations (implicit in Levelt 1984, 1996, the view to be adopted here). These issues will be taken up in the section below, where we will turn to ask what distinctions in frames of reference are grammaticalized or lexicalized in different languages.

Let us turn now to the various distinctions suggested in the psychology of language. Miller and Johnson-Laird (1976), drawing on earlier linguistic work, explored the opposition between 'deictic' and 'intrinsic' interpretations of such utterances as *The cat is in front of the truck*; and the logical

properties of these two frames of reference, and their interaction, have
been further clarified by Levelt (1984, 1989, 1996). Carlson-Radvansky
and Irwin (1993: 224) summarize the general assumption in psycholinguistics as follows:

> Three distinct classes of reference frames exist for representing the spatial rela-
> tionships among objects in the world . . .: **viewer-centred frames, object-
> centred frames, and environment centred** frames of reference. In a
> viewer-centred frame, objects are represented in a retinocentric, head-centric
> or body-centric coordinate system based on the perceiver's perspective of the
> world. In an object-centred frame, objects are coded with respect to their intrin-
> sic axes. In an environment-centred frame, objects are represented with respect
> to salient features of the environment, such as gravity or prominent visual land-
> marks. In order to talk about space, vertical and horizontal coordinate axes
> must be oriented with respect to one of these reference frames so that linguistic
> spatial terms such as 'above' and 'to the left of' can be assigned.

These three frames of reference, renamed the relative, intrinsic and
absolute respectively, are essentially those that will be adopted as a framework for the analyses in this book. But notice that on this particular formulation frames of reference inhere in spatial perception and cognition
rather than in language: *above* may simply be semantically general over
the different frames of reference, not ambiguous (Carlson-Radvansky
and Irwin (1993: 242).[22] Thus the corresponding three-way distinctions
between, for example, the 'deictic', 'intrinsic' and 'extrinsic' are merely
alternative labels for the linguistic interpretations corresponding, respectively, to viewer-centred, object-centred and environment-centred
frames of reference.

There are other oppositions that psycholinguists employ, although in
most cases they map onto the same triadic distinction. One particular set
of distinctions, between different kinds of survey or route description, is
worth unravelling because it has caused no little confusion. Levelt (1989:
139ff.) points out that when a subject describes a complex visual pattern the linearization of speech requires that we 'chunk' the pattern into
units that can be described in a linear sequence. Typically, we seem to
represent 2D or 3D configurations through a small window, as it were,
traversing the array; that is, the description of complex static arrays
is converted into a description of motion through units or 'chunks' of
the array. Levelt (1996) has examined the description of 2D arrays and
found two strategies: a **gaze tour** perspective – effectively the adoption
of a fixed viewpoint where one's gaze travels over the path (a 'deictic' or
viewer-centred perspective) – and a body or **'driving' tour** – effectively

an intrinsic perspective, where a pathway is found through the array, and the imagined tour of oneself along the path is used to assign 'front', 'left' etc. from any one point (or location of the window in describing time). Since both perspectives can be thought of as egocentric, Tversky (1991) opts to call Levelt's intrinsic perspective '**deictic** frame of reference' or '**route** description' and his 'deictic' perspective she labels '**survey** perspective'.[23] Thus Tversky's 'deictic' is Levelt's 'intrinsic' or non-deictic perspective! This confusion is, I believe, not merely terminological, but results from the failure in the literature to distinguish coordinate systems from their origins or centres, as discussed in the next section.

There is a final issue of some importance. In psycholinguistic discussions about frames of reference, there seems to be some unclarity, or sometimes overt disagreement, about *at which level* – perceptual, conceptual or linguistic – such frames of reference apply. Thus Carlson-Radvansky and Irwin (1993, quoted above) make the assumption that a frame of reference must be adopted within some spatial representation system, as a precondition for co-ordinating perception and language, whereas Levelt (1989, 1996) has argued that a frame of reference is freely chosen in the very process of mapping from perception or spatial representation to language. On the latter conception, frames of reference in language are peculiar to the nature of the linear, propositional representation system that underlies linguistic semantics: they are different ways of conceiving the same percept in order to talk about it.[24] The view that frames of reference in linguistic descriptions are adopted in the mapping from spatial representation or perception to language seems to suggest that the perceptions or spatial representations themselves are frame-of-reference-free. But this of course is not the case: there has to be some coordinate system involved in any spatial representation of any intricacy, whether at a peripheral, or sensory, level or at a central, or conceptual, level. What Levelt's (1996) results and Friederici and Levelt (1990) seem to establish is that frames of reference at the perceptual or spatial conceptual level do not necessarily determine frames of reference at the linguistic level. This is exactly what one might expect: language is flexible and it is an instrument of communication – thus it naturally allows us, amongst other things, to take the other guy's perspective. Further, the ability to cast a description in one frame or another implies an underlying conceptual ability to handle multiple frames, and within strict limits to convert between them (a matter to which we will return). In any case, we need to distinguish in discussions of frames of reference between at least three levels, perceptual, conceptual and linguistic, and we need to consider the possibility that we may utilize distinct frames of reference at each level (although I shall later argue that they tend to be brought into congruence).

There is much further pertinent literature in all the branches of psychology and brain science, but it should already be clear that there are many different classifications and different construals of the same terms, not to mention many unclarities and many deep confusions in all of this. However, despite this forest of distinctions with obscuring undergrowth, there are some obvious common bases to the distinctions we have reviewed. It is clear, for example, that, on the appropriate construals, 'egocentric' corresponds to 'viewer-centred' and '2.5D' sketch to 'deictic' frame, while 'intrinsic' maps onto 'object-centred' or '3D model' frames of reference, while 'absolute' is related to 'environment-centred', and so on. We should build on these commonalities, especially as in this book we will be concerned with how frames of reference in language may reflect, or induce, frames of reference in other kinds of mental representation. However, before proposing an alignment of these distinctions across the board, it is essential to deal with linguistic frames of reference, which present a troubling flexibility that has led to various confusions.

2.3 LINGUISTIC FRAMES OF REFERENCE IN CROSS-LINGUISTIC PERSPECTIVE

Cursory inspection of the linguistic literature will give the impression that the linguists have their house in order. They talk happily of **topological** vs. **projective** spatial relators (e.g. as pronouns like *in* vs. *behind*), **deictic** vs. **intrinsic** usages of projective prepositions, and so on (see, e.g., Bierwisch 1967, Lyons 1977, Herskovits 1986, Vandeloise 1991, and psycholinguists Clark 1973, Miller and Johnson-Laird 1976). But the truth is less comforting. The analysis of spatial terms in familiar European languages remains deeply confused,[25] and those in other languages almost entirely unexplored. Thus the various alleged universals should be taken with a great pinch of salt – indeed many of them can be directly jettisoned. One major upset is the recent finding (exemplified in Chapter 4 below) that many languages use an 'absolute' frame of reference (involving fixed bearings like 'West') where European languages would use a 'relative' or viewpoint-centred one (using notions like 'left'). Another is that some languages, like many Australian ones, use such frames of reference to replace so-called 'topological' notions like 'in', 'on' or 'under'.

A third is that expressions for familiar spatial notions like 'left' and 'right', and even sometimes 'front' and 'back', are missing from many, perhaps a third of all languages. Confident predictions and assumptions can be found in the literature that no such languages occur (see, e.g., Clark 1973, Miller and Johnson-Laird 1976, Lyons 1977: 690).

These developments call for some preliminary typology of the frames of reference that are systematically distinguished in the grammar or lexicon of different languages (with the caveat that we still know only a little about only a few of them). In particular, we will focus on what we seem to need in the way of coordinate systems and associated reference points to set up a cross-linguistic typology of the relevant frames of reference.

In what follows I shall confine myself to linguistic descriptions of static arrays, and concentrate just on the central frames of reference, leaving a broader review of linguistic spatial systems for Chapter 3. Moreover, I will focus on distinctions on the horizontal plane. This is not whimsy: perceptual cues for the vertical may not always coincide, but they overwhelmingly converge, giving us a good universal solution to one axis. But the two horizontal coordinates are up for grabs: there simply is no corresponding force like gravity on the horizontal.[26] Consequently there is no simple solution to the description of horizontal spatial patterns, and languages diverge widely in their solutions to this basic problem: how to specify angles or directions on the horizontal.

Essentially, three main frames of reference emerge from this new data as solutions to the problem of description of horizontal spatial directions. They are appropriately named **'intrinsic'**, **'relative'** and **'absolute'**, even though these terms may have a somewhat different interpretation from some of the construals reviewed in the section above. Indeed the linguistic frames of reference potentially *cross-cut* many of the distinctions in the philosophical, neurophysiological, linguistic and psychological literatures for one very good reason. The reason is that linguistic frames of reference cannot be defined by reference to the nature of the origin of the coordinate system (in contrast to, e.g., 'egocentric' vs. 'allocentric'). It will follow that the traditional distinction 'deictic' vs. 'intrinsic' collapses – these are not opposed terms. All this requires some explanation.

We may start by noting the difficulties we get into by trying to make the distinction between 'intrinsic' and 'deictic'. Levelt (1989: 48–55) organizes and summarizes the standard assumptions in a useful way that illustrates the problem: we can cross-classify linguistic uses according to (a) whether they presume that the coordinates are centred on the speaker or not, (b) whether the **relatum** or ground is the speaker or not. Suppose then we call the usage **'deictic'** just in case the coordinates are centred on, or have their origin in, the speaker, **'intrinsic'** otherwise. This yields the following classification of examples:

(1) *The ball is in front of me*
    Coordinates: **'Deictic'**
    Origin: Speaker
    Relatum (Ground):   Speaker

(2) *The ball is in front of the tree*
    Coordinates: **'Deictic'**
    Origin: Speaker
    Relatum (Ground):   Tree

(3) *The ball is in front of the chair (at the chair's front)*
    Coordinates: **'Intrinsic'**
    Origin: Not the speaker, but the chair
    Relatum (Ground):   Chair

Clearly it is the locus of the origin of the coordinates that is relevant to the traditional opposition 'intrinsic' vs. 'deictic', otherwise we would group (2) and (3) as both sharing a non-deictic relatum. The problem comes when we pursue this classification further:

(4) *The ball is in front of you*
    Coordinates: **'Intrinsic'**
    Origin: Not the speaker, but the addressee
    Relatum: Addressee

(5) *The ball is to the right of the lamp, from your point of view*
    Coordinates: **'Intrinsic'**
    Origin: Not the speaker, but the addressee
    Relatum: Lamp

Here the distinction between 'intrinsic' vs. 'deictic' is self-evidently not the right classification, as far as frames of reference are concerned. Clearly, (1) and (4) belong together: the interpretation of the expressions is the same, with the same coordinate systems, there are just different origins, speaker and addressee respectively (moreover, in a normal construal of 'deictic', inclusive of first and second persons, both are 'deictic' origins). Similarly, in another natural grouping, (2) and (5) should be classed together: they have the same conceptual structure, with a viewpoint (acting as the origin of the coordinate system), a relatum distinct from the viewpoint, and a referent – again the origin (or viewpoint here) alternates over speaker or addressee.

We might be tempted to just alter the designations, and label (1), (2), (4) and (5) all 'deictic' as opposed to (3) 'intrinsic'. But this would be a further confusion. First, it would conflate the distinct conceptual structures of our groupings (1) and (4) vs. (2) and (5). Secondly, the conceptual structure of the coordinate systems in (1) and (4) is in fact shared with (3). How? Consider: *The ball is in front of the chair* presumes (on the relevant reading) an intrinsic front, and uses that facet to define a search domain for the ball; but just the same holds for *The ball is in front of me/you*.[27] Thus the logical structure of (1), (3) and (4) is the same: the notion 'in front of' is here a **binary** spatial relation, with arguments constituted by the figure (or referent) and the ground (or relatum), where the projected angle is found by reference to an intrinsic or inherent facet of the ground object. In contrast, (2) and (5) have a different logical structure: 'in front of' and 'to the right of' are here **ternary** relations, presuming a viewpoint V (the origin of the coordinate system), a figure and ground, all distinct.[28] In fact, these two kinds of spatial relation have quite different logical properties, as demonstrated by Levelt (1984, 1996), but only when distinguished and grouped in this way (more in a moment). Let us dub the binary relations **'intrinsic'**, but the ternary relations **'relative'** (because the descriptions are always relative to a viewpoint, in contradistinction to 'absolute' and 'intrinsic' descriptions).

To summarize then, the proposed classification (retaining the earlier numbering of examples) is:

(1) *The ball is in front of me*
   Coordinates: **Intrinsic**
   Origin: Speaker
   Relatum: Speaker

(3) *The ball is in front of the chair (at the chair's front)*
   Coordinates: **Intrinsic**
   Origin: Chair
   Relatum: Chair

(4) *The ball is in front of you*
   Coordinates: **Intrinsic**
   Origin: Addressee
   Relatum: Addressee

(2) *The ball is in front of the tree*
   Coordinates: **Relative**
   Origin: Speaker
   Relatum: Tree

(5) *The ball is to the right of the lamp, from your point of view*
    Coordinates: **Relative**
    Origin: Addressee
    Relatum: Lamp

(6) *John noticed the ball to the right of the lamp*
    Coordinates: **Relative**
    Origin: Third person (John)
    Relatum: Lamp

Note that use of the intrinsic system of coordinates entails that relatum (ground) and origin are constituted by the same object (the spatial relation is binary, between figure F and ground G), while use of the relative system entails that they are distinct (the relation is ternary, between F, G and viewpoint V). Note too that whether the centre is deictic, i.e. whether the origin is speaker (or addressee) or not, is simply irrelevant to this classification. This is obvious in the case of the grouping of (1), (3) and (4) together. It is also clear that, although the viewpoint in relative uses is normally speaker-centric, it may easily be addressee-centric or even centred on a third party as illustrated in (6). Hence *deictic and intrinsic are not opposed*; instead we need to oppose (a) *coordinate systems* 'intrinsic' vs. 'relative', on the one hand, and (b) *origins* 'deictic' and 'non-deictic' (or, alternatively, egocentric vs. allocentric) on the other. Since frames of reference are coordinate systems, it follows that, in language, frames of reference cannot be distinguished according to their characteristic, but variable, origins.

I expect a measure of resistance to this reformation of the distinctions, if only because the malapropism 'deictic frame of reference' has become a well-worn phrase. How, the critic will argue, can you define the frames of reference if you no longer employ the feature of deixis to distinguish them? In section 2.3.2 it will be shown that the three systems have distinct logical and spatial properties, which can be defined without reference to specific deictic or non-deictic origins. But first we must compare these two systems with the third system of coordinates in natural language, namely absolute frames of reference. Let us review them together.

2.3.1 *The three linguistic frames of reference*

As far as we know, and according to a suitably catholic construal, there are exactly three frames of reference grammaticalized or lexicalized in language (often, lexemes are ambiguous over two of these frames of reference, sometimes expressions will combine two frames,[29] but often each frame will have distinct linguistic expressions associated with it).[30]

Each of these frames of reference encompasses a whole family of related but distinct semantic systems.[31] It is probably true to say that even the most closely related languages (and even dialects within them) will differ in the details of the underlying coordinate systems and their geometry, the preferential interpretation of ambiguous lexemes, presumptive origins of the coordinates etc. Thus the student of language can expect that linguistic expressions glossed as, say, intrinsic 'side' in two languages will differ considerably in the way in which 'side' is in fact determined, how wide and how distant a search domain it specifies etc. Here we will treat the linguistic frames of reference in a relatively abstract way, returning in Chapter 3 to the details of linguistic variation.

Let us first define a set of primitives necessary for the description of all systems.[32] The application of some of the primitives is sketched in Figure 2.2, which illustrates three canonical exemplars from each of our three main types of system. Minimally, we need the primitives in Table 2.2, the use of which will be illustrated below:

Table 2.2. *Inventory of primitives*

---

1. System of labelled angles:
Language-specific labelled arcs (e.g. *front*, *left*, *north*) specified by coordinates around origin; such labels may or may not form a fixed template of oppositions (with, e.g., orthogonal axes).

2. Coordinates:
(a) Coordinates are *polar*, that is are specified by rotation from a fixed x-axis; single sets of terms may require more than one coordinate system;
(b) one *primary coordinate system* C_1 can be mapped from origin X_1 to secondary origin X_2, by the following transformations (or combinations of them):
  • Translation
  • Rotation
  • Reflection
  to yield a *secondary coordinate system* C_2.

3. Points:
F = Figure or referent with centre point at volumetric centre F_c
G = Ground or relatum, with volumetric centre G_c, and with a surrounding region r
V = Viewpoint of observer
X = Origin of the coordinate system, with X_2 as origin of a secondary coordinate system
A = Anchor point, to fix labelled coordinates
L = Designated landmark

4. Anchoring system:
which locks the labelled angles in 1 into the coordinate system in 2:
A = Anchor point, e.g. within G or V; in landmark systems A = L.
S = 'Slope' of a fixed bearing system, with infinite parallel lines across environment

---

INTRINSIC

"He's in front of the house."

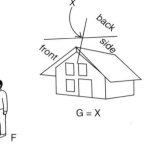

RELATIVE

"He's to the left of the house."

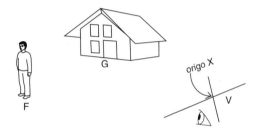

ABSOLUTE

"He's north of the house."

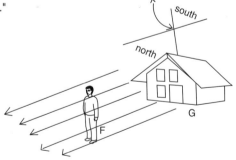

Figure 2.2. Underlying elements in the three frames of reference

Some of these concepts, like figure (the object to be located) and ground (the object with respect to which the figure is to be located), are familiar from earlier studies, but many of the notions have been left implicit in the literature. The application of some of these primitives to the three main canonical frames of reference is illustrated in Figure 2.2. Not diagrammed here is the role of the anchoring system, but how it works can be simply described. Take the first kind of system, the intrinsic system, which has in English amongst its subsystems the linguistic labels *front/back/sides*. To lock these to a ground object, the *front* or *back* of the object must be found, together with the centroid of the mass which will form the origin X of the coordinate system. Once the coordinates are locked to X and (say) the designated front of the object, we can find the other facet names by rotation through the quadrants *front, side, back, side*. Now take the third kind of system, the absolute. Again we find the centroid X of the ground object, and we find the salient 'slope' S across the landscape; now we lock the relevant local term (say 'north') to S, and we have a northern facet of the ground object. Again we can find the other labels now by clockwise rotation through, say, *north, east, south, west*, or alternatively simply by having other 'slopes' (e.g. *west*) given to us directly.[33]

The need for the other primitives will become clear later in Chapter 3, when different sub-types of linguistic system are described, and the role of secondary coordinates in the relative frame of reference is explored in depth. Combinations of these primitives yield a large family of systems which may be classified in the following tripartite scheme:

2.3.1.1 Intrinsic frame of reference
Informally, this frame of reference involves an object-centred coordinate system, where the coordinates are determined by the 'inherent features', sidedness or facets of the object to be used as the ground or relatum. The phrase 'inherent features', though widely used in the literature, is misleading: such facets have to be conceptually assigned according to some algorithm, or learned on a case-by-case basis, or more often a combination of these. The procedure varies fundamentally across languages, for example in English it is largely functional, so that the *front* of a TV is the side we attend to, while the *front* of a car is the facet that canonically lies in the direction of motion etc. But in some languages, it is much more closely based on shape, as in Tzeltal, where a volumetric analysis very similar to the object-centred analysis proposed by Marr in the theory of vision is required, and function and canonical orientation is largely

irrelevant (Levinson 1994). Such systems are contrasted in the next chapter. In many languages the morphology makes it clear that human or animal body-parts (and occasionally plant-parts) provide a prototype for the opposed sides: hence we talk about the fronts, backs, sides, lefts and rights (and in many languages heads, feet, horns, roots etc.) of other objects.[34] But whatever the procedure in a particular language, it relies primarily on the conceptual properties of the object: its shape, canonical orientation, characteristic motion and use etc.

The attribution of such facets provides the basis for a coordinate system in one of two ways. Having found, for example, the 'front', this may be used to anchor a ready-made system of oppositions 'front', 'back', 'sides' etc.[35] Alternatively, in other languages, there may be no such fixed armature as it were, each object having parts determined by specific shapes; in that case, finding 'front' does not predict the locus of 'back' etc., but nevertheless determines a direction from the volumetric centre of the object through the 'front' which can be used for spatial description. In either case, we can use the designated facet to extract an angle, or line, radiating out from the ground object, within or on which the figure object can be found (as in *the statue in front of the town hall*).

The geometrical properties of such intrinsic coordinate systems vary cross-linguistically. Systems with fixed armatures of contrastive expressions generally require the angles projected to be mutually exclusive (non-overlapping), so that in the intrinsic frame of reference (unlike the relative one) it makes no sense to say things like *?The cat is to the front and to the left of the truck* (meaning 'The cat is at the truck's front and at the truck's left hand side'). Systems utilizing a looser set of single parts make no such constraints (as in *The cat is in front of, and at the foot of, the chair*). In addition, the metric extent of the search domain designated (e.g. how far the cat is from the truck) can vary greatly: some languages require figure and ground to be in contact, or visually continuous, others allow the projection of enormous search domains ('In front of the church lie the mountains, running far off to the horizon').[36] More often, perhaps, the notion of a region, an object's penumbra as it were, is relevant, related to its scale.[37]

More exactly: An intrinsic spatial relator R is a binary spatial relation, with arguments F and G, where R typically names a part of G. The origin X of the coordinate system C is always on the volumetric centre of G. An intrinsic relation R(F, G) asserts that F lies in a search domain extending from G on the basis of an angle or line projected from the centre of G, through an anchor point A (usually the named facet 'R'), outwards for a determined distance. F and G may be any objects what-soever (including ego), and F may be a part of G. The relation R does not support transitive inferences, nor converse inferences (see below).

Labels for angles may or may not come in fixed armatures. When they do, they may be found by polar rotation: for example given that facet A is the 'front' of a building, clockwise rotation in 90 degree steps will yield 'side', 'back', 'side' and 'front' again. Or they may be assigned by isolating the major directed axes, yielding, for example, 'top' vs. 'bottom', 'back' vs. 'front', with 'side' as a residual term. When A (e.g. 'front') fixes the coordinates, we call it the anchor point. But coordinates need not come with a fixed set of oppositions: for example given that facet B is the *entrance* of a church, Gc its volumetric centre, we may derive an axis B-Gc, so that *at the entrance to the church* designates a search area on that axis, with no necessary implications about the locations of other intrinsic parts, *front*, *back* etc.

2.3.1.2 *Relative frame of reference*

This is roughly equivalent to the various notions of viewer-centred frame of reference mentioned above (e.g. Marr's 2.5D sketch, or the psycholin-guists' 'deictic' frame). But it is not quite the same. It presupposes a 'viewpoint' V (given by the location of a perceiver in any sensory modal-ity), and a figure and ground distinct from V. It thus offers a triangulation of three points, and utilizes coordinates fixed on V to assign directions to figure and ground. English *The ball is to the left of the tree* utilizes a frame of reference of this kind of course (as illustrated in Figure 2.3). Since the perceptual basis is not necessarily visual, calling this frame of reference 'viewer-centred' is potentially misleading, but perhaps innocent enough. Calling it deictic, however, is potentially pernicious, because the 'viewer' need not be ego, and need not be a participant in the speech event – as in "Bill kicked the ball to the left of the goal". Nevertheless, there can be little doubt that the deictic uses of this system are basic (prototypical), and are ontogenetically and conceptually prior.

The coordinate system, based on viewer V, seems generally to be based on the planes through the human body, giving us an 'up'/'down', 'back'/'front' and 'left'/'right' set of half-lines. Such a system of coor-dinates can be thought of as centred on the spine or main axis of the body and anchored by one of the body-parts (e.g. 'front' anchored to my chest). In that case we have polar coordinates, with quadrants based on orthogonal axes counted clockwise from 'front' to 'right', 'back' and 'left' (Herskovits 1986). Although the position of the body of viewer V

Figure 2.3. The relative frame of reference: "The ball is to the left of the tree"

may be one criterion for anchoring the coordinates, the direction of gaze may be another, and there is no doubt that relative systems are closely hooked into visual criteria. Languages may differ in the weight given to the two factors, for example in the extent to which occlusion plays a role in the definition of 'behind'.

But this set of coordinates on V is only the first step in the definition of a full relative system; in addition a secondary set of coordinates is usually derived by mapping (all or some of) the coordinates on V onto the relatum or ground object G. The mapping involves a transformation which may be 180 degree rotation, translation (movement without rotation or reflection) or reflection across the frontal transverse plane. Thus *John is in front of the tree* in English entails that the figure John is between V and G (the tree), because the primary coordinates on V seem to have been reflected in the mapping onto G, so that G has a 'front' before which John is located. Such a system can be diagrammed, to a first approximation, as in Figure 2.4.

The variation in such systems and their proper analysis are discussed in detail in the following chapter. But the point to emphasize here is

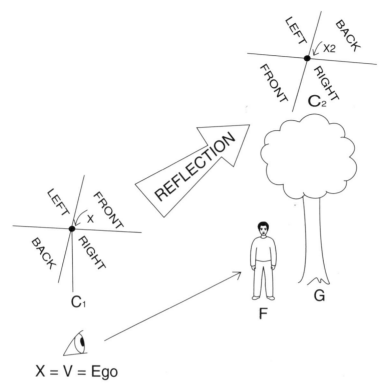

Figure 2.4. Secondary coordinates in a relative frame of reference: "John is in front of the tree"

that a large amount of variation in such systems is definable, according to, for example, the role of visual factors and the particular mapping transformations, constituting a broad family of relative systems.

Not all languages have terms glossing 'left', 'right', 'front', 'back'. Nor does the possession of such a system of linguistic oppositions guarantee the possession of a relative system. Many languages use such terms in a more or less purely intrinsic way (even when they are primarily used with deictic centres): i.e. they are used as binary relators specifying the location of F within a domain projected from a part of G (as in 'To my left', 'In front of you', 'At the animal's front', 'At the house's front' etc.). The full range of left/right systems is discussed in the next chapter. The tests for a relative system are (a) its utilizability with what is culturally construed as an object *without* intrinsic parts,[38] (b) whether there is a ternary relation with viewpoint V distinct from G, such that when V is rotated around the array, the description changes (see below). Now, languages that have a relative system of this kind also tend to have an intrinsic system sharing at least some of the same terms.[39] This typological implication, apart from showing the derivative and secondary nature of relative systems, also more or less guarantees the potential ambiguity of 'left', 'right', 'front', 'back' systems in languages with both frames of reference (although they may be disambiguated syntactically, as in English *to the left of the chair* vs. *at the chair's left*). Some languages that lack any such systematic relative system may nevertheless encode the odd isolated relative notion, like 'F is in my line of sight towards G'.

Relative systems that clearly use secondary coordinates mapped from V to G suggest that these mappings are in origin a means of extending the intrinsic frame of reference to cases where it would not otherwise apply (and this may suggest that the intrinsic system is rather fundamental in human linguistic spatial description).[40] Through projection of coordinates from the viewpoint V, we assign pseudo-intrinsic facets to G, as if trees had inherent fronts, backs and sides. For some languages, this is undoubtedly the correct analysis: the facets are thus named and regions projected with the same limitations that hold of intrinsic regions.[41] Thus many relative systems can be thought of as *derived intrinsic* ones – systems that utilize relative conceptual relations to extend and supplement intrinsic ones. One particular reason to so extend intrinsic systems is their extreme limitations as regards logical inference of spatial relations from linguistic descriptions: intrinsic descriptions support neither transitive nor converse inferences, but relative ones do (Levelt 1984, 1996, and see below).[42]

Although from a perceptual point of view a frame of reference like the relative one seems entirely fundamental, from a linguistic point of view it is not. In fact it is entirely dispensable. Western children learn this kind of system very late (mastering 'projective' or relative 'left' and 'right' as late as eleven or twelve). Many languages simply do not employ this frame of reference at all,[43] or only in marginal uses of linguistic expressions dedicated primarily to the intrinsic or absolute frame of reference. That means such languages have no way of expressing notions like 'in front/behind/to the left/right/side of the tree' as determined by the location of a 'viewer' or speaker. This will probably come as a bit of a shock to psychologists, who have, on the basis of familiar languages, confidently predicted the universality of the relative frame in language (e.g. Clark 1973, Miller and Johnson-Laird 1976, Takano 1989).

More exactly: A relative relator R expresses a ternary spatial relation, with arguments V, F and G, where F and G are unrestricted as to type, except that V must be centred on an observer and V and G must be distinct.[44] The primary coordinate system always has its origin on V; there may be a secondary coordinate system with origin on G. Such terminological systems are normally applied by polar rotation, for example, 'front', 'right', 'back' and 'left' may be assigned by clockwise rotation from 'front'. Coordinate systems built primarily on visual criteria and without a mapping onto a secondary origin, need not perhaps be polar, for they could in principle be defined by rectangular coordinates on the two-dimensional visual field (the retinal projection) so that 'left' and 'right' are defined on the horizontal or x axis, and 'front' and 'behind' on the (apparent) vertical or y axis ('behind' has (the base of) F higher than G and/or occluded by G). Some analyses of prepositions like *behind* or *beyond* which are built on vector analysis seem especially appropriate for such a visually determined kind of spatial terminology (see O'Keefe 1996), but in fact this makes little sense for English, where *front* and *back/behind* are clearly modelled on the terminology for intrinsic parts – and in general, relative systems seem to originate as extensions of intrinsic ones, as just mentioned.

Terms that may be glossed 'left' and 'right' may involve no secondary coordinates, although they sometimes do (as when they have reversed application from the English usage). Terms glossed 'front' and 'back' normally do involve secondary coordinates.[45] Secondary coordinates may be mapped from primary origin on V to secondary origin on G under the following transformations: rotation, translation and (arguably) reflection. Examples of these different mappings will be given in the next chapter.

Typological variations of such systems include: degree to which a systematic polar system of coordinates is available, degree of use of secondary coordinates, type of mapping function (rotation, translation, reflection) for secondary coordinates, differing anchoring systems for the coordinates (e.g. body-axis vs. gaze), differing degrees to which visual criteria (like occlusion, or place in retinal field) are definitional of the terms.

2.3.1.3 Absolute frame of reference
Amongst the several uses of the term 'absolute' frame of reference, one refers to the fixed direction provided by gravity (or the visual horizon under canonical orientation). Less obviously of psychological relevance,

the same idea of fixed directions can be applied to the horizontal. In fact, many languages make extensive, some almost exclusive, use of such an absolute frame of reference on the horizontal. They do so by fixing arbitrary fixed bearings, 'cardinal directions', corresponding one way or another to directions or arcs that can be related by the analyst to compass bearings. Speakers of such languages can then describe an array of, for example, a spoon in front of a cup, as 'spoon to north of cup' (etc.) without any reference to the viewer/speaker's location.

Such a system requires that persons maintain their orientation with respect to the fixed bearings at all times. People who speak such languages can be shown to do so, a matter of considerable psychological interest taken up in Chapters 4 and 6. How they do so is simply not known at the present time, but we may presume that a heightened sense of inertial navigation is regularly cross-checked with many environmental clues.[46] Indeed, many such systems are clearly abstractions and refinements from environmental gradients (mountain slopes, prevailing wind directions, river drainages, celestial azimuths etc.).[47] These 'cardinal directions' may therefore occur with fixed bearings skewed at various degrees from, and in effect unrelated to, our 'north', 'south', 'east' and 'west'. It perhaps needs emphasizing that this keeping track of fixed directions is, with appropriate socialization, not a feat restricted to certain ethnicities, races, environments or culture types, as shown by its widespread occurrence (in perhaps a third of all human languages) from Mesoamerica, to New Guinea, to Australia, to Nepal. No simple ecological determinism will explain the occurrence of such systems, which can be found alternating with, for example, relative systems, across neighbouring ethnic groups in similar environments, and which occur in environments of contrastive kinds (e.g. wide open deserts and closed jungle terrain).

The conceptual ingredients for absolute systems are simple: the relevant linguistic expressions are binary relators, with figure and ground as arguments, and a system of coordinates anchored to fixed bearings, which always have their origin on the ground. In fact, these systems are the only systems with conceptual simplicity and logical elegance. For example, they are the only systems that fully support transitive inferences across spatial descriptions: intrinsic descriptions do not do so, and relative ones only do so if viewpoint V is held constant (Levelt 1984). Intrinsic systems are dogged by the multiplicity of object types, the differing degrees to which the asymmetries of objects allow the naming of facets, and the problem of 'unfeatured' objects. Relative systems are dogged by the psychological difficulties involved in learning left/right distinctions,

the complexities involved in mapping secondary coordinates, and, because the linguistic expressions are often developed from intrinsic ones,
they tend to display ambiguities across frames of reference (like English
in front of). The liabilities of absolute systems, on the other hand, are
not so much logical as psychological: they impose a cognitive overhead,
namely the constant background calculation of cardinal directions, together with a system of dead reckoning that will specify for any arbitrary
point P which direction P is from ego's current locus (so that ego may
refer to the location of P).

Absolute systems may also show ambiguities of various kinds. First,
places of particular sociocultural importance may come to be designated
by a cardinal direction term, like a quasi-proper name, regardless of their
location with respect to G. Secondly, where the system is abstracted out
of landscape features, the relevant expressions (e.g. 'uphill' or 'upstream')
may either refer to places indicated by relevant local features (e.g. local
hill, local stream) or to the abstracted fixed bearings, where these do not
coincide. Thirdly, some such systems may even have relative interpretations (e.g. 'uphill' may imply further away in my field of vision; cf. our
interpretation of 'north' as top of a map etc.).

One crucial question with respect to absolute systems is how, conceptually, the coordinate system is thought of, in order to map a system of
terms onto fixed bearings. It may be a single polar system, as in our
'north', 'south', 'east' and 'west', where north is the designated anchor
and east, south, west found by clockwise rotation from north.[48] Other
systems may have a primary and a secondary axis, so that, for example,
a north/south axis is primary, but it is not clear which direction, north
or south, is itself the anchor.[49] Yet other systems favour no particular primary reference point, each half-axis having its own clear anchor or fixed
central bearing.[50] Some systems like that used in Tenejapa (see Chapter
4) are 'degenerate', or not fully linguistically specified, in that they offer
two labelled half-lines (roughly 'north', 'south'), but label both ends of the
orthogonal with the same terms ('across'). Even more confusing, some
systems may employ true abstracted cardinal directions on one axis, but
landmark designations on the other, guaranteeing that the two axes do
not remain orthogonal when arrays are described in widely different
places. Thus on the island of Bali, and similarly for many Austronesian
systems, one axis is determined by monsoons, and is a fixed, abstracted
axis, but the other is determined by the location of the central mountain,
and thus the one bearing varies continuously when one circumnavigates
the island (Wassmann and Dasen 1998). Even where systematic cardinal

systems exist, the geometry of the designated angles is variable. Thus, if we have four half-lines based on orthogonal axes, the labels may describe quadrants (as in Guugu Yimithirr), or they may have, for example, narrower arcs of application on one axis than the other (as appears to be the case in Wik Mungan[51]). Even in English, though we may think of north as a point on the horizon, we also use arcs of variable (and unclear) extent for informal description.

More precisely: An absolute relator R expresses a binary relation between F and G, asserting that F can be found in a search domain at the fixed bearing R from G. The origin X of the coordinate system is nearly always centred on G,[52] and the system of terms anchored by reference to a conceptual 'Slope' S. G may be any object whatsoever, including ego or another deictic centre; F may be a part of G. The geometry of the coordinate system is linguistically/culturally variable, so that in some systems equal quadrants of 90 degrees may be projected from G, while in others something more like 45 degrees may hold for arcs on one axis, and perhaps 135 degrees on the other. The literature also reports abstract systems based on star-setting points and winds, which will then tend to have uneven distribution around the horizon.[53]

Just as relative relators can be understood to map designated facets onto ground objects (thus 'on the front of the tree' assigns a named part to the tree), so absolute relators may also do so. Australian languages, for example, may have specific 'edge' suffixes, which applied to cardinal directions roots yield such meanings as 'northern edge/side' etc. Some of these stems can then only be analysed as an interaction between the intrinsic facets of an object and absolute directions.

2.3.2 *The 'logical structure' of the three frames of reference*

I have argued that as far as language is concerned we must distinguish frame of reference qua coordinate system from, for example, deictic centre qua origin of the coordinate system. Still, the sceptic may doubt that this is either necessary or possible.

First, to underline the necessity: each of our three frames of reference may occur with or without a deictic centre (or egocentric origin). Thus for the intrinsic frame we can say 'The ball is in front of me' (deictic centre); for the absolute frame we can say 'The ball is north of me'; and of course in the relative frame we can say 'The ball is in front of the tree (from where I am standing)'. Conversely, none of the three frames need have a deictic centre: thus in the intrinsic frame one can say 'in front of

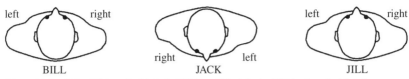

left   right   left   right

BILL   right   left   JILL
                            JACK

'**Transitivity fails:** Jill is at Jack's left, Bill is at Jill's left, but Bill isn't at Jack's left.
Converseness fails: Jill is at Jack's left, but Jack isn't at Jill's right'

Figure 2.5. Logical inadequacies of the intrinsic frame of reference

the chair', in the absolute frame 'north of the chair', and in the relative
frame 'in front of the tree from Bill's point of view'. This is just what we
should expect given the flexible nature of linguistic reference – it follows
from Hockett's (1960) design feature of displacement, or Bühler's (1982
[1934]) concept of transposed deictic centre.

Second, we need to show that we can in fact define the three frames
of reference adequately without reference to the opposition deictic vs.
non-deictic centre or origin. I have already hinted at plenty of distinguishing characteristics of each of the three frames. But to collect them
together, first consider the logical properties. The absolute and intrinsic
relators share the property that they are binary relations whereas relative
relators are ternary. But absolute and intrinsic are distinguished in that
absolute relators define asymmetric transitive relations (if F_1 is north of
G, and F_2 is north of F_1, then F_2 is north of G), where converses can
be inferred (if F is north of G, G is south of F). The same does not hold
for intrinsic relators, which hardly support any spatial inferences at all
without further assumptions (see Levelt 1984, 1996). Consider, if Jack
and Jill are standing side by side, then Jill may be at Jack's left, but it
does not follow that Jack is at Jill's right – she may be facing in the other
direction, as sketched in Figure 2.5. With respect to logical properties,
absolute and relative relators share logical features, since relative relators
support transitive and converse inferences *provided that* viewpoint V is held
constant.

This is already sufficient to distinguish the three frames. But we
may add further distinguishing features, for certain important spatial
properties follow from the nature of the anchoring system in each case.
In the intrinsic case we can think of the named facet of the object as
providing the Anchor, in the relative case we can think of the viewpoint
V on an observer and the Anchor being constituted by, for example, the
direction of his front or his gaze, while in the absolute case either one
or more conceptual 'slopes' across the environment fixes the coordinate

Rotation of:

	viewer	ground object	whole array
Intrinsic "ball in front of chair" 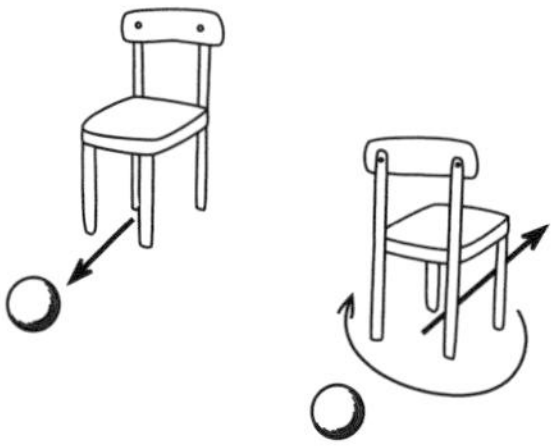 	same description? yes	same description? no	same description? yes
Relative "ball to left of chair" 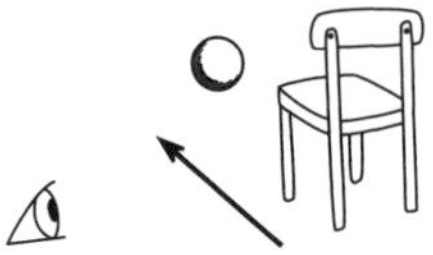	no	yes	no
Absolute "ball to north of chair" 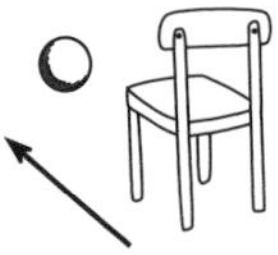	yes	yes	no

Figure 2.6. Properties of the frames of reference under rotation

Table 2.3. *Summary of properties of different frames of reference*

	INTRINSIC	ABSOLUTE	RELATIVE
Relation:	binary	binary	ternary
Origin on:	Ground	Ground	Viewpoint V
Anchored by:	A within G	'slope'	A within V
Transitivity:	no	yes	yes if V held constant
Constancy under rotation of:			
Whole array:	yes	no	no
Viewer:	yes	yes	no
Ground:	no	yes	yes

system. From this, certain distinct properties emerge of such conceptual systems under rotation of part or whole of the assemblage, as illustrated in Figure 2.6.[54] These properties have a special importance for the study of non-linguistic conceptual coding of spatial arrays, since they allow systematic experimentation as will be shown in Chapters 4 and 5.

Altogether then the distinctive features of each frame of reference are as summarized in Table 2.3; these features are jointly certainly sufficient to establish the nature of the three frames of reference independently of reference to the nature of the origin of the coordinate system.

We may conclude this discussion of the underlying properties of the different linguistic frames of reference with the following observations:

a. Languages use, it seems, just three frames of reference: absolute, intrinsic and relative.
b. Not all languages use all frames of reference: some use predominantly one only (absolute or intrinsic; relative seems to require intrinsic), some use two (intrinsic and relative, or intrinsic and absolute), while some use all three.
c. Linguistic expressions may be specialized to a frame of reference, so we cannot assume that choice of frame of reference lies entirely outside language, for example in spatial thinking, as some have suggested. But spatial relators may be ambiguous (or semantically general) across frames, and often are.

2.3.3 Realigning frames of reference across disciplines and modalities

We are now at last in a position to see how our three linguistic frames of reference align with the other distinctions in the literature arising from the consideration of other modalities (as listed in Table 2.1 above). The motive, recollect, is to try to make sense of the very idea of 'same frame of reference' across modalities, and in particular across the various kinds of nonlinguistic thinking as well as linguistic conceptualization.

An immediate difficulty is that, by establishing that frames of reference in language should be considered independent of the origin of the coordinate systems, we have opened up a gulf between language and the various perceptual modalities, where the origin of the coordinate system is so often fixed on some specific egocentre. But this mismatch is in fact just as it should be: language is a flexible instrument of communication, designed (as it were) so that one may express other persons' points of view, take other perspectives and so on. At the level of perception, origin and coordinate system presumably come pre-packaged as a whole, but at the level of language, and perhaps more generally at the level of conception, they can vary freely and combine.[55]

So to realign the linguistic distinctions with distinctions made across other modalities, we need to 'fix' the origin of the coordinate system so that it coincides, or fails to coincide, with ego in each frame of reference. We may do so as follows. First, we may concede that the relative frame of reference, though not necessarily egocentric, is prototypically so. Second, we may note that the intrinsic system is typically, but not definitionally, non-egocentric. Third, and perhaps most arbitrarily, we may assign a non-egocentric origin to the absolute system. These assignments should be understood as special subcases of the uses of the linguistic frames of reference.

If we make these restrictions, then we can align the linguistic frames of reference with the other distinctions from the literature as in Table 2.4.

Notice then that, under these restrictions concerning the nature of the origin:

a. Intrinsic and absolute are grouped as allocentric frames of reference, as opposed to the egocentric relative system.
b. Absolute and relative are grouped as orientation-bound, as opposed to intrinsic which is orientation-free.

This correctly captures our theoretical intuitions: in certain respects absolute and intrinsic viewpoints are fundamentally similar – they are binary relations which are viewpoint independent, where the origin is typically not ego, although that is not ruled out. They are thus allocentric systems which yield an ego-invariant picture of the 'world out there'. On the other hand, absolute and relative frameworks are fundamentally

Table 2.4. *Aligning classifications of frames of reference*

INTRINSIC	ABSOLUTE	RELATIVE
Origin ≠ Ego	Origin ≠ Ego	Origin = Ego
Object-centred Intrinsic-perspective 3D Model	Environment-centred	Viewer-centred Deictic-perspective 2.5D Sketch
Allocentric		Egocentric
Orientation-free	Orientation-bound	

similar on another dimension, because they both impose a larger spatial framework on an assemblage, and thus specify its orientation with respect to external coordinates: thus in an intrinsic framework it is impossible to distinguish enantiomorphic wholes (like a left vs. a right shoe), while in either of the orientation-bound systems it is inevitable.[56] Absolute and relative frameworks presuppose a Newtonian or Kantian spatial envelope, while the intrinsic framework is Leibnizian.

The object-centred nature of the intrinsic system hooks it up to Marr's (1982) 3D model in the theory of vision, and the nature of the linguistic expressions involved suggests that the intrinsic framework is a generalization from the analysis of objects into their parts: a whole configuration can be seen as a single complex object, so that we can talk of the leading car in a convoy as 'at the head of the line'. The viewer-centred nature of the relative framework connects it directly to the sequence of 2D representations in the theory of vision. Thus the spatial frameworks in the perceptual systems can indeed be correlated with the linguistic frames of reference.

Let me summarize: I have sought to establish that there is nothing incoherent in the notion 'same frame of reference' across modalities or inner representation systems. Indeed, even the existing distinctions that have been proposed can be seen in many detailed ways to correlate with the revised linguistic ones, once the special flexibility of the linguistic systems with respect to origin is taken into account. Thus it should be possible, and intellectually profitable, to formulate the distinct frames of reference in such a way that they have cross-modal application. Notice that this view conflicts with the views of some (e.g. Levelt 1996) that frames of reference in language are imposed just in the mapping from perception to language via the encoding process. On the contrary, I shall presume that any and every spatial representation, perceptual or conceptual, must involve a frame of reference, for example retinotopic images just are, willy-nilly, in a viewer-centred frame of reference.

But at least one major problem remains: it turns out that the three distinct frames of reference are 'untranslatable' from one to the other, which throws further doubt on the idea of correlations and correspondences across sensory and conceptual representational levels.

2.4 MOLYNEUX'S QUESTION

In 1690 William Molyneux wrote John Locke a letter posing the following celebrated question: if a blind man, who knew by touch the difference between a cube and a sphere, had his sight restored, would he recognize the selfsame objects under his new perceptual modality or not?[57]

The question whether our spatial perception and conception is modality specific is as alive now as then. Is there one central spatial model, to which all our input senses report, and from which instructions can be generated, appropriate to the various output systems (touch, movement, language, gaze and so on)?

There have of course been attempts to answer Molyneux directly, but the results are conflicting: on the one hand, sight-restored individuals take a while to adjust (Gregory 1987: 94–6), monkeys reared with their own limbs masked from sight have trouble relating touch to vision when the mask is finally removed (Howard 1987: 730f.), and touch and vision are attuned to different properties (e.g. the tactile sense is more attuned to weight and texture than shape; Klatsky and Lederman 1993); on the other hand, human neonates immediately extrapolate from touch to vision (Meltzoff 1993) and the neurophysiology suggests direct cross-wirings (Berthoz 1991: 81, but cf. Stein 1992), so that some feel that the answer to the question is a 'resounding "yes"' (Eilan 1993: 237). More soberly, it seems that there is some innate supra-modal system observable in monkeys and infants, but it may be very restricted, and sophisticated cross-modal thinking may even be dependent on language.[58]

Here I want to suggest another way to think about this old question. Put simply, we may ask whether the same frames of reference can in principle operate across all the modalities, and if not, whether at least they can be translated into one another.

What we should mean by 'modality' here is an important question. In what follows I shall assume that corresponding to (some of) the different senses, and more generally to input/output systems, there are specialized 'central' representational systems, for example an imagistic system related to vision, a propositional system related to language, a kinaesthetic system related to gesture, and so on (cf. Levelt 1989, Jackendoff 1991). Our version of Molyneux's question then becomes:

a. Do the different representational systems natively and necessarily employ certain frames of reference?
b. If so, can representations in one frame of reference be translated (converted) into another frame of reference?

Let us discount here the self-evident fact that certain kinds of information may perhaps in principle be modality specific: for example spatial representations in an imagistic mode must, it seems, be determinate with respect to shape, while those in a propositional mode need not and, perhaps, cannot be so.[59] Similarly, the haptic-kinaesthetic modality will have available direct information about weight, texture, tactile warmth and three-dimensional shape which we can only guess at from visual information (Klatsky and Lederman 1993), while the directional and inertial information from the vestibular system is of a different kind again. All this would seem to rule out a *single* supra-modal spatial representation system: What hybrid monster would a representation system have to be to record such disparate information? But all that concerns us here is the compatibility of *frames of reference* across modalities.

So, first, let us take the question of translatability across frames of reference. This is the easier question, and the answer to it offers an indirect answer to the first question. Here there is a striking but, on a moment's reflection, self-evident fact: one cannot freely convert information from one framework to another. Consider, for example, an array with a bottle on the ground at the (intrinsic) front side of a chair; suppose too that you view the array from a viewpoint such that the bottle is to the right of the chair, and as it happens the bottle is also north of the chair (see Figure 2.7). Now I ask you to remember it, and suppose you 'code' the scene in an intrinsic frame of reference: 'Bottle in front of chair', discarding other information. It is immediately obvious that from this intrinsic description you cannot later generate a relative description – if you were viewing the array so that you are facing one side of the chair, then the bottle will be either to the left of, or to the right of the chair – depending on your viewpoint. So without a 'coding' or specification of the locus of the viewpoint V, one cannot generate a relative description from an intrinsic description. The same holds for an absolute description: knowing

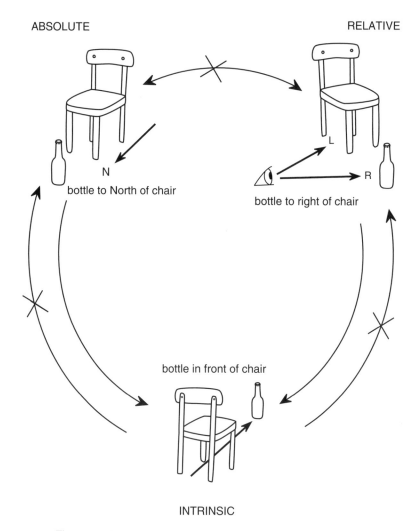

Figure 2.7. The partial untranslatability across frames of reference

that the bottle is at the front of the chair will not tell you whether it is north or south or east or west of the chair – for that you will need ancillary information. In short, one cannot get from an intrinsic description – an orientation-free representation – to either of the orientation-bound representations.

What about conversions between the two orientation-bound frame-works? Again, it is clear that no conversion is possible: from a relative description or coding 'The bottle is to the left of the chair' you do not know what cardinal direction it lies in, nor from 'The bottle is north of the chair' can one derive a viewpoint-relative description like 'The bottle is to the left of the chair'.

In fact, the only direction in which one may convert frames of reference is, in principle, from the two orientation-bound frames to the orientation-free one.[60] For if the description of the orientation of the ground object is fully specified, then one can derive an intrinsic description: for example from the relative description 'The chair is facing to my right and the bottle is to the right of the chair in the same plane' one may in principle get to the intrinsic specification 'The bottle is at the chair's front', and similarly from the absolute description 'The chair is facing north and the bottle is to the north of the chair'. Normally, though, the orientation of the ground object is irrelevant to the orientation-bound descriptions, so this remains only a translation in principle. Translations in all other directions are in principle impossible.

This simple fact about translatability across frames of reference may have far-reaching consequences. Consider for example the following syllogism:

1. Frames of reference are incommensurable (a representation in one framework is not freely convertible into a representation in another).
2. Each sense utilizes its own frame(s) of reference: for example while vision primarily uses a viewer-centred frame, touch (arguably) uses primarily an object-centred frame, based on the appreciation of form through three-dimensional grasping.
   Ergo:
3. Representations from one modality (e.g. haptic) cannot be freely translated into representations in another (e.g. visual).

The syllogism suggests then that the answer to Molyneux's question is negative – the blind man upon seeing for the first time will not recognize by sight what he knew before by touch. More generally, we will not be able to exchange information across any internal representation systems that are not based on one and the same frame of reference.

I take this to be a clearly false conclusion, in fact a *reductio ad absurdam*: we can feel something in the dark and visualize how it must look. Not only can we construct mental images from touch, and thus draw what we have felt, we can also gesture about what we have seen, and talk about shapes and spaces however perceived. Since premise (1) seems self-evidently true, we must then reject premise (2), the assumption that each sensory modality or representational system operates exclusively in its own primary, proprietary frame of reference. In short, either the frame of reference must be the same across all modalities or representational systems in order to allow the cross-modal sharing of information, or each must allow more than one frame of reference.

Intuitively, this seems the correct conclusion. On the one hand, peripheral sensory systems may operate in proprietary frames of reference: for example low-level vision may know only of 2D retinotopic arrays, while the otoliths (small pendulums in our inner ears) only know of a gravitational frame of reference. But, on the other hand, at a higher level, visual processing seems to deliver 3D analyses of objects as well as 2D ones. Thus when we (presumably) use the visual system to imagine rotations of objects, we project from 3D models (intrinsic) to 2.5D (relative) ones, showing that both are available. Thus more central, more conceptual, levels of representation seem capable of adopting more than one frame of reference.

Here then is the first part of the answer to our puzzle. Representational systems of different kinds, specialized to different sensory modalities (like visual memory) or output systems (like gesture and language), may be capable of adopting different frames of reference.

In fact, it will transpire below that there is direct experimental evidence for this flexibility in frames of reference – we can show that the Mayan inhabitants of Tenejapa utilize the same frame of spatial reference in language, memory, inference and gesture, and yet this frame of reference is not the same as that used by, for example, the inhabitants of Holland. To account for these facts, some explanation greater than the mere flexibility of internal representations is required – we will need an explanation of why the distinct levels of representation used by an individual tend to conform. One driving fact here will turn out to be language, for many languages simply fail to express one or more of the different possible frames of reference. Such restrictions place a bottleneck on the entire system of representations – if we are to talk about what we see and feel and remember, we must make sure that those representations are consistent with the available linguistic ones, or can be converted into them. That is why the limited translatability of frames of reference, together with a linguistic bottleneck, tend to drive uniformity of frame of reference through the entire spatial system. Thus the facts that (a) frameworks are not freely convertible, (b) languages may offer restricted frameworks as output, and (c) it may be desirable to describe any spatial experience whatsoever at some later point, all conspire to require that speakers code spatial experiences at the time of experience in whatever output frameworks their dominant language offers.

CHAPTER 3

Linguistic diversity

3.1 AN OVERVIEW OF SPATIAL LANGUAGE

The prior chapter has provided the conceptual underpinnings to appreciate both the striking variety of spatial coordinate systems to be found in language, and the relatively small set of underlying principles from which they are constructed. In this chapter, I sketch how the three basic frames of reference get instantiated in different languages. Here we will be concerned however not with the detailed grammar, morphology and lexical details of different languages – for that the reader is urged to see the companion volume (Levinson and Wilkins in preparation) – but primarily with the relevant semantic parameters, and how various combinations of these get variably encoded. To set the frame-of-reference facts in proper perspective, it will also be useful to mention other (non-frame-of-reference) semantic fields in spatial language, to make clear how they relate and how they are different from frame-of-reference information.

A serious overview of what is known about spatial language would be a book in itself. It is moreover a field of study dominated by preconceptions based on familiar languages – for example the presumption that the most important aspects of spatial language are encoded in adpositions (prepositions or postpositions). This presumption has been elevated to theoretical prediction by, for example, Landau and Jackendoff (1993), to the effect that spatial relations will express only a few aspects of 'gross geometry' of the ground or reference object, and will be coded in just a few closed form-classes, principally adpositions. They claim that 'we can develop a fairly comprehensive idea of the spatial relations expressed in language by focusing on spatial prepositions' (p. 223), proceed to an analysis of the geometric constraints on figure/ground relations coded in English prepositions, and then leap to universal claims such as: no language will have spatial relators expressing specific volumetric shapes of ground objects – for example there will be no preposition *sprough* meaning 'through a cigar-shaped object' (p. 226). But the Californian language Karuk has precisely such a spatial prefix, *-vara* 'in through a tubular space' (Mithun 1999: 142)![1] The whole set of claims is based on woeful ignorance of the cross-linguistic facts. As we shall see in this chapter (section 3.5), spatial information is not restricted to one part of speech, but is typically distributed throughout the clause in many different kinds of morphemes, and the spatial distinctions that are made in each of these classes can be extremely detailed, and indeed unexpected.

Many observers (e.g. Talmy 1988 and Jackendoff 1983: 14) have thought that spatial language may give us deep insights into the nature of spatial cognition in general (van der Zee 1996: 14, puts this forward as a general methodological premise). For example, Talmy (1988: 171) suggests that the properties of spatial language tell us interesting things about what is neglected or abstracted in naïve human spatial cognition: 'If grammatical specifications generally correspond to (linguistic) cognitive structuring, then the nature of that structure is largely relativistic or topological rather than absolute or Euclidean.' Unfortunately, no such inference from the absence of characteristics in the linguistic system to the general nature of cognition is possible. We have already seen in Chapter 2 that the sensory and motor systems of human cognition require a highly precise Euclidean metric system of coordinates, and it is clear that language abstracts from these in interesting ways. But this abstraction tells us about language, not the underlying cognitive systems. The inference that we can make is only in the other, positive direction, namely from the presence of any linguistic distinction to the need for its support by underlying cognitive systems, and this will already take us very far in understanding the nature of non-linguistic spatial reasoning, as will be illustrated in Chapter 4. But to understand how far, we must independently investigate language and then non-linguistic cognition, and that is the substance of this book, as detailed in Chapters 4, 5 and 6. In Chapter 7, we will return to address these global issues about the relation between language and the underlying cognitive systems that support it.

In this chapter, the main focus is on frames of reference, specifically how the semantic parameters are selected and arranged in specific languages. But it will be useful to start with a broader perspective, giving an impression of where frame-of-reference information fits into the larger picture of spatial language. We will then proceed to the main focus, namely the diverse semantical variants of the main frames of reference. For although, as we saw in Chapter 2, there seem to be just three frames of reference universally available in cognition and language, the ways in which these are conceptually structured in specific semantical systems can be quite divergent even within a major type (absolute, relative or intrinsic). Finally (although this is not the major focus of this book), a sketch is provided of the way in which these distinctions tend to be encoded in the forms of language, that is in linguistic subsystems.

3.2 CONCEPTUAL DOMAINS UNDERLYING THE LANGUAGE OF SPACE

Space is not a restricted domain like, for example, colour, kinship or the plant world, in each of which it is arguably natural to ask how languages code the relevant distinctions. Indeed, few languages probably have a word for 'space' in the abstract sense in which it used in this book – it has taken a sustained philosophical and scientific tradition of western thought to extract such a notion, as we saw in Chapter 1. In unwritten languages one is more likely to find a term for 'place where something belongs' (as in Tzeltal), or 'sacred site' (as in Guugu Yimithirr) – the notion *place* is much more frequently lexicalized (often with restrictions as just sketched) than the abstract notion *space*. One may therefore be forgiven for wondering whether space, or even generalized place, plays any general role in language – that is, whether we may hope for universals in the spatial domain in any way similar to those in say colour terminologies or ethnobotanical nomenclature. But there is one striking universal in spatial language – as far as we know all languages have *Where*-questions, usually with a common morpheme that bridges across motion and location (Ulltan 1978).[2] Such questions presuppose a notion of place. But as we shall further see, all languages also encode at least one frame of reference or coordinate system – and such coordinate systems presuppose an abstract notion of space, a search domain in which entities may be found.

Taking the hint from the universality of *Where*-questions, we may think about the spatial domain as essentially about location and direction. Notice that this sets to one side the Platonic and Cartesian idea (mentioned in Chapter 1) that space is essentially about the tri-dimensionality of matter. Such a view would lead in a different direction, placing, for example, dimensional expressions in language (i.e. 'long', 'wide', 'thick', etc.) at the heart of spatial conception (see Bierwisch 1967, Bierwisch and Lang 1989, Lang 1995). Interestingly, there are languages (like Yélî Dnye) without proper dimensional expressions,[3] suggesting that this is actually a specialized subdomain that may have more to do with such cultural activities as carpentry and masonry than the roots of human cognition.

The spatial domain has both uniformities and major internal divisions or subdomains. Apart from *Where*-questions, one important uniformity is the distinction between *figure* and *ground*, where the thing to be located is the figure and the thing with respect to which something is located is the ground (this Gestalt terminology was introduced by Talmy 1983, but is equivalent to the older terminology of *theme* and *relatum*, or the more recent *trajector* and *landmark*, introduced by Langacker 1987). Most spatial descriptions display both elements, allowing one to talk of *spatial relations* as specifications of the relation between figure and ground. If all spatial language had this property, it would be thoroughly Leibnizian – space would be conceived as the relations between things, not as an abstract void à la Newton or Kant. But in some languages abstract spatial vectors play a crucial role – one can say in effect things like 'The white pigeons fly north at this time of year', in which *north* is not a landmark or goal but an abstract direction. Nevertheless, in all languages *Where*-questions tend to elicit answers in which the location of the figure is specified as in some relation to a ground.

Considering just static location initially, let us consider different possible answers to a *Where*-question. We may think about these as different solutions to the problem of how to specify the location of a thing. The major solutions employed in languages are of distinct types, as detailed below (F stands for Figure, G for Ground), or sketched in a different format in Figure 3.1:

1. **No frame of reference or coordinate system employed:**
   A. **Placenames**, where F is located at a named place G.
   B. **Deixis**, where F is located relative to a (usually egocentric) G in terms of radial categories ('here' vs. 'there'), or in combination with a pointing gesture ('there' with a point).
   C. **Contiguity or topology**, where F is located as contiguous with G.
2. **Frames of reference, or employment of coordinate systems:**
   A. **Vertical**
   B. **Horizontal**

      B.1. **Intrinsic**
      B.2. **Relative**
      B.3. **Absolute**

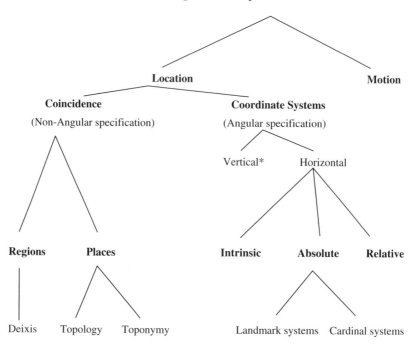

(*The vertical dimension is divided off here for practical reasons — it shares the same major divisions into intrinsic, absolute and relative.)

Figure 3.1. Major semantic subfields in spatial language

Each of these solutions may be thought of as a distinct strategy for locating referents, and they are differentially developed by different languages. They tend to form clear semantic subdomains, expressed with distinctive sets of morphemes. Nevertheless, these subdomains overlap, in the sense that in one clause many of these fields may contribute semantic content.

In the first major locative class, no coordinate system is employed to specify the figure's location with respect to the ground – that is, no angular specification is given. Instead, the figure is said to be coincident with, contiguous to, or proximate to the ground object, or some part of it. Perhaps this is most obvious in the case of placenames – *The tournament is at Wimbledon* simply locates the figure at the ground location. In English, the prepositions (*at Wimbledon, in London, on Salisbury Plain*) clearly assimilate placenames to the topology system, but in many languages placename specifications require no spatial relators (one says in effect 'He is Wimbledon'), or occur with a special locative case, adposition or other distinct construction, hence we need analytically to distinguish toponymy from topology.

'Topology' in the literature on spatial language refers to the sort of domain covered by the English prepositions *in*, *at*, *on*, *near*, *between* and so forth – that is to notions of coincidence, contact, containment, contiguity and proximity (the notion is thus wider than mathematical topology, see below). This domain can be conceived of as essentially about spatial coincidence or its approximation (as in *near*), with the subsequent subdivisions of types of coincidence (as in *in* vs. *on*). It is the domain of spatial language that has been most heavily studied, although not in proper cross-linguistic perspective – it is not central to the concerns of this book, but will be briefly treated further below.

Deictic specification, as in *It is here*, provides another kind of non-angular spatial location, often involving special locative constructions. Deixis in fact is just a way of providing a special kind of ground or landmark, and can thus play a role in all the other spatial subdomains. Although in combination with a motion verb, deictic specifications may seem to yield directions, they are in fact normally radial: *He came here* only specifies a goal, not a direction – to get a direction we would need to have two points specified, source and goal. *The orange is here* fails to specify an angular location from the deictic centre (here normally the speaker) in just the same way as a topological description like *The orange is in the bowl* fails to specify an angle with respect to the bowl (contrast a frame of reference description like *The orange is to the left of the bowl*). The strategy for location reference in all of these non-angular locative descriptions is 'choose a ground or landmark object in close contiguity with the object to be located'.

A quite different strategy from these specifications of spatial coincidence or contiguity is to use a coordinate system. The strategy is to choose a prominent ground object at some remove from the figure or object to be located, and then to specify a search domain from the ground by specifying an angle from that landmark, as in *The orange is to the left of the bowl*, *Amsterdam is north of Utrecht* or *The statue by Giambologna is in front of the cathedral*. As outlined in Chapter 2, there seem to be just three main types of frame of reference, but within each the possibilities of variation are very substantial, and languages make differential use of these possibilities, as will be described below. One may also talk similarly of *The bird above the tree*, using the vertical angle overdetermined by gravity, our upright stance and normally upright head position. The vertical dimension is special in various ways and is an angular specification that creeps into essentially non-angular topological specifications, as illustrated by the *The orange on the table* (about which more later). The three frames of reference, and the semantic specializations within them that are to be found in different languages, constitute the main focus of this chapter.

A final major branch in the spatial domain is motion description. Like most locative descriptions, nearly all descriptions of motion also involve reference to ground locations (as mentioned above, exceptions are statements like *In April the white pigeons fly southwards*). Two crucial grounds for motion descriptions are 'goal' (the landmark towards which motion is directed) and 'source' (or the landmark from which it originates). Notice that specification of either source or goal alone does not determine a direction – it merely determines a progression towards or away from a ground. Specification of both (as in *He went from Antwerp to Amsterdam*) determines a unique vector – so, unlike in locative description, one can specify a direction without employing frames of reference. Often, though, frames of reference will be employed either exclusively (as in *In the summer the geese fly north*) or as part of, or in addition to, goal or source specification (as in *He ran off behind the building*). Deictic verbs of motion (as in *He came late*) may lexically specify a goal, namely the place of speaking, and verbs of motion may also build in 'attainment of goal' as in *reach*, *arrive*, or 'departure from source' as in *leave*. Verbs of motion may also package other semantic material, like manner of motion, and even languages with very restricted verbal inventories seem to have a set of contrastive motion verbs (see the description of Jaminjung in Schultze-Berndt 2000, in preparation). It is static description that will be most important to what follows, but the reader should note that most of the subdomains listed in figure 3.1 under location recur in the motion subdomain: motion description can involve, for example, deixis (as in *Come here!*), frames of reference (as in *Move to the left!*) and even topology (as in *Put it inside the bowl!*). Further discussion of motion description is therefore postponed till section 3.5, after these other subdomains have been described.

Figure 3.1 has laid out the major semantic subdomains pertinent to this book. It is important to remember that any spatial description is likely to draw on the resources of a number of these subdomains, as in *It is there, in front of the house near the door* (in this case, deixis, frames of reference, and topology). Nevertheless, they constitute analytically distinct conceptual domains, and moreover cross-linguistically tend to have distinctive form-classes associated with their expression. In the rest of the chapter these different kinds of subsystem will be reviewed. The locative solutions involving coincidence or contiguity, where no coordinate systems are employed, are not the subject of this book, but are briefly described immediately below in order to give a wider context for the remainder of the discussion.

3.3 SOLUTIONS TO PLACE SPECIFICATION *NOT* INVOLVING FRAMES OF REFERENCE OR COORDINATE SYSTEMS

3.3.1 Placenames

Named locations offer a simple solution to location specification – one simply says the X is at the place named Y. The study of placenames or onomastics is one of the older branches of linguistic enquiry, since the extraordinary conservatism of toponyms preserves the appellations of long-forgotten peoples (from Massachusetts to London). But despite the long tradition of study, little of theoretical interest has emerged. The field is no doubt ripe for revolution, and some interesting ideas have been developed by Hunn (1996) and Kari (1989): the interesting questions are just what drives differential densities of placenames, and what the principles underlying monomorphemic vs. complex, or descriptive vs. opaque placenames are. My own field experience suggests that traditional naming systems are often very dense – for example the underpopulated Pacific island of Rossel has a striking density of names, mostly binomial, covering virtually every ridge, reef and stream (see also Goodenough 1956).

Given the utility and simplicity of a dense placenaming system, why are such systems not even more developed? Obviously, one factor is lexical proliferation, with consequential learning overload. But here there are possibilities of generative systems of placenames, which are never exploited as far as we know in societies of simple technology. For example, the kind of grid pattern underlying the naming of Manhattan streets would provide one kind of general solution. The absence of such widespread systems reflects an underlying universal, discussed below: no natural languages make systematic use of Cartesian coordinates (at least outside expert contexts). Another limitation, brought out by this discussion, is that placenames themselves of course do not provide a way of *finding* the location: they trade on an underlying mental map of locations, a matter taken up in Chapter 6 below.

3.3.2 Deictic systems

Deixis concerns the relativization of reference to properties of the speech event. Many aspects of deixis, for example tense, have nothing to do with spatial conception. But deixis is involved in the interpretation of spatial expressions in many different ways. Firstly, many statements of location and motion make overt reference to deictic parameters, as in *It's over there* or *He's coming here*. In this case, as mentioned, deixis is simply a means of providing a rather special ground or reference point, namely the location of the speech participants. Such locutions (in English at least) presuppose a division of space into an inner and outer circle around the speaker as it were, defining *here* vs. *there*, but where the exact division is contextually established. They do not tell us in which direction locations lie, and even for motions they only give a goal or a source and no fixed direction, unless combined with other specifications (note that many languages have 'hither'/'thither' morphemes which do not take up an argument slot, allowing easy further specification of goal or source). In this way, they are fundamentally different from locutions that employ frames of reference, as in *It's to the left of the desk*, or *He's going north from the town*. Deictic adverbs and demonstratives may succeed in pragmatically determining a distance or a location, but they typically fail to provide angular information on the horizontal dimension. (One has to say 'typically' because some languages, e.g. the Eskimo languages (Fortescue 1988, Jacobson 1984), have enormous arrays of demonstratives which have not only deictic content but also built-in directions in the absolute frame of reference, a point discussed below). It is the lack of angular specification that motivates the fact that deictics are often (and often obligatorily) accompanied by gesture, where the gesture can give finer degrees of angular arc than any linguistic specification.

Secondly, there is often covert reference to deictic parameters, as in *It's thirty miles away* which is understood as 'thirty miles away *from here*' (but compare: *He wanted to go to Istanbul but it was thirty miles away*). This covert reference intrudes into what I shall have to say about frames of reference below: a statement like *He kicked the ball to the left of the goalie* may, but need not, be interpreted from the speaker's viewing point at the time (it is just as naturally interpreted from the protagonist's or the goalie's point of view). In general, all frames of reference may or may not make use of an egocentric perspective or use a speech participant as a ground, as will be further touched on below.

Deictic spatial specifications may be built into many kinds of linguistic expression, typically into demonstrative pronouns and adverbs, or affixes that derive such categories, motion verbs and directional particles or affixes. Because the use of features of the speech situation to add further points of reference is always a possibility in spatial description, deictic parameters can intrude into all other kinds of spatial description, thus constituting a special kind of spatial parameter.

It is important to appreciate that deixis itself does not constitute a frame of reference. That is because deictic specifications of location merely use the deictic centre as a special kind of ground, and they do not themselves contribute to angular specifications of the kind that constitute coordinate systems. In Chapter 2 we noted, in discussing frames of reference, that we need to make a clear distinction between the nature of the coordinate system itself – whether, for example, it is based on bodily coordinates or fixed bearings – and the nature of the *origin* of the coordinate system: the origin of any frame of reference can, but need not be, a participant in the current speech event. Thus the expressions *north of me, in front of me, in front of the tree from where I'm standing* make use of the absolute, intrinsic and relative frames of reference, respectively, but all contain an explicit deictic component. The phrase 'deictic frame of reference' is therefore, despite its prevalence, conceptual nonsense. Specification of the origin of the coordinate system within a frame of reference is one way in which deixis contributes to spatial descriptions of all types. Other ways include specification within or beyond a certain circumference from the deictic centre (as in a simple interpretation of *here* vs. *there*), orientation of a figure object towards the deictic centre (as in *He's facing towards me*), and motion towards the deictic centre (as in *Come here!*).

3.3.3 *Topology*[4]

In a work that has had tremendous, though often indirect and unrecognized, impact on the study of spatial concepts, Piaget and Inhelder (1956) argued that the child passes through a series of stages of spatial reasoning – at first it grasps only topological notions, then much later grasps Euclidean notions of metric distance and angle, and finally grasps projective geometrical notions. Topology, sometimes described as 'rubber-sheet geometry', is the study of geometrical properties that remain constant under transformation or 'deformation', and so are preserved under the loss of metric angle and distance. Thus a sphere and a cube are topologically equivalent, and together are both distinct from a doughnut or a bicycle tyre. Piaget discovered that children less than four will, under the right circumstances, conflate circles, ellipses and squares, while distinguishing objects with holes in them. Children's drawings in their disregard for the order and location of eyes, nose and mouth also seem to follow topological principles.[5] Spatial relations between two objects of undistinguished shape and size are limited to primitive kinds: Piaget listed proximity, order, enclosure and continuity. Thus semantic notions like NEAR, AT, BETWEEN, IN etc. have been called topological. Children do indeed learn linguistic terms for these notions earlier than other kinds of spatial vocabulary, at least in those European languages whose acquisition has been intensively studied (Johnston and Slobin 1979, Slobin 1985). This may differ for other languages (see Brown and Levinson 2000, and Chapter 7 below).

The topological prepositions or relators have a complex relation to frames of reference. First, note that frames of reference are defined in this book in terms of coordinate systems, and many topological relators express no angular or coordinate information, for example *at* or *near*. However, others do involve the vertical absolute dimension and often intrinsic features, or axial properties, of landmark objects. Thus proper analysis of the so-called topological notions involves partitioning features of them between non-coordinate spatial information and features of information distributed between the frames of reference: thus English *in* (in uses like *The money in the piggy-bank*) is a topological notion based on properties of the ground object, *under* (in *The dust under the rug*) compounds topological, intrinsic (under-surface, bottom) and absolute (vertical) information, and so forth.

Much analytic and descriptive work has been done on this kind of spatial language, which is often encoded in closed-class morphemes, for example prepositions or local cases. A review of this work lies beyond the present scope, but see Miller and Johnson-Laird (1976) for older semantic treatments, Herskovits (1986: 127–55) for a careful consideration of the range of uses of English *at*, *in*, *on*, and Vandeloise (1991) for corresponding French expressions. Talmy (1988: 171) has advanced the view, mentioned above, that all closed-class spatial morphemes tend to be topological in character, being neutral over shape, material or medium, angle and magnitude, the nature of cognitive structure underlying spatial morphemes thus being 'largely relativistic or topological rather than absolute or Euclidean'. But this is not so. Precise axial and angular properties are quite typically expressed in adpositions (cf. English *across* or *opposite* which presuppose figures or grounds with long axes, and orthogonal angles) as are horizontal and vertical axes (as perhaps in prototype English *on* or *over*, but in any case in many languages), as pointed out in the prior paragraph. Shape discriminations may be rarer, but they turn up often enough, as in the Karuk postposition 'through a tube' mentioned earlier, or the locative proclitics of Nishga (encoding, e.g., 'on something horizontal', 'concave side down', 'flat against' etc. (see Mithun 1999: 146–7)). Contrastive locative verbs quite normally make shape-specific restrictions (see, e.g., Levinson 1999 on Yélî Dnye), and Tzeltal distinguishes, for example, 'be in a hemispherical container' from 'be in a cylindrical container', and many other such details (see Brown 1994). As for the specification of matter or medium, this seems in fact quite common too, Karuk again providing examples of spatial suffixes meaning, for example, 'in through a solid' or 'out of fire', Nishga proclitics encoding, for example, 'be in woods', 'into woods' etc., while 'acquatic' adpositions occur in, for example, Cariban languages (see Meira in preparation).[6]

It is true that a certain kind of abstraction seems to be involved in the grammaticalization process, in spatial morphemes as elsewhere, but the abstraction is not necessarily away from Euclidean geometry or other details like medium. Recent work has focussed on the diachronic 'evolution' of (largely topological) spatial morphemes (especially adpositions) from other sources, for which see Heine *et al.* 1991, Heine 1997 and Svorou 1994 and references therein. This literature makes clear that body-parts are a frequent source for such closed-class items, and it has been claimed that this mapping of body to world is an essentially metaphorical process (Brugman 1983), but again careful analysis suggests that a fully precise axial and volumetric geometry may actually underlie such spatial morphemes (see, e.g., Levinson 1994).

Despite the availability of cross-linguistic information, there has been a widespread assumption that the notions in the English prepositions *in*, *at*, *on* map one-to-one onto other language morphemes. Nothing could be further from the truth. Even the closest languages, Dutch and German, show substantial differences in the number of expressions covering the same area, and their semantic composition (see, e.g., Bowerman 1996). However, it does seem that the underlying conceptual space covered by such expressions is indeed organized in such a way that concepts can be universally located as neighbours in the space – for example, although languages may group 'on' and 'over' notions in the same morpheme, or 'in' and 'under' notions, they will not group 'over' and 'around' unless they also include 'on' (see Levinson and Wilkins in preparation, Chapter 13). The similarity space that organizes this field seems to have as its major parameters such underlying concepts as 'contact', 'vertical relation', 'adhesion', 'containment', not molar concepts like ON or IN. Some languages display fractionation of such molar IN, ON, AT relations, as in Tzeltal where positional locative predicates carry most of the semantic load of locative descriptions, and distinguish, as mentioned, such notions as 'in a hemispherical container' vs. 'in a cylindrical container' (Brown 1994).

The encoding of topological relations in language is usually thought to be restricted to adpositions (pre- and post-positions) and case. In fact, this is not the case at all. Quite typically the information is also found in predicates, as in the Tzeltal case just mentioned, and spatial nominals. For example, there are two kinds of spatial nominals, one kind illustrated by *top* in *on top of*, which plays a role in restricting the ground. This kind often combines with prepositions (as in English) or case (as in Turkish or Tamil or Australian languages), or occurs alone in apposition with the ground nominal (as in isolating languages like Thai). The other kind of spatial nominal can be illustrated by English *outside* which can have an adverbial function. Then there are locative predicates: many languages have a demarcated set of verbs that can occur in locative constructions, and that contrast with one another, indicating distinctive (often shape) properties of the figure, or of the relation between figure and ground (Levinson 1999, Ameka and Levinson in preparation). Thus topological information is often distributed throughout the clause, a point returned to at the end of the chapter.

3.4 SOLUTIONS TO LOCATION DESCRIPTION UTILIZING FRAMES OF REFERENCE OR COORDINATE SYSTEMS

I have earlier described the motivations for distinguishing three major frames of reference in language and cognition, the **intrinsic**, **relative** and **absolute**, acknowledging that each is a large family of systems. Contrary to statements in the literature (Miller and Johnson-Laird 1976: 404, Carlson-Radvansky and Irwin 1993: 242, Svorou 1994: 23), ambiguities of interpretation between the frames of reference are the exception, not the rule – most languages have special expressions and special constructions for each frame. The English ambiguity in *The dog is in front of the truck* reflects the diachronic origin of many relative systems from intrinsic systems, and disappears in related constructions, like *in the front of the truck*, *at the truck's front* etc. which have only the intrinsic interpretation. The point is important (and was already mentioned in Chapter 2) because it establishes that frames of reference are a *linguistic* matter, not merely a matter of psychological construal, as will be elaborated below.

In this section, considerably more detail is provided about each of the three main families of frames of reference, so that the reader has a sense both of the strong universality of the typology and the considerable extent of the variation within each frame.

3.4.1 The vertical dimension

This book largely ignores the vertical dimension. But the three frames of reference can equally be distinguished on the vertical axis. Suppose a fly hovers above an upright bottle. The three frames of reference coincide – the fly is in line with the top of the bottle (intrinsic), it appears above the bottle in my visual field (relative), and it is higher in the axis defined by gravity (absolute). However, if the bottle is on its side, and the fly is vertically above, the intrinsic frame has the fly by the side, not above the bottle. In English, the intrinsic frame of reference is now eclipsed – although if you lie down with the fly in the same axis as your trunk, "The fly is above your head" may be acceptable (Levelt 1984, Carlson-Radvansky and Irwin 1993). If I, the speaker, lie on my side, it gets better still. Because intrinsic tops, relative viewpoints, and gravitational fields normally align, we scarcely notice the possibility that the frames of reference may fail to accord. This is because in most situations the vertical dimension is massively overdetermined and unproblematic – we think about things as in their canonical upright position, viewed from an upright stance, with 'upright' determined by the gravitational field. In short, the intrinsic (canonical position of objects), the relative (perception from an upright stance) and the absolute (as defined by the gravitational axis) tend to coincide. Intuitions and clever experimentation can of course pull the frames of reference apart, and there appear to be rules that force us to override the intrinsic system where it is in gross conflict with the absolute (Carlson-Radvansky and Irwin 1993, Levelt 1996: 88–95), and in zero gravity the relative frame of reference must take over (Friederici and Levelt 1990).

Perhaps because of the general conflation of the frames of reference in the vertical dimension, elements of vertical meaning intrude into intrinsic descriptions, so that in English the top of the bottle is that part that is canonically vertical. Absolute systems often build the vertical dimension into the relevant linguistic system, so that in Australian languages, for example, 'up' and 'down' are often the same specialized part of speech (a special kind of noun) as 'north', 'south', 'east' and 'west'. In fact, some Mayan languages may have systematically collapsed 'up' and, for example, 'south' for symbolic purposes (Brown and Levinson 1993a, Stross 1991; see also Bickel 1997 on a Himalayan language). In the rest

of this book we will meet the vertical only as it impinges on our analysis
of horizontal description.

3.4.2 The horizontal plane

Just where angles in the vertical plane are massively overdetermined,
angles on the horizontal are radically underdetermined. There simply is
nothing like the reliably fixed axis of the vertical to be found on the horizontal. In a few parts of the world, there may be strong environmentally
determined axes, as where trade winds are constant, or escarpments well
defined and uniform, but these are exceptional cases. The conceptual
puzzle therefore is how to define angles on the horizontal plane, such
that search domains can be reliably projected off a ground object.

As we have seen, there are three main answers to this puzzle: the
intrinsic system, which projects out a search domain from a named facet
of a landmark object; the relative system, which imports the observer's
bodily axes and maps them onto the ground object thus deriving named
angles; and the absolute system, which uses a fixed set of bearings or a
conceptual 'slope' to define a direction from a ground object. But the
ways in which languages instantiate these strategies can be really quite
diverse, and that is the subject of the following sections.

3.4.2.1 Intrinsic systems – towards a typology

As we have seen, in the intrinsic frame of reference the figure object
is located with respect to what are often called *intrinsic* or *inherent* features of the ground object. The locutions are bad, because often nothing
is 'inherent', and everything is culturally imposed and assigned, in the
isolation and designation of these features. Consider, for example, the
phrases *in front of the TV* , *in front of the steps*, *in front of the church*, *in front of the
ship*, *in the front of the book* etc. (in the relevant non-relative or 'non-deictic'
sense).[7] Clearly the notion 'front' of an object is not an inherent property:
in the case of the TV it is based on canonical viewing position, in the case
of the steps on the direction they are ascended (rather than descended),
in the case of the church the west end regardless of the ordinary entrance,
in the case of the book the first few pages, and in the case of the ship the
direction of canonical movement. Various underlying principles may be
discerned, and their relative priorities observed. Thus, direction of motion is secondary to direction of sense organs as shown by the designated
fronts of crabs (Fillmore 1975, Miller and Johnson-Laird 1976: 402–5).
Although the designation of English *front* is such a complex amalgam

of orientational, perceptual, functional and other cultural factors, it is not merely a matter of rote-learning: two-year-olds can assign *fronts* to unfamiliar objects by a generally correct algorithm of some kind (Levine and Carey 1982).

The English intrinsic system can be thought of as a six-sided, box-like 'armature' that is imposed on objects when in their canonical position (the position in which they normally, naturally occur or are intended to be used). The cubic armature is oriented by gravity, so the *top* side of an object is uppermost, and the *bottom* the underneath facet. *Front* and *back* are found in this way too, by taking 'perceptual apparatus' (as with animals, cameras etc.), canonical direction of motion, canonical direction of use etc. into account. The two remaining facets are the *sides* (if no front or back can be found, then the object will have up to four sides). If the object is animate, it may have its own *left* and *right side*, if not, it may inherit its left and right from the human beings who wear it or drive it or sit in it. If human beings characteristically confront it, as they do with desks, cupboards and mirrors, the *left* side is transferred from the closest human left side. Objects can obviously resist these assignments if, like cubes and balls, they lack both inherent and functional asymmetries (see Miller and Johnson-Laird 1976: 403 for a sketch of an algorithm assigning intrinsic sides in English).

Although a fair bit of work has been done on corresponding notions cross-linguistically (see, e.g., Svorou 1994, Heine 1997 and references therein), it mostly fails to examine the detailed semantics of the systems, making them appear cross-linguistically more similar than they actually are. For example, Tzeltal has body-part terms that at first sight look a bit like English 'front', 'back', 'sides' and so on. Yet the system works in a totally different way (see de León 1993 for a similar Tzotzil system). There is no fixed armature at all, and certainly no fixed orientation (of the kind that gives us English *top*). Instead, the system is driven by an axial geometry together with an analysis of shapes, which scarcely refers to human use or orientation (Levinson 1994). The relevant kind of geometrical analysis is very similar to that proposed by Marr, Biederman, Leyton and other theorists of human visual recognition, in terms of generalized cones, directed axes, natural segmentations and protrusions. Thus the 'face', 'back', 'stomach', 'nose' of a stone or novel object are assigned regardless of its orientation, its use, or any viewing angle. This is consistent with other aspects of Tzeltal spatial description, in which, despite appearances, the human frame plays almost no part in the actual concepts employed (Levinson and Brown 1994).

1. Fixed armatures: e.g. Zapotec (MacLaury 1989)

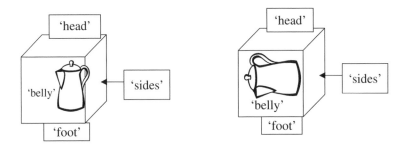

2. Object-centred geometry: e.g. Tzeltal (Levinson 1994)

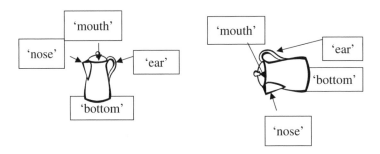

Figure 3.2. Variation in two Mesoamerican intrinsic systems

Many other languages use body-parts in what at first appear to be similar ways. But close analysis throws up radical dissimilarities. For example, Zapotec seems to operate with a fixed vertically oriented armature – 'head' at top, 'foot' at bottom, and 'sides' for the vertical facets (MacLaury 1989). If the object is rotated within the armature, its facets are renamed. In contrast, the Tzeltal terms are fixed once and for all by the internal geometry of the object, regardless of orientation – Tzeltal terms could in principle be assigned in outer space to an alien object regardless of the observer's position! Figure 3.2 represents the fundamental difference between these two Mesoamerican systems in a simplified, schematic way.

Compare English now once again. First note that it uses a fixed armature to assign top, bottom and sides to objects: thus, unlike Tzeltal, a cube can be said to have a top, bottom and sides, according to its orientation, in this respect showing some kinship to the Zapotec system. But mostly in English this fixed armature applies to the canonical, not actual, orientation – an upside down television has its top downward, and in this respect the system is unlike Zapotec and more like Tzeltal (TVs have tops and fronts fixed once and for all). But unlike Tzeltal, in English, canonical orientation and functional usage are crucial, rather than the internal axial geometry that determines Tzeltal part and facet names.

These three different intrinsic systems give one a sense of the range of diversity that remains to be described in systems of this kind (for other Mesoamerican systems see Levy 1994, Brugman 1983, Brugman and Macaulay 1986, Friedrich 1971). In summary, we can suggest an incipient typology of such systems as follows. Clearly, the job of such a system is to find asymmetries or differences between the parts or facets of an object, such that those facets can be named. Then, given those names, a search-region can be projected from that facet, such that the figure object can be said to be within the search-region (as in "The statue in front of the town hall"). There are three major ways to discern or assign those asymmetries:

1. Using a fixed armature, oriented gravitationally, which when super-imposed on the ground object gives a 'top', 'bottom' and 'sides'.
2. Using the internal axial geometry of the ground object to assign major axes and minor axes, a process often reflected in the dimensional vocabulary of a language (Lang 1995, Stolz 1996). Such axial geometry needs to be supplemented with an analysis of major volumetric properties, a system of object-segmentation into parts, and a classification of protrusions (see Levinson 1994 for references).
3. Using functional criteria, and in particular notions of canonical orientation, functional orientation (e.g. fronts of buildings), functions of parts, and direction of motion.

Some (so-called 'unfeatured') objects resist such an extraction of distinctive vertical facets – that is, parts usable to assign angles on the horizontal. This itself is partly a matter of convention – for example, we do not assign intrinsic backs and fronts to trees, but speakers of Chamus do (according to the direction of lean, see Heine 1997: 13). When the local system fails to produce facets, the relative frame of reference (if available in the language) may be called on to provide them – thus for us 'the front of the tree' is given by the observer's orientation. Many languages that effectively lack a relative frame of reference may show some effects of such a system at the margins of an intrinsic system. For example, Tzeltal has no relative system, but when it comes to the assignment of front ('face') and back ('back') terms to a door, speakers may decide that whatever facet is facing the speaker is the 'face' (Levinson 1994: 826).

Another major dimension of variation in intrinsic systems is the degree to which part-names can be used to designate spatial regions. Here Heine (1997: 44) has argued that there is a grammaticalization chain, which predominantly starts off from human body-parts, generalizes them to object parts, then to a highly restricted area near those parts, and finally extends the meanings to cover large search-domains projected from those parts. In the process, body-parts become increasingly grammaticalized as adpositions (the process is discussed below, see Figure 3.9). In the terms of this book, these extended spatial uses correspond to a transition from topological spatial uses (where the figure is said to be at a named part of the ground) to an intrinsic coordinate system (where the figure is implied to be in a large search-domain projected off the named part). Note that in English we can use any object part in topological constructions, for example *The man is at the door of the house*; note too that the intrinsic construction is subtly different – we can say *The man is in front of the house* but not **The man is in door of the house*, showing that only a few of the part-names have been grammaticalized into the inventory of terms in the intrinsic system. The Tzeltal object-part terminology is an interesting intermediate case: of the c. eighty human body-part terms, only sixteen terms have been transferred to inanimates. These sixteen (together with two or three terms from animal and plant-part terminologies) form a systematic set for the partition of objects into named parts. All of these can be used for topological description – one can say the figure is at X-part of the ground. Only a handful of them allow extended search-domains, especially *xujk* 'flank', and *pat* 'back'.

Incidentally, there is a great deal of information available about the diachronic sources of intrinsic spatial relators. As mentioned, most of this points to an 'anthropocentric' source in human body-parts. Nevertheless, there are clear sources of other kinds, either features of terrain or animal and plant parts (see Bowden 1991, Svorou 1994: 8off., Heine 1997: Ch. 3).

We can see now how topological systems may grade into intrinsic systems for good grammaticalization reasons, and we have also seen how the relative system can intrude into the intrinsic system at the margins. There are also possible interactions with the absolute system. Consider the inside of a building like a hall or church: the front is the side to which the audience is oriented, and audience left determines building left – but these terms are not dependent on the presence of an audience, for the building has inherited a fixed set of intrinsic internal facets. In some societies, as in the Amazon or the Arctic, buildings are seen as a microcosm of the world, and the building terms are mapped onto the cosmos utilizing fixed coordinates. But another more plodding way in which intrinsic systems and absolute systems overlap is that landmarks in the immediate environment can be thought of as a large intrinsic system, with the observer inhabiting the interior of a space, as in buildings. Such a local landmark system can in principle easily be distinguished from an absolute system: once outside it, your bearings are lost.

The intrinsic frame of reference can also be used to describe motion. Thus *The truck is moving backwards*, or *It's turning right* (not in the sense of 'right from my viewpoint') uses the truck's assigned intrinsic facets to indicate directional characteristics of motion. Perhaps one might gloss *It's turning right* in terms of the truck being at location L_1 at t_1 and at L_2 at t_2, such that L_2 is to the right side of the truck at t_1. It is interesting to note that motion allows objects that would otherwise resist the assignment of intrinsic facets to now acquire them. Thus if a cube is sliding down an inclined plane, its leading edge can be called its *front*, and it could now be said to veer to its *left*. Perhaps we should think about the path itself as having intrinsic properties assigned to it, which then determine the named facets of the moving object. If the truck is reversing and is said to be *turning right*, my intuition is that the truck's intrinsic left and right are now reversed. If so, this suggests that facets assigned on the basis of motion can overrule those based on other intrinsic criteria. When we give route directions, we typically use these intrinsic sorts of locutions: *go forward, turn to the left, then take the next right* and so on. We can describe abstract diagrams and patterns in the same terms, using fictive motion or an imaginary tour (Levelt 1996).

The intrinsic frame of reference is close to linguistic bedrock, in that it is near universal. Although there are languages, like the Australian language Guugu Yimithirr (Haviland 1979a, Levinson 1997a), that use it minimally, most have fairly elaborate systems of one kind or another. There are languages that almost exclusively rely on it, like Mopan (Danziger 1996, 1999). Children appear to acquire it earlier than other systems (Johnston and Slobin 1979). All this is puzzling because the principles for assignment of intrinsic facets are culture-specific and often highly complex, as illustrated above. The puzzlement increases when one considers the logical properties of intrinsic expressions, which are incapable of supporting any sustained spatial inference (Levelt 1984, 1996). The

Table 3.1. *Cline of L(eft) / R(ight) concepts in languages*

	L/R bias in, e.g., Demonstratives	Relative L/R in visual field	Objects with L/R regions	Persons with L/R regions	Persons with L/R sides	L/R as names of hands
Guugu Yimithirr (Australian)						+
Tzeltal (Mayan)					+/–	+
Tzotzil (Mayan)					+	+
Longgu (Austronesian)				+	+	+
Belhare (Tibeto-Burman)				+	+	+
Mopan (Mayan)			–?	+	+	+
Kilivila (Austronesian)			+	+	+	+
English		+	+	+	+	+
Tamil (Dravidian)	+	+	+	+	+	+

explanation for the prominence of the intrinsic frame of reference is probably that the relations are conceptually simple in one respect: they are binary, unlike the covertly ternary relations in the relative frame of reference.[8]

Human body-parts are not only a source of terms that are then mapped onto object facets, they are also directly useful, since humans often provide pertinent ground objects. Note that whereas *The hat is on his head* is a topological description, *The door is in front of him* is an intrinsic description (unlike *head*, *front* does not name a body-part, but a spatial region). In English *left*, *right*, *front* and *back* have these intrinsic uses as well as the relative uses to be described below. *The door is to the left* implies the door is to the left of the addressee's body (either now or soon, along the route traversed) – this is an intrinsic usage. *The ball is left of the tree* is in the relative frame of reference – the ground is the tree, not a human body.

Left and right terms offer a fascinating excursus into the semantic complexities that underlie apparently simple lexemes – and the detour is essential to avoid possible misunderstandings about the significance of a language having terms for 'left' and 'right'. Not all languages have terms for left and right sides, but perhaps all languages do have some way of referring to the left and right hands of the human body. What we see here is a whole family of related notions (some of them usefully distinguished by Piaget on the basis of child development), which can be organized as an implicational scale, as in Table 3.1. From the right column of the table we have terms that simply label the hands alone – they are body-parts only, and may be monolexemic, more often some such description like 'weak hand' vs. 'strong hand'. Some languages, like Guugu Yimithirr, leave it at that. Others extend the notion of left and right so that the terms can also be used to talk of left and right legs or arms or eyes – they now describe sides of the body (Tzotzil is a language like this, and a few Tenejapan Tzeltal speakers allow such an extension). Some languages, like Longgu, further extend the notion of left and right into regions projected from the left and right hand sides of the body (Hill 1997: 105). This is the first truly spatial use of the terms (before this they are simply partonyms), and this kind of use is sometimes also extended to animals. Even so, speakers of Mopan, a language like this, show a profound absence of left/right coding in psychological tasks (Danziger 1999, Kita *et al.* 2001). Some languages go further and assign left and right regions to inanimate objects – this may be done on clockwise rotation from an assigned intrinsic 'front', as in Kilivila. Or it may be done by assigning 'front' on the grounds of the relative frame of reference, and then counter-clockwise deriving 'right' (as in some dialects of Tamil, discussed in the next section). A further extension is to use 'left' and 'right' not as the names of sides of objects and associated regions, but rather as projective terms, whereby 'F is right of G' means 'F is more right in the visual field than G' – now we are well into the relative frame of reference, the subject of the next section. Just a few languages go on to bias the interpretation of other expressions in terms of left and right – Tamil is a case in point where *itu* 'this' can mean 'the left one' in contrast to *atu* 'that', 'the right one'. These progressive extensions of the terms are also associated with increasing symbolic associations of left and right – Guugu Yimithirr and Tzeltal speakers have scarcely any (see Chapter 4), while Tamil culture has elaborate ritual and taboo restrictions on the use of the left hand, clockwise circumambulation and so forth.

3.4.2.2 The relative frame of reference and its subtypes

One reading of *The cat is behind the truck* is similar to *The cat is behind the tree*: namely it has the truck or tree between speaker or viewer on the one hand, and the cat on the other. This is clearly a ternary relationship between points: viewer, truck, cat. Many languages, English among them of course, have 'front', 'back', 'left' and 'right' expressions with this ternary relation, but they are also often ambiguous between this and a binary intrinsic relation of the kind just reviewed. Piaget correctly predicted that the ternary relation should be hard for children to learn, and in fact the full set of 'left'/'right' uses may not be fully acquired until late childhood (Piaget and Inhelder 1956). Nevertheless, it is this system that many authors from Kant (1768) onwards, have considered fundamental to human spatial cognition.

The complexity of these systems is such that the correct analysis of such ternary 'left', 'right', 'front', 'back' systems is still, despite considerable work, quite unclear. One of the problems is that, whereas in an intrinsic left/right/front/back system 'right' (as in 'at my right') is found by clockwise rotation from 'front', in a relative system like that of English (there are alternatives, mentioned below) 'right' (as in 'To the right of the tree') is found by counter-clockwise rotation from the 'front' (as in 'in front of the tree')! Here is one explanation (Clark 1973, Miller and Johnson-Laird 1976, Herskovits 1986: 155–92): We assimilate the tree to the 'canonical encounter' where speakers face each other, hence the front of the tree is towards us; but we fail to make the rotation of 'left' and 'right' because that is too conceptually complex. The problem with this account, however, is that, apart from cultural variability in preferred positions for verbal interaction,[9] children in fact learn to make the rotation to others' lefts and rights by age five or six, long before they master this mixed-up system! Another explanation is that the terms *front* and *back* in this usage have nothing to do with 'front' and 'back': *in front of* in *The cat is in front of the tree* simply means 'between me and (the ground)', while *behind* in *The cat is behind the tree* means 'is occluded from my viewpoint by (the ground)' or something similar (Miller and Johnson-Laird 1976: 399–400, O'Keefe 1996). Such a brute-force solution hardly satisfies our feelings about what kinds of notions are lexicalized in natural languages, but a more serious objection is that on this account there is no explanation for the frequent ambiguity in many languages of 'front'/'back' terms between an intrinsic and relative interpretation, for there would be simply nothing in common between the relevant semantical notions (and hence no reason for the diachronic relation between them).

I believe that the correct solution is that these relative ternary relations often introduce a secondary coordinate system, as mentioned in Chapter 2. First let us consider a first approximation to how this works, which later will require modification. The viewer of a scene has intrinsic (egocentric) parts of his own, a left side, right side, front and back. In order to obtain named vertical sides for a ground object, which by the local intrinsic system is 'unfeatured', the speaker maps his own egocentric left/right/front/back onto the ground object. There are in principle at least three ways this can be done: the egocentric axes can be translated onto the ground object (shifted across without rotation or reflection), they can be translated under rotation, or they can be translated under reflection. Take the last possibility first – the system that will result is illustrated in Figure 3.3 (repeated from Chapter 2 with minor alterations).

Although this is arguably not the correct analysis for English, it is a good first approximation: we have the 'front' of the tree facing the speaker, with the 'right' of the tree to the observer's right (and thus counter-clockwise from the tree's front, the puzzle mentioned above). This is achieved by 'flipping over' the egocentric coordinates as if they were on a sheet of acetate, and mapping them on the tree.

Supposing instead of a complex reflection of the coordinates, we simply shift them to the tree and then rotate them so that 'the front' of the tree is facing the speaker. Now we have the 'right' of the tree to the speaker's left, as illustrated in Figure 3.4.

Such a system would fit Clark's (1973) analysis in terms of the canonical confrontation with another speaker, and it can be found in

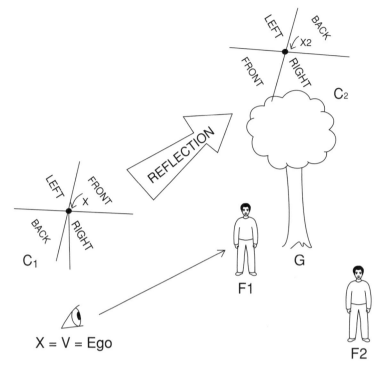

Figure 3.3. Reflection analysis: speaker's egocentric axes mapped onto ground
under reflection

English-speaking children between, say, six and nine years of age. At least one dialect of Tamil (NaTar caste, Ramnad district) seems to utilize a system of this kind, and there are no doubt many exemplars yet to be discovered, since it seems entirely natural.

But suppose instead of any such complexities, we simply translate the speaker's egocentric axes (i.e. shift them without rotation or reflection) onto the tree. We then end up with the system diagrammed in Figure 3.5.

Systems like this are widespread – the classic case being Hill's (1982) description of Hausa, and again its naturalness is shown by the fact that children learning a reflection system (like English) sometimes pass through a Hausa-style translation analysis of the meaning of 'in front of' or 'behind'.

Let us come back to the first kind of system, as exemplified by English. A number of minor facts suggest that in fact the reflection analysis is

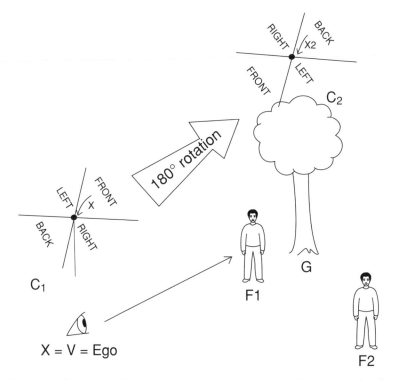

Figure 3.4. Rotation analysis: speaker's egocentric axes mapped onto ground under rotation as in 'canonical encounter'

probably not correct for English, and that such a system is likely to come about either from an amalgam of the other two analyses, or from the only partial application of the rotational analysis. On the latter analysis, the primary coordinate system is based on the viewer, so that *The cat is to the left of the tree* could be glossed as something like 'from this viewpoint, the cat is further left in the visual field than the tree'. But for the *front/back* terms we map a secondary coordinate system onto the tree under 180 degrees rotation (following the canonical encounter idea if you like), so that the tree is now assigned a 'front' and a 'back'. Now *The cat is in front of the tree* means just what it says: the cat will be found in a region projected from the front of the tree, where 'front' is found by a 180 degree rotation of the viewer's front about the tree. It may be objected that this results in a fundamental difference between the 'left'/'right' terms (which do not involve a secondary coordinate system) and the 'front'/'back' terms (which do). But for many languages this is

Linguistic diversity

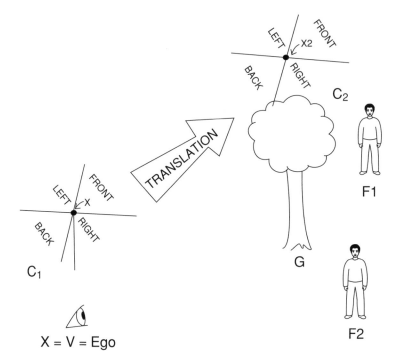

Figure 3.5. Translation analysis: speaker's egocentric axes translated onto ground
without rotation or reflection

probably correct. For example, although Hausa prefers an interpretation
under which 'in front of' means what English 'behind' means, Hausa also
allows a less-favoured English-like interpretation of the 'front'/'back'
terms. In either case, the 'left'/'right' terms stay constant (Hill 1982).
The same appears to be true of actual Japanese usage in spatial tasks
(K. Inoue personal communication). This potential independent flexibility of the 'front'/'back' terms would depend on the variable mapping
of the secondary coordinates. If this line is correct, then we might expect
that some 'left'/'right' terms might also be able to shift independently
of the 'front'/'back' terms – that is, they might be variably interpreted
either like English or like the Tamil dialect mentioned above, and this
seems to be true for some other dialects of Tamil.

The use of primary and secondary coordinate systems makes the details of these relative systems complex. Why have peoples and languages
bothered to develop such systems? One answer is that intrinsic systems

alone appear fairly inadequate. First, not all useful landmark objects (like rocks or trees) will necessarily offer distinguishable facets by the local intrinsic criteria. Second, relative systems do support proper logical inferences: If A is to left of B, and B to the left of C, then A is to the left of C (Levelt 1984). A third potential advantage of these systems is that they hook up to visual experience in a very direct way. A visual memory of a scene provides all the information that we need to describe it in relative terms. Indeed, the degree to which such systems are visually defined may itself be an interesting cross-linguistic variable (e.g. in some languages 'behind' may actually require partial occlusion). Such visual criteria can also be shown to intrude on the intrinsic and absolute vocabulary in languages (Levinson 1994: 844–5), which is further evidence for their importance.

Relative systems of spatial description build in a viewpoint and are thus essentially 'subjective'. For this reason they have been called 'deictic', as discussed in Chapter 2 above, although it is important to see that such descriptions are not necessarily egocentric: the viewpoint need not be the speaker ("It's to the left of the tree from where you are sitting"), nor indeed any participant in the speech event (as in "The goalkeeper deflected the ball to the left of the goal"). The non-deictic uses may be thought of in terms of a relativization to text (Anderson and Keenan 1985, Fillmore 1982) or Bühler's 'transpositions' (Hanks 1990, Haviland 1996). Alternatively, one could think about the deictic uses as just special (if normal) uses of a viewpoint-dependent system, which is the position adopted here.

Such systems allow the description not only of static arrays, but also of motion events (as in "The squirrel ran from the left and then behind the tree"). In such descriptions the viewpoint is normally held constant. One reason is that their logical structure has the same contextual dependency as deictic inferences generally. Just as "I am taller than you, you are taller than Bill, so I am taller than Bill" fails as an inference if the speaker and addressee change midway, so logical inferences of the kind "if A is to the left of B, and B to the left of C, then A is to the left of C" fail if the viewpoint changes. By holding the viewpoint constant, we can describe not only motions, but also describe patterns as fictive motions, as in "The line runs up, then left, then up, then right" (Levelt 1996). This holding static of the viewpoint limits the utility for the description of, for example, long and complex journeys, and, as suggested above, route directions are usually given using intrinsic left/right/front/back notions.[10]

3.4.2.3 *The absolute frame of reference*

Many speech communities make extensive use of fixed bearings, or absolute coordinates, like north, south, east and west. Conceptually cardinal directions are very abstract notions. A notion like 'north' or 'west' (in its relevant everyday conception) cannot be thought of as a proximate place or landmark (*pace* Li and Gleitman 2002), because then if we moved sideways the bearing would change. Rather, it defines an infinite sequence of parallel lines – a conceptual 'slope' – across the environment. Nor does it matter what defines the slope, just so long as everybody in the speech community agrees: these are cultural conventions not 'natural' directions, whatever basis there may be in the environment.

The most obvious cue to fixing a bearing is a solar compass. But the sun moves constantly in two dimensions, upwards and across the horizon, and both rates vary across the seasons very substantially at high latitudes. The sun's rising and setting cannot directly determine fixed bearings of any accuracy due to solstitial variation, and, because of this, human systems that do make primary use of the sun's course tend to make the north-south axis primary, removing the distraction of the particular course of the sun during the current season.[11] Although many animals use a time-corrected solar compass, the calculations are complex and instinctual (see Gallistel 1990) – the most complex pre-industrial human navigation systems have rather been sidereal. In any case, cultures often seem to settle on fixed bearings that are abstracted from varied additional sources, from seasonal winds, to mountain inclines, to coastal alignments, to river drainage directions, to star-setting points. Given these varied sources, there is no need for such systems to give us quadrants or orthogonal axes, although many cardinal direction systems have those properties.

Absolute direction systems give us external bearings on an array, but without employing viewpoints. They are 'allocentric' systems. Local landmarks can give us some of the same properties, especially within a restricted territory, but they do not have the same abstract properties as notions like 'north'. The point is made vividly by many Austronesian island languages which fix an east-west absolute axis by reference to the monsoons, but use a 'mountain'-'sea' axis to contrast with it. As one moves around such islands the one axis remains constant, the other rotates (Ozanne-Rivière 1987, 1997, Wassmann and Dasen 1998). Truly intermediate cases may be the riverine systems of Alaska, which operate as abstract systems within a vast drainage area, but are reset

when crossing into another drainage system (Leer 1989). Many systems that take their terminology from local landmark features are in
fact fully abstracted. For example, Tenejapan Tzeltal abstracts a north-
south axis from the mountain incline of the local environment, but
the axis remains constant outside the territory (Brown and Levinson
1993a, and Chapter 4). In fact, the very wide distribution of systems of
these sorts may have been missed because the terminology, in terms
of hillsides, river directions, coastal features, wind directions and so
on, may have appeared directly referential, while in fact being fully
abstract.[12]

Absolute systems yield elegant spatial descriptions of all sorts and
scales of spatial arrangements. Just like relative 'left', absolute 'north' is
an implicitly comparative relation (cf. 'bigger than') that allows complex
spatial inferences. Thus if A is north of B, and B is north of C, A is
north of C. But it has the logical superiority that the validity of such
inferences is not relative to a fixed viewpoint, as it is with 'left' or 'right'
(or 'in front'/'behind'). In fact it is by far the most elegant solution to
the problem of angular descriptions on the horizontal. There are just
two catches: (a) such systems do not capture egocentric constancies –
for example it is impossible to give a general recipe for setting the table
in such terms, with forks on the left and knives on the right; (b) to use
such systems, speakers and addressees must be constantly and correctly
oriented to the local fixed bearings (more below). These difficulties might
lead one to expect that such systems would be learned late by children,
but apparently they are learned earlier than relative expressions like 'to
the left of X' (de León 1994, Brown and Levinson 2000).

Motion descriptions are as natural in these systems as are location
specifications. Some languages (like Kayardild, Evans 1995) even use
cardinal directions as verb roots. One special feature of absolute motion
descriptions is that they allow the specification of direction without any
reference to places, landmarks or grounds. One can thus talk happily
of birds heading north, ships sailing east, winds blowing west, and so
on, without reference to sources and goals, which are often thought to
be essential to the description of motion events. Two moments in time
are sufficient to fix an absolute angle of motion, thus dispensing with the
otherwise general dependency of the specification of the figure's location
by relation to a ground object. Similarly, one can specify alignments, for
example of mountains or rivers, without reference to locations, since any
linear figure passing through two points will give us a bearing.

Such systems are of special interest when they occur without a corresponding relative system of 'left', 'right', 'front', 'back' terms. Then
descriptions of most spatial arrays, even in small-scale space, must use
absolute terminology. Such descriptions classify spatial arrays in a very
different way than our own relative sort of system. For us, a cup to the left
of a bottle becomes a cup to the right of a bottle when we walk around to
the other side of the table, but in an absolute system the cup remains, say,
north of the bottle from any viewpoint. On the other hand, constancies
that we have built into our cultural environment, such as (in most of the
world) gear-stick to right of steering wheel, are constantly varying assemblages under absolute descriptions. Cultures favouring absolute frames
of reference may build cultural environments that have constancies that
may be 'invisible' to our kind of cultural description (e.g. windbreaks to
the east in central Australia, see Nash 1993).

3.4.3 *The distribution of frames of reference in languages*

In this book, I will use a number of shorthand expressions that need to be
unpacked. For example, I will use a series of locutions of the sort 'absolute
community', 'absolute language', 'absolute expression'. To qualify each
of these accurately would be laborious on every occasion of use. What
they are based on is the idea that some languages make predominant
use of, in this case, the absolute frame of reference in spatial description.
But even this locution animates a language as it were: it is not languages
that make use of a frame of reference but speakers, of course. Languages
do indeed restrict the frames of reference for which they provide ready-
made expressions, but even here, many linguistic expressions may allow
use in more than one frame of reference (like English *in front of*). And
of course where they do provide relevant expressions, they may for various reasons not be usable in all circumstances – for example although
English has cardinal direction terms, it is not colloquial in any dialect
that I know of to say "The book is on the north end of the desk". For
most English speakers, most of the time, the cardinal direction terms are
usable only on geographic scales, and then normally with reference to
maps, where they come to signify relative directions on a map (north
at the top).[13] Other languages may provide terms for 'left' and 'right'
that only have esoteric ritual uses, and thus we also need to distinguish
between expert terminology and everyday terminology and its uses. Here
we are interested only in everyday parlance, such as children are daily

Table 3.2. *Uneven distribution of frames of reference across languages*

Intrinsic only:	Mopan (Mayan)
Absolute only:	Guugu Yimithirr (Pama Nyungan)
Intrinsic and Relative:	Dutch, Japanese
Intrinsic and Absolute:	Tzeltal (Mayan), Hai//om (Khoisan)
Intrinsic, Relative and Absolute:	Yucatec (Mayan), Kgalagadi (Bantu)

Distributional patterns:
- Intrinsic and absolute can occur alone
- Relative requires intrinsic
- Otherwise all combinations are possible

exposed to, which is the only kind of language – if any – that can be presumed to have an influence on everyday thinking. We also therefore need to distinguish the semantics of expressions in the language from their conventional uses. Not all languages provide locutions for all three frames of reference in everyday parlance. For example, amongst the languages relevant to the experiments to be described in Chapter 5, we find the patterns shown in Table 3.2.

A table of this sort is of course a crude summary of a complex pattern in each language. It would no doubt be possible to quibble with the two assignments 'intrinsic only' (Mopan) and 'absolute only' (Guugu Yimithirr). The former case is interesting because it indicates a tolerance for the absence of *any* orientation-bound frame of reference, making distributional asymmetries (as in 0–1 vs. 1–0) hard to define except by ad hoc means. Eve Danziger (1996) has explored this case in some detail. The second case (Guugu Yimithirr) is interesting because it is the only known exception to the rule that all languages have intrinsic systems – otherwise we would be able to say that intrinsic systems offer a bedrock for linguistic conceptualization of space, forming in many languages at least the first frame of reference acquired by children. I will provide some more specific information about Guugu Yimithirr in the next chapter, so that readers can make up their own minds on the evidence provided, but the case will largely hinge on whether body-part specifications alone, without projective spatial search domains, should count as constituting an intrinsic system (no, in my opinion).

One question that naturally arises is: To what extent are the concepts underlying these frames of reference universal, natural or innate? We have seen in Chapter 2 that our sensory systems are geared to processing information in specific frames of reference. Thus vision gives us information in a relative frame of reference, but visual-object recognition may require reconstructing objects in an intrinsic frame of reference from this relative perspective, while the otoliths in our inner ears give us information about our verticality in an absolute, gravitational, frame of reference. But given the modularity of many aspects of perception, we can make no assumption that perceptual frames of reference are automatically available to conceptual processes. As Piaget argued, the infant's early perceptual distinctions are reconstructed on the cognitive level only slowly over many years of cognitive development and socialization.

Information from child development and the acquisition of spatial language may be quite revealing about the naturalness of spatial concepts. Piaget's own results (see Piaget and Inhelder 1956) suggest that at the cognitive level, topological concepts precede frame-of-reference concepts, and the intrinsic frame of reference is available years before the relative frame of reference is properly mastered. Language acquisition research on European languages essentially supports this (Johnston and Slobin 1979), with projective relative notions not learnt before four years old at the earliest (by which time the intrinsic frame of reference concepts seem mastered), and not completed till eleven years old. Languages with absolute frames of reference also show relatively late acquisition of spatial concepts (with comprehension at around four years old), although notably earlier than the relative frame of reference (see, e.g., Brown and Levinson 2000). This developmental trajectory is quite interesting for our understanding of the cultural component of spatial cognition, and is reviewed in more detail below (see section 7.1). But for now, what we can say is that, with the possible exception of the intrinsic frame of reference, none of the frame of reference concepts appear to be 'natural categories', innately available, and so utilized from the earliest periods of language acquisition.

Further very interesting light on the 'naturalness' of frame-of-reference concepts in communication systems is provided by emergent languages. One such language is Nicaraguan Sign Language (NSL), which has emerged in the last twenty years as deaf children from different homes have been brought together for the first time in institutions for the deaf. Work by Annie Senghas (2000), using the same elicitation methods as other language research reported in this book, shows that it takes a considerable time to stabilize a communication system that can reliably communicate frame-of-reference information. First cohort signers, who learned NSL relatively late in life, are not able to communicate frame-of-reference information with much greater than chance success (as judged by errors on the Men and Tree matching game, described in Pederson *et al.* 1998). In contrast, second-generation signers can communicate this information reliably, but only after explicitly agreeing a format of presentation. Even this second cohort group, who are fluent and standardized signers, do not have a conventionalized format for frame-of-reference encoding – they may, for example, set up what is to the left in a visual scene as to the signer's right, as if the signer was on the other side of the array. What this reveals is that the encoding of frame-of-reference information requires a complex set of conventions about how scenes in the world will be mapped onto representations and whose perspective will be employed in these representations. If only one frame of reference was given to us innately as the most salient form of conceptual coding, we might have expected this single natural solution to provide a default on which the signing system built. But there does not appear to be any such natural default. We return to these issues in Chapter 7.

I have now reviewed the distribution of frames of reference in languages and shown that this is variable: not all languages use all the frames of reference. We have also seen in the prior section that each frame of reference can be variably conceived or constructed, with different subtypes of coordinate system and different kinds of mappings. There is yet another kind of variation to be found: namely the various ways in which particular languages, given that they encode a specific frame of reference, encode this in lexical or morphological distinctions. In the final section of this chapter, some indication is provided of the ways that these different frames of reference are variably instantiated in the grammars and lexica of languages. But first, we need to return to motion description, to show that the various semantic subdomains I have distinguished recur in the motion field.

3.5 MOTION

Many aspects of motion description involve just the same distinctions that have already been made for descriptions of static spatial scenes. Motion events can of course be located as wholes, as when we say *He is running in the gym* in which case all the resources for the description of static location apply. As mentioned earlier, they are often deictically anchored, for example by distinctions between 'coming' vs. 'going', 'hither' vs. 'thither' particles and the like. There is also a special relation to topology, since languages typically have ways of making causatives which describe events that bring about, or destroy, topological relations. The corresponding motion events, such as 'put in', are variously construed in languages. Korean, for example, classifies 'putting in' or 'putting on' situations in quite different ways than English: in Korean the relevant distinction is not 'in' vs. 'on' but 'tight fit' vs. 'loose fit' (Bowerman 1996). A close look at the linguistic development of children raised in Dutch-, English-, Tzotzil- and Korean-speaking homes shows that children do not start from a common conceptual core, given say by innate presumption or biological endowment, but from the earliest point of language production already make distinctions more like adult speakers of their own languages (Bowerman *et al.* 1995). Recent work by the same authors shows that children are already sensitive to the language-specific distinctions in comprehension before they are able to produce the relevant expressions at all (Bowerman 2000). As Bowerman (1996: 170) concluded with respect to the production evidence 'there was little evidence that [the children] had strong prelinguistic biases for classifying space differently from the way introduced by their language. This leaves the door open to the possibility that, after all, spatial thought – undeniably one of our most basic cognitive capacities – bears the imprint of language.'

The direction of motion events, unlike the direction of locations, can be described without coordinate systems or frames of reference, through the mention of two points along the trajectory. Normally these are the source or goal of the motion, although sometimes a ('perlative') waypoint may also be mentioned. Some languages have a constraint that allows only source or goal but not both to be encoded within a clause by a nominal adjunct, although an additional deictic specification of source or goal (either encoded in the verb or by means of an affix or 'hither'/'thither' particle) is still usually possible. This constraint may be based on the underlying semantics of motion verbs, which may be non-durative (as in Yucatec, see Bohnemeyer and Stolz in preparation), or on the absence of adpositional or case coding on the nominal, requiring the use of verbs meaning 'leave' vs. 'arrive' etc. In these cases, it will take two clauses to clearly establish a direction, of the sort 'He left the town and arrived home'.

Although direction of motion can thus be described without recourse to frames of reference, in fact frames of reference are frequently employed in motion description. Consider for example route descriptions of the kind "Take the first turning to your left, then the next right", where the advice is given in the (addressee's) intrinsic frame of reference. As we saw in Chapter 2, the difference between an intrinsic and a relative frame of reference in motion description can be confusing, so consider describing a skier coming down a mountain towards you. Now he turns to his left. If you describe the direction as "He is turning left" you are adopting his intrinsic coordinates. If you describe the direction as "He is turning right", you are adopting relative coordinates based on yourself. In this sort of way, the use of coordinate systems in motion description can be systematically investigated – for the languages described in this book this was done, for example, by means of a game in which the movements of a model man in a toy landscape had to be described in such a way that another screened-off native speaker could move a model man in an identical landscape. This, and natural conversational use, shows that all three frames of reference are in fact heavily used in motion description. For example, languages that use the absolute frame of reference may have the distinctions built into motion verbs or affixes (as in Tzeltal) or, even if fixed bearings are expressed in adjunct nominals, they may be more or less obligatorily present in motion description (as in Guugu Yimithirr). All the distinctions in frames of reference and their instantiation therefore carry over from the static to the dynamic subdomain of spatial description.

However, despite these connections to the locative systems, the description of motion is partially organized along different lines, and thus raises an additional set of parameters of variation across languages. Motion is naturally more complex than location, because it involves the extra temporal dimension. This naturally brings with it not only change of location, but also manner of motion, medium, instrument and other attributes. These are differentially coded in languages – for example, Talmy (1983) has pointed out that languages tend either to lexicalize manner and motion (as in *crawl*) or 'path' and motion (as in *enter*), but not both together. Similarly, some languages lexicalize medium + motion (as in *fly*), others not (saying in effect 'go in air'); some lexicalize instrument + motion (as in *sail*), others not, and so forth. If 'path' is not lexicalized in the verb, Talmy suggests it tends to turn up in 'satellites' as in English *go up*. Such directional information, however, can also be coded in adpositional phrases independent of the verb lexicalization type. These details do not concern the issues central to this book, but once again they illustrate just how variable spatial coding can be across languages.

3.6 THE GRAMMAR OF SPACE: PATTERNS OF LINGUISTIC CODING

There is a prevalent misleading presumption, which has grown out of the study of European languages and can be found in many textbooks, that spatial notions are encoded primarily in just one word class, namely prepositions or postpositions. In fact, spatial information is typically distributed throughout a sentence and in many different word classes. This is true even in the focal cases, static description in the European languages, many of which encode important spatial distinctions in demonstrative adjectives, adverbs, spatial nominals, adpositions, cases and contrastive locative verbs. Once we look further afield to a broader range of languages the picture looks ever more complex.

What then are the form-classes in which spatial information is encoded across languages, and can one say something about *what* kind of spatial information is encoded in *which* form-classes? Unfortunately, we are in no position to even begin to answer these questions authoritatively. The reason is that most grammars of languages do not provide detailed semantic information about spatial expressions. But we have enough information from such grammars together with the detailed work done in the kind of project described in this book to hazard a guess at general patterns. An overview is here tentatively given of the ways in which two different kinds of spatial information tend to be encoded in linguistic expressions – namely topological and frame-of-reference information. I will provide some information about the coding of topology, even though frames of reference are our main focus, for two reasons: much more cross-linguistic information is available, and topology grades into the intrinsic frame of reference, as will be explained below.

Figure 3.6 gives an impression of how spatial information may be distributed throughout the clause in different kinds of form-classes. It shows, for example, that information about the shape of the figure object may occur in the referring noun phrase itself or in locative verbs (which also often encode overall configurational geometry of figure-ground relations), while information about the shape of the ground is more likely to be found in adpositions and spatial nominals of a relational kind, but possibly (marked by dotted lines) also in case and adverbial spatial nominals. To see that in any one language spatial information can be distributed throughout the clause, consider the following example from the Papuan language isolate Yélî Dnye.

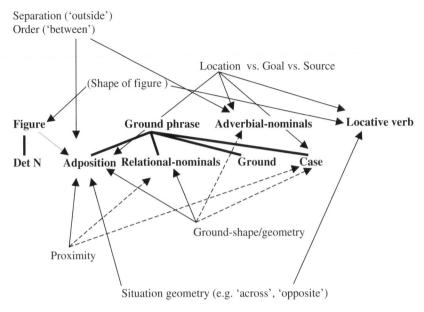

Figure 3.6. 'Topological' information and its distribution in form-classes

(1) kpîdî pee   pi   kêpa   mbêmê   ka   **t:a**
     cloth piece person forehead on   TAMP   **hang**
     'The piece of cloth is around the person's forehead'

Here the spatial information is provided, in a common pattern, by a combination of postposition and positional verb. The postposition *mbêmê* is glossed as 'on', but in this language there are no less than eleven other, contrasting adpositions with an 'on' gloss! The other 'on's are specific to vertical grounds or plane surfaces, or presuppose adhesion, or require the ground to be a peak or summit, or require the figure to be granular and distributed, or the like. The other crucial part of the locative construction is a locative verb, here 'hang'. The choice of locative verb encodes the disposition of the figure relative to the ground – here it implies that the cloth is tied around the head. If instead the positional verb *tóó*, 'sit', had been selected, it would have implied that the cloth was not properly affixed, but merely precariously perched on the head (see Levinson 1999 for details). Often such verbs, by specifying spatial features of the figure, provide essential construal of the nominal: thus in Yélî Dnye *mbwaa*

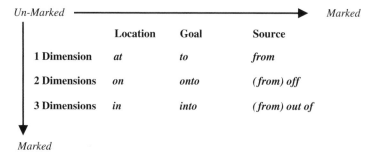

Figure 3.7. The structured typological space of ground-marking

'water, creek, river' in collocation with the verb *t:a* 'hang' indicates river, but with *tóó* 'sit' indicates 'pool', and so on.

Now compare the Australian language Arrernte (from Levinson and Wilkins in preparation):

(2) *Panikane-Ø   tipwele   akertne-le   aneme*
    cup-NOM   table   superadjacent-LOC   sit
    'The cup is on the table'

Here we have a case-marking language without adpositions, and the locative case is used here, as in most descriptions of location. To further specify the nature of the ground, a special spatial nominal *akertne* occurs, here glossed 'superadjacent', since it covers both 'on' and 'over' notions. Its adjunction to the non-case-marked noun 'table' signals a part-whole relation, so specializing *akertne* to 'top surface' by means of a special construction (instead 'table' could be marked by the ablative, in which case the spatial nominal would be construed as 'above'). Finally, once again the verb contributes to the locative construction, being one of a set of positional verbs indicating the shape and orientation of the figure object with respect to the ground.

These two examples should suffice to indicate what is meant here by spatial information being distributed throughout the clause. Further examples will be found in the following chapter, while more systematic observations can be found in Levinson and Wilkins in preparation.

There is no doubt considerable typological structure behind this variation. As an example, take the patterns of ground-marking, where local cases and adpositions seem to conform to a matrix with the structure in Figure 3.7 (see Clark 1973). The two dimensions are shown as increasing in markedness, that is, the linguistic expression of these morphemes

Table 3.3. *Composite category model of case/adposition evolution*

No. of distinctions:	1	2	3
	$\left\{\begin{array}{l}\text{Goal}\\\text{Location}\\\text{Source}\end{array}\right\}$ >	$\left\{\begin{array}{l}\text{Goal}\\\text{Location}\end{array}\right\}$ >	Goal
			Location
		Source	Source
Case:	Tarascan	Guugu Yimithirr	Turkish, Tamil, Warlpiri
Adpositions:	Tzeltal Nigerian Pidgin	Classical Chinese	Ainu

tends to be more complex or multi-morphemic as one moves in either direction away from location at a point (i.e. either towards dimensional complexity of ground, or away from stasis), as illustrated by the English examples.

Along the horizontal axis in Figure 3.7 are different kinds of grounds: static location at a ground, goal of motion and source of motion. Quite often, the three notions are subsumed within a single case (as in Tarascan) or a single adposition (as in Tzeltal). If there are two markers, then location is conflated with goal, and source is fractionated out (as in the Guugu Yimithirr case, Haviland 1979a, or classical Chinese adpositions, Norman 1988: 93). If there are just three markers then they will distinguish location, goal and source (as in Turkish or Tamil case, or Ainu adpositions). The implicational scale here is best conceived of as a 'composite category' model with successive fractionation, as in recent models of colour terminology (Kay and Maffi 1999), as in Table 3.3.[14]

Down the vertical dimension in Figure 3.7 is the construal of the ground object as having increasing dimensionality, from one-dimensionality (expressed in an 'at' concept, treating the ground as a point), to two-dimensionality (treating the ground as a plane, as in 'on' concepts), to a three-dimensional treatment as a solid or container (as in 'in' concepts). Many languages with local cases do not make these further distinctions in the case system, instead combining the case with a spatial nominal (as just illustrated for Arrernte in example (2) above), or combining case with an adposition (as in Tamil or Turkish). A few languages, however, have large sets of local cases. Hungarian (like Finnish) has nine local cases, ignoring the two-dimensional row, and instead subdivides the three-dimensional row by making a distinction between 'inside' and 'outside' the volume; further spatial distinctions are made by case-marking postpositions (Kenesei *et al.* 1997). Avar has twenty local cases (Blake 1994: 154), where the more central locative, allative and ablative case notions intersect not only with topological notions of coincidence (one-dimensional), location on a surface (two-dimensional), and containment (three-dimensional), but also with 'under' and 'among'.

So far I have considered case and adpositions in particular, and I have mentioned the important role of spatial nominals. In most languages, spatial nominals play an important role in spatial description, often in combination with adpositions or case. But in isolating languages like Thai such nominals may function without marking to indicate location (Kölver 1984: 2; see also Stassen 1997: 58 on Vietnamese and Maltese):

(3) khăw   yùu   bâan
    he   stay   house
    'He is at home'

Quite probably, all languages have spatial nominals. Despite their importance – they may be the only universal type of spatial coding – spatial nominals are under-researched. They typically belong to at least one minor form-class, for example in many Australian languages they combine with special case-endings. Take, for example, English *front*: it occurs in a number of compound expressions that function like prepositions, such as *at the front of*, or *in front of* where, unlike normal nouns, it drops the determiner. This noun belongs to one minor form class which may be called 'relational nominals', since they are understood to be bound to the ground nominal (and hence often marked with a possessive) – in English they participate in the construction of complex prepositions like *in the front of*.[15] Another minor class in English consists of adverbial nominals like *outside*, *under* or *north*, which do not require a specified ground (as in *he went outside*). Both classes participate in a few special derivations like *frontwards*, *northwards*, but only adverbial nominals like *north* can stand alone in adverbial function. Clearly there are diachronic tendencies for spatial nominals to become prepositions in one direction (*behind*) and adverbs in another (*home* in *He went home*) (see Kahr 1975 for cross-linguistic patterns). Spatial nominals play a special role in frame of reference information and will be discussed further below.

So far then we have the following kinds of form-class involved in the coding of topological (and other) spatial relations:

1. Local cases
2. Adpositions
3. Spatial nominals:

    3a. Relational nominals
    3b. Adverbial nominals

All three of these major form-classes consist of closed-class morphemes, although in many languages one may recursively derive large numbers of spatial relators, for example by applying case to adpositions (as in Turkish; Kornfilt 1997: 243ff.), or case to spatial nominals (as in Arrernte), or adpositions to spatial nominals (as in English complex prepositions like *in front of*). Some languages lack case (e.g. English), others adpositions (like Arrernte or Guugu Yimithirr), some both (as in isolating languages), while some utilize all three types (like Turkish or Hungarian). Sometimes there is difficulty distinguishing between some of these types, and grammars of the same language (like Tamil) may be inconsistent. This is in part because there is a grammaticalization chain, whereby spatial nominals evolve into adpositions, and adpositions into cases.

Topological information is also often encoded in verbs. I have already illustrated in examples (1) and (2) above the important role that positional verbs can play in encoding spatial relations. Such verbs are sensitive not only to properties of the figure object, but also to the configuration between figure and ground. There appear to be two major types of contrastive locative predicates, or verb classes (Ameka and Levinson in preparation): small sets of posture verbs of three to five members, on the one hand, and large sets of 'positional' verbs on the other. The small-set verbs are often drawn from the human posture verbs 'sit', 'stand', 'lie', but also from verbs meaning, for example, 'hang'. Although this origin suggests a simple reflection of the axial properties of the figure (the subject), this is not entirely how they work in their locative uses – for example, in Yélî Dnye attached objects always 'hang', regardless of axial properties, and protrusions 'stand', regardless of orientation and length of the major axis (Levinson 1999). There are usually sortal presuppositions (e.g. the subject has a long axis) as well as complex figure-ground configuration conditions. The large sets of positional verbs, in contrast, tend not to have sortal presuppositions, but express directly the actual configuration of figure to ground. Take, for example, the following Tzeltal sentence (Brown 1994: 753):

(4) chepel-Ø   ta   chojak'   te   ixim ta
located-bulging-in-netbag-3s PREP large.netbag the corn PREP
tz'ante'-e
roofbeam-PARTICLE
'The corn is sitting in a netbag on top of the rafter'

Tzeltal has just the one highly general preposition, which subsumes spatial, temporal and many other relational concepts. All the spatial work here is done by the stative predicate, which expresses location, the relation between figure and ground, and the consequent shape of the figure. The shape characteristics specified in the verb root can often be attributed either to the figure or the ground (Brown 1994: 772–7). Tzeltal also has spatial nominals, which I will mention under the rubric of the intrinsic frame of reference.

Verbs play another crucial role in topological spatial description, since in many languages they function like adpositions. One route is via nominalization (as in English *Following the car came a truck*), and another is via verb-serialization (Kahr 1975: 33). What are functionally local prepositions in Chinese are probably best treated as on a grammaticalization path from verbs: *zài*, 'at, locative' is also a full verb meaning 'be present' (Norman 1988: 162–3). Thai uses (as mentioned above) bare spatial nominals for static location, but for source/goal marking uses serial verbs, so that, for example, 'He is coming from school' would be expressed as 'He come depart school' (Kölver 1984). In many African languages (as in Ewe) the verbal origin of adpositions is clear.

Let us now return to the focus of this book, frames of reference, and see what generalizations we can make about how they are encoded. Unfortunately, our information here is altogether poorer – grammars mostly fail to provide unequivocal descriptions. Thus in Figure 3.8, the arrows indicate only encodings of information in word classes for which I and my colleagues have had first-hand experience within our own project – other possibilities no doubt exist, yet to be properly described (dashed arrows indicating rare occurrences). The picture that emerges, however, is not very different from the distribution of topological information sketched in the earlier Figure 3.6, except that frame-of-reference information appears to be coded in a lesser range of root classes: spatial nominals, adpositions, verbs, determiners and so forth, but perhaps never in, for example, grammaticalized local cases. For example, in the diagram it is made clear that absolute frame-of-reference information can be found encoded in determiners (e.g. demonstratives), in relational nominals, in

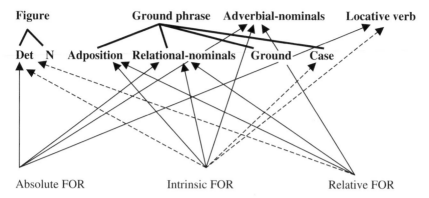

Figure 3.8. Frames-of-reference (FOR) information and its distribution in form-classes

adverbial nominals and in verbs, while as far as I know relative frame-of-reference information never occurs in verbs, and although it may be associated with determiners (as with the possible interpretation of Tamil *itu* 'this' as 'this leftmost one'), it is perhaps not grammaticalized in them. In what follows, some examples of these tendencies are provided, although given our current restricted information we cannot be sure that other patterns will not show up in other languages.

Let us take the intrinsic frame of reference first. This frame of reference typically involves the use of named facets of objects, like 'front', 'top', 'side', and these parts of objects usually belong to the class of relational spatial nominals mentioned above. Svorou (1994) and Heine (1997) demonstrate how these terms are typically recruited first from human body-part terms, second from animal body-parts, third from landmark terms (e.g. 'top' from 'sky', 'front' from 'door'). They go on to show how these nouns typically grammaticalize into adpositions (or, in languages that lack adpositions, into spatial nominals with abstract spatial interpretations), gradually acquiring more spatial, regional interpretations, as sketched in Figure 3.9.

There are two important thresholds in the illustrated progression: one from body-part to generalized thing-part, and then from thing-part to spatial region projected off from that part. The first gives us a general system for segmenting objects, which can then play a role in topological description: rather than say figure F is at ground G, one can be more precise and say F is at the X-part of a landmark (to be precise, F is at G which is a part of Y). The second progression, from part to region, takes us out of topology into the intrinsic frame of reference. The progression

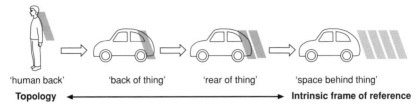

'human back'   'back of thing'   'rear of thing'   'space behind thing'

Topology ◄───► **Intrinsic frame of reference**

Figure 3.9. Grammaticalization chain from 'back' to 'behind' (after Heine 1997: 44)

may seem slight, but it is a jump into the world of coordinate systems. It is conceptually a very different usage of the part-term – in the topological use 'at the back of X' simply names as a ground *the back* of X (not X), while in the intrinsic frame of reference 'at the side of X' has X as ground and projects a search-domain off that facet of X that can be called a side. In the topological use, the hearer is invited to search the area of the thing named by the part-term to find the figure, while in the intrinsic use the hearer should search a large spatial area for which the part-term merely gives a direction.

Topological systems seem to be near universal, conceptually simple and early learned by children. Because of the close link of topological to intrinsic systems, intrinsic systems inherit some of the properties and prevalence of topological systems, including the style of linguistic encoding. Nevertheless, languages often make a relatively clear distinction between the systems. As mentioned in connection with example (2) above, Arrernte uses a different construction with different case marking for topological and regional interpretations. Tzeltal has a very systematic set of relational nominals, most based on body-parts, which have topological uses – as figure and ground become a little separated in space, speakers prefer to utilize the absolute frame of reference. But a few of the nominals, especially 'back' and to a lesser degree 'front' and 'flank', are increasingly becoming projective intrinsic expressions, with regional interpretations, a grammaticalization process that has gone considerably further in neighbouring Tzotzil. There is some evidence for an implicational scale over the part-terms that are likely to lead in this grammaticalization process, as follows: 'back' > 'front' > 'sides' > 'top' > 'bottom', where 'back' is the first to acquire intrinsic interpretations, 'front' second, and so on, so that if a language has a regional intrinsic interpretation for, for example, 'side' then it will have such interpretations for 'front' and 'back', but the converse does not necessarily apply.

From this it is clear that nominals, naming sides or facets, are the major source of intrinsic spatial descriptors, which are then used to project search regions from the named facet. But sometimes there are verbal sources for intrinsic notions, as in Longgu *na'ova-* 'front', derived from the verb *na'o* 'to face' (Hill 1994). More often, we can see part nominals being incorporated into verbs, as in Tarascan or Totonac (Levy 1999), where they come to have specific spatial meanings (see also Mithun 1999: 111 on Cherokee 'classificatory verbs'). Many Amerindian languages seem to have parallel object-shape concepts coded independently in both nominal phrases and in verb roots or affixes: thus Tzeltal has elaborate body-part terminology with specific axial interpretations (Levinson 1994), which are partly mirrored in axial coding in locative verbs (see Brown 1994). Similarly Kwakwala has -χsa, numeral classifier 'flat', and such verbs as *pəlq-*, 'be located, of flat object on its front', *k'uk^w-*, 'be located, of flat object vertical' (Mithun 1999: 110). This attention to the geometry of objects is crucial for the development of both topological and intrinsic systems, and can be found in nominals and their collocating modifiers and predicates, but topology seems more grammaticalized. For example, many languages have large arrays of spatial cases as noted above, but these appear to always cover the topological domain, rather than the intrinsic frame of reference – thus they do not include, for example, local cases meaning 'in front of'. Topological notions do seem then to have a closer relation to grammatical morphemes, while intrinsic frame-of-reference concepts are more likely to be expressed in lexical items or complex adpositions.

The relative frame of reference seems in most cases to be a system built by extensions from the intrinsic vocabulary. That is, a notion like 'front' seems in both language learning and language history to have initial reference to intrinsic fronts, and then comes to be extended (if at all) to relative uses, especially with objects lacking inherent facets. This can be viewed as a recurrent direction of semantic change, which partly explains why the relative frame of reference does not occur without the intrinsic frame of reference. Hence the ambiguity of, for example, *in front of the truck* which can be read as either 'at the truck's front' (intrinsic) or 'between the speaker and the truck' (relative). Some observers have thought that the overlap in uses of expressions shows that the expressions are in fact semantically general over both frames of reference – that is indifferent as it were to different psychological construals: 'typically reference frames are not coded linguistically in spatial expressions', as Svorou 1994: 23 puts it (see also Carlson-Radvansky and Irwin 1993: 242).

However, in most languages there are many subtle details of the use of expressions that generally mark which frame of reference they are being used with – thus *at the truck's front* or *in the front of the truck* can only have an intrinsic reading, not a relative one – so this cannot be treated as an extralinguistic matter. In Kilivila for example the left/right terms take different possessives if they are to be interpreted intrinsically or relatively. Moreover, many languages have forms that are entirely restricted to one or the other reference frame. For example, Tzeltal has body-part terms that one might gloss as 'face/front', 'back', and which are used for spatial reference as in *ta spat na*, 'at the house's back, i.e. behind the house'. The position of the speaker is normally irrelevant for the use of these and all the related terms, although in a few marginal uses one can see relative interpretations, suggesting that the relative frame of reference is incipiently available if undeveloped (see Levinson 1994: 824ff. for details).

Normally, then, the relative frame of reference is expressed through the same classes of expressions as the intrinsic ones, from which they are normally derived by diachronic extension. Thus in English we have prepositions like *behind*, relational nominals like *front* in complex prepositions like *in front of*, but no verbs meaning, for example, 'to be in front of from this viewpoint', or the like. Nevertheless, in languages where relative notions may have far-reaching significance, relative interpretations may intrude into other form-classes. Thus (as mentioned) in Tamil, the proximal demonstrative *itu* can come to have a 'that to the left' interpretation in contrast to distal *atu*, which can then imply 'that to the right'. And as mentioned above, languages with more or less exclusive absolute rather than relative spatial descriptors may permit relative interpretations of the absolute system at the margins. For example, in Tzeltal a marginal use of the 'uphill' (south) term is the use to denote 'higher in my visual field', i.e. 'the one behind', an interpretation pre-empted by the absolute interpretation if it makes sense in context (Brown and Levinson 1993a; see also Bickel 1997 for a similar pattern in Belhare).

Turning to the absolute frame of reference, let us first take the Australian languages as one example. In these, there is typically a closed class of spatial nominals, which includes four cardinal direction terms, sometimes including also two vertical axis terms ('up', 'down' as in Warlpiri), demonstrating the natural extension of the absolute frame of reference to the vertical. This nominal class is special because it has unusual case properties – for example, the cardinal direction terms either do not take the locative case, or there are special forms of the local cases for them. There is also usually a set of special derivational affixes, yielding, for example, 'north side', 'north-origin', 'northern edge' forms (as in Kayardild, Evans 1995: 221–3), or complex vector specifications with over fifty forms (see Chapter 4 and Haviland 1993 on Guugu Yimithirr). These spatial nominals may then be derived into referential nominals, as in Garawa (Karrwa) *gula-majnga-ngurra*, 'one belonging to a south place obscured from view' (Furby and Furby 1976 cited in Evans 1995: 215). In some languages they combine with special morphemes to form verbs, as in Kayardild *jirrkur-ijula-tha*, 'move northward (imperative)' (Evans 1995: 226). Thus cardinal direction roots are likely to show up in all major phrase types. Incidentally, the semantics of these terms varies across the languages – in Guugu Yimithirr they denote quadrants shifted about 15 degrees from grid north, but in Warlpiri the division of space is not into equal quadrants, but is restricted to narrower arcs at the northern and southern axes.

A different pattern is found in, for example, the Mayan language Tzeltal. There are three distinct directions rather than four ('uphill', 'downhill', 'across', associated with fixed compass bearings, again shifted from ours), forming a semantic template that is then lexicalized directly in two different kinds of nominal root, and independently in verbal roots. Thus *ajk'ol* is an abstract noun meaning 'high', used to derive a locative adverbial phrase *ta ajk'ol* 'upwards'/'uphillwards, i.e. southwards', *s-ba* is a relational noun meaning 'its top, uphill edge, southern edge', and *mo* a verb meaning 'ascend, go uphill, i.e. south', and *moel* a derived verbal directional meaning 'ascending, going south'. So here the underlying oppositions are reflected in unrelated word forms of different kinds. Similar patterns are found in a number of other languages relevant to the sample in Chapter 5 below, for example, Belhare, where a series of demonstratives, directionals and verbs reflect a similar underlying 'uphill', 'downhill', 'across' set of distinctions, constituting a grammatical category (Bickel 1997).

In many languages in which the absolute frame of reference is dominant, demonstratives also encode fixed directions, as in Papuan and Austronesian languages (Steinhauer 1991, Heeschen 1982, Haiman 1980: 258).[16] The Eskimo languages are another well-known exemplar – for example, Yup'ik has demonstratives indicating 'that upriver' and the like (see Mithun 1999: 134 for references). An additional locus for absolute information is verbal affixes and clitics. For example, Central Pomo has directional suffixes on verbs which indicate motion up, down, north, south and so on (Mithun 1999: 139). In these cases, many other kinds of spatial information may also be coded in the same locus, especially topological and intrinsic information, so that some languages have large arrays of such morphemes (e.g. Kwakwala has over sixty-five verbal/nominal suffixes indicating not only such notions as 'upriver', 'inland', 'offshore' but also 'on surface of water', 'in canoe' etc.). Tidore (a West Papuan language) uses a set of such affixed verbs in normal answers to static locative *Where*-questions: one says in effect, say, "The cup is-seawards on the table", meaning the cup is on the table, seawards from the viewpoint (van Staden 2000: 162–3). This is a language that assimilates absolute direction terms to an underlying category of oppositions which includes deictic specifications, so that the absolute terms presume a deictic origo (as in 'to be located, seawards from my viewpoint'). The oppositions surface in nouns, verbs of motion and these viewpoint verbal affixes.

Absolute information thus appears cross-linguistically in many different kinds of word class, nominal, verbal, directional affixes or particles and so on. These are often closed classes, like the Australian spatial nominals with special cases, Eskimo demonstratives or the Tidore verbal affixes. A possible constraint is that absolute directions on the horizontal are not known to appear in nominal case affixes – the only codings of absolute bearings in grammatical cases are probably those that indicate position on the vertical axis, as in superessive and subessive cases in Finno-Ugric.

From this brief survey it will be clear that spatial information is not, contrary to the impression from the textbooks, in any way restricted to local cases and adpositions, but is rather distributed throughout the clause, both intralinguistically and cross-linguistically. In this way, frame-of-reference information can be found not only in adpositions and case, but also in two kinds of spatial nominal, verbs, verbal clitics and demonstratives. The ways in which spatial information is encoded in language are as varied as the conceptual parameters that are coded.

3.7 CONCLUSIONS

In this chapter, I have attempted to provide an overall picture of the nature of spatial language, its major domains and subdomains, and the range of semantic variation in each of them. In particular, I have tried to sketch the variants of the different frames of reference and how they tend to be encoded in different languages, a necessary preliminary to the rest of the volume. As was noted in Chapter 1, there are reasons to think that spatial cognition is one of the least likely domains to show fundamental variation in human thought, and thus we might have expected uniformity in spatial semantics. On that basis, authors such as Li and Gleitman (2002) have announced that, in this area at least, 'all languages are broadly similar' in coding and conception. However, the material reviewed shows that the assumption of uniformity here is entirely mistaken.

This chapter is not an exhaustive survey – there are many languages and many language stocks for which we have no adequate information, grammatical descriptions usually failing to provide reliable information here. Much more detailed information can be found in the companion volume, *Grammars of space* (Levinson and Wilkins in preparation), where systems are treated as wholes within the context of the surrounding lexical and grammatical machinery of each language. That book also contains more information about the methods for the collection of such linguistic data, which require departure from normal elicitation procedures. In the following chapter some greater detail about two rather different languages is provided, and some mention made of these methods of inquiry.

CHAPTER 4

Absolute minds: glimpses into two cultures

In this book, the opposition between systems based on relative and absolute coordinates plays a major role. One pole of this opposition is familiar: we live in a culture in which relative coordinates organize most of our more self-aware spatial behaviour. This dependence on directions based on viewer-centred left vs. right is built into our cultural environment in scores of ways: the directionality of writing, the sidedness of traffic, the nature of route directions, the egocentric asymmetries of consoles, table settings, doors and so forth. It is we relative-thinkers who are indeed 'the lopsided apes' (as Corballis has put it). But the other pole of the opposition, cultures that organize things in absolute coordinates, is altogether less familiar, and in this chapter I try to bring this less familiar alternative world to life, by providing details from two such 'absolute' communities in which I have been fortunate enough to have had the opportunity to work.

In Chapter 2 we were concerned with how frames of reference can be correlated across different kinds of mental representations, and it was argued that one can distinguish the same three types of reference frame, intrinsic, relative and absolute, across the different perceptual modalities and their internal representations. In this chapter, I will produce the first evidence for a tendency for individuals to specialize their frames of reference towards the relative or the absolute across all these different kinds of representation. That is, it seems that individuals prefer to use just one frame of reference across modalities, for example across language, non-verbal communication media like gesture, non-linguistic spatial memory, and spatial reasoning. We have already seen some reasons for this pressure towards homogeneity in frames of reference – for example, it was shown in Chapter 2 that on first principles translation across the different frames of reference is highly restricted, and specifically, there is no way to get from, for example, a relative frame of reference to an absolute one, or vice versa. Memorizing situations in one frame would then make them

unavailable for description in another. That would not matter if the local
language provides all three frames of reference – but sometimes it does
not, and that is the subject of this chapter.

In this chapter we will begin to see how language might be the driving
force behind the choice of one predominant frame of reference not only
within individuals, but within communities of individuals. Language is a
public representation system – a system shared by all in a community –
at the same time that it is an internal representation, a system into which
we can code thoughts as we prepare to speak. Without fundamental convergence in linguistic representations across individuals, communication
would be impossible. This convergence at a high level, in a public representation system, must have consequences at the level of individuals'
internal representations, and this chapter will suggest that those consequences can be rather far reaching – constructing for each community
a specific 'cognitive style' of spatial representation.

To show that there are such convergences between linguistic representations and non-linguistic representations requires new methods,
specifically the independent examination of linguistic categories and
non-linguistic concepts. The methods that have been developed for the
analysis of the semantic 'tool kit' of specific languages are fairly straightforward, involving, for example, the development of communication
tasks between native speakers which will reveal the full resources of
the language in a specific domain. But the methods for the analysis
of non-linguistic cognition need a little more explanation because they
are entirely novel, and they will be introduced in detail in this chapter,
thus preparing the ground for the full-scale cross-cultural analysis in
Chapter 5.

4.1 GUUGU YIMITHIRR SPEAKERS OF HOPEVALE[1]

The present inhabitants of Hopevale include the descendants of a tribe
who occupied about 10,000 square kilometres of territory stretching
north from the present township of Cooktown, Northern Queensland,
Australia. They probably never numbered more than they do today,
around 800 souls (for the tragic colonial history, see Haviland 1985,
Haviland and Hart 1998). The language belongs to the large Pama-
Nyungan family and has many interesting features, including an elaborate case system (of the absolutive/ergative type), a syntactic structure in
which constituency plays an altogether minimal part, word order thus
being completely free, zero-anaphora without verbal cross-referencing,

and an alternate taboo vocabulary (see Haviland 1979a, b, Levinson 1987a, b). All inhabitants of Hopevale also speak English, often the specific variety of Aboriginal English found in the far north, and some also speak other Aboriginal languages, and there is a lot of interchange between this and other Aboriginal communities. In this multilingual and fluid setting, the sociolinguistics are complex, and Guugu Yimithirr appears to be undergoing rapid change. Trying to avoid these sociolinguistic complexities, the studies reported here focussed primarily on older people with long associations with the community, who were acknowledged to have special cultural competence.

In Guugu Yimithirr (henceforth GY), nearly all spatial descriptions involve essential reference to something like our cardinal directions.[2] In GY, in order to describe someone as standing in front of the tree, one says something equivalent (as appropriate) to 'George is just north of the tree', or, to tell someone to take the next left turn, 'go north', or, to ask someone to move over a bit, 'move a bit east', or, to instruct a carpenter to make a door jamb vertical, 'move it a little north', or, to tell someone where you left your tobacco, 'I left it on the southern edge of the western table in your house', or to ask someone to turn off the camping gas stove, 'turn the knob west', and so on. So thoroughgoing is the use of cardinal directions in GY that just as we think of a picture as containing virtual space, so that we describe an elephant as behind a tree in a children's book (based on apparent occlusion), so GY speakers think about it as an oriented virtual space: if I am looking at the book facing north, then the elephant is north of the tree, and if I want you to skip ahead in the book I will ask you to go further east (because the pages would then be flipped from east to west).

Such a language makes elaborate and detailed reference to an absolute set of angles – absolute in the sense that they do not depend on the angle of the human frame (unlike *left* and *right*) nor, essentially, on the speaker's viewpoint (unlike *in front of the tree*), although ego's position may optionally be used as a reference point (as in *north of me*). If you describe the layout of a room in an absolute system, the description does not vary whether you look through the window or the door: for example, the lamp is north of the sofa, with the table to the west. In a system based on relative angles, in contrast, the lamp may be behind the sofa with the table to the left when viewed from the door, but when viewed from the window the sofa may be behind the lamp with the table to the right. Anyone who doubts the fundamental difference between these two kinds of system should try to devise a general instruction, purely in absolute terms, about how to lay the table in genteel fashion (with forks to the left, knives to the right).

Guugu Yimithirr is a language more or less completely absolute in spatial description. The argument advanced here will be that in order to speak GY, it is necessary to carry out a specialized kind of background computation of orientation and direction. Further, it is argued that these computations must be carried out well in advance of (indeed independently of) speaking, that the results must be memorized, be available for inference and other psychological process, and in general must pervade many aspects of cognition. Thus the fact that absolute directional information is a fundamental prerequisite for speaking GY must, it will be claimed, have pervasive psychological implications.

The argument is made in two ways. The first line of argument consists of qualitative information (in the way of natural records of interaction and anecdote) about the nature of the linguistic distinctions and their mode of application. Various kinds of linguistic performance have been induced by setting systematic tasks of spatial description (the information here supplements work by Haviland 1979a, 1986, 1993). It is argued that in order for these linguistic performances to be possible at all, psychological processes of special kinds must be involved. This is then an argument from linguistic performance to the underlying cognitive processes required to support it. The second line of argument, more persuasive if it can be sustained, is based on trying to tap those underlying cognitive processes directly. The hypothesis is that a predominant frame of reference in a language might induce a dependence on a corresponding frame of reference in non-linguistic cognition. Accordingly, informal experiments have been devised that attempt to assess psychological variables directly, independently of language. We can then see whether those psychological variables have the expected values.

4.1.1 Guugu Yimithirr communication about space

4.1.1.1 Guugu Yimithirr spatial description: the linguistic resources
Like most Australian languages, Guugu Yimithirr makes essential use of terms for cardinal directions.[3] There are four root expressions, as in our Western compass points, but the roots label 'edges' (i.e. quadrants) rather than points (despite which they will simply be glossed here as 'north' etc.) and are skewed about 17 degrees clockwise from our magnetic or grid directions (Haviland 1979a, 1986). The linguistic details are not essential for current purposes, and I give a brief account here (see Haviland

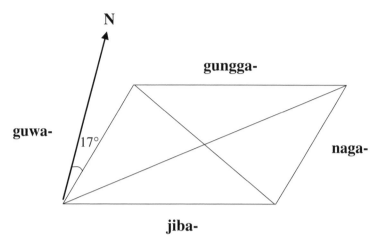

Figure 4.1. Guugu Yimithirr cardinal edges

1979a, 1986, 1993, 1998). The cardinal direction roots, which are spatial nominals of a special subclass, are:

gungga- (northern edge)
jiba- (southern edge)
naga- (eastern edge)
guwa- (western edge)

Figure 4.1 gives a sketch of the basic system. Incidentally, as in many (but not all) Australian languages, the vertical dimension is assimilated to this system, with the nominals *wanggaar-* 'up' and *bada-* 'down' taking many, but not all, of the special derivational suffixes associated with this class of adverbial spatial nominals (the details are mentioned below).

Unlike the privileged position our Western tradition confers on north, on account of the magnetic compass and our map-making tradition, there is no obvious priority to any one direction or axis in GY. It is interesting, for example, that in the 'Brother-in-law language' (an alternate vocabulary used when talking in the presence of taboo relatives), only two of the four roots are thought necessary to replace, but since they are the terms for south and west, no clear pattern of priority emerges.[4]

The directional roots appear with various morphological derivations, of which the most important are as follows (for the semantics, I follow Haviland's 1993 analysis based on the exegesis of texts, which suggests a sort of aspectual content for the derivational suffixes; glosses are approximate indications only).

o-form: (UNMARKED or implicit Start focus)
gungaarr 'to/at the N'
jibaarr 'to/at the S'
naga 'to/at the E'
guwa 'to/at the W'

These are the simplest, unmarked forms, used, for example, in route directions of the form 'turn west' and have a locative or allative interpretation.[5] Another frequently used set contrasts by implying some kind of focus on the end-point of a journey or trajectory:

R-form: (END-POINT focus)
gunggarra 'to/at a point in the N'
jibarra 'to/at a point in the S'
nagaar 'to/at a point in the E'
guwaar 'to/at a point in the W'

These are then the terms naturally used if one is specifying a destination (indeed *ngayu gunggarra thadaara* 'I am going north' may already be sufficient to unequivocally specify that I am going, e.g., to the beach). The third frequently used set puts some kind of focus or emphasis on the trajectory or vector itself, as in motion through a point; these terms are thus naturally used to describe a general direction of heading or an alignment.

L-form: (VECTOR)
gunggaalu 'northwards'
jibaalu 'southwards'
nagaalu 'eastwards'
guwaalu 'westwards'

When specifying motion *from* a direction, there are corresponding forms with different ablative inflections. When specifying small movements, or small distances, reduplications do the job. There are also special derivatives for specifying northern, southern, etc., edges, for example the east side of a house or the eastern flank of a mountain range: *X-n.garr* can be glossed as 'on the X-side', *X-:lnggurr* as 'along the X-side'. Altogether, there are at least twelve derivational suffixes, together with a number of case inflections (e.g. the comitative case), yielding for the four cardinal roots something like fifty distinct forms with distinct meanings.[6]

The cardinal direction terms thus essentially constitute a closed form-class, characterized by the special derivational morphology already partially sketched above:

(i) Locative/allative: (ii) Ablative
   -(rra) 'vector'   *-almun* 'from X-direction'
   -:r 'to/at a point'   *-nun* 'from a point', also *-nu-nganh*
   -:lu 'through a point'   *-almun-nganh* 'out of a point (not towards origo)'
(iii) *-n.garr* 'on the X-side'
   -:lnggurr 'along the X-side'

As mentioned, the terms for the vertical directions are marginal members of the same class: *wanggaar* 'up', *bada* 'down' take sets (ii) and (iii), but not (i). But these two terms have additional idiosyncrasies: ablative *wangaarmun* also means 'onto, on top', and there is a special derivation *badiimbarr* 'below, along beneath'. In the Australian languages the 'up'/'down' terms quite often belong to the cardinal direction set, but in some languages they do not – for GY it is interesting to see the logic of absolute directions expressed in a single form-class. Indeed the 'up'/'down' terms also have horizontal uses, especially within the settlement area, where 'up' can mean west, and 'down' east (reflecting a slight incline in the terrain).

Since GY does not employ terms in other frames of reference to any substantial extent, it is essential to use these cardinal direction terms for almost every description of location on the horizontal.[7] It is also customary to specify direction when using verbs of motion. The actual interpretation of these cardinal expressions is not as straightforward as might at first seem. Although these terms refer to fixed angles, the origin point from where the angle is subtended can be various. For example, 'I went north' can be interpreted as 'I went north from here', 'I went north from there' (place given by narrative) or just 'I headed in a northerly direction' (see Haviland 1996).

The special property of GY spatial language is not only the possession of this rich absolute system, but also the complete absence of relative terms and the very restricted set of intrinsic and topological expressions. As mentioned, there are no spatial terms for 'left' and 'right', although there are monolexemic terms for the left and right hands as body-parts. Nor are there any terms translating 'front' and 'back' in relative terms (as in 'The boy is in front of the tree'). Consider, for example, the following

Figure 4.2. Picture book for description, speaker facing north

description in (1) of a picture in a standardized stimulus book, illustrated in Figure 4.2:

(1) *bula gabiirr gabiirr nyulu nubuun yindu   buthiil naga   nyulu yindu*
      dual girl   girl   3sg   one   another nose east+o 3sg   another
      '(There are) Two girls, the one (has) face to the east, the other

      buthiil jibaarr   yugu gaarbaarr   yuulili
      nose   south+o   tree   between, in   stand+REDUP
      (has) face to the south, a tree stands in between,

      buthiil jibaarr   nyulu baajiiljil
      nose   south+o   3sg   cry_REDUP_NONPAST
      She's crying nose to south'

As indicated in Figure 4.2, the picture book is being held up so that the speaker is facing north. In the absence of left/right and front/back relative descriptions, no full spatial description is possible in GY which is true regardless of the orientation of the book.

It has been mentioned in Chapter 3 that of all the frames of reference in language, the one with the best claim to universality would be the intrinsic frame of reference. However, when this is understood to exclude topological description, and thus to imply not only the existence of part terminologies but also their use as projective concepts, then GY would seem to be an exception. For, arguably, GY has no intrinsic system at all. There are a few body-part terms which have slightly extended spatial uses, for example *walu* 'temple', *baaru* 'front', *buthiil* 'nose', all used to indicate the front of a man or animal, usually in conjunction with an orientational specification by cardinal direction. But these are topological in character – they refer to a part, not to a spatial region (as in 'nose to east' meaning facing east). There are a number of other topological expressions, for example *wawu-wi* (lit. soul-LOC) 'inside', *waguurr* 'outside', and a few expressions for indicating 'side', 'between', 'near' and so forth. But generally speaking the cardinal direction system together with case inflection carries most of the load that would be carried in other languages by, for example, a relative and intrinsic system. Consider, for example, the following locative description, in response to "Where's the telephone?" (relevant constructions in bold):

(2) *yii*   **wanggaar-mun** *wunaarna table-***bi**   *telephone*   *yii*
    here   top-ABL   lie+REDUP table-LOC, telephone here

    wunaaran   *walmba-***wi**   **wanggar-mun**
    lie+REDUP division-LOC   top-ABL
    'Here on top, on the table it's lying, the telephone is lying on the table, on top'

Here the combination of a simple locative case on the ground nominal 'table' together with a postural verb 'lie' would often be sufficient to implicate that the telephone was in the canonical position, on top of the table, but to make it really clear the speaker has used the spatial nominal *wanggaar* plus the ablative case. *Wanggaar* should perhaps be glossed 'superadjacent' since it covers both 'on' and 'above' – it is a nominal belonging to the absolute system, here being used to clarify topological contact relations.

For source, goal and location, nominals can be inflected with the following local cases, which do provide basic topological and motion contrasts:

Dative, locative, allative: *-bi/-wi*
Allative: *-ga* (unproductive)
Ablative: *-mun/-nun*

And, with a few uses only:

Superadjacent: *-:nh* (unproductive; only with body-part words, topographical features)
Adessive: *-:gal* (motion or speech to/location in presence of person)
Abessive: *-g:a* (motion away from person/location of habitat)
Comitative: *-dhirr* (sometimes used with spatial meanings)

The language has a relatively rich set of motion verbs (c. twenty out of c. seventy-five intransitive verbs). These include some manner verbs like 'crawl', 'run' and 'swim', but also some verbs of the 'verb-framed' type, for example verbs glossing 'ascend', 'enter', 'go', 'come' and so forth, although none of these encode cardinal directions (unlike in some languages).

Guugu Yimithirr is a language under rapid change, and the present Hopevale Community where it is most often (but not exclusively) spoken is a sociolinguistically complex one, with a long mission history and a rapidly expanding population.[8] No adequate study of the varieties of the modern language has been done.[9] All speakers of GY are also speakers of English, and for many Hopevale residents English is now the predominant language. The generalizations in this study are based on data gathered almost exclusively from men over forty, indeed mostly in the age bracket fifty-five to seventy-five, who would normally speak Guugu Yimithirr amongst themselves in preference to English, and who have spent their lives in close association with each other and the land of Hopevale Aboriginal mission. Reference to 'GY speakers' and so on in this book should be interpreted in that restrictive fashion – I simply do not know to what extent the results described below would generalize to a larger sample, inclusive of both sexes.[10]

4.1.1.2 The communicative use of cardinal direction information
There has been extensive study of the use of directional terms in GY verbal interaction and story-telling (see Haviland 1986, 1993, 1996, also

Levinson 1986, 1987a, b). These studies show that directional terms have
a high frequency of use (Haviland estimates that about one word in ten
is a cardinal direction term), and also that directions are specified with
a consistency and accuracy that allows them to play an essential role in
reference identification and tracking (e.g. to report a conversation, the
interlocutors may be identified as the one to the north and the one to
the south).

Haviland (1986, 1993) has also shown in detail through the study of
filmed interaction how this linguistic system is supplemented by gestural
specification, where directional gestures have great accuracy, although
their interpretation requires understanding of the point of view from
which the gesture is made (Haviland 1996). The fact that gesture is deeply
integrated into the system of directional reference is fundamentally important to an understanding of the cognitive background to the system.
It demonstrates clearly that it is not simply a linguistic system, but a
broader communicative one, the implications of which will be explored
in Chapter 6.

In addition to this body of natural spoken interaction,[11] a corpus of spatially directed talk was systematically collected from older GY speakers.
A battery of elicitation techniques was used, as developed by the research
group at the Max Planck Institute for Psycholinguistics, as part of the
cross-linguistic study of spatial description and conception reported on
in this book.[12] Informants were asked to perform a series of eleven interactive tasks or 'games'. For example, in one of these tasks, a 'director'
had to describe a route (marked with a cord) through a model town, so
that another informant (the 'matcher') could emulate the route on an
identical but screened-off model. This essentially involved giving precise
route and location descriptions. In another task, the director had to describe the position and stance of an articulated wooden man, so that the
matcher could emulate the body positions on another identical figurine.
In a third task, the director had to describe the relative locations of a
set of farm animals so that the matcher could emulate the arrangement.
And so on.[13]

These tasks push the resources for spatial description of any language
to the limit, and it was interesting to note the almost total reliance of
our GY speakers on the cardinal direction system. Rotation, angular
direction, side or edge location, relative distance and so on were all
specified essentially through cardinal direction terms. Even in the task
involving the model man, where terms for left and right body-parts
might have been used (the lexicon includes terms for 'left-hand' and

'right-hand' in a purely body-part sense), specification was exclusively in terms of cardinal locations ('hand on the Western side' etc.). As a result, the orientation of models or assemblages was always identically matched by the matcher in absolute terms (e.g. the model man arranged by the matcher not only pointed with his left hand, but pointed West with his left hand), regardless of the relative positions of 'director' and 'matcher'. A small extract from the director's instructions in the wooden man task is given in (3):

(3) *Wooden Man description task*

yindu nyulu same way   yuulili   *ngaaguul   guwaalngurrthirr*
another 3sg *** ***   stand+REDUP   arm   west+side -COMIT
'Another one – he's standing (facing) the same way, his arm on the West side

thiliinh   guwa   *miirriilil*   *nhaathi*
then   west+o   show+REDUP+NONPAST   see-PAST/REFL
he's pointing West, see?

yindu   *yindu*   *ngaaguul naga*   *miirriilil,*
another   another   arm,   east+o   show+REDUP+NONPAST
yindu   *guwa*   *ee?*
another west+o eh?
The one arm is pointing east, the other west, see?

gaari   *nagaalngurrthirr*   *bada   gurrala ya   guwaalngurr   midaarra,   gaari*
no,   east+side+COMIT   down   say -IMP   west+side   lift_IMP   not
wanggaar
above
No, put the eastern side (hand) down, lift the westernside one, not upwards (not too high)'

4.1.2 The hypothesis of non-linguistic consequences

Against this background, I decided to investigate the cognitive consequences of operating a communicative system of this sort, both verbal and gestural, through field experimentation. The hypothesis was that the cognitive consequences would be far reaching. Although most perceptual properties are no doubt universal, and given by the interaction between the structure of the perceptual organs and that of the relevant perceptual field, the further processing of perceptual information may bring it into line with what is required for the communicative system. For example, if I am to be able to describe a scene at some later point, I must remember the properties required for accurate linguistic description in my particular language. Thus to describe an arrangement of model farm animals in English, I must remember, for example, that the pig was in front of the cow, with the horse, say, to my left or its right. But to do so in GY I must remember the cardinal directions of each animal, or at least be able to reconstruct them. Thus although the perceptual information available to GY and English speakers may be identical, the coding for memory must, it seems, be distinct. The hypothesis is that GY speakers must take primary visual perceptions and code them *together with* cardinal direction information for memory. They must do this all of the time (at least for locally significant events), since one never knows in advance what memorized facts one may wish to describe. Inference on such coded memories should make use of this cardinal direction information. In short, one expects that GY speakers might behave differently in memory tasks (whether recognition or recall) and in inferential tasks compared to speakers of a language with 'relative' spatial description.

As mentioned at the beginning of the chapter, two lines of argumentation can be pursued. The first takes the linguistic expressions, here specifications in an absolute frame of reference, as the starting point, and asks what kinds of background cognitive processes would be necessary to support them. We can then check the deduction, by seeing whether direct tests substantiate that such special cognitive processes are indeed being utilized. This is explored in the next section. The second approach is more geared to the nature of the representations in language and cognition – given the translation problem between frames of reference described at the end of Chapter 2, there should be a congruence between linguistic and non-linguistic codings of directional and orientational information. This deduction again can be checked by directly testing the non-linguistic coding of spatial arrays in memory and inference. This is pursued in section 4.1.2.2.

4.1.2.1 *The essential prerequisite: orientation and mental maps*

GY speakers invariably seem to know, day and night, familiar or unfamiliar location, whether sitting still or travelling in a vehicle, where the cardinal directions lie.[14] This orientational surety is considered trivial, and is general, I have the impression, throughout the speech community despite the sociolinguistic diversity. There are many details of everyday interaction that exploit this surety. Quite typical, for example, is the anecdote mentioned in Chapter 1, where the following advice was given to me in English:

RH: 'They have plenty of fish fillet in the store.'

SCL: 'I've never seen it – where?'

RH: 'On this side' (gesturing), 'in the frozen food container, far end this side.'

We were standing in a hospital 45 km from the said store. I was expected to note that the gesture was to the north-east, so that next time I was in the store I would look in the north-east corner.

But in order to speak GY, more than a sense for immediate direction is required. In order to say, for example, that George was standing in front of the post office in Cooktown, it will be necessary to remember (or be able to calculate) the orientation of the building and George's location relative to that, so that we can say in effect 'George was standing east of the post office'. Similarly if he was at some point A heading for B, a proper description will include the quadrant containing the directional angle between A and B.

To achieve such descriptions one will need to know, or be able to recover, the angles subtended between any two places. In that sense a mental map of one's world with accurate absolute angles must be accessible. One place in that map that will be especially, but not exclusively, important will be the location of speaking, since perhaps the majority of cardinal expressions have an implicit deictic interpretation ('north of here'). As the speaker moves, his angular position vis-à-vis other places will change. In that sense, it will be essential to **dead reckon** one's current location – that is keep track of how far one went on each heading – in order to know what angles the current position subtends to places one might wish to refer to. Figure 4.3 should help to make clear why one needs not only to keep track of direction but also distance: in order to speak a language that primarily uses cardinal directions, you need to be able to calculate your present location, so that someone heading towards you from your last location by a different route can be referred to as, for example, 'heading south from there' and 'coming from the north to here'.

How accurate is the sense of direction? In particular, how accurate is the dead reckoning on which the use of GY directionals would seem to depend?[15] An attempt was made to systematically investigate this, by getting people to point at distant invisible locations from different transitory locations, for example on stops while travelling or camping. On various trips to the bush, or at halts on other kinds of journeys, ten men aged

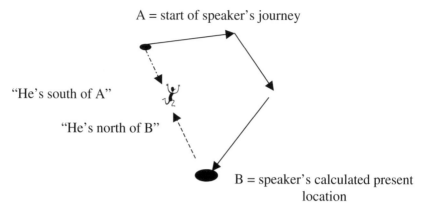

Figure 4.3. Dead reckoning (calculating present position) for speaking

thirty-five to over seventy were asked on various occasions to estimate directions of named locations beyond the range of vision. The locations were chosen because they had names familiar through local history or associations, even though not all informants had visited all of them. The sites were variously mountains, river mouths or crossings, islands, cattle stations, promontories, old mission sites and the like. The distances of these locations ranged from a few kilometres up to several hundred as the crow flies (and up to about 350 km as the routes actually go). The method consisted of halting at some spot with restricted visibility (e.g. amongst trees), asking the men to point to a series of locations, if possible by picking out a landmark in the direct line of sight, so that the investigator could sight through a prismatic compass. It was made plain that an accurate rather than an instant response was being asked for, but in most cases the response was within a couple of seconds (some exceptions noted below), often an immediate gesture. Later the readings were compared to the most detailed survey maps available, the location at which the questioning took place identified (where necessary by triangulation from landmarks and by odometer or pedometer readings), the angles between that place and the pointed-out locations measured, six degrees allowance made for the difference between magnetic and grid north, and the subjects' errors calculated.

The results are shown in Table 4.1.[16] Over a total of 120 trials from bush locations or stops on bush roads, the average error was 13.9 degrees,

Table 4.1. *Hopevale subjects' estimates of direction*

No. of estimates	N	Degrees	Percent	Median	s.d.
			Mean corrected error		
*From non-base locations**	120	13.9	3.9	11.0	11.3
Including base and hypothetical locations	160	13.5	3.8	11.0	11.2
From base locations only	40	12.6	3.5	9.5	11.0
From hypothetical locations	6	19.0	5.2		16.0

*'Base' here means Hopevale, 'hypothetical locations' are actual distant places where the subject was asked to imagine he was located before pointing to other places.

or less than 4 per cent. Including estimates from base camp (Hopevale), there were a total of 160 trials, with an average error of 13.5 degrees, a median error of 11 degrees, and a fairly even distribution of errors in both directions, clockwise (67) and anticlockwise (79) from north (the remainder being zero errors). Forty-five or 28 per cent of errors were of 5 degrees or under.

Given the varied nature of the locations where readings were taken (true bush to roadside), the different speed of travel (foot, vehicle on good gravel road vs. bush track), the approximate nature of some of the readings due to many sources, the great distance, and in some cases the relative unfamiliarity of some of the locations pointed to, these are very impressive results. Nothing like this can be obtained from European populations, a point returned to in Chapter 6. By way of contrast, accuracy improved slightly by about 1 degree average error when persons were asked locations from base at Hopevale, and decreased to about 20 degrees average error when asked at Hopevale to estimate angles subtended from a distant place A ('hypothetical location') to another one B. The proper statistical analysis of this data, and comparison with performance from other human groups, is postponed till Chapter 6. This degree of accuracy probably considerably exceeds one's ability to communicate it through gesture, as it seems hard to make adequate allowance for parallax when estimating exactly where another person is pointing unless one is standing directly behind them.

The figures can be usefully compared to the only other comparable data from Australia, those collected by Lewis (1976) in desert conditions from Western Desert peoples. Lewis' study was a direct inspiration for

Table 4.2. *Western Desert peoples' estimates of direction (from Lewis 1976)*

No. of estimates	N	Mean corrected error			
		Degrees	**Percent**	**Median**	**s.d.**
From non-base locations	34	13.71	3.8	7.0	16.48
Ten worst estimates	10	35.8	9.9	27.0	
Ten best estimates	10	1.3	0.5		

this one. Over two fieldtrips he took thirty-four measurements during desert travel by vehicle, from five Western Desert Aboriginal men of different tribes. Table 4.2 extrapolates from his results.

The figures are interestingly comparable, despite the very different conditions under which they were collected. In Lewis' experiment, the distances of the locations ranged from 10 km to 670 km, but were mostly around 300 km distance. Our GY experiment had the ranges 7–350 km, but were mostly in the 50–100 km range. He was travelling off-road over great distances, while we were either on or only a few kilometres from dirt roads or bush tracks. On the other hand, his consultants often had the benefit of vistas over vast terrain, while GY terrain is very much rougher, and except along the coast, visual sighting is cut by dense bush, dunes and mountain ranges. Above all, in GY territory it is almost never possible to travel in a straight line, as the route must deviate constantly around bogs, deep rivers, mountains, sand dunes, rain forest or impenetrable scrub, mangrove swamp or, if on foot, around snake-infested grassland.

What these results show is that GY speakers maintain a mental map of a large terrain, say 300 by 150 km in extent, and can compute their own location within it, and the angles between that location and any others, more or less at the speed of conversational response. What is this ability based on? Clearly, a constant sense of orientation (which is perceived by GY speakers as trivial) is one ingredient. The basis for this is still unclear to me. Systematic use of the sun as a compass is by far the most likely basic check on inertial navigation. In the southern winter (our northern summer), the sun lies discernibly (about 12 degrees) north at midday at this latitude of 15 degrees, and sets and rises north of west and east. Use of a sun compass of course requires constant correction for time of day and progress of season, and the interaction between the two. However, three men independently volunteered anecdotes about how when travelling far afield (Melbourne, Brisbane or New Guinea) they became convinced the sun was rising other than in the east (Haviland also collected anecdotes of this kind), while another seemed to claim that this was actually the case in distant places. This suggests that at least on some occasions primary reliance is placed on other clues, which together yield an unconsciously assessed sense of direction. Bush lore includes ways of discerning orientation from the relative brightness of sides of trunks of particular kinds of trees, from the reliable orientation of certain kinds of termite mound, from the prevailing wind directions at particular seasons, the nightly swarm of bats, the migratory flight of bird species, the rising and setting points of particular stars, the north-easterly alignment of sand dunes in the coastal area, the prevailing currents around particular stretches of the coast, and so on, and presumably all this kind of information is constantly if unconsciously monitored.[17]

Multiple sources of information must thus be used to constantly update a mental map of one's own current location in a large territory. But to achieve this other kinds of information are necessary too. The other ingredients include abilities to estimate distance travelled on each leg or angle of a journey. On some of the few occasions on which I obtained delayed responses, informants would give a protocol of a mental dead reckoning, for example of the kind: 'We came a little bit west, then we went that long way straight north along the dune, and then had to go west again along the river bank, crossed it, and then could go east again, so where we started from would be about there.' The pattern of errors shows that fast vehicle travel may upset these estimations of distance travelled on a particular leg or angle, and indeed some of the most accurate measurements I collected come from within a cave mouth in dense bush, but a location reached by foot.

To summarize, there is an obvious prediction that any user of a language that predominantly uses absolute bearings in spatial descriptions would know where the cardinal directions are at any time. Less obviously, perhaps, that will not be sufficient: it will be necessary to dead reckon one's current location with respect to all other major locations. These predictions turn out to be correct for GY speakers, and they will be compared to the predictions for other groups in Chapter 6. The results imply that a cognitive precondition to using absolute spatial descriptions in language is a constant background sense of orientation – a mental compass, as it were, that operates constantly in the background. Such a special mental faculty, which most of us do not possess, must be constructed during socialization and language learning, and the argument will be (again developed further in Chapter 6) that it is language (not, e.g., the environment alone) that forces this constant attention to the directional attributes of every scene.

4.1.2.2 The non-linguistic coding of spatial scenes in memory and inference
4.1.2.2.1 Spatial coding in memory. The hypothesis is that GY speakers code scenes for memory complete with directional information in an absolute frame of reference. They should do this not only in the context of speaking, but at all times that they memorize spatial scenes. The reasoning behind the hypothesis is this:

1. GY speakers use, and indeed (in the absence of other descriptive resources in the language) must use, absolute directions to describe spatial locations and events.
2. GY speakers may, like all of us, want to describe any experience at any time.
3. In order to be able to do so, they must have accurately remembered scenes together with their cardinal orientation, since these cannot be reconstructed from codings in a relative or intrinsic frame of reference (as established in Chapter 2).

To test this hypothesis we clearly cannot merely interrogate speakers about past experiences, without having some control over the accuracy of absolute spatial descriptions. It is in fact fairly straightforward to demonstrate the accuracy of GY spatial descriptions from memory. For example (following similar exercises by Haviland), I have examined filmed stories about events that happened long ago, involving complex journeys and movements over terrain. The sequence of events can be related precisely to a map, their internal coherence checked, and the descriptions of locations verified against reality and other people's memories. The precision of gestural indications of angle can also be checked up to the limits of estimation from a film record. In all cases, the linguistic and spatial specifications seem to check out with remarkable reliability. However, the interpretation of both directional terms and gestures is not a simple matter, as they are often (but not always) from the point of view of the protagonists at that particular point in the story (Haviland 1996).

An especially convincing case study by Haviland (1993) serves to make the point best. Haviland filmed the late Jack Bambi in 1980 telling a story about how he and a companion were shipwrecked in a ketch. In 1982, I serendipitously filmed the same man retelling the same story. By comparing the two tellings, event by event, Haviland shows that orientations are preserved across the two tellings down to the details of which way the ketch rolled over, and on which side the two men jumped out, and who was west of whom on the swim back to shore, and so on throughout the story.

I made a wide range of further attempts to explore the nature of memorized directions. On one occasion, a group of a dozen Hopevale men made an overland trip to Cairns, the nearest city 250 km to the south, to discuss land rights issues with other Aboriginal groups. The meeting took place in a room without windows, in a building reached either by back alley or through a car park, so that the relation between building and city layout was somewhat obscured. Between a month and six weeks later, I asked half a dozen of them (as I happened to meet up with them) about the orientations of the meeting rooms and the positions of the speakers at the meeting, and also details of their hotel rooms. They could all give immediate and, as far as I was later able to ascertain, accurate responses to these questions. In particular there was complete agreement about, for example, the orientation of the main speaker, the blackboard, the breakfast room at the hotel and so on.

Somewhat more systematically, ten informants were shown a six-minute film, depicting various events without words, and asked to describe it to another native speaker.[18] Although there was no systematic delay between watching the film and describing it, the length of the film made it likely that at least a six-minute interval arose between watching and describing the relevant portion of the film. Every one of the descriptions obtained includes many orientational specifications, which are correct for the virtual space behind the screen (if a man appears to be coming towards the viewer, and the viewer faces south, then the man will be described as coming northwards). Or as one young man remarked on another occasion, 'You always know which way the old people been watching the TV when they tell the story.' This is intriguing. Clearly we cannot *see* cardinal directions, and our visual system must process information in terms of relative position, for example locating objects in the left or right, or foreground or background, of our visual field. So we expect visual perception to operate in terms of a relative, viewpoint-centred system. But equally clearly we cannot see without looking in a particular direction, and it seems that visual percepts are coded for memory by GY speakers with that direction attached.

This line of investigation has distinct limitations, because it relies on a verbal protocol – we can show that speakers can recover memories and then code them in absolute terms, but it is possible that in some way the

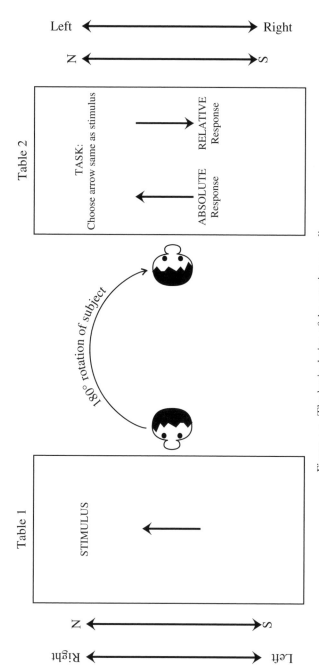

Figure 4.4. The basic design of the rotation paradigm

absolute directions are reconstructed during the process of preparation for speaking. For example, perhaps GY speakers think of scenes and memorize them accordingly, just like you or I do so in primarily egocentric coordinates, but unlike us they can reconstruct what direction they were facing at the time and so crank out absolute descriptions. In that case, absolute conceptualization is not part of thinking *simpliciter*, it is rather part of the process of regimenting thought for language production, or in Slobin's (1996) felicitous phrase, 'thinking for speaking'.

4.1.2.2.2 The rotation paradigm. While still in the field in 1992, I was racking my brains for a way to show what I now felt intuitively was certain, namely that GY speakers not only speak differently about space, they simply do not *think* like we do about spatial arrangements. Yet so far, apart from the dead-reckoning abilities, I had only language-related evidence, together with an indirect inference to a different underlying conception of spatial relations. But how can one explore the *conceptual structure* of a non-linguistic representation? There is curiously little experimental tradition here on which to draw, most psychological experimentation being about process, not about the structure of representations.[19]

In my mind at the time was John Lucy's (1992a) demonstration that how a language treats nominal semantics can be shown to have an effect on non-linguistic memory for number or for substance vs. shape: he had been able to show this in memory tasks in which language played no role. My 'eureka!' experience was seeing someone drawing a map apparently upside down (the anecdote is related below), which made it startlingly clear that the crucial difference between our own system of spatial conception and the GY one is that we constantly rotate our coordinate systems with ourselves, while they do not. This insight rapidly generated a whole set of tasks in which one could explore at least this one property of the underlying mental representations without asking subjects to talk about what they were doing. The logic of the rotation paradigm is immediately grasped from Figure 4.4, which illustrates a possible experiment about non-verbal coding for memory. Suppose the subject sees an arrow point to his right on Table 1, and is required to memorize it; now he is asked to turn around, and asked to identify which of the arrows on Table 2 is most like the arrow previously seen. If subjects identify the rightwards pointing arrow as the arrow seen before, they are clearly rotating the coordinate system with them; but if instead they choose the arrow pointing left, they have preserved the absolute direction of the arrow seen on Table 1.

Note that this rotation design instantiates just one of the rotation variables that distinguish the different frames of reference, as described in Chapter 2 (see Figure 2.6). Obviously, such a paradigm lends itself to many variants. If identifying a prior stimulus from a second one tests recognition memory, being asked to place the second arrow in the direction seen before would test memory for recall. These two aspects of memory are interestingly different – you recognize your auntie without difficulty on seeing a photo of her, but it is another matter to draw a picture of her face (or even to try and recall a mental image of it). Delaying responses, or talking to the subject in between stimulus and response, should help to mask any subvocal rehearsal. In later work, we have developed many such tasks, some of them described later in this book, but in the field in 1992 only a few of these possibilities could be explored.

Following this line of reasoning, a series of tasks were developed, which were later also run on a Dutch comparison group – only a couple of these are described here, see Levinson 1997a for a full description. The Hopevale tasks were conducted in a pair of rooms that were interconnected, but were so arranged that they were rotations of one another, down to the last detail of the furniture (the later Dutch comparison group was also run in a similar setting).[20] So from the interconnecting door, each room visually presented the identical scene, with the desk at the right-hand side on the far wall. One desk thus faced north, the other south (see Figure 4.5). The passage between one desk and the other, around the existing furniture, took approximately 30–45 seconds, so that, together with verbal instructions, about one minute passed between a subject seeing a stimulus set on one table and the corresponding set on the other table. This setting gave the minimum environmental encouragement to thinking in terms of cardinal directions, compared, for example, to carrying out experiments in the bush or on the beach, and the rotational matching of the rooms gave a definite bias towards thinking in relative terms, for example in terms of left and right. Thinking in terms like 'towards the bed' or 'towards the cupboard' in such mirror-image settings would also yield the same results as thinking in terms of left and right.

In order to not prejudice the results, considerable thought was given to the instructions, which contained no directional expressions. In the event, all instructions were given in English, and the subjects therefore responded in English where a verbal response was requested. This minimized any possible residual effect of 'thinking for speaking' in GY (Slobin

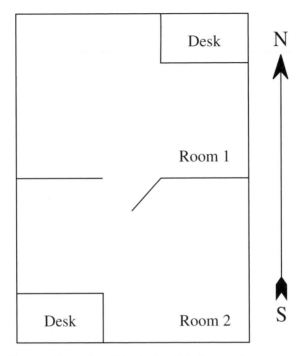

Figure 4.5. Rooms with rotational identity in which the experiments were conducted

1996), even though the main task set to informants was non-verbal: for the most part, they had merely to indicate what they previously saw by pointing.

4.1.2.2.3 Recognition memory task. The hypothesis entertained was that, although visual perception and processing is presumably universally viewpoint dependent or relative in nature, nevertheless a visual percept may be coded for long-term memory together with viewpoint-independent (cardinal direction) information by GY speakers. This would transform the percept into a fundamentally different concept, with testable consequences. As a test of recognition memory, I employed identical sets of stimulus cards which could be oriented in different ways, and the task was to remember the orientation.

4.1.2.2.4 Method. The stimuli consisted of a pair of two (i.e. four) black cards, each of which had glued on it two chips of plastic: one bright red, about 2 cm square, one light blue about 1 cm wide and 2 cm long. The size difference of the chips was designed to guard against any unforeseen effects from colour blindness. The chips were identically arranged on each card using a template with exactly the same spacing between them and the edges of the card. Each pair of cards was displayed as follows. One card was placed above the other, but twisted around, so that the top card had the red chip to the left, blue to the right, while the bottom card had blue to the left, red to the right. The initial pair or stimulus set was displayed in Room 1 on the desk viewed looking north, while an identical arrangement (top card with red to the left) was placed in Room 2 on the desk viewed looking south.

Subjects were led into Room 1, and asked to choose one of the two cards. Having chosen it they were asked to remember it. Then they were turned around and led to Room 2, where they now faced the identical arrangement facing in the opposite cardinal direction. They were then asked to identify the card they chose before. They were then told to keep remembering it, and were led back to Room 1 where they saw the previous stimulus set rearranged, so that the card that was on the top was now on the bottom. Again they were asked to identify the previously chosen card. Finally they were led back to Room 2, where they were shown the same two cards but now placed side by side, rather than on top of each other (see Figure 4.6).

4.1.2.2.5 Participants. Twelve Hopevale men were recruited for the task. They were all primary GY speakers, and were aged forty or over. Later, a Dutch comparison group of fifteen men and women of mixed ages performed the identical task in a similar setting in Holland, with paired rooms across a corridor.

4.1.2.2.6 The results. There are two different, equally correct, ways to perform the task. The one identifies the cards seen before and after rotation in terms of the left/right directions of the different coloured chips. The other identifies the matching card in terms of absolute orientations, disregarding the rotation of the viewer, in which case a different card will be recognized as the same as the original stimulus card under rotation. Where the left/right orientation was preserved, the trial was coded as relative, where the absolute direction (e.g. red chip to east) was preserved in recognition, the trial was coded as absolute. Table 4.3 shows the individual decisions by group, Hopevale versus Dutch, and it is clear

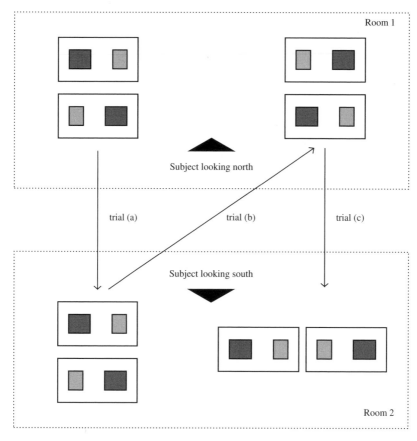

Figure 4.6. Recognition memory task

that the two groups treat the task significantly differently – Hopevale participants mostly code in absolute terms, and Dutch participants code almost uniformly in relative terms.

Field experiments expose participants to unfamiliar materials and practices, and one can expect less consistency from non-Western subjects – only seven out of the Hopevale men were consistent absolute coders on three trials, while fourteen Dutch participants were consistent relative coders. If we classify subjects by majority of choices, we find the pattern in Table 4.4, which shows that most Hopevale men are absolute coders, and all Dutch participants are relative coders. In this table I have set aside two Hopevale men who only completed two out of three trials.

Table 4.3. *Memorizing chips: individual decisions*

		Orientation		
		Absolute	Relative	Total
Group	Hopevale	27	7	34
	Dutch	1	44	45

Hopevale vs. chance: p = 0.0004 (Binomial test, P = 0.5 for Absolute, Relative)
Dutch vs. chance: p = 0.0000 (Binomial test, same assumptions)
Hopevale vs. Dutch: p = 0.0000 (Fischer's exact test)

Table 4.4. *Memorizing chips: subjects by majority of choices*

		Orientation		
		Absolute	Relative	Total
Group	Hopevale	9	1	10
	Dutch	0	15	15

Hopevale vs. chance: p = 0.0107 (Binomial test, P = 0.5 for Absolute, Relative)
Dutch vs. chance: p = 0.0000 (Binomial test, same assumptions)
Hopevale vs. Dutch: p = 0.0000 (Fischer's exact test)

4.1.2.2.7 Discussion. Despite weaknesses in the design (with too few trials), the results do suggest that GY speakers perform non-verbal recognition tasks in a different way than those who speak languages that make predominant use of relative spatial coding. The results are indeed in line with the hypothesis, namely, that speakers of a language with primary absolute frame of reference might code spatial arrays for non-verbal memory in terms of absolute coordinates, and vice-versa for speakers of a language with predominant relative coordinates.

4.1.2.2.8 Mental maps and inference. Might it be possible to show that not only in memory tasks involving recognition or recall, but also in various higher but non-verbal cognitive processes essential recourse is had to absolute orientation by GY speakers? In a pilot task, informants were presented with a set of about twenty cards. Each card had a Polaroid photo of a familiar building or other site on the mission, for example the store, church, cemetery, sawmill and so on. On the back of the card was a photo of the same building from the other side. The cards were supplied with stands so they could be set upright. Four consultants were given the cards and asked to arrange them like a map of the mission site without further instruction. In all cases, not only did the consultants arrange the cards in the correct absolute orientation, so that, for example the cemetery was south (and slightly east) of the hospital, but also the individual cards were oriented so that the front of the church faced west, the back of the hospital east, the back of the store south etc., thus matching reality.

This seems to show that, whereas for us a map or plan has an arbitrary orientation, for GY speakers any such plan should be correctly oriented. This was also demonstrated on various occasions by sketch maps drawn in the sand. For example, on one occasion when talking over the challenge mounted by one highly educated Hopevale resident in the state high court to a land rights decision on the Quinkan reserve, he drew the map of the reserve lands in the dust on the table in a workshop. I was confused until I realized that he had located south at the top of the map, because that was also the true direction.

Thinking like this might lead to distinct solutions to inferential problems, along the lines of Johnson-Laird's (1983) theory of mental models. The differences between an egocentric coding of coordinates and an absolute one would become obvious only upon rotation.

4.1.2.2.9 Method. To test this, four mazes were drawn on large cartridge sheets. Each maze had a black circle as starting point from which began a path made of equal length arrows (each 10 cm), each following the other either in a straight line or at 90 degree angles. Thus a rectilinear path was traced, like the path through and round half a dozen city blocks (Figure 4.7 illustrates with one of the mazes). The path came to an end at (variously on different trials) two or three arrow lengths from the starting circle. The task was to choose from a set of three cards the one that would complete the path back to the starting point. For each trial, two of the cards were identical, except that one was rotated 180 degrees; both of these cards were acceptable solutions to the puzzle. The third card was a distractor; there was no way that this one could lead back from the end of the path to the starting point.

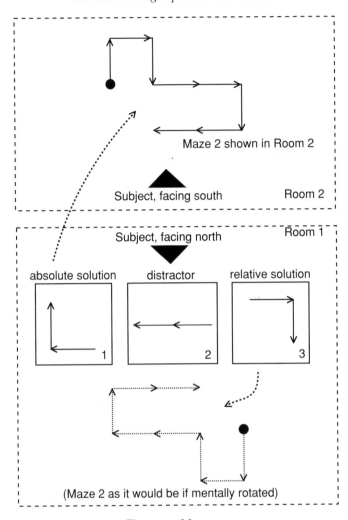

Figure 4.7. Maze test

First, in a training session, participants were shown a practice maze (not further used in the experiment), and the three candidate completion cards. It was demonstrated that, holding their orientation constant, only one of the cards would complete the maze, and it was explained that the task would be to choose the right card when the maze had been taken away. Once participants claimed to understand the task, the main

Table 4.5. *Maze completion: individual decisions*

		Absolute	Relative	Distractor	Total
		\multicolumn{4}{c}{Solution}			

Group		Absolute	Relative	Distractor	Total
	Hopevale	24	11	1	36
	Dutch	3	42	0	45

Hopevale vs. chance: p = 0.0000 (Multinomial test, assuming P = 0.3333 for Absolute, Relative, Distractor)
Dutch vs. chance: p = 0.0000 (Multinomial test, same assumptions)
Hopevale vs. Dutch: p = 0.0000 (Chi-square)

Table 4.6. *Maze completion: consistency of subjects over three trials*

Group		Absolute	Relative	Inconsistent	Total
	Hopevale	5	1	6	12
	Dutch	0	12	3	15

trials proceeded. In the main trials, participants were shown the mazes in Room 2, facing south. They were then taken into the other room and, facing the opposite direction, were shown the three completion cards for that maze, and asked to choose the card that would complete the route. The variable to be coded was whether participants would preserve the absolute orientation of the maze, and thus choose out of the two correct cards the one that retained the absolute direction, or whether they would choose the card that was the correct solution from an egocentric or relative perspective. Each participant performed three trials with different mazes.

4.1.2.2.10 Results. The results for Hopevale participants are listed in the first rows of Tables 4.5 and 4.6, with comparative results from a Dutch control group beneath. Note in Table 4.6 only one choice of the 'blind' or control card was made, indicating good comprehension of the task. The great majority of Hopevale choices were absolute decisions, although out

Table 4.7. *Maze completion: subjects by majority of choices*

| | | Orientation | | |
		Absolute	Relative	Total
Group	Hopevale	8	4	12
	Dutch	0	15	15

Hopevale vs. chance: p = 0.1938 (Binomial test, assuming P = 0.5 for Absolute, Relative)
Dutch vs. chance: p = 0.0000 (Binomial test, same assumptions)
Hopevale vs. Dutch: p = 0.0002 (Fischer's exact test)

of twelve Hopevale participants there were only five wholly consistent absolute-strategy users (Table 4.6); on the other hand, there was only one consistent relative coder, the rest not being fully consistent performers. As shown in Table 4.7, eight out of the twelve subjects had a majority of absolute choices. The results show that the Hopevale participants were performing on a non-random basis over the three trials and three possible responses, and that the majority of consistent users were absolute thinkers in the ratio of five absolute to one relative subject. There are statistically reliable differences between the two populations, represented by our Hopevale and Dutch participants. Inconsistent responses from Hopevale subjects though have the consequence that the Hopevale trend towards absolute coding is not statistically significant when computed by subject.

4.1.2.2.11 Discussion. The task could in principle be solved in two ways – by memorizing the maze, or by computing a set of possible solutions before leaving the maze. Given the properties of visual memory (Baddeley 1990: 31), the latter is more likely, implying that the task is inferential.

The Dutch subjects, who were of mixed sex and age, were more consistent relative coders on the reported experiments than the Hopevale participants were absolute coders (and this same pattern was repeated in other experiments not reported here). For all field experiments, there is of course a tendency for less-schooled populations, unused to a Western-style testing environment, to perform less consistently than more schooled Western populations. In the Hopevale context there may also have been special factors. One of these is the fact that Hopevale residents are all bilingual in English, and the experimental instructions were in English – might this have induced some relative coding? But Hopevale English makes little use of the relative frame of reference, so this may not be a confounding factor.

Another explanation for more mixed responses from the Hopevale participants may have to do with visually presented tasks. Our visual system codes initially at least in viewer-centred terms, and thus in the relative frame of reference (as discussed in Chapter 2). In order to establish the basis for linguistic description in GY, GY speakers must recode these scenes in absolute coordinates in long-term memory. It is likely that, at least for short-term memory, both kinds of coding are available and accessible, since, for example, motor-control is certainly guided by the viewpoint-dependent information. Their long-term memory may be exclusively absolute in nature (allowing derivative computations of viewpoint-dependent angles) or possibly mixed (especially to the extent that it is visual). In other words, when Hopevale residents wake in the night and search for the alarm clock, it is an open question whether they think 'it must be just there by my left arm' or 'just north there' or both. What we do know, on the basis of the experiment and anecdote here reported, is that the absolute coding is almost certainly available to the GY speaker, and it is almost certainly not readily available to the Dutch speaker.

The idea that the visual coding system and the linguistic coding system, and their associated memory requirements, might be *incongruent* in some cultures and not in others is important. It suggests for one thing that there might be substantial differences in child development cross-culturally. For example, Piaget noted the very long developmental gap between early established *perceptual* spatial abilities and the corresponding *conceptual* abilities. But what accounts for this strangely laborious recapitulation on the conceptual level of what is so effortlessly given on the perceptual level? It is hard to avoid his conclusion that conceptual abilities are constructed through experience on the basis of native abilities. Indo-European languages just happen to display an isomorphism in spatial perception and conception, which is absent or downplayed in many languages, including GY. Thus children cannot be structured as organisms to *presume* such an isomorphism, but must slowly find out whether things are so (if their language is English or Dutch) or not so (if their language is GY). We will pursue the issues of child development and language acquisition in Chapter 7.

4.1.2.2.12 Directionality and Imagination. If among GY speakers scenes are normally remembered with orientational information, and inferential processes adapted accordingly, the intriguing possibility arises that even hypothetical or imaginary scenarios are thought of as oriented in particular ways.[21] It is hard to know how to investigate this seriously, but a series of pilot probes were tried as follows.

First, informants were asked to translate verbally three passages, two from the New Testament, and one adapted from a newspaper story about a car chase. The New Testament passages recounted Jesus' trip across the sea of Galilee and his casting out of the demons of Mob (Mark 4:35–5:11), and the miracle of the good catch (John 21). Three exemplars were obtained, and each imposed an arbitrary orientation upon the lake crossing and subsequent events, and upon the fishing expedition. Thus, for example, the passage 'Jesus said "Let us go to the other side of the lake"' was rendered (in gloss) 'Go to the east-side of the sea', and the passage 'Throw your net out on the right side of the boat' was rendered (in gloss) 'Throw your net out on the east side of the boat'. The car chase with left and right turns was more problematic, but again recourse was had to an arbitrary imposed orientation.

It may be complained that this imposition of cardinal directions on a scene shows nothing about conception, only about the necessity of making additional assumptions for adequate translation (just as, when translating *you* into French, I must choose between *tu* and *vous*). So another kind of task was assigned, namely to provide generalized recipes for actions of various kinds. For example, five informants were asked to describe how to catch the large sea-going turtles that are prized as festive eating by Hopevale people. The procedure involves chase by a dinghy, until the turtle surfaces for air, whereupon it is either harpooned or grabbed by a man diving overboard, and wrestled to the surface and into the boat. Again all the verbal recipes or instructions were given to me in GY in an oriented way, so that the turtle was visualized, or at least described, as being on a particular side (east etc.) of the imaginary boat that we were sitting in.

Perhaps, under such circumstances, informants naturally think of some particular actual event they participated in, thus accounting for the concrete instantiation of the generalized instruction. Therefore inquiries were also made about dreams. Four dreams were collected, either wholly or partly in GY. Each had some motion description or involved some imaginary landscape (e.g. heaven), and each account oriented the motion or landscape in specified cardinal directions. I am glad to be able to report that heaven is entered heading north (at least from Cape York), and that you will be met by the Lord (half Aboriginal) coming south towards you!

Although these probes are hardly decisive, they are at least consistent with the possibility that GY speakers supply absolute orientations to historical, hypothetical or entirely imaginary scenarios.[22] If their recognition, recall and especially inferential faculties habitually make use of absolute orientational information, then it would make sense to think of hypothetical scenarios in the same way, in terms of fixed directions.

4.1.2.2.13 Conclusions. There are many caveats that must be made about the observations and experiments reported here. Amongst other things, they were conducted with a very small sample of consultants, namely those relatively senior men whose sociolinguistic prowess in GY was undisputed, and who happened to be available and willing to help at the time of study. Further, the methods employed were still in their infancy. Despite these limitations, if these results are taken together with the many qualitative studies that we have for this community, and with the kind of anecdotal evidence partially reported here, they do point in a single convincing direction. Guugu Yimithirr speakers, at least of this older generation, not only speak a language that as a prerequisite requires storage and computation of orientation and absolute directions, they can also be shown when not engaged in speaking the language to think in a way that is concordant with it. This represents a serious challenge to the view that linguistic spatial categories directly reflect innate concepts. It also suggests that more is involved than just 'thinking for speaking' (Slobin 1996), the view that a particular language at most requires a special way of thinking just while speaking. Rather, the fact that GY provides an absolute system and no system of relative description seems to have knock-on effects: speakers must remember spatial dispositions in the absolute terms which will allow them to later code them in the language. Spatial memory will then determine an absolute mode of spatial inference. Absolute coding in both memory and language in turn requires a constant, background 'dead reckoning' of current heading and position, which our pointing experiments appear to have tapped directly into. Language, gesture, cognitive style, and many aspects of spatial behaviour, come to form a coherent and distinctive complex. The system constitutes an intellectual achievement of the first order, and one of the central surviving features of a culture under

prolonged erosion, which connects to that enduring traditional preoccupation of Australian Aboriginal peoples, the landscape and its hidden
meanings.

4.2 TZELTAL SPEAKERS OF TENEJAPA[23]

4.2.1 Background

Let us now turn to an entirely different kind of community at the other
side of the world, where there is a similar dependence on an absolute
frame of reference in spatial language. Once again our question will be:
Is it possible to show a corresponding reliance on an absolute frame of
reference in non-linguistic conceptualization of spatial arrays?

Tenejapa is an upland municipio in highland Chiapas, Mexico, located
in rugged country ranging in elevation from about 2,000 metres to under
1,000 metres, and thus ecologically from subalpine pine forest to tropical
conditions. Overall, the territory forms an incline from high south to
low north, cut by many deep valleys. In this territory live speakers of a
dialect of Tzeltal, a Mayan language with other dialects spoken in other
areas (but for simplicity, henceforth the Tenejapan dialect will simply
be designated 'Tzeltal'). The c. 15,000 inhabitants practise slash-and-
burn maize and bean cultivation, as their ancestors have for well over
a thousand years. They have a dispersed settlement pattern, practising
subsistence farming, with distinctive material culture (houses, chattels,
weaving style and so forth). Many of the material conditions of traditional
life seem relevant to understanding their conceptual system, although
in the last decade there has been a transformation of these conditions
through improved communications and growing dependence on the
cash economy. Tenejapa offers a substantial contrast to the material and
ecological conditions of the Guugu Yimithirr speakers of Hopevale.

Tzeltal, like other Mayan languages, has a verb-first structure, with
the verb cross-referencing agents, subjects and objects in an ergative-
absolutive manner. Most complex phrase building is done through possession, using relational nouns, or through one general-purpose preposition *ta*. The lexicon has a relatively small set of roots (c. 3,000), from
which a powerful derivational morphology yields perhaps a tenfold common vocabulary. The language has attracted attention for its elaborate
classifiers (Berlin 1968) and because of the excellent ethnobiological studies conducted in Tenejapa (Berlin *et al.* 1974). Recently the spatial system

has also been shown to be of considerable scientific interest and is the focus of a monograph (Brown and Levinson in preparation).

Unlike Guugu Yimithirr, where the absolute system is predominant to the extent that the topological system is highly reduced, Tzeltal has a rich topological system, with some extended uses into the intrinsic frame of reference. Tzeltal therefore offers two spatial frames of reference, absolute and intrinsic, with a rich topology in addition. In Chapter 3 a number of these features were already mentioned, but to provide a little more detail the following illustrates the topological system:

(4) **waxal**   *ta*   **x-chikin** *mexa* *te* *p'ine*
    stand-of-vertical-cylinder PREP its-ear   table the pot
    'The pot is standing at the corner of the table'

Here the locative predicate in bold, *waxal*, provides information about the orientation and shape of the figure, and its placement on a horizontal ground. Interestingly, for a language with only about 3,000 lexical roots, about a tenth of them are dedicated to very precise spatial configurations of this sort. Most Mayan languages share a special root class of no fixed stem class (i.e. they have to be derived into one of a number of parts of speech), appropriately called 'positionals', in which many of these configurations are specified (here illustrated by *wax-*). Also in this example, marked in boldface, we can see the use of the 'body-part' topological/intrinsic system of parts: the semantically general preposition *ta* (both locative and relational) introduces a ground phrase, which describes by means of a 'body-part' spatial nominal the part (*chikin* 'ear') of a table that constitutes the ground. There are about twenty such contrastive body-parts, with extended uses based on the dissection of objects into parts on the grounds of their precise volumetric and axial properties. As mentioned in Chapter 3, these body-part expressions have a precise axial and volumetric interpretation, but are orientation free, allowing them to be used for any novel object in any position (see Levinson 1994 for details).

This same topological construction has some extended uses in the intrinsic frame of reference, when figure and ground are not necessarily in direct contact or contiguity:

(5) *nakal*   *ta*   *spat*   *na*   *te*   *kerem-e*
    sitting PREP its-back house the boy-PART
    'The boy is sitting behind the house (other side from the door)'

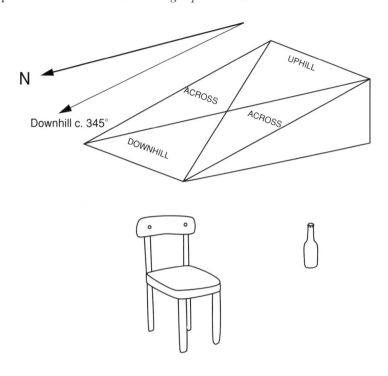

'The bottle is uphill of the chair.'

Figure 4.8. Tenejapan Tzeltal uphill/downhill system

However, for most situations where figure and ground are separated in space, the absolute frame of reference comes into play. The absolute system, as mentioned briefly in Chapter 3, involves an idealized inclined plane, abstracted from the landscape, with parallel directed arcs headed at about north 345 degrees. The directions across this plane are designated *ajk'ol* 'uphill (roughly south)', *alan* 'downhill (roughly north)', and *jejch* 'across (either east or west)', as illustrated in Figure 4.8.

For the scene depicted in Figure 4.8, if someone asks 'Where is the bottle?', (6) would be a natural answer:

(6) *waxal*   *ta*   *y-ajk'ol*   *xila*   *te*   *limite*
    stand-of-vertical-cylinder   **PREP**   its-uphill   chair   the   bottle
    'The bottle is standing uphill (i.e. south) of the chair'

It is important to add that such descriptions do not depend on an actual incline – here the bottle and the chair were on a flat surface. Nor do they depend on visible features of the environment – the same locutions would be used in a novel house in the night, and in any case in any actual location, valleys and banks lie in all directions. Nor do they depend on being in the actual territory from which the inclined plane is abstracted – native speakers taken outside their territory utilize the system with fixed compass-like bearings wherever they are.

There is no systematic relative frame of reference reflected in language: one simply cannot say in Tzeltal 'The boy is to the left of the tree', or 'Take the first turning left' or 'Put the ball in front of the chair' (meaning between me and the chair). There are body-part terms for left and right hands, and a few speakers find it acceptable to talk about, for example, left and right breasts during breast-feeding, but there is certainly no way to use these terms to indicate left and right visual fields. Front and back terms are determined by the geometric, non-oriented part-system already mentioned, and only in marginal cases – where the geometry fails to yield a solution – can they be assigned on the grounds of viewing angle (Levinson 1994: 825–6, 844). A few relative-like marginal uses can also be found in the use of the absolute system (Brown and Levinson 1993a: 59–60). Although these marginal uses are interesting, because they suggest that a relative frame of reference is incipiently available, they effectively play no significant role in language usage.

Spatial description is thus for the most part split between two main systems: the topological system when figure and ground are contiguous, and the absolute system when they are separated. The absolute oppositions 'uphill', 'downhill' and 'across' form a kind of grammatical category, or set of underlying semantic parameters, which reappear in a number of other lexical sets: there are terms for uphill/downhill and side edges (e.g. of fields), and verbs of motion towards each of the directions, as well as directionals for directions of motion and alignment. Descriptions of motion, as in route-directions, descriptions of alignment, and descriptions of location, thus come quite normally with absolute specifications.

The use of Tzeltal in spatial descriptions was carefully investigated using many different sources of information: overheard conversation, recorded natural talk, detailed elicitation and, perhaps most importantly, communicative tasks. These tasks were designed to elicit linguistic solutions to various descriptive problems of a spatial character. For example, consider Figure 4.9, a line drawing after the original photo stimulus.

Figure 4.9. Men and tree game

   This was contrasted with another similar photo, in which the man was
on the other side of the tree. These two photos in turn were embedded
in a larger set where other oppositions were also implicitly present –
such as the man facing towards the tree or away from the camera. In the
communication task, the 'director' had to describe the photo correctly in
such a way that a 'matcher', sitting side by side but visually screened from
the director, could distinguish the described photos from amongst the
full set of oppositions. This, together with many other communication
tasks, is one of the main bases that we have used for the typing of languages in terms of available frames of reference (see Pederson *et al.* 1998).
Here is how the photo in Figure 4.9 was described by a fifteen-year-old
Tenejapan boy director:

(7) *sok   xan   tekel   te'*
    with   again   standing(of.trees)   tree
    'Again there's a tree standing there,
    jich   ay   ta   ajk' ol   te   te'-e
    thus   there.is   PREP   uphill   Def.Art   tree-PART
    Thus the tree is at the uphill side

te	winik-e	jich	tek'el		ta	alan	ine
Def.Art	man-CL	thus	stand(of.bipeds)		PREP	downhill	there

The man is thus standing downhill there

jich	ya	x-k'aboj	bel	ta	be	ine
thus	INCOMPL	ASP-look	going	PREP	path	there

He's looking thus towards the trail there'

The description of the relative placement of man and tree requires an orientation-bound frame of reference, and the boy uses the absolute frame (as that is what the language provides) – he describes the tree as at the 'uphill' of the man, and conversely, the man as at the 'downhill' of the tree (recollect from Chapter 2 that only the absolute frame of reference allows converse inferences regardless of viewpoint). 'Uphill' corresponds roughly to south and downhill to north, as we have seen, and at the time of description the photo in Figure 4.9 was placed so that 'director' and 'matcher' were facing west, with south to their left and north to their right. Notice that, just as in Guugu Yimithirr, the virtual world of a photograph inherits the cardinal directions of its orientation in the real world.

Many other such tasks were conducted, testing the description of motion, the description of causative placement, the description of body-parts (using the wooden man task described for Guugu Yimithirr above), and so on. All the findings are consistent with the conclusion that Tenejapan Tzeltal offers only two frames of reference, absolute and intrinsic, and that there are strict constraints on which is relevant when, the absolute frame coming into play as soon as figure and ground are substantially distanced in space.

4.2.2 Informal investigations of Tenejapan 'cognitive style'

Over many years of intensive investigation of the language, culture and interaction of Tenejapans, Penelope Brown and myself have had occasion to note many details of behaviour and response that suggest that these language patterns are echoed in unconscious non-linguistic thought and behaviour. A couple of anecdotes were mentioned in Chapter 1, for example how a Tenejapan woman spending the night for the first time in a hotel in an alien city asked her husband 'Is the hot water in the uphill tap?' – here she was, displaced from home territory, in a warren of a building at night, and she presumed that the 'uphill' direction was as immediately accessible to her husband as to herself. We are dealing here with something like the same uncanny sense of direction that we met with Guugu Yimithirr speakers – Tenejapans clearly run a mental compass in the unconscious background as it were. The implications of this are further explored in Chapter 6. Just as in Hopevale, Tenejapans can point to known locations when randomly questioned, and although they do so with somewhat less accuracy than Guugu Yimithirr speakers, they are in a quite different league from Dutch or English speakers, as will be shown in Chapter 6. There we will also turn to look at Tenejapan gesture, for, just like Guugu Yimithirr speakers, when Tenejapans gesture, their gestures are directionally accurate. For example, a man relaying what the leader of the community had said miles away in the ceremonial centre, echoed not only the words but also the directional properties of the gesture, saying 'that truck' and pointing south, just as the original speaker had. Just as in Hopevale, so in Tenejapa, the full import of what is said cannot be separated from the gestural channel. The gestural channel appears to play an important role in the learning of this system by children, as will be discussed in Chapter 7.

These behaviours suggest a mental coding of scenes in terms of fixed bearings very similar to that we have explored among Guugu Yimithirr speakers. But there are significant differences. Consider, for example, the following rather surprising finding. Tenejapans when confronted with photos or figures that are reflected across the frontal plane – like **b** vs. **d** – seem to have a hard time distinguishing them. Having discovered this by accident (see anecdote 4 in Chapter 1), we went on to explore it by systematic experimentation. We constructed line figures that contained parts, for example a triangle that contained a dot in an asymmetrical location. Then we made for each such figure a separate drawing of the relevant part, then a counterpart that was a mirror-image of the part, and finally a part unrelated to the contained part, as in Figure 4.10. We trained our participants to recognize the difference between the part and its mirror-image by using acetate overlays that did or did not match. Then we ran a series of trials to see whether they could maintain the distinction between unreflected and reflected images, with both the original embedded part and its match or mirror in front of them. Two thirds of Tenejapan participants conflated the majority of mirror-images with their unreflected counterparts – that is, they apparently could not systematically maintain the difference between a figure and its mirror-image. Nearly a third failed to detect even one of these reflections – overall most Tenejapan subjects conflated mirror-images most of the

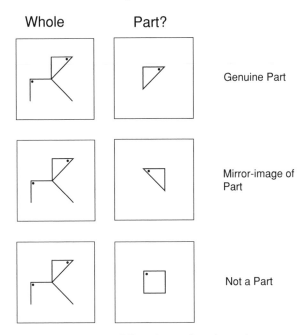

Figure 4.10. Mirror-image detection task

time. Only a quarter of subjects were able to consistently maintain the distinction despite the immediately prior training. In contrast Dutch subjects consistently identified the mirror-images, only one subject out of forty having any persistent problems.

Obviously such a result might be attributed to illiteracy or other cultural factors. We therefore asked Paulette Levy to run the same experiment among Totonac speakers, another indigenous people of Mexico with a similar ecology and lifestyle to the Tenejapans. The Totonac speakers, despite a greater inconsistency, displayed essentially the same result as the Dutch speakers – few people made errors, and when they did, they did so in a small percentage of trials, rather than consistently like Tzeltal speakers. (Full details of these experiments can be found in Brown and Levinson in preparation; see also Danziger and Pederson 1998.)

We therefore believe that there is a systematic downgrading of left/right asymmetries in Tenejapan conception, or mental classification of percepts. This seems to be a striking piece of evidence for the downgrading of the relative frame of reference in Tenejapan cognition, in line with its absence in the language. Recollect Kant's argument in Chapter 1: If we did not bring an egocentric spatial framework to bear on our analysis of space, we would not be able to distinguish 'incongruent counterparts' or enantiomorphs like a left-hand glove from a right-hand one. The Tenejapans seem to show that the Kantian inference is indeed essentially correct (see Levinson and Brown 1994). But still, there are real puzzles here: why don't the Tenejapans simply code the figures in terms of cardinal directions, so that one triangle, for example, could be thought of as having the dot to 'uphill' (south)? We believe the answer is that Tenejapan spatial cognition closely follows Tenejapan spatial language in making a split between objects in contiguity versus objects separated in space. The linguistic system makes an important divide here: objects in contiguity get treated in the topological/intrinsic system, while objects separated in space get treated in the absolute system. Because the stimuli were parts of an object, or objects alone, they were assimilated to the topological/intrinsic system – a system that is orientation free. It makes good functional sense to keep an orientation-free frame of reference for assemblages that are either single objects that move together and have a 'common fate' (like parts of a picture), or are objects in contiguity where no projective angles have to be established. This analysis fits all of the cases of mirror-image conflation we have observed in Tenejapa – once objects are separated in real space, as with chattels on a table, no such conflations are made.

There is therefore a significant difference, we believe, between the 'cognitive style' of Guugu Yimithirr speakers and Tzeltal speakers. Although both groups make fundamental use of absolute bearings, Tzeltal speakers also use a rich topological/intrinsic system, with c. 300 predicate roots indicating spatial configurations between figure and ground, and a set of c. 20 geometrically assigned part-terms, and this seems to be reflected in cognition, as it is in many cultural details – for example, in the preoccupation with types of vessel, the shapes involved in dough preparation, or the patterns in weaving. There is nothing like this in traditional Guugu Yimithirr culture, where material possessions were minimal, and the absolute system is used to describe many topological relations.

4.2.3 Non-verbal memory and inference

The rotation paradigm can be exploited more systematically than I was able to do in Hopevale, and along with colleagues we have since developed a whole suite of non-verbal tasks that can be employed to distinguish absolute from relative coding in non-linguistic memory and inference. Here I present a selection of these tasks, which were collaboratively designed and first run in Tenejapa in 1993 (Brown and Levinson 1993b, Levinson 1996b) and subsequently in many other cultures. These tasks form the basis of the comparative results described in Chapter 5, so they are introduced here in some detail, which may perhaps be somewhat distracting from the immediate job in hand – namely, to give some sense of the cognitive style of an 'absolute' community (i.e. a community that speaks a language that has an absolute and no relative frame of reference). But bear with me, for the results of these experiments conducted in Tenejapa do indeed give quite a profound glimpse into such a cognitive style.

The tasks have been designed to probe for the nature of non-linguistic spatial representations – and specifically just the difference between a relative and absolute coding. We have seen in Chapter 2 that all the evidence points to multiple levels of internal representation of spatial scenes – visual, auditory, haptic, motoric and multi-modal conceptual representations are, for example, clearly distinct, and within each of the modalities there seem to be multiple levels of successively processed representations, as in Marr's (1982) model of the visual system. It is also quite plausible that the representations that serve different conceptual functions might be different at least in detail – for example, the kind of memory representation I would need to recognize this page as one I had seen before is quite different than the representation I would need to rewrite it word by word. Thus we have made efforts to probe the conceptual structure of the non-linguistic representations that drive different cognitive functions, like recognition memory, recall memory and transitive inference.

Clearly it is crucial that the instructions for the experiments, or the wording used in training sessions, do not suggest one or another of the frames of reference: instructions were of the kind 'Point to the pattern you saw before', 'Remake the array just as it was', 'Remember just how it is', i.e. devoid of spatial information as much as possible, and as closely matched in content as could be achieved across languages. Just as in the Guugu Yimithirr experiments, two tables were set up at some metres distance, so that the participant first saw a stimulus on Table 1 (where pre-test trials were also conducted), and after a short delay was then rotated 180 degrees, and led across to Table 2, where the response was required.[24] (I provide here only an outline description,

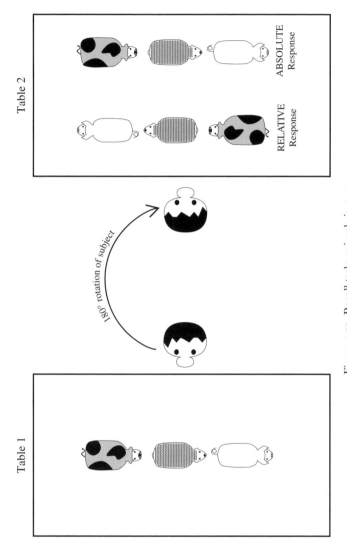

Figure 4.11. Recall task: animals-in-a-row

as further details of the methods employed can be found in Brown and Levinson 1993b, Brown and Levinson in preparation, and Levinson *et al.* 2002).

All the experiments below were run on mixed-age and mixed-sex samples of Tenejapan and Dutch participants. There were 25–8 participants (depending on the experiment) in the Tenejapan sample, and 39–40 in the Dutch comparison group (drawn from an aphasia control panel constructed of different educational and occupational backgrounds – they were not uniform university students as in so many psychological experiments).

The hypothesis being tested in all of these experiments is of course that there is a congruence between the coordinate systems used in language and those used in memory and inference – thus where a community uses predominantly the relative frame of reference in language (as in Holland), we expect the relative frame of reference to be used in memory and inference, and where the community uses predominantly the absolute frame in language (as in Tenejapa), we expect the absolute frame in non-linguistic coding. Both languages also make available an intrinsic frame of reference, but the tasks – since they oppose directions – have been designed to make an orientation-bound frame of reference (either absolute or relative) seem the relevant type to use.

4.2.3.1 Recall memory: the 'animals' task[25]

4.2.3.1.1 Method. The 'animals' task was intended to distinguish between an absolute and relative coding in the detailed memory involved in recall. It was designed to deflect attention from memorizing *direction* towards memorizing the *order* of objects in an array, although the actual primary motive was to tap recall memory for direction. The stimuli consisted of two identical sets of four model animals (pig, cow, horse, sheep) of species familiar in both cultures. From the set of four, three were aligned in a pre-randomized order, all heading in (a randomly assigned) lateral direction on Table 1. Subjects were trained to memorize the array before it was removed, then after a three-quarters of a minute delay to rebuild it 'exactly as it was', first with correction during pre-test trials on Table 1, then without correction under rotation during trials on Table 2 (see Figure 4.11).

Five main trials then proceeded, with the stimulus always presented on Table 1, and the response required under rotation, and with delay, on Table 2. Responses were coded as 'Absolute' if the direction of the

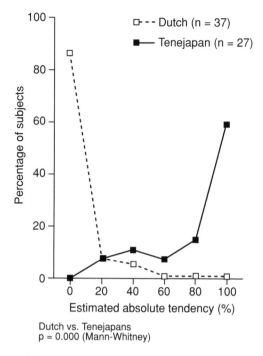

Figure 4.12. Animal task: results for direction

recalled line of animals preserved the fixed bearings of the stimulus array, and as 'Relative' if the recalled line preserved egocentric 'left' or 'right' direction.

4.2.3.1.2 Results. 95% of Dutch subjects were consistent Relative coders on at least four out of five trials, while 75% of Tzeltal subjects were consistent Absolute coders by the same measure. The remainder failed to recall direction so consistently. For purposes of comparison across tasks, the data have been analysed in the following way. Each subject's performance is assigned an index on a scale from 0 to 100, where 0 represents a consistent Relative response pattern, 100 a consistent Absolute pattern, and inconsistencies between codings over trials are represented by indices in the interval. (This treatment will allow controlled comparison across groups, in ways made clear in Chapter 5, where the methodology is discussed in detail.) The data can then be represented by the graph in Figure 4.12, where subjects from each population have been grouped by

20-point intervals on the index (the reasons for this kind of analysis are explained in Chapter 5).

As the graph makes clear, the curves for the two populations are approximately mirror-images, except that Tenejapan subjects are less consistent than Dutch ones. This may be due to various factors: the unfamiliarity of the situation and the tasks, the 'school'-like nature of a task performed by largely unschooled subjects, or to interference from an egocentric frame of reference that is available but less dominant. Only two Tenejapan subjects were consistent Relative coders (on four out of five trials). This pattern is essentially repeated across the experiments.

The result appears to confirm the hypothesis that the frame of reference dominant in the language is the frame of reference most available to solve non-linguistic tasks, like this simple recall task.

4.2.3.2 Recognition memory: the 'chips' task[26]

4.2.3.2.1 Method. The 'chips' task was intended to distinguish between absolute and relative codings in the quick-access memory used in recognition of a prior stimulus. Five identical cards were prepared: on each there was a small green circle and a large yellow circle. The trials were conducted as follows. One card was used as a stimulus in a particular orientation; the subject saw this card on Table 1. The other four were arrayed on Table 2 in a number of patterns so that each card was distinct by orientation (see Figure 4.13). The subject saw the stimulus on Table 1, which was then removed, and after a delay the subject was rotated and led over to Table 2. The subject was asked to identify the card which was the most similar to the stimulus. The eight trials were coded as indicated in Figure 4.13: if the card that maintained orientation from an egocentric point of view (e.g. 'small circle towards me') was selected, the response was coded as a Relative response, while the card that maintained the fixed bearings of the circles ('small circle north') was coded as an Absolute response. The other two cards served as controls, to indicate a basic comprehension of the task. Training was conducted first on Table 1, where it was made clear that sameness of type rather than token identity was being requested.

4.2.3.2.2 Results. We find the same basic pattern of results as in the previous task, as shown in Figure 4.14. Once again the Dutch subjects are consistently Relative coders, while the Tenejapans are less consistent.

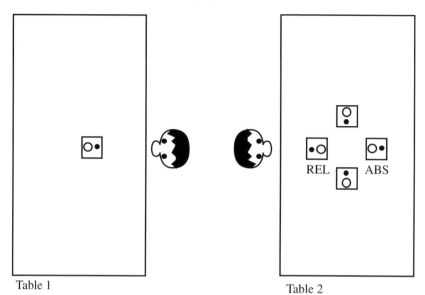

Table 1

Table 2

Figure 4.13. Chips recognition task: 'absolute' vs. 'relative' solutions

Nevertheless, of the Tenejapan subjects who performed consistently over six or more of eight trials, over 80% were Absolute coders. The greater inconsistency of Tenejapan subjects may be due to the same factors mentioned above, but there is also here an additional factor because this experiment tested for memory on both the transverse and sagittal (or north-south and east-west) axes. As mentioned above, the linguistic Absolute axes are asymmetric: one axis has distinct labels for the two half-lines north and south, while the other codes both east and west identically ('across'). If there was some effect of this linguistic coding on the conceptual coding for this non-linguistic task, one might expect more errors or inconsistency on the east-west axis. This was indeed the case.

4.2.3.3 Motion-to-path transformation and recognition memory: 'Eric's maze' task[27]

This task was designed to test whether the memory for motion events is coded in absolute or relative terms. To solve the task, participants must observe a motion event – a toy man 'walking' along and making rectangular turns – and extract the path traversed, and then code the direction of each of its arcs for use in recognition memory. They are then asked, after rotation, to find the path traversed on a map or maze that

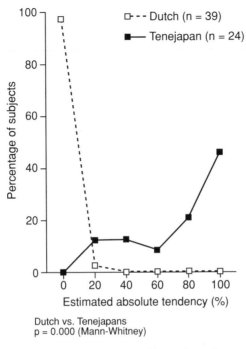

Figure 4.14. Chips recognition task: results

contains numerous possible paths, including the one observed, whichever way it is coded, absolute or relative.

4.2.3.3.1 Method. The experimenter enacted a predetermined motion path on Table 1 (by carefully moving a toy man), starting off from a circle marked with an X. For the pre-test trials, a learning maze was then produced on Table 1, and the participant was asked to recognize the path traversed on the maze – these trials were repeated if necessary until recognition was achieved. Then a further practice trial was conducted, but now after rotating the participant and leading him or her over to Table 2, where the practice maze was again produced. After three pre-test trials, the main trials, five in number, began. In the main trials, the participant saw the motion event as before, but was now always rotated and walked to Table 2 after a short delay, where he or she was shown a new maze and asked to recognize the path traversed. Figure 4.15 displays a main-trial maze and should help to make the nature of the task clear.

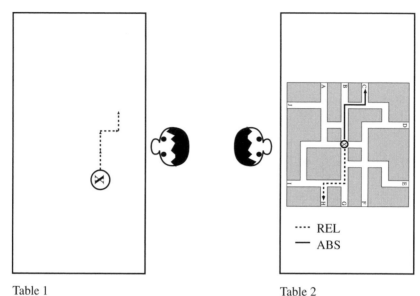

Table 1   Table 2

Figure 4.15. Maze recognition task: 'absolute' vs. 'relative' solutions

For each observed motion, there are two corresponding paths embedded in the maze, one correct under a relative frame of reference, the other under an absolute frame – an example of such a pair is shown in the figure. Solutions were coded relative if they preserved the shape of the motion in egocentric coordinates, and absolute if they preserved its fixed bearings.

4.2.3.3.2 Results. Figure 4.16 displays the results for this task. As can be seen, despite the fact that this task is considerably more taxing than the earlier tasks, the results are essentially the same – Tenejapans are clearly coding in absolute coordinates, and Dutch participants in relative ones.

4.2.3.4 Transitive inference
This task was designed to distinguish the kind of coding – absolute or relative – in representations used in making inferences from spatial arrays.

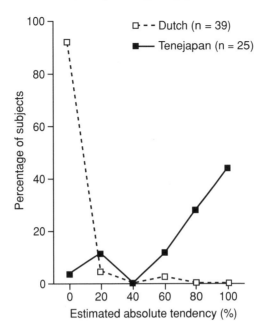

Figure 4.16. Maze recognition task: results

Levelt 1984 observed that relative, as opposed to intrinsic, spatial relations support transitive and converse inferences; Levinson 1992a noted that absolute spatial relations also support transitive and converse inferences. This makes it possible to devise a task where, from two spatial arrays or non-verbal 'premises', a third spatial array or non-verbal 'conclusion' can be drawn by transitive inference utilizing either an absolute or a relative frame of reference. The following task was designed by Eric Pederson and Bernadette Schmitt (and piloted in Tamilnadu by Pederson 1993, 1995).

4.2.3.4.1 The design. The design is as follows. The subject sees the first non-verbal 'premise' on Table 1, for example a blue cone A and a yellow cube B arranged in a predetermined way. The top diagram in Figure 4.17 illustrates one such array from the perspective of the viewer. Then the subject is rotated and sees the second 'premise', a red cylinder C and the yellow cube B in a predetermined orientation on Table 2 (the array

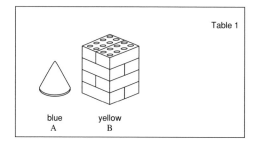

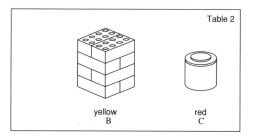

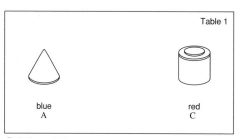

Relative solution

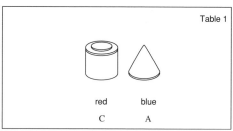

Absolute solution

Figure 4.17. Transitive inference task

appearing from an egocentric point of view as in the second diagram in Figure 4.17). Finally, the subject is rotated again and led back to Table 1, where he is given just the blue cone A and asked to place the red cylinder C in a location consistent with the previous non-verbal 'premises'. For example, if the subject sees ('premise 1') the yellow cube to the right of the blue cone, then ('premise 2') the red cylinder to the right of the yellow cube, when given the blue cone, he may be expected to place the red cylinder C to the right of the blue cone A. It should be self-evident from the top two diagrams in Figure 4.17, representing the arrays seen sequentially, why the third array (labelled the 'Relative solution') is one natural non-verbal 'conclusion' or transitive inference from the first two visual arrays.

However, this result can only be expected if the subject codes the arrays in terms of egocentric or relative coordinates that rotate with him. If instead the subject utilizes fixed bearings or absolute coordinates, we can expect a different 'conclusion' – in fact the reverse arrangement, with the red cylinder to the left of the blue cone (see the last diagram labelled 'Absolute solution' in Figure 4.17)! To see why this is the expectation, consider Figure 4.18, which gives a 'bird's eye view' map of the experimental situation. If the subject does not use bodily coordinates that rotate with him, the blue cone A will be, for example, south of the yellow cube B on Table 1, and the red cylinder C further south of the yellow cube on Table 2, so the conclusion must be that the red cylinder C is south of the blue cone A. As the diagram makes clear, this amounts to the reverse arrangement from that produced under a coding using relative coordinates. In this case, and in half the trials, the absolute inference is somewhat more complex than a simple transitive inference (involving notions of relative distance), but in the other half of the trials the relative solution was more complex than the absolute one in just the same way.

4.2.3.4.2 Method. Three objects distinct in shape and colour were employed. Training was conducted on Table 1, where it was made clear that the position of each object relative to the other object – rather than exact locations on a particular table – was the relevant thing to remember. When transitive inferences were achieved on Table 1, the subject was introduced to the rotation between the first and second premises; no correction was given unless the placement of the conclusion was on the orthogonal axis to the stimulus arrays. There were then ten trials,

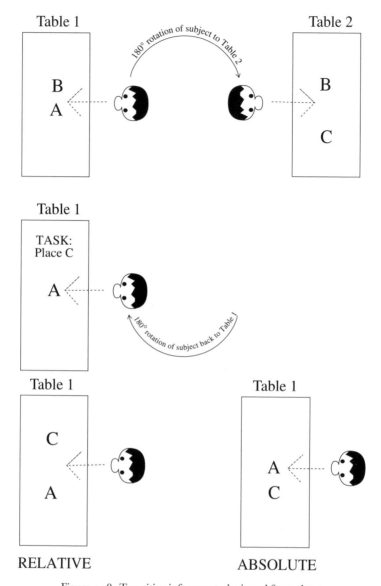

Figure 4.18. Transitive inference task viewed from above

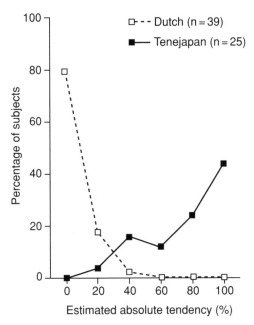

Figure 4.19. Transitive inference task: results

randomized across the transverse and sagittal axes (i.e. the arrays were either in a line across or along the line of vision).

4.2.3.4.3 Results. The results are given in the graph in Figure 4.19. Essentially we have the same pattern of results as in the prior memory experiments, with Dutch subjects consistently relative coders, and Tenejapan subjects strongly tending to absolute coding, but with more inconsistency. Of the Tenejapans who produced consistent results on at least seven out of ten trials, 90% were absolute coders (just two out of twenty-five subjects being relative coders). The reasons for the greater inconsistency of Tenejapan performance are presumably the same as in the previous experiment: unfamiliarity with any such procedure or test situation, and the possible effects of the weak absolute axis (the east-west axis lacking distinct linguistic labels for the half-lines). Once again, Tenejapans made most errors, or performed most inconsistently, on the east–west axis.

4.2.3.5 Discussion of the Tenejapan experiments
The results from these four experiments, together with others unreported here (see Brown and Levinson 1993b, in preparation), all tend in the same

direction: while Dutch subjects utilize a relative conceptual coding (presumably in terms of notions like left, right, in front, behind) to solve these non-verbal tasks, Tenejapan subjects predominantly use an absolute coding system. This is of course congruent with the coding built into the semantics of spatial description in the two languages. The same pattern holds across different psychological faculties: the ability to recall spatial arrays, to recognize ones one has seen before, and to make inferences from spatial arrays. Further experiments of different kinds, exploring recall over different arrays and inferences of different kinds, all seem to show that this is a robust pattern of results. These results show that there is a tight correlation between coding in language and coding in non-linguistic memory and reasoning. They seem to indicate that the effects of language on thinking are not just transient effects of the kind involved in getting one's thoughts into line for expression in the local language (Slobin's 1996 on-line 'thinking for speaking'), but are potentially deeper effects on the preferred coding of spatial arrays in memory for the purposes of retrieval and reasoning.

4.3 CONCLUSIONS

This chapter has focussed on two communities, Hopevale and Tenejapa, where the languages place a primary reliance on the absolute frame of reference. Such systems will be unfamiliar to most readers, and because I shall make much of the opposition between absolute and relative below, some clear exemplars were needed. Obviously, the two languages, Guugu Yimithirr and Tzeltal, have emerged from millennia of independent cultural evolution, but the single shared property of a predominantly absolute spatial frame of reference has been shown to have rather similar, fundamental cognitive consequences. One such consequence, it has been argued, is a 'mental compass', a learned ability to maintain fixed bearings at all times. This will be further explored cross-culturally in Chapter 6, where its relation to the nature of mental maps will be examined. Another consequence seems to be an interesting congruence between the nature of spatial coding in language and spatial coding in non-linguistic cognition, or more general thinking. If this congruence can be reliably shown to exist, it raises the possibility that some kind of 'Whorfian' view of the relation between language and thought is not as untenable as current dogma in the cognitive sciences maintains. In the next chapter, a wide sample of communities with different inventories of frames of reference in their languages are examined for just these issues.

This chapter has also introduced the methods crucial to the rest of the book. We have started from the position that the relation between linguistic categories and non-linguistic thinking cannot be presumed to be one of identity as in so much theorizing in, for example, cognitive linguistics. Rather the relation between linguistic and non-linguistic categories is a matter for empirical investigation. To pursue that, we must independently investigate the language and the psychology, as Lucy (1992a, b) has eloquently argued. The study of semantic categories raises no essentially new problems, but the study of non-linguistic categories is another matter, and here we have had to develop novel methods, like the rotation paradigm that lies behind the set of experiments just described, which I have now described in some detail. After pursuing the nature of non-linguistic representations of space independently of language, one can return to consider the correlation between these and linguistic categories. And as we have seen, the news here is that, even where linguistic categories differ fundamentally, the cognition seems to pattern with the language, and not with some language-independent, pre-linguistic cognitive categories. The next chapter, using the same methods, tests these correlations across a much wider sample of languages and cultures.

CHAPTER 5

Diversity in mind: methods and results from a cross-linguistic sample[1]

5.1 LINGUISTIC INFLUENCES ON THINKING: TESTING THE HYPOTHESIS

In the prior chapter we have seen how spatial description and spatial thinking can co-vary cross-culturally, and we have seen too that there are methods that can be employed to demonstrate this in a non-anecdotal way. In this chapter, we turn to further develop these methods, and then apply them to test the major hypothesis that is at stake in a large cross-cultural sample. Here we will be concerned not with linguistic details, but only with the non-linguistic psychological parameters that seem to correlate with them. The hypothesis in its strongest, crudest form would run as follows:

The frames of reference used in a language constrain or determine the frames of reference used by its speakers in the non-linguistic coding of spatial scenes.

Many riders are immediately in order. What does 'used in a language' mean? We need to note that most languages provide special expressions for more than one frame of reference, and there are conventions for the kinds of circumstances each frame of reference is used in (see, e.g., Tversky 1996). So we need to relativize the statement to situations of use. Second, what does 'constrain or determine' mean? The idea behind the hypothesis is that community-wide conventions about what linguistic expressions mean and how they are to be used will tend to induce a way of thinking in which the immediate, unreflective memory coding matches the kind of coding required to describe an arbitrary spatial array. Third, non-linguistic coding is very unlikely to be a unitary, unilevel phenomenon: we code differently in different sensory systems and code differently for different purposes. So the claim again has to be constrained. So here is a slightly more sophisticated version:

The frames of reference appropriately used in a language to describe specific situations are likely to induce the use of the same frames of reference in the non-linguistic coding of the same scenes for memory and reasoning.

Such a hypothesis entails others more easily directly tested, and crucially a weaker correlational hypothesis:

*The frames of reference appropriately used in a language to describe specific situations are likely to **correlate** with the use of the same frames of reference in the non-linguistic coding of the same scenes for memory and reasoning.*

In this chapter, we attempt to test such a correlational hypothesis against a cross-cultural sample, returning to the issue of the causal efficacy of language at the end.

To test the hypothesis, one clearly needs to determine which linguistic frames of reference are generally utilized for arrays of different kinds by the speakers of different languages. The procedures have in part been illustrated in the prior chapter, where some examples were given of interactive verbal tasks, where spatial arrays of different kinds have to be described, correctly recognized or rebuilt from linguistic descriptions, or where motive action must be undertaken following linguistic instruction. Further information on the verbal tasks can be found in Senft and Wilkins 1994, Senft 1994a, 1994b, 1995, Levinson and Wilkins in preparation, and the methods for coding the linguistic performance are described in Pederson *et al.* 1998. On the basis of both linguistic analysis and linguistic behaviour on these tasks, one may isolate the frames of reference that are effectively available within a particular speech community. For the purposes of the following non-linguistic tasks, I am primarily interested in the opposition between the relative and absolute frames of reference (the tasks were of a kind that makes the intrinsic frame of reference inadequate to solve them, although its utilization may explain certain errors described below).

Once a linguistic analysis has been determined, we can take subjects from the same speech community and see whether the spatial coordinate system they utilize to solve non-linguistic tasks of various kinds is or is not concordant with the language they speak. The hypothesis we entertained was that where the conventions of the language dictate the predominant use of *either* an absolute *or* a relative frame of reference for descriptive purposes, the *same* frame of reference will be employed by speakers of that language to solve corresponding non-linguistic tasks. The alternative hypothesis, probably the basic working assumption in cognitive science circles, would be that universal properties of human spatial cognition, dictated by a common biological inheritance, should lead speakers of different languages to converge on a single kind of spatial coordinate system in memory and reasoning.

As we shall see, the outcome suggests that the coordinate systems that subjects employ in non-linguistic tasks not only vary, but systematically co-vary with the frames of reference in language. The results are compatible with various sub-hypotheses about the nature of the correlation between linguistic and non-linguistic coding strategies:

1. *Constructivism*: Language actually introduces coordinate systems that might not otherwise be available (the best candidate might be absolute systems).
2. *Activation*: Language favours, exercises and develops one or another system, all of which are antecedently available in cognition.
3. *Partial constructivism*: Language instantiates a particular realization or token of antecedently existing potential *types* of coordinate system in cognition, and thus partially constructs a system.

The main data in hand are compatible with at least some versions of each of these hypotheses, but it is clear that in principle one may be able to distinguish between them with slightly richer data. Thus, for example, under a full-scale version of the first hypothesis we would expect categorical differences across speech communities (absence of linguistic coding implying complete absence of the corresponding concepts); under a modified version, for example where absolute coding is a cultural overlay on a universal relative substrate, we would expect a quantitative bias rather than a categorical one for subjects from an absolute speech community, but something nearer to a categorical absence of absolute coding in a relative speech community (our results could be read this way). Some support for a strong constructivist position of this kind can be found in the relatively late acquisition of both relative and absolute systems by children (see Chapter 7).

Under the second hypothesis we would expect all three frames of reference to be constantly in play, with only a quantitative bias towards the linguistically dominant frame of reference in both absolute and relative speech communities. In general our data do not seem to support this view – for example, many relative-coding populations seem categorically to exclude the possibility of absolute coding (possibly, these results might be explained away by suggesting that the more categorical performance in relative speech communities is explained by correlation with higher schooling).[2]

As for the last hypothesis, we might again expect some distribution of performance over all three frames of reference, but a much stronger quantitative bias towards the frames of reference used in the local language. But now we would expect to find in addition some traces of fine-grained language-specific coding distinctions showing up in non-linguistic coding distinctions. Specially close analysis would be necessary to show this, and I present some evidence for the existence of these culturally specific coding features towards the end of this chapter.

5.2 METHODS

5.2.1 Methodological preliminaries

It should be emphasized that the techniques were developed for application in a wide cross-cultural survey of spatial language and cognition conducted in field conditions, largely in small-scale traditional communities with unwritten languages (in Middle America, southern Africa, Papua New Guinea, Solomon Islands and elsewhere). They were administered by specialists in the language and culture of each of these groups (and not, e.g., through an interpreter as often done with unsatisfactory results in cross-cultural psychology), and the results reported here were only made possible by a large number of collaborators.[3] Field conditions give rise to special problems: small samples, small numbers of trials, simple test materials, practical difficulties in retrials, incommensurable social categories of subjects, and so on. A great deal of thought has gone into the designs employed, and the methods employed in the analysis of the data, and I here record the reasons for certain procedures, because they may be of general interest for future applications.

Here we concentrate on the following issues: How are we to compare performance on non-linguistic spatial tasks by subjects who (a) are employing quite different conceptual parameters (i.e. solving the tasks in different ways), (b) display varying levels of consistent performance across cultures, (c) exhibit differing levels of variation within cultures according to social or cultural variables of one kind or another?

The solution to these methodological problems involves the introduction of a single crucial notion, a gradient measure of performance, which (a) gives a uniform measure of performance across two quite distinct types of conceptual coding system, and across tasks of quite different kinds, (b) accurately reflects the consistency of performance, allowing even weak or inconsistent subjects to stay within the subject pool (an important consideration in field studies), and (c) nevertheless remains sensitive to intra-cultural variation of systematic kinds, even ultra-fine coding distinctions.

In Chapter 4, in describing the Tzeltal case, we have seen the basic array of tasks developed under the rotation paradigm. The methods employed there for analysing the data were, however, especially developed for the larger-scale project described in this chapter. Here we return to explain why those methods were chosen and the further applications they have, using the Tzeltal data for examples.

5.2.2 *The gradient of spatial orientation*

In this section, different views of the same empirical findings will be contrasted. My aim is to show that assumptions about conceptual coding and the nature of the task do have a bearing on the way data are grouped and analysed subsequently. We start with an example drawn from the prior chapter, where speakers of Tzeltal and a control group of Dutch performed the animals recall task, where each subject completed five trials.

Assuming that the linguistic hypothesis is correct, the strongest expectation would be the following: Subjects perform all trials consistently, the Tzeltal choosing five times 'absolute' and the Dutch five times 'relative'. If we allow one exception (one trial out of line), the typing would still appear quite strict. The result of this latter categorization can be seen in Table 5.1. As predicted, the majority (74%) of Tzeltal subjects fall within the absolute category and nearly all (95%) of the Dutch subjects fall within the relative category by these strict criteria. However, one fifth of the Tzeltal group remains 'untypable' as five informants perform inconsistently in more than one trial.

Table 5.1. *Categorical typing of Tzeltal and Dutch subjects (from Brown and Levinson 1993b)*

Subjects	Relative	Untypable	Absolute	Total
Tzeltal	7%	19%	74%	100% (n = 27)
Dutch	95%	5%	0%	100% (n = 37)

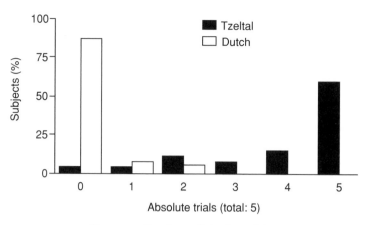

Figure 5.1. Bar chart of 'absolute trials'

This categorization is not entirely satisfactory in two respects. First, the asymmetry between the highly consistent Dutch subjects and the less consistent Tenejapans may reflect nothing more than the kind of performance degradation one expects in an unschooled population faced with an alien, abstract task. One wants to capitalize on whatever patterning there is among the 19% 'untypable' subjects. Second, the dividing line at four trials may appear like a halfway solution – too strict, following the arguments in the preceding paragraph, but at the same time too weak for a simple task with only a few items. Setting only three out of five trials as a 'weak' criterion would make it impossible to discriminate weak performance from random choices. In both cases there is no way to incorporate 'untypable' subjects; they simply fall out of the predefined classes.

The solution may be to choose a more descriptive measure of performance. Consider, for instance, simply counting those trials whose outcome is being judged as 'absolute' (Figure 5.1). This procedure allows us to postpone categorization, while accessing data in a different way: we zoom in on absolute trials, ignoring the rest (if any). Given our example, this turns out to be quite informative. In the Tzeltal case, the percentage of subjects increases with the number of absolute trials, 60% of the informants showing perfectly consistent behaviour in all five cases. On the other hand, the Dutch display a sharp decrease in the same direction, with 86% showing zero absolute trials, and no subject producing more than two absolute trials.

However, this procedure displays the data at the expense of a gap between theory and evidence. Individual trials or numbers of trials have no significance in themselves. We need to interpret them with regard to the initial hypotheses, and this representation fails to capture the possibility of a transition between two possible coding systems. In addition, this trial-wise grouping implies another problem: it is unequivocal only as long as the response categories are dichotomous. If a trial is judged either relative or absolute but nothing else, then, certainly, the number of relative trials equals the total minus the absolutes. But what if there are instances of a third category, such as 'error' or 'untypable'?

A large set of field experiments shows that errors of this type do occur. In the animals recall task, order as well as direction of the alignment was coded: six orders of the three model animals are possible, four of which are neither absolute nor relative. Belhare (Tibeto-Burman) subjects made such ordering errors in about one third of trials, Tzeltal (Mayan) subjects (see Brown and Levinson 1993b: 16–17) and Tamils in one quarter, and Longgu (Austronesian) in 16%. At the same time, Japanese subjects, Mparntwe Arrernte (Pama-Nyungan) and English-speaking Australians made almost no errors. Thus there is a substantial variation in the frequency of erroneous choices. A good measure of spatial orientation has to account for this fact. That measure will therefore have to incorporate absolute, relative and also erroneous or untypable trials as a third value. How can these three values be weighted against each other?

5.2.2.1 Properties of the gradient measure

The plot in Figure 5.1 already implies one reasonable presupposition, namely that the properties '(fully) absolute' and '(fully) relative' can be treated as poles of a single dimension. If a person shows, for example, five times absolute coding in a five-trial-test, she or he will, of course, produce neither relative nor erroneous results. If she ends up four times with absolute, the remaining trial might be relative *or* an error; three times absolute leaves room for two trials with three possible pairings (relative-relative, relative-error or error-error), and so forth.

In analysing the data, we have made use of a measure that I will call the **'relative-to-absolute gradient'**, or in short the RA gradient. It is a measure composed of three possible outcomes ('absolute', 'relative' and 'untypable') of each trial. It aims at giving an estimate of the absolute tendency of an individual or a sample, depending on the number of observations or the number of subjects. The RA gradient will be calculated as follows: each absolute trial receives value 'I', each 'relative' o, while 'untypable' responses score 0.5, thus symbolizing that they are neutral with regard to the two poles or just in-between. Then, these values will be added up and divided by the total number of trials. The result will lie between o and I; multiplied by 100, it gives us a measure we can call the *estimated absolute tendency*, as a percentage.

An example helps to clarify the procedure: assume that a person performs a six-trial-test in the following way, producing three clear relative solutions, one absolute and two untypable:

Outcome of trials:	rel	abs	rel	unt	unt	rel
Coding of trials:	o	I	o	0.5	0.5	o
RA gradient:	$(3*0 + 2*0.5 + 1*1)/6 = 2/6 = \mathbf{0.33}$					
Estimated absolute tendency:	*33% absolute tendency*					

Since the RA gradient was set up such that a low value indicates a subject is generally a relative coder and a high value (towards I) indicates the subject is basically an absolute coder, this subject correctly stands as an inconsistent coder towards the relative end.

Confidence intervals and reliability of such estimates will be intimately tied to the amount and representativeness of the collected data. In fieldwork amongst small unschooled populations, it is often very difficult to get more than a few results from each individual, so we advocate sampling over subjects, which leads to *estimates for certain populations*. In the rest of this chapter I will make use of RA gradient distributions of this sort. Figure 5.2 repeats the same Tzeltal vs. Dutch data for the animals task, now expressed by the RA gradient.

It is worth considering a little further the proper interpretation of this gradient measure. On one interpretation, it is simply an analytical convenience, a way of finding a common measure across tasks, populations and coding strategies. But a more psychological interpretation may also be in order. One possible view would be that it represents a psychological possibility space. The tasks in question require an 'orientation-bound' frame of reference (see Table 2.4 and Figure 2.6 in Chapter 2) – they cannot be solved by using an intrinsic frame of reference, which only codes the internal relations of the objects in the array to one another, and which therefore yields no single coherent solution. Rather, what is required is some coordinate system that is external to the array itself. There are, as far I know, only two such (families of) coordinate systems used by humans, namely a relative and an absolute type. Thus the

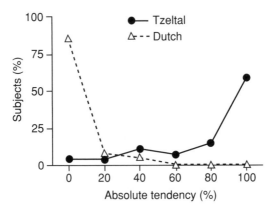

Figure 5.2. Tzeltal and Dutch RA gradients

RA gradient arguably captures the possibilities available to individual subjects – one type of orientation-bound solution or the other, or a response that for one reason or another fails to satisfy the demand for a determinate solution. Another even stronger psychological interpretation would be in line with the second of the hypotheses mentioned at the beginning of this chapter, namely that both absolute and relative frames of reference are incipiently available to all subjects. Then we could view all types of response as a function of *competing mechanisms* of spatial coding. On this view, a 'competition' between possible frames of reference occurs in each trial and for each informant separately, and would be biased by specific contextual features (cf. Li and Gleitman 2002) – this view is experimentally investigated in section 5.6 below.

5.3 OVERALL TEST OF THE CODING DIFFERENCE HYPOTHESIS

The central hypothesis, recollect, was that (a) populations would differ in the coordinate systems employed in non-linguistic tasks, (b) the choice of coordinate system would correlate (be consistent) with the coordinate systems available and employed in corresponding linguistic tasks. The first job is to assign speech communities to three working categories on the basis of *linguistic* evidence – elicitation and extensive linguistic tasks of the kind already illustrated in Chapter 4 (see Levinson and Wilkins in preparation for further detail):

1. linguistically absolute (i.e. linguistic conventions specify use of some kind of cardinal direction system), with no systematic use of a relative system available;
2. linguistically relative (where the linguistic conventions specify a 'left', 'right', 'front', 'back' system), with no use of an absolute system;
3. linguistically mixed (i.e. the language uses full sets of expressions for both absolute and relative, and most likely all three, frames of reference).

There are two potentially rather different such classifications of communities in terms of linguistic frames of reference. In one kind of classification one looks at the *linguistic resources* available in a particular language – which frames of reference are expressible in the language (in ordinary parlance, not technical or specialist registers). In the other kind, one looks at the *actual use* of linguistic expressions in specified situations, and compares languages for usage in those situations. In certain cases, like Tzeltal and Guugu Yimithirr, these two methods of classification collapse: the linguistic resources are very constrained – to describe the location of an object displaced in space from another ground object, the linguistic resources provide only one frame of reference available for use (recollect from Chapter 4 that Guugu Yimithirr effectively offers only one frame of reference, and Tzeltal only uses the intrinsic/topological system for objects close in space). In other cases, though, classifying communities by linguistic resources as opposed to language use will give a different typing – for example in English or Dutch, both relative and intrinsic frames of reference are available and colloquially used, but the relative frame is clearly predominant for most kinds of spatial description. In the case where more than one frame of reference is available, one may find one frame of reference preferred for one situation, and another for another situation. In that case, in testing a language-to-cognition correlation, one may want to match situations as closely as possible in parallel linguistic and non-linguistic tasks. Thus we need to distinguish between (a) a linguistic typing based on linguistic resources, which is thus a *cross-situation* typing on the basis of a general preference for one frame of reference over another across situations, and (b) a typing that is keyed to a specific kind of spatial array or situation. In this chapter, we shall mostly be concerned with the former kind of classification, but first let us consider a case study using the latter more constrained kind of classification.

5.3.1 Situation-specific typing: performance across matched linguistic and non-linguistic tasks

We have used the *situation-specific* strategy for investigating the language-to-cognition correlation in the paper published as Pederson *et al.* 1998. There we compared the results on a specific linguistic task involving asymmetries on the egocentric transverse axis (the men and tree verbal communication task, described in Chapter 4 above) with results from a non-verbal task requiring coding of the same kinds of asymmetries (the animals task, also described in Chapter 4). The main burden of that paper is the procedures to be used for careful linguistic typing, and I will not repeat the details here. Using those procedures, out of a sample of thirteen mostly unrelated languages, we found five that used either an absolute frame of reference, or a relative one, but not both. The linguistic typing on this verbal task yielded three absolute-coding communities (Arrernte, Tzeltal and Longgu) and two relative-coding cultures (Dutch and Japanese).[4] We then went on to compare the coding on the specific linguistic task and the exactly corresponding non-verbal task. The 'animals' task results are shown in the following tables, Table 5.2 summarizing the cognitive results for the linguistically absolute communities, and Table 5.3 summarizing the cognitive results for the linguistically relative communities.

In the tables, the means of the RA gradient for each sample – a score of 5 (on this task with 5 trials) would reflect completely consistent, error-free absolute behaviour, a score of 0.0 completely consistent relative coding. We have then assigned each subject to one of three categories according to his/her RA in percentage terms: subjects with scores 0–30% are typed

Table 5.2. *Linguistic prediction: absolute linguistic coding samples*

Sample	Arrernte	Tzeltal	Longgu	Total sample size
Sample size	11	27	13	**51**
RA mean	**3.8**	**4.0**	**4.2**	
RA categories: **R** U **A*** (%)	**18** 0 **82**	7 19 **74**	**15** 8 **77**	

*Relative, Untypable, Absolute categories on the relative-absolute gradient

Table 5.3. *Linguistic prediction: relative linguistic coding samples*

Sample	Dutch	Japanese	Total sample size
Sample size	37	16	**53**
RA mean	**0.2**	**0.9**	
RA categories: **R** U **A** (%)	**95** 5 **0**	**82** 6 **12**	

as relative non-verbal coders, those with 70–100% scores are typed as absolute coders, and 30–70% as 'Untypable' (inconsistent coders).

Our prediction of course was that groups (absolute and relative) as categorized on linguistic testing would accurately predict behaviour on non-linguistic testing, and specifically that linguistically absolute coders would perform absolutely on the non-linguistic task, and linguistically relative coders would perform relatively on the cognitive task. The Mann-Whitney U-test confirms that the predicted difference is highly significant (U-Test 2496.5, p = 0.000).[5]

5.3.2 The cross-situation prediction: from linguistic coding tendency to non-verbal coding

Here, I wish to pursue the other strategy, the *cross-situation* testing of possible correlations between preferred frame of reference in linguistic and non-linguistic coding. This is because there are many languages where the linguistic resources may include *both* expressions in relative and absolute frames of reference, but where nevertheless in the linguistic tasks there is a clear overall preference for one or another frame of reference. In short, the *situation-specific* comparison reduces the number of languages in our sample, and we can increase the sample size of the populations to be compared if we can include them.[6]

By *preferred frame of reference* I do not necessarily mean that there is a mere statistical preference – in some cases, at least, there are clearly linguistic conventions involved. All our linguistic tasks were communication tasks which required speakers to effectively describe spatial arrays in 'table top' space to screened off interlocutors, and so for most languages they constitute a coherent type of situation, in which specific frames of reference are expected in language use. Nevertheless, this kind of global typing is a somewhat more impressionistic procedure than the situation-specific comparison just reviewed. The kinds of procedures employed for determining an overall categorization for linguistic coding are described in Pederson *et al.* 1998.

Table 5.4. *The cross-cultural sample*

Linguistic Type	Language (*Investigator*)	Available FORs	Preferred FORs in linguistic tasks	Tasks done (N subjects)
Absolute Predominant	Arrernte (Australian) (*D. Wilkins*)	A, I	A	1(16), 3(8)
	Hai//om (Khoisan) (*T. Widlok*)	A, I, (R)	A	1(26), 5(18)
	Tzeltal (Mayan) (*Brown and Levinson*)	A, I	A	1(27), 2(24), 3(27), 5(25)
	Longgu (Austronesian) (*D. Hill*)	A, I, (R)	A	1(18), 2(18), 3(17)
Relative Predominant	Dutch (Indo-European) (*Levinson et al.*)	R, I, (A)	R	1(40), 2(40), 3(40), 4(40), 5(40)
	Japanese (*K. Inoue, S. Kita*)	R, I, (A)	R	1(16), 2(8), 4(19), 5(8)
	English (Australian) (*D. Wilkins*)	R, I, (A)	R	1(14)
Intrinsic Predominant	Totonac (Totonacan) (*P. Levy*)	I, (A)	I	1(16), 4(16)
	Mopan (Mayan) (*E. Danziger*)	I, (A)	I	1(33), 4(28)
All three FORs	Belhare (Tibeto-Burman) (*B. Bickel*)	A, I, R	A	1(16), 2(15), 5(16)
	Kgalagadi (Bantu) (*S. Neumann*)	A, I, R	R, A, I	1(16), 2(16), 3(16)
	Kilivila (Austronesian) (*G. Senft*)	A, I, R	A, I, R	1(16), 2(16), 3(16), 4(16), 5(16)
	Yucatec (Mayan) (*C. Stolz*)	A, R, I	I, R	1(16)
	Tamil-Urban (*E. Pederson*)	R, I, A	R	1(22), 2(13), 4(14), 5(14)
	Tamil- Rural (*E. Pederson*)	A, I, R	A	1(25), 2(13), 4(13), 5(28)

The hypothesis to be tested is whether subjects from speech communities who normally and preferably use absolute (allocentric, fixed bearing) coordinates to solve linguistic communication tasks of a certain sort will tend to use absolute coordinates to code spatial arrays for memory and inference in non-linguistic tasks, and vice-versa for subjects where speech communities prefer relative coordinates in the same situations.

5.3.2.1 The populations
Linguistic tasks systematically exploring frames of reference were run in seventeen non-western cultures, all small-scale communities except for Japanese and Tamil. Of these, it proved possible to collect data from uniform cognitive tasks in thirteen of these cultures, as indicated in Table 5.4 (since then other scholars have been able to replicate the findings too; see, e.g., Wassmann and Dasen 1998). All our experiments were also run on a Dutch subject pool, who were not the normal student fodder, but rather an aphasia control-group of all ages, of both sexes and different occupations and educational level – in this way we approximated the mixed nature of the samples from the small communities.[7]

In Table 5.4, there is indicated a coarse typology of the linguistic systems for each culture. In the column 'Available FORs' are tabulated which frames of reference are coded linguistically and thus potentially available for use in our linguistic tasks – we discount here frames of reference only in use by experts, specialists or that would require technological or prosthetic devices (like compasses) for systematic use by the subjects. In the column 'Preferred FORs' are indicated those frames of reference systematically favoured by the majority of subjects in our linguistic tasks. The final column lists which non-verbal tasks were conducted in that speech community, according to the following coding (thus '1(16)', indicates that sixteen participants did task 1):

Name of task	*Psychological property explored*
Task 1: Animals in a row	Recall memory
Task 2: Red and blue chips	Recognition memory
Task 3: Eric's maze	Motion-to-path transformation, recognition
Task 4: Steve's maze	Path completion and recognition
Task 5: Transitivity	Memory and transitive inference

5.3.2.2 Procedure
To accumulate the larger samples, we here aggregate the *preferred* absolute samples with those populations whose languages effectively only offer absolute (plus or minus intrinsic) frames of reference. Thus, from the last

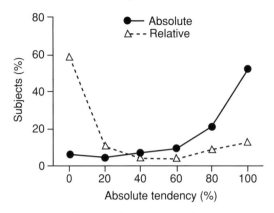

Figure 5.3. RA gradients for the animals task by linguistic category

category in the table, we extract the Belhare and Tamil-Rural samples and add them to the absolute linguistic coders in the table; and similarly we add the Tamil-Urban sample to the relative linguistic coders.

Overall, in the linguistically absolute populations we have then Mparntwe Arrernte (a Pama-Nyungan language of central Australia), Longgu (an Austronesian language of the Solomons), Belhare (a Tibeto-Burman language of Nepal), one Tamil subsample (subjects from rural settings in Tamilnadu, South India, where absolute linguistic conventions prevail), Hai//om (a Khoisan language of Namibia)[8] and Tzeltal (a Mayan language of Mexico). Subjects from these six groups added up to N = 85. They were contrasted with subjects from populations whose linguistic conventions dictate relative coordinates for small-scale arrays, like speakers of Dutch, Japanese, English-speaking Australians and another Tamil subsample (urban subjects who use relative coordinates in their language), with a total of just under a hundred subjects (N = 99). All of these participants performed the animals recall task, and a part of them – excluding Arrernte and Longgu – did the transitivity task too (as described in Chapter 4).

Figures 5.3 and 5.4 show the results for these two non-linguistic tasks in graph form using the RA gradient. Note that the two curves identify *linguistically* determined categories, with the shape of each curve reflecting non-linguistic performance.

5.3.2.3 Results
To test the hypothesis that linguistic and non-linguistic coding are correlated, we now test that, given the linguistic breakdown into two groups,

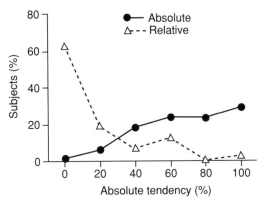

Figure 5.4. RA gradients for the transitivity task by linguistic category

there is a significant difference in non-linguistic coding between the two groups. The predicted difference between absolute and relative speakers was highly significant in the animals task (Mann-Whitney U-test = 1453, p < .001) as well as in the transitivity task (U-test = 506, p < .001). These results confirm that language is a good predictor of non-linguistic performance on such non-verbal tasks.

On all the other tasks described above we also have results consistent with the language-to-cognition correlation. But in these other tasks the prediction groups are smaller, because not all tasks could be run in all communities. Consider, for example, the Eric's maze task described in Chapter 4, involving the conversion of an observed motion path into a route through a map under rotation. This cognitive task is expected to match closely to the mental coding of direction of motion, and thus, under the hypothesis of a language/cognition correlation, also to the description of motion. Here we have data just from the Dutch relative control group and three absolute-speaking groups, the Arrernte, Longgu and Tzeltal. The findings are presented graphically in Figure 5.5.

Again, the prediction from the linguistic coding to the non-verbal coding is confirmed – there is a highly reliable difference in non-verbal behaviour between the two groups formed on linguistic criteria (Mann-Whitney U-test 1851.00, p = 0.000). Thus so far, for every task for which we have adequate data, the patterning is in the direction predicted by the hypothesis that the frames of reference in language correlate closely with those used in non-verbal memory and reasoning.

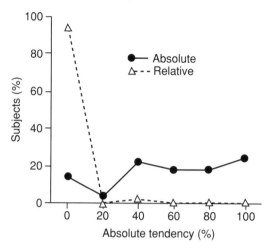

Figure 5.5. RA gradients for Eric's maze task (the absolute category is here Arrernte, Longgu and Tzeltal with 50 subjects, vs. the relative category Dutch with 39 subjects)

5.3.3 Pairwise comparisons between samples

Although the global hypothesis of coding differences is confirmed, there is room for some doubt that this treatment of the data is adequate. Samples from different locations with very different cultural backgrounds have been grouped together for the purpose of global comparison. In spite of the large difference *between* the two groups there might be differences *within* them too, not revealed by the averaging procedure. The magnitude of such differences might indicate different qualities and therefore justify separate treatment.

Evidence for or against this line of thought can be evoked by pairwise comparisons between groups. Two expectations follow, if the global comparison was correct. First, there should be substantial differences between any two membering groups of different 'prediction groups', absolute or relative (call this the **difference prediction**). Second, differences between members of the *same* prediction group should be non-significant (call this the **similarity prediction**).

5.3.3.1 Procedure

Only samples with a minimum of ten subjects have been included. In the 'difference prediction' cases, the Type I (or α) error probability[9] was corrected in the case of multiple comparisons with the same sample (Marascuilo and Serlin 1988: 445). In the 'similarity prediction' cases,

Table 5.5. *The two 'prediction groups'*

| Linguistically Relative | English, Dutch, Japanese, Tamil-Urban | *Prediction*: Non-verbal coding will be relative | N = 99 |
| Linguistically Absolute | Arrernte, Hai//om, Tzeltal, Longgu, Belhare, Tamil-Rural | *Prediction*: Non-verbal coding will be absolute | N = 85 |

Table 5.6. *Difference and similarity predictions in the animals task: results of some pairwise comparisons*

Samples	Sample sizes	Prediction outcome	Result test statistic
		different:	
Arrernte vs. Dutch	11 vs. 37	confirmed	$U = 365$***
Arrernte vs. Japanese	11 vs. 16	confirmed	$U = 143$**
Tzeltal vs. Dutch	27 vs. 37	confirmed	$U = 971$***
Tzeltal vs. Japanese	27 vs. 16	confirmed	$U = 379$***
Longgu vs. Dutch	13 vs. 37	confirmed	$U = 456$***
Longgu vs. Japanese	13 vs. 16	confirmed	$U = 181$***
		similar:	
Arrernte vs. Longgu	11 vs. 13	confirmed	$U = 58$ n.s.
Arrernte vs. Tzeltal	11 vs. 27	confirmed	$U = 142$ n.s.
Longgu vs. Tzeltal	13 vs. 27	confirmed	$U = 198$ n.s.
Dutch vs. Japanese	37 vs. 16	marginal	$U = 238$ p = .099

Conventions: Asterisks indicate the level of significance, ranging from less than 5% error probability (one asterisk) to less than 0.1% (three asterisks); n.s. means non-significant. The exact error probability is given in one marginal case.

Type I error probability was set to .10 to increase testing power.[10] The results are shown in Tables 5.6 and 5.7.

5.3.3.2 Results
The 'difference' expectation was pairwise confirmed. Any two members of different 'prediction groups' (i.e. communities categorized according to their use of *linguistic* frames of reference) turned out to be significantly different in non-linguistic coding as measured by the RA gradient. The 'similarity' prediction holds too – any two groups of the same linguistic type showed similar non-linguistic performance (the marginal Dutch vs. Japanese case in the animals task notwithstanding).

Table 5.7. *Difference and similarity predictions in the transitive inference task (conventions as in Table 5.6)*

Samples	Sample sizes	Prediction outcome	Result test statistic
		different	
Hai//om vs. Dutch	18 vs. 39	confirmed	$U = 698^{***}$
Tzeltal vs. Dutch	25 vs. 39	confirmed	$U = 964^{***}$
		similar	
Hai//om vs. Tzeltal	18 vs. 25	confirmed	$U = 180$ n.s.

We can therefore conclude that the earlier comparison between the two 'prediction groups' is not vitiated by internal differences or incomparables within each group – there should be no objections to the averaging procedure. Samples from different locations with distinct historical linguistic traditions have been assembled in two large categories, following only the absolute vs. relative hypothesis, but this categorization proves sufficient to predict for homogeneity within the categories (similarity prediction) as well as differences between any two members of the two distinct categories (difference prediction). Thus again, all the evidence points to the reliable correlation between frames of reference available in language and those utilized in non-linguistic cognition.

5.4 LINGUISTIC VS. ECOLOGICAL/CULTURAL DETERMINISM: DIFFERENT SUBSAMPLES FROM THE SAME REGION

A special variant of pairwise comparisons is to contrast groups from the same country or region, but with different linguistic characteristics as regards frames of reference. This may be regarded as a more restricted test of the linguistic determinism hypothesis, as both groups live, say, in the same nation state and share many aspects of ecological environment and cultural tradition, yet differ in the critical linguistic feature in question (communication conventions for either absolute or relative coordinate systems in language). Such cases can help us be more confident that language is the key determinative factor in the different non-verbal coding tendencies.

I have already mentioned some such cases above. For example, three of our groups speak Mayan languages – Tzeltal, Mopan and Yucatec.

Tenejapan Tzeltal is predominantly absolute in language, Mopan predominantly intrinsic, and Yucatec speakers use all three frames of reference but with heavy use of the intrinsic frame of reference. All three cultures have very similar material culture and the same subsistence base, although there are ecological differences between the Chiapas highlands, the Maya Mountains where the Mopan live in Belize, and the less elevated Yucatan. On the non-linguistic tasks which require an orientation-bound frame of reference (absolute or relative) to solve, Tenejapans behave absolutely, the Mopans behave effectively randomly as predicted by their orientation-free linguistic strategy, and Yucatecos predominantly (eleven out of sixteen) choose a random direction or a monodirectional response – that is they chose an arbitrary fixed direction for the animals task (presumably corresponding to a mental intrinsic coding). These patterns are in accord with the hypothesis that language-usage patterns are the key determinant of non-linguistic coding patterns.

5.4.1 Two Tamil-speaking populations

Eric Pederson (1993, 1995, Pederson *et al.* 1998) has pursued another interesting case like this, namely subdivisions of the Tamil-speaking population of Madurai District, Tamilnadu. Two groups of Tamil speakers were established on the basis of linguistic tests: one group, essentially speakers of a rural dialect, who predominantly use absolute coding in language, and another group, largely speakers of urban dialects, who predominantly use relative coding in language. The rural population shares most of the material and cultural background with the urban population, Tamil villages being in many cases semi-urban conglomerations of 5,000 persons or more.

The question was whether, corresponding to this dialect difference, a cognitive bias could also be found. The same non-linguistic tasks (including the animals and transitivity tasks) were thus run across the two samples, with each subject being independently evaluated on a linguistic test.

5.4.1.1 Results
There is mixed evidence from the two sources. In the animals task, differences tended to the predicted poles but were non-significant (U = 135, p = .78). However, the hypothesis that language correlates with non-linguistic coding could indeed be confirmed in the transitive inference task (U = 139, p < .01). This task, as mentioned above, is a better test for

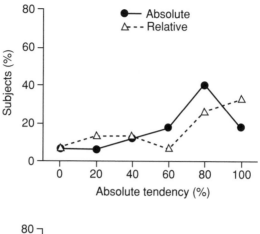

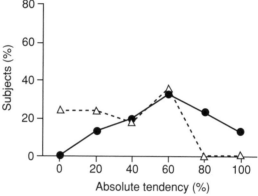

Figure 5.6. Tamil subsamples: animals (top graph) and transitivity (bottom graph)

a subject's preferred mental strategy due to the relatively high memory and reasoning demands it places on the subject (for further details about method and interpretation, see Pederson 1995). The RA gradient reveals that the differences are smaller than in the Tzeltal–Dutch case. There are several informants of both groups in the middle region, who show inconsistent results which might express mixed coding or the interference of competing strategies. However, the two peaks at the 'relative' and 'absolute' poles are sufficient to characterize both groups as being distinct. The similarity of RA distributions in both tasks is also apparent, despite partially different samples.

I conclude that there is distinct evidence from both this Tamil case, and the three Mayan cultures mentioned above, that ecological factors, or factors to do with material culture, or indeed religion or other cultural variables, do not seem to have a decisive role to play in non-verbal coding. No doubt better controlled cases can be found, but on present evidence there is no reason to doubt the significant influence of language on non-verbal coding strategy.

5.4.2 *Central Australia: Arrernte and English speakers*

Another interesting case of groups living in the same or neighbouring environments, with differential amounts of access to each other, has been studied by David Wilkins.[11] He collected data from speakers of Arrernte, a language used around Alice Springs in Central Australia, which utilizes absolute cardinal directions for orientational specifications (as usual, cardinal direction specifications are supplemented with intrinsic and deictic descriptions, see the description in Baayen and Danziger 1994: 78). Wilkins contrasted this 'Central Australian' group with native English-speakers from the same Central Desert region – 'English 1' – and with another group of English-speakers from Sydney, which is more than 2,000 km south-east on the coast – 'English 2'. The 'English 1' group were residents of Alice Springs who worked professionally with Aboriginal people, and were thus in daily cross-cultural contact. In contrast, the Sydney residents would have very few occasions to interact with Arrernte or indeed speakers of other Australian Aboriginal languages. The 'English 1' group have in some subtle respects come to converge in English language and interactional style with the Aboriginal inhabitants of Alice Springs and environs, thus the language/cognition correlation was tested not with them but with the Sydney speakers of standard Australian English without significant interaction with Aboriginal people ('English 2'). Nevertheless, the 'English 1' population was also sampled, on the suspicion that such subjects might show intermediate behaviour. Subjects were tested using the animals task.

5.4.2.1 *Results*
The tests confirmed the linguistic-correlation hypothesis, contrasting the Arrernte absolute speakers with the Sydney English-speakers ('English 2'). Figure 5.7 shows the RA curves for Arrernte-speakers and 'English 2' contrasting in the now familiar manner. But it also shows that the 'English 1' group, the Central Australian resident speakers of English, do indeed lie somewhere in between: the RA curves are ordered exactly according to the expectation that Arrernte have the

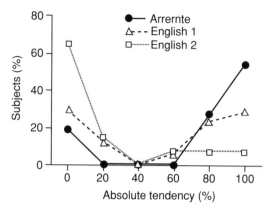

Figure 5.7. Animal task: Arrernte and English subsamples

strongest absolute bias, 'English 2' the strongest relative, and 'English 1' may be intermediate. The Kruskal-Wallis analysis of variance indicates an overall significant difference between the three groups ($H = 9.88$, $p < .01$).

Pairwise tests for the components then showed that this effect is mostly due to the predicted Arrernte vs. 'English 2' difference ($U = 128$, $p < .01$), while the two pairings with 'English 1' were non-significant or only marginal (with Arrernte: $U = 122$, $p = .16$; with 'English 2': $U = 171$, $p = .03$).[12] The Central Australian English-speakers are obviously influenced by both sides. One can assume that like most English native speakers they have a base relative system, but since they are also in daily contact with non-relative Arrernte-speakers, this seems to influence their coding of spatial configurations – Wilkins suggests that this influence may be partly linguistic (through Aboriginal English) but also quite largely through other semiotic systems like gesture (see Chapter 6). Wilkins collected protocols from the 'English 1' subjects after the experiment, and they self-report (a) an awareness that, compared to Aboriginal people, they are 'bad at spatial orientation', (b) an awareness that there are two solutions to the task, (c) some attempts to emulate Aboriginal modes of thinking, by the use of ad hoc landmarks, or even the reversal of their default left/right coding under rotation. Wilkins concludes that culture-contact has resulted in a greater awareness of cultural mismatch in spatial thinking, but no real acquisition of an Aboriginal-like conceptual coding with fixed absolute bearings. Although these results show some malleability of conceptual coding under the influence of verbal interaction with speakers presupposing a different conceptual coding system, they also show that the natural environment alone, even when supplemented by a strong, contrastive cultural environment, is not sufficient to induce a complete switch from the conceptual coding built into a natal language and culture.

5.5 OTHER POSSIBLE DETERMINANTS OF NON-VERBAL CODING STRATEGY: GENDER, LITERACY AND CULTURAL CONSERVATISM

In this section, I pursue further the business of trying to narrow down the possible causal chain lying behind the correlation between linguistic and non-linguistic coding, which has now been firmly established. If the samples were significantly biased by gender, or if all the absolute coders were illiterate or belonged to older, conservative age grades, we might have confounding variables. It is certainly not self-evident that there are any such biases in the samples, but still the possibility needs to be tested. One way to test for confounding variables is to see whether gender, literacy or other factors are indeed good predictors of frames of reference used in non-verbal tasks. All these hypotheses can be explored using the RA gradient. Here we explore the effect of these variables in a slightly larger sample of cultures than hitherto considered.[13]

The basic finding is that none of these factors can be serious confounds – there is a surprisingly small number of differences in the spatial memory and inference tasks due to these variables, even though in visual categorization tasks of a quite different kind subject properties like literacy, schooling, gender and cultural conservatism do have significant effects on performance.[14] In the following sections, we look at a number of these factors in turn.

5.5.1 Gender

Gender has often been thought to be an important factor in differential performance on spatial tasks (see, e.g., Galea and Kimura 1993). Yet in our sample, gender yields a nearly significant ($p = .065$) difference in only one single case, the Dutch sample. Here, in the animals task, women tend to be less consistently 'relative' than men. Transitivity shows a similar, though weaker and thus also non-significant tendency.

Tests for gender differences showed a non-significant result in the following samples: Arrernte and Australian English-speakers (animals task, tests within 'Arrernte', 'English 1' and 'English 2' groups), Belhare (animals, transitivity), Hai//om (animals, transitivity), Japanese (animals), Longgu (animals), Kgalagadi (animals), Kilivila (animals, transitivity), Tamil (animals, transitivity), Tzeltal (animals, transitivity), and Yucatec (animals).

These results are interesting in the light of many studies, which go back at least to Langhorne 1948, that seem to show differential abilities between men and women in spatial orientation. It would be very interesting to have more substantial cross-cultural data on this subject in order to assess whether the gender effect found in Europe and North America is in fact a cultural or culture-independent effect. Our results at least raise an interesting question mark about the cross-cultural validity of the gender bias in spatial memory and reasoning which has been taken for granted for so long in the literature.

5.5.2 Literacy

It has been argued that literacy has many important cognitive effects, and it is clear that writing systems with (mostly) left-to-right or right-to-left writing order, and mirror-image discriminations between letters like **d** and **b** or **p** and **q**, might induce a special sensitivity to left/right discriminations, and thus to egocentric, relative coordinates. Subjects from communities in our sample with no relative linguistic coding and little literacy do indeed display some interesting tendencies to mirror-image conflation (see Levinson and Brown 1994, Danziger and Pederson 1998). One hypothesis then is that literacy might correlate with more relative coding in non-linguistic tasks, especially perhaps in communities in close contact with speakers of relative-coding languages.

Two of our samples, Tamil and Belhare speakers, do indeed show differences correlated with literacy. Both communities include absolute linguistic coders, who verbally interact frequently with relative linguistic coders from other communities. In both cases, the difference is non-significant in the animals task, but significant in the transitivity task (Tamils: $p < .001$, Belhare: $p < .05$). This may be a function of effectively larger samples in the transitivity task,[15] and therefore increased power in the latter case. Literacy affects performance in the expectable way: being literate increases the likelihood of becoming a relative coder (Figures 5.8 and 5.9).

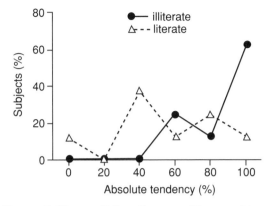

Figure 5.8. Literacy: Belhare literate vs. illiterate subjects

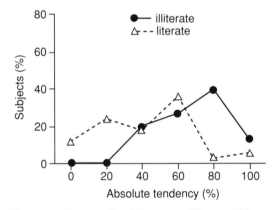

Figure 5.9. Literacy: Tamil literate vs. illiterate subjects

We should keep in mind that, among Tamils, literacy is confounded with subsample categories (urban vs. rural samples). Most relative linguistic coders are literate, while the literate-to-illiterate ratio for absolute linguistic coders is 18 : 13. One way to partially disentangle these two categories, and thereby to avoid a circular interpretation, is a test *within* the Tamil-absolute sample, which is large enough for this contrast. The test confirms the expectation: the literates among absolute-Tamils tend to be more relative than the illiterates ($p < .05$).

However, apart from these two cases, in the rest of the small-scale communities we find no significant correlations with literacy – for example, literacy shows no substantial influence in the Hai//om, Kilivila and

Tzeltal communities (animals and transitivity tasks) and the Kgalagadi and Yucatec samples (animals task).

To summarize, there is evidence for the influence of literacy in two larger samples where literacy is also associated with close interaction with linguistically relative coders from other communities. But for the majority of the samples, there is no systematic effect of literacy. Hence we can conclude that literacy is not a general confound in the correlation between language type and non-verbal type of coding.

5.5.3 *Age, schooling and conservatism: indices of cultural change*

Many of the communities studied in our cross-cultural survey are small ethnic groups under recent but growing pressure of acculturation by larger national communities or urban influences. One might therefore expect that younger subjects, or those with greater education, might have adapted more than older conservative subjects to the predominantly relative coding tendencies in the larger linguistic communities around them. If so, this again could introduce confounds if our samples were biased one way or the other. It is therefore worth testing any correlations between general measures of conservatism and non-verbal coding tendencies.

In fact, these variables show no substantial effect (with one exception mentioned below). However, it has to be conceded that there are difficulties in assessing some of these variables or categorizing them in a valid and reliable way. For example, in many of the communities no exact record of age is kept, while a measure like 'years of schooling' alone is insensitive to the nature and quality of education. In some communities but not others there were decisive measures of cultural conservatism (e.g. subjects retained traditional ethnic dress). All contrasts of this sort were made by a post-hoc median split. For example, in a sample of $N = 18$, the nine people below thirty-five were labelled 'young', the others 'old'. Obviously, there is much scope for heterogeneity within these groups, and there remains a good chance that a positive effect might be found with better data.

A significant difference due to age was however found in Belhare, in the transitivity task ($p < .05$). But here, contrary to the prediction that older people would be more reliably absolute-coders, the older people were in fact more likely to code in a relative manner. A similar, counter-intuitive effect ($p < .05$) shows in the Tamil sample in the animals task, but only for *order* of animals: younger people tend to be more absolute. All further tests provide no evidence for the effect of cultural change.[16]

5.5.4 Summary of the effects of intra-sample variables

Literacy seems to play some role across the samples. For the other variables, like sex and age, the overall finding is negative. But before concluding that spatial cognition is independent of these factors, we should note that there are two possible methodological explanations for this outcome. First, some variables are confounded (for example, literacy with age or with urban/rural residence in the Tamil case; or more often sex with literacy – a high proportion of women are illiterate in the samples). Of course, field research imposes significant constraints, and it is often not possible to carry out carefully controlled experiments. Researchers in the field often have to work in small communities where they are known and trusted – they cannot easily then balance group composition and the interaction of relevant factors. Second, most samples are simply too small for clear results – if N does not exceed 20, as in the majority of actual comparisons, subgroups of eight to ten people would have to be extremely homogeneous to show substantial differences. Thus caution is in order.

Still, on the evidence we have in hand, there is no reason to think that any of these factors – gender, literacy, cultural conservatism – are serious confounds in the language–cognition correlation. However, there is another possible confound that has recently been suggested in a critique of this work by Li and Gleitman (1999, 2002), to which we now turn.

5.6 ANOTHER POSSIBLE CONFOUND? THE 'BIG OUTDOORS' AND THE RELEVANCE OF LANDMARKS

In recent papers, Li and Gleitman (1999, 2002) seek to undermine the relevance of the rotation paradigm – and thus all the experiments described above – for examining general questions about the language–cognition correlation. Instead, they suggest that mental coding in both absolute and relative terms is native to all humans (indeed, rats too).[17] They hold that differential use of the frames of reference is entirely a matter of non-linguistic context, and can accordingly be induced one way or the other simply by changing the context. In particular, they suggest that all humans will tend to use absolute coding and landmarks in an outdoors setting, and relative coding in an indoors one, regardless of the native language of the subjects. These views echo a strong current of contemporary thought in the cognitive sciences that minimizes the role of culture in cognition and denies the existence of significant differences in the conceptual structure of languages. It is therefore worth considering their views, and showing where and why they are wrong (but see Levinson *et al.* 2002 for a detailed critique).

Could all the results above be an artefact of the conditions under which the experiments were run? Li and Gleitman (1999, 2002) were under the erroneous impression that all our absolute populations were tested outdoors, and all the relative ones indoors in closed, windowless lab spaces. In fact, this was not so. As explained in Chapter 4, the absolute Guugu Yimithirr speakers were tested inside rooms that should (on Li and Gleitman's views) have enhanced the use of relative coordinates, and so were the Arrernte speakers who contribute to the large cross-cultural sample above. And our original Dutch control group were tested in rooms with large windows. Moreover, in our sample we have 'mixed languages' (with all three frames of reference) where no clear prediction was made concerning absolute vs. relative cognitive coding – in these cases in some tasks we found strong relative non-verbal coding despite testing in outside conditions (e.g. with Kilivila speakers in Melanesia, or with the Kgalagadi, a Bantu people).[18]

In any case, Li and Gleitman (1999) believed otherwise and had the hypothesis that they could induce English-speaking subjects to vary their performance, from relative to absolute coding, along the lines that the more outside landmarks were visible, the more they would be used by subjects for non-verbal coding. They therefore ran American undergraduate participants on a variant of our animals task under a number of conditions:

1. Indoors with windows covered: 'Blinds down condition'
2. Indoors with windows uncovered: 'Blinds up condition'
3. Outdoors: 'Outdoors condition'
4. Indoors with local cues to the right ('relative ducks' condition) vs. local cues to the north ('absolute ducks condition')

They report that under condition 1 vs. 2 they get some difference in the predicted direction (greater absolute performance under condition 2), although not a statistically reliable one. But in the outdoors condition they report that they can get American subjects to behave just like Tenejapans, that is, the majority will code in what appears to be absolute coordinates (on the larger sample in Li and Gleitman 2002, the effect is diminished, outdoors testing inducing mixed results).

We have been unable to replicate the difference between condition 1 and 2 – all our control experiments with Dutch people show resolutely relative coding under a 'Blinds up' condition. We have also tried hard but unsuccessfully to replicate the Li and Gleitman 'Outdoors' condition. We ran our version of the animals task outside with Dutch university students in the middle of campus in spring, with major landmarks on all sides clearly indicating the north/south/east/west grid of the campus layout. We also ran the Eric's maze task. There was no statistical difference between the indoors and outdoors conditions, all subjects coding consistently in relative coordinates (see Levinson *et al.* 2002).

I believe that Li and Gleitman obtained their result only by simplifying our experiment in a number of ways, and making clear in their instructions that the experimenters were interested in directional constancy under rotation – and indeed they report subjects querying their intentions. Our original animals task was designed to emphasize memory for order and distract attention away from direction, but Li and Gleitman simplified it by not requiring memory for the kinds of animals involved. We do not think they could obtain the same result in a battery of tasks, where there is more memory load, such as in our transitivity experiment.[19] Then, we predict, subjects will resort to their unreflective, natural mode of coding.

In addition, Li and Gleitman conflate the use of landmarks with an absolute system, but as I have tried to make clear in Chapter 2, landmarks can play a role in all three frames of reference – I can think I parked my car to the left of the visible church (relative), at its front entrance (intrinsic), or to the north of it (absolute), so the use of visible landmarks cannot itself constitute an absolute frame of reference. The kind of coordinate system is independent of the origin or ground. Or, to return to the relevant kind of examples, if I remember the toy animals as lined up facing towards a ball, this is an intrinsic coding involving the front of the animals facing towards a local cue or 'landmark'. It is intrinsic because it is orientation-free: if we rotate the whole array the coding remains unchanged, quite unlike a real absolute coding. Similarly, if subjects use a window as a cue, but without placing the whole room and building in a fixed orientational frame – as may have happened in Li and Gleitman's condition 2 – we are dealing with a large intrinsic array that includes the participant. Our 180-degree rotational paradigm distinguishes clearly between *egocentric* and *allocentric* frames of reference, but both absolute and intrinsic frames are allocentric as explained in Chapter 2. If one suspects conflation, it is relatively easy to add an extra manipulation that will distinguish between intrinsic and absolute, for example a 90-degree rotation as exploited below.

Li and Gleitman's two conditions in their experiment 4 above are thus actually not relevant to the point they were trying to establish. They placed two large 'duck ponds' – symmetrical, colourful toys – on the ends of the two testing tables (separated and arranged with their long axes north/south). Under their 'relative' condition, the two duck ponds were placed at (say) the north end of one table and the south end of the other, so that under rotation they would both be 'to the right'. Under their 'absolute' condition, the two duck ponds remained at the north end of each table. When they ran the animals task with English-speaking subjects in the lab they found that if the stimulus had the animals facing the duck pond to the right, then subjects would line up the animals facing the duck pond, regardless of whether the duck pond on the response table preserved orientation to the participant's right. This they believed showed that their subjects were using an absolute frame of reference.

Unfortunately, this only shows a fundamental misunderstanding of the nature of the frames of reference. Since there were two identical duck ponds on each table, these were not landmarks so much as parts of the original stimulus to be reproduced on the recall table. So naturally, subjects did their best to preserve the stimulus array – and they could do so happily in an intrinsic frame of reference. Since colloquial English offers both a relative and intrinsic frame of reference, Li and Gleitman's experiment does nothing to undermine the language–cognition correlation. What they have shown is that English-speakers can under certain circumstances be induced to use an intrinsic frame of reference instead of their dominant relative frame of reference.

Still, we wanted to show that our interpretation of their results was the correct one. So we replicated their experiment exactly – and unlike in the 'outside' condition, we got the same results that they did (details in Levinson *et al.* 2000, 2002). Then we introduced two variants: one required the higher memory load as in our original animals experiment, and the other involved a 90-degree rotation instead of a 180-degree rotation. These experiments are variants of our tasks that are worth describing as ways of exploring how participants choose between competing frames of reference.

5.6.1 The 180-degree 'absolute duck' conditions

5.6.1.1 Method

Twenty Dutch student subjects were recruited, ten for each of two conditions as follows. They were tested in a windowless room on tables minimally apart, just as in Li and Gleitman's 'absolute' condition, i.e. with two large 'duck pond' toys, one at the northern end (subject's left) of the stimulus table, and one at the northern end (subject's right) of the recall table, as in Figure 5.10.

There were two conditions:

a. *Exact replication of 'absolute' condition, using three animals*
   Li and Gleitman had simplified our original animals design – they gave the subject back just the three animals used in the stimulus, so subjects did not have to remember which animals they had seen (just order and direction). This was replicated.
b. *Replication of 'absolute' condition, using four animals*
   In this slight variant, we reverted to our original design, with the subject having to chose the three out of four possible animals in the stimulus, thus adding slightly to the memory burden (kind, order and direction).

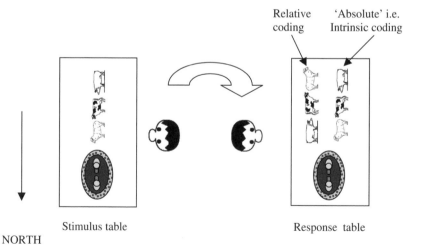

Figure 5.10. Set up for the 'absolute duck' condition

Absolute duck: 3 animals vs. 4 animals (direction)

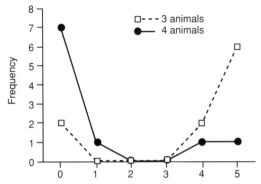

Figure 5.11. 'Absolute duck' experiment under different memory-load conditions

5.6.1.2 Result

In condition a we obtained just the results that Li and Gleitman did, namely the direction of recall was cued by the 'duck pond'. But in condition b, with the greater memory load as in our original animals task, subjects ignored the 'duck pond' cues, and reproduced the animals in a relative way, i.e. preserving left/right orientation. The results are contrasted in Figure 5.11, and the contrast is clearly significant (Mann-Whitney U-test $U = 19$, $p < .01$).

5.6.1.3 Discussion

This experiment establishes that this Li and Gleitman result is replicable (unlike their 'outdoors' condition) – as explained, I think this is an intrinsic result so I am not in the least surprised. But the second condition is interesting. It shows that, despite the bright cues, what we suppose to be an intrinsic result is fragile: as soon as the memory load is upgraded slightly, subjects revert to their habitual, predominantly relative way of coding spatial scenes. This result also throws light on Li and Gleitman's experiment 2: as I suggested above, I suspect that if they were to upgrade the memory load, subjects would not be able to engage in the double-guessing behaviour that I suspect underlies their 'absolute' result, and will react in a relative way.

We turn now to our second variant of the Li and Gleitman 'duck pond' experiment, involving 90-degree rotation. This 90-degree rotation we reasoned should disambiguate between a real absolute response and an intrinsic one. Let me clarify the reasoning. An intrinsically coded array is orientation-free in the sense that only its internal arrangement has to be preserved – in this case animals facing towards or away from the 'duck pond'. Both an intrinsic and absolute solution can look the same under 180-degree rotation – that is, the subject may be thinking 'Animals facing duck-pond' (intrinsic) or equally 'Animals facing north' (absolute). The intrinsic and absolute solutions can become separated under any rotation, but since the intrinsic solution by definition can be in any direction, it will tend to be oriented by local ecological factors, like the main axis of the table, and viewpoint-preserving factors, like egocentrically transverse vs. sagittal arrangement. Thus under 180-degree rotation with a duck pond at one end of the table and the main axis of the table in the egocentric transverse, they will tend to align. But if we now put the recall table at 90 degrees to the stimulus table, the absolute solution will require a sagittal alignment away from the subject in response to a transverse stimulus, while the intrinsic solution is likely to be influenced by ad hoc factors, like the main axis of the table or preservation of the transverse viewpoint. Thus the two frames of reference should now separate. My hypothesis, of course, is that what Li and Gleitman are calling an absolute response is in fact coded intrinsically by subjects like theirs as well as ours. The experiment was conducted as follows.

5.6.1.4 Method
Ten Dutch student subjects were recruited. They performed the 'duck pond' experiment just as in the Li and Gleitman 'absolute condition', but with the tables pre-arranged as shown in Figure 5.12 so that the subject was rotated through 90 rather than 180 degrees. All other procedures were the same as the Li and Gleitman 180-degree 'absolute' condition. Responses in all three frames of reference can now be distinguished as shown in the figure.

5.6.1.5 Results
The results are depicted in Figure 5.13, which charts the 90-degree condition against the 180-degree condition from the prior experiment (both with the lesser memory load, i.e. the correct three animals given to the subject after viewing the stimulus). Along the x-axis we now have a number of *intrinsic* trials, that is the trials that preserve a direction headed to or away from the 'duck pond' cue. It is clear that in the 90-degree condition the great majority of trials do **not** align sagittally (allowing an absolute interpretation), but are oriented intrinsically, and that there

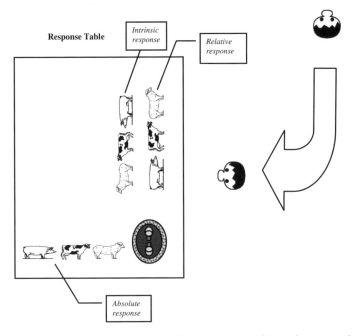

Figure 5.12. The layout of the experiment with 90-degree rotation

is no significant difference between the two conditions (Mann-Whitney U-test $U = 46$, $p = .74$). This strongly suggests that behaviour under both conditions comes from the same source: an intrinsic coding.

Taken together, these experiments – namely our failure to replicate the Li and Gleitman 'outdoors' effect and the demonstration that their 'duck pond' effect is an intrinsic effect – show that Li and Gleitman have not produced any persuasive evidence for genuine absolute coding

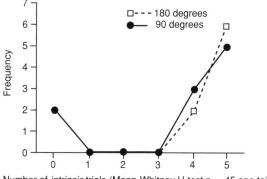

Number of *intrinsic* trials (Mann-Whitney U-test p = .45 one tailed)

Figure 5.13. 'Absolute duck' experiment with 180- vs. 90-degree rotation

of spatial arrays in memory amongst subjects whose language has primary relative and secondary intrinsic frames of reference. Certainly, I believe that our Dutch student subjects are impervious to 'blinds up' vs. 'blinds down', or 'inside' vs. 'outside' conditions. They remain stolidly relative in coding. However, they can be induced to switch into an intrinsic mode of coding. They do so under specific conditions, for example when there are fixed cues that can be seen as part of the array. Li and Gleitman's 'absolute duck pond' condition clearly meets this requirement, and the 'blinds up' condition can be interpreted as an intrinsic result too.

Both English and Dutch are languages that offer two frames of reference in common parlance: namely both intrinsic and relative. Of these two, the relative is predominant. For example, in an abstract description task – neutral over real scale or real objects – Levelt (1996: 99) found that less than 25% of Dutch subjects were verbally consistent intrinsic coders. Still, both frames of reference are perfectly colloquial. Thus on the hypothesis of a language–cognition correlation, we would predict both frames of reference to be used in non-verbal coding, with the relative predominant. As we have seen, for our Dutch subjects it takes low memory load and large local cues to induce a switch from relative to intrinsic frames of reference. The theory that context alone determines frame of reference choice does not fly – Dutch speakers do not seem to have the absolute frame of reference available, at least for these kinds of tasks.

We have dwelt here at length on the possibility that coding for memory is easily switched from one frame of reference to another, and that this switch is conditioned by environmental factors. All the experimental evidence seems to show that such context conditions cannot readily induce a frame of reference that is not frequently used in the language of the subjects for spatial arrays of a similar kind. Where the switch is labile – as between a relative and intrinsic frame of reference for Dutch speakers – it corresponds to degrees of freedom in the relevant language. Even here it is clear that there is a preference for one or the other frame of reference, the preference reasserting itself under cognitive load. Both the original evidence from the cross-cultural sample – which was in fact collected under multiple and varying conditions (e.g. indoors and outdoors, in the same culture) – and the further experimental evidence described in this section argue against the suggestion that environmental factors are determinative of mental coding strategy.

5.7 A POSITIVE TEST OF LINGUISTIC DETERMINISM: THE CASE OF THE TZELTAL DEFECTIVE AXES

If we are trying to establish that language is the most important determining factor behind the choice of non-verbal coding strategy, we should seek some positive stigmata that might carry over from the language into the non-linguistic representations of spatial arrays that are used in memory and reasoning. Detailed analysis of the Tzeltal data has in fact turned up one such possible case (Brown and Levinson 1993b). As described in Chapter 4, in this community spatial orientation is described using a cardinal direction system based on an idealized inclined plane: 'downhill' equates with (just west of) north, 'uphill' with (just east of) south, and 'across' with either east or west. This conflation, or lack of distinction, of easterly and westerly directions (which can of course be further distinguished by reference to landmarks) is a peculiarity of the linguistic coding system. If the Tenejapan linguistic coding system and the corresponding coding system for non-linguistic tasks are in any way closely isomorphic, then we might expect errors to accrue on the undifferentiated east–west axis in non-linguistic coding tasks. Note that in principle the two systems – linguistic and non-linguistic – could both be absolute without being isomorphic: the linguistic system is coarsely digital, as well as conflating east and west; while a non-linguistic system could be more precisely analogue, recording actual fixed directions without categorization.

However, errors were in fact found to accumulate on the east–west axis task (or alternatively, absolute performance was strongest on the north–south axis) in the transitivity task, and in other tasks (like the chips task described above in Chapter 4) in which trials opposed both north–south and east–west axes. However, there was a rival possible explanation. The east–west axis in the experimental set-up happened to coincide with the egocentric front–back axis (i.e. the subject faced east and was then rotated to face west), and since the front–back axis is known to be the strong egocentric axis (many relative-coders confusing left and right to some extent), it could be that the strong egocentric axis was overriding the weak (east–west) absolute axis. Such an analysis would be compatible with the hypothesis, mentioned in the introduction to this chapter and in section 5.2.2, that all frames of reference are innate, and compete with one another with differential outcomes according to the context.

We therefore recalled half the subjects, and ran these tasks again, but now on orthogonal absolute bearings, so that subjects faced north and south. Figure 5.14 shows the experimental set-up under the original and the second condition.

With these two sets of results in hand, we are now able to distinguish between the possible effects of a weak vs. strong absolute axis and an interacting weak vs. strong relative axis, as indicated in Table 5.8. The table shows that in the first run of the experiments the egocentric strong axis (front–back) coincided with the absolute weak axis (east–west), while in the second run the egocentric strong axis coincided with the absolute strong axis (north–south).

Our hypothesis was that stronger absolute performance would be found on the north–south absolute axis (which is more explicitly coded in the corresponding linguistic coding) – and thus in Cells 1 and 3 in Table 5.8, regardless of the subjects' egocentric orientation. If instead, on the 'competition' model between frames of reference, both absolute and relative frames are always in play, each coming to the fore in certain circumstances, then we might expect to see the effect of the strong egocentric axis especially in Cell 2 where the absolute system is weak.

The results in fact confirm our hypothesis that the main factor determining variable Tenejapan performance is the strong vs. weak absolute axes. We found that in the transitivity task (but not in other tasks) heightened absolute performance occurred just on the strong absolute axis, regardless of egocentric orientation. The arcsine transformations of RA gradient scores were taken as the input of a 2*2 Analysis of Variance (ANOVA) with repeated measurements. The two factors were 'Cardinal axis' (north–south vs. east–west) and 'Egocentric axis' (sagittal or away vs.

FIRST RUN

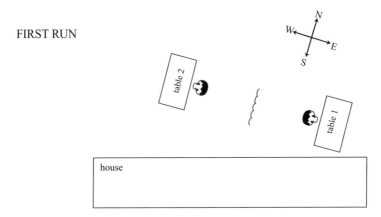

SECOND RUN

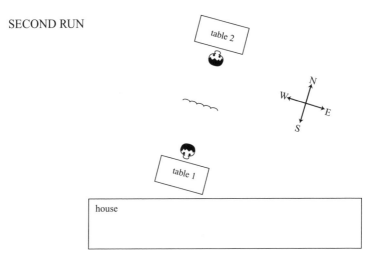

Figure 5.14. Physical layout for first and second runs of experiments in Tenejapa

transverse or across). The analysis revealed a highly significant Cardinal factor ($F = 18.8$, d.f. $= 1$, $p = .001$). The prediction on the 'competition' model that Cell 2 would reveal significantly more relative responses was not confirmed ($p = .74$ Analysis of Variance; $p = .232$ Friedman analysis of variance). Interestingly, however, there was a significant effect of

Table 5.8. *Pitting the strong and weak egocentric axes against the strong and weak absolute axes*

ABSOLUTE SYSTEM

		Strong axis (N–S)	Weak axis (E–W)
RELATIVE SYSTEM	Strong axis (Front–Back)	**Cell 1** (Run 2)	**Cell 2** (Run 1)
	Weak axis (Left–Right)	**Cell 3** (Run 1)	**Cell 4** (Run 2)

the strong egocentric axis across both Cells 1 and 2 ($F = 5.7$, d.f. $= 1$, $p < .05$), suggesting that indeed there is some competition between absolute and egocentric axes going on. However, the main point of interest here is that, even in this non-verbal task, there is evidence for some kind of analogue in cognition of the weak coding of east–west directions in language.

We can display this effect of the weak east–west axis graphically – Figure 5.15 shows how performance shifts towards greater absolute consistency on the strong cardinal axis. The vertical axis represents the cumulative percentage of the sample, and the horizontal the RA gradient, so that each point represents two (or at most three) subjects that share a band on this gradient. Inspection will show that there is a rightwards shift between the two curves, corresponding to the increasingly absolute performance from the weak to the strong cardinal axis.

This result is interpreted to show that there is indeed a systematic isomorphism between the linguistic coding system and the non-linguistic representation of spatial arrays. Specifically, the representation utilized in memory for spatial arrays by absolute coders is not a fully analogue, fixed bearing system, but instead carries over some of the categorical features of the linguistic semantics. Just where the linguistic

Diversity in mind

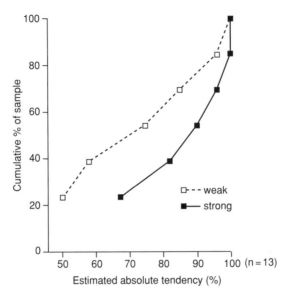

Figure 5.15. Transitive inference task: cardinal axis (Tenejapan sample, reruns)

representation is underspecified, there is a corresponding lack of precision in the non-verbal coding system. This telling little detail is amongst
the most powerful kind of empirical argument we have for a linguistic
source for non-verbal spatial representations.

5.8 CORRELATION AND CAUSATION: CHICKEN OR EGG?

Many disciplines and strands of research have a stake in general solutions
to the study of the language/cognition interface, for example students
of language acquisition and conceptual development, those studying
language functioning under brain damage, those interested in the mechanisms of language production, not to mention those concerned with the
traditional conundrums of 'language and thought'. It seems clear that
cross-linguistic comparison, by varying the linguistic parameters, is one
of the most fruitful avenues of research in this domain.

In this chapter I have been primarily concerned with testing the hypothesis of a language–cognition correlation on a large cross-cultural
sample. There are many methodological difficulties to be overcome in
such an enterprise – small samples, different kinds and numbers of

subjects with different performance characteristics, poor performance due to unfamiliarity with testing in general and the test materials in particular, differential literacy and other factors, and not all tasks being runnable on all populations. I hope that future work can profit from the methods we have collectively developed. In this work, it has proved vital to involve specialists in each language and culture. Much care and attention was expended by the many collaborators in this project to make sure, for example, that verbal instructions were neutral in the crucial respects, and above all to establish the essential linguistic groundwork that is required to assess the significance of the non-verbal tasks.

The results presented in this chapter establish quite clearly that, given facts about a language and its use, one can predict the way in which subjects will code spatial arrays for non-verbal purposes such as recognition, recall or inference. The inverse inference is not in general possible, and that is because there are some languages in which it is perfectly idiomatic to use all three frames of reference in a wide range of situations – that is, to describe spatial arrays that differ on such dimensions as scale, or stasis vs. motion, utilizing all three frames of reference. Here, there is no simple prediction from the language, although observation of the results we have suggests that one can expect mixed non-verbal coding in these cases.

I have focussed on the languages in which there is a clear predominance of either a relative frame of reference or an absolute one. And in these cases, we have found a clear correlation between linguistic and non-verbal coding. But correlation does not establish causation: if A correlates with B, A might cause B, or B might cause A, or there might be an independent factor C that causes both A and B. The material provided in this chapter is already sufficient to narrow down some of these possibilities. Let me summarize.

We have found that language categories (LC) correlate with distinctive cognitive codings (CC). Some, like Li and Gleitman (2002), have tried to cast doubt on this, by suggesting that CC is entirely independent of LC – but as I showed in my review of their work, no demonstrations of this exist, and the evidence all tends in the other direction, namely that CC and LC are interdependent. The hypothesis I am entertaining is that LC is determinative of CC. But consider the inverse alternative, that CC determines LC. This amounts to the claim that cognitive coding style is the dominant factor and is merely reflected in language. We have certainly shown that CC in frames of reference are not universal – some populations use predominantly one frame of reference or the other. How then would all members of a community come to share the locally predominant CC? There are a few distinct possibilities:

1. there is human genetic diversity in this domain;
2. some third factor – say, climate or ecology – induces a distinctive CC in the local population;
3. the local population converges through communication.

Given the present state of our knowledge about sub-specific differences in the genetic control of mental life, we cannot definitively rule out (1), but it is extremely unlikely for a number of reasons: as mentioned, there are closely related populations (like the Mayan ones) where quite distinct cognitive coding styles are employed, and children cross-reared in communities with distinctive coding styles appear to become normal members of the local community.

But what about the second possibility, that some third factor like ecology induces a certain bias in the choice of frames of reference for non-verbal coding? Could it be as simple as this: people who live in the 'big outdoors' tend to be absolute coders, and that this will then be reflected in language? Perhaps such people need to be better navigators, and that is the driving force. But there is no such simple correlation of 'outdoorsy' people and absolute coding (nor even, as we shall see in the next chapter, between 'outdoorsy' people and a good directional sense). In our sample, we have Oceanic island peoples like the Longgu (who are linguistically and cognitively absolute) and the Trobrianders (who use a mixed linguistic system and display mixed coding strategies, with the intrinsic frame of reference dominant). And our Mayans vary from highlanders amongst the clouds (who use an absolute system) to lowlanders who see a lot of the sun like the Yucatecos (who use a mixed system). Peoples who are hunters and gatherers in large territories (like the Australian Aboriginals or the Hai//om) probably do tend to have predominant absolute systems – but unfortunately, and unbelievably, the existing data on relevant details amongst these crucial representatives of our most ancient way of life is very poor, and with the loss of most such ethnic groups who still follow a traditional lifestyle it is probably too late to test this hypothesis. It is worth noting though that true absolute systems do seem to be lacking (or at least unreported) from some hunter-gatherer groups, for example some Alaskan Athabaskan groups. In any case, many absolute populations are small-scale farmers who live in a sedentary fashion in a small territory, like the Tenejapan Tzeltal.

Other possible third factors, like literacy, were examined above, and not found to correlate highly with coding pattern across the sample. It is also possible that other cultural factors play an important role: for example, our built environment builds in many left/right asymmetries – consider our own driving regulations and corresponding asymmetries in car design, queuing and walking habits, door and handle design, and so forth. Many absolute-speaking communities also construct environmental regularities almost invisible to us, such as directions for sleeping or assignment of male vs. female sitting areas by cardinal direction. Important though these may be to a child's learning of the local system, we know of no communities where such cultural regularities are not also reflected in the language. After all, if the rule is 'drive on the right' one expects to be able to verbalize it. Finally, we should note that the Tamil case reported above suggests that, when most other variables are held constant (culture, climate, major language type etc.) but the crucial linguistic factors vary, we then find the expected variation reflected in non-verbal coding.

Thus we are thrown back on explanation (3) – that populations converge on a particular non-verbal coding strategy largely because they have learnt to do so by communicating with each other. This seems by far the most likely explanation. Language is not the only communication system, and other semiotic systems may play an important role – of these gesture is the most frequent and salient, and quite probably plays an important role in, for example, children's learning of an absolute system. We examine this in the next chapter. Still, of all the semiotic systems that humans use, language is the most complex, the most highly practised, and the most crucial in human development. And we have at least some direct positive indications of an isomorphism between the detailed semantics of the language and non-verbal representations (like the errors in non-verbal performance mirroring semantic generality on the linguistic level in the Tenejapan case). It seems inevitable then that we must conclude that it is language above all that drives the convergence between linguistic and non-linguistic coding of our spatial world.

5.9 CONCLUSIONS

I began this chapter with a correlational hypothesis: The frames of reference appropriately used in a language to describe specific situations are likely to correlate with the use of the same frames of reference in the non-linguistic coding of the same scenes for memory and reasoning. Most of this chapter has been dedicated to showing that, on a wide cross-cultural sample, this hypothesis is confirmed. Claims that there are confounding variables do not seem to stand up to scrutiny.

At the end of the chapter, we turned to ask whether these correlational findings can be interpreted as 'linguistic determinism'. There is just a little bit of direct evidence for the causal direction from language to cognition, namely the finding that in Tenejapa just where there is a linguistic weakness in the coding system (a partial conflation of east and west axes), so there is a greater fallibility on the east–west axis in absolute coding in non-linguistic tasks. In the next chapter another tell-tale sign from Tenejapa will be adduced – people's sense of direction seems to be mediated by linguistic categories. Finally, in the preceding section it was argued that linguistic determinism seems the most likely explanation for the correlation – ecological accounts fail, and it would seem to take a communicative system to induce cognitive uniformity throughout a community in such an abstract psychological domain.

Also at the beginning of the chapter we considered three rather different ideas about where frames of reference come from, and how differential usage is to be explained:

1. *Constructivism*: Language actually introduces coordinate systems that might not otherwise be available at all.
2. *Activation*: Language merely favours, exercises and develops one or another system, all of which are antecedently available in cognition.
3. *Partial constructivism*: Language selects one or more *types* of frame of reference from a set incipiently available in the sensory modalities, constructs particular realizations or distinctive *tokens* of those types, and thus partially constructs a system.

The facts that I have adduced so far tend in favour of the last view. Strong constructivism, as in view (1), is certainly not supported for all frames of reference – the intrinsic frame in language is widespread, indeed incipiently universal, and even where there is no systematic relative frame of reference in language, marginal traces turn up in linguistic details, as noted in Chapter 3. Similarly, the details of performance on cognitive tasks suggest that the relative frame of reference is often incipiently available to peoples who are largely absolute coders, as with the Tzeltal or Guugu Yimithirr. This is not surprising, since the relative frame is built into our visual system, as we saw in Chapter 2. The best case for a strong constructivist position is probably to be made around the absolute frame of reference on the horizontal plane – where this is interpreted not just as an allocentric sense of direction, but as possession of a mental map anchored to fixed bearings and cardinal directions. This issue is explored further in the next chapter.

Meanwhile, view (2) suggests that all people should have available all frames of reference, and usage should merely be biased by external factors. We have seen that when this is interpreted, as in the study by Li and Gleitman (2002), as meaning that specific external cues will universally induce one or other of the frames of reference, this view is almost certainly false. And we have seen that relative-language speakers seem to show almost total absence of absolute coding tendencies. This leaves us with view (3), partial constructivism, as the most plausible position. Partial constructivism is compatible with a lot of the details mentioned in this chapter, for example the Tenejapan bias to best absolute performance on the linguistically strongest absolute axis. It is also compatible with the huge range of detail about the diverse ways in which specific frames of reference are semantically constructed in language, as reviewed in Chapter 3. This is an issue that we will return to in the final chapter of this book.

CHAPTER 6

Beyond language: frames of reference in wayfinding and pointing

In the prior chapters, we have seen that language, together with other semiotic systems, seems to have a decisive impact on the choice of an internal code for spatial memory and reckoning. In this chapter, we explore other possible ramifications of frame-of-reference specialization. The literature reviewed in Chapter 2 suggests that there are a myriad of internal representations of space for different sensory modalities and purposes. If language can be shown to influence the choice of frame of reference for the spatial memory of small-scale arrays, what about larger-scale arrays and mental models of the world around us? After all, spatial cognition must centrally be concerned with locating ourselves in a 'mental map' of the environment, and finding our way around in it. This chapter pursues differences in the cognition of wayfinding and orientation that seem deeply linked to specializations in frames of reference in language. But the chapter also pursues another theme, the cross-modal nature of these frame-of-reference specializations. For the best evidence for wayfinding abilities and the nature of mental maps comes from pointing and gesture – that is from the motoric output driven (at least proximately) by kinaesthetic representations. Unreflective gesture gives us insight into another level of mental life, representations of space that are at least partially independent of language, and that seem close to the very heart of our spatial thinking and spatial imagery. We can therefore look at gesture as a special window on underlying spatial cognition.

6.1 THE ROLE OF LANGUAGE IN EVERYDAY HUMAN NAVIGATION

6.1.1 The nature of wayfinding abilities

There is a large literature on the navigation of non-human species (see, e.g., Schöne 1984, Waterman 1989, Gallistel 1990 for references), which reveals wondrous dead reckoning mechanisms in the simplest of ants through to the miracles of the arctic tern which flies from one pole to the other and back again every year. Some of these mechanisms appear to employ decidedly specialized sensory equipment, for example the ability to get fixes directly from polarized light or the earth's magnetic field (Hughes 1999), mechanisms that seem to be denied to humans (but see Baker 1989).

When we turn to the study of routine human navigation, we find no correspondingly rich literature. Of course, there is a wealth of knowledge about marine navigation, but in our own culture this has been largely formalized since at least the fifteenth century, and is the province of experts. Such expert knowledge is not necessarily in the navigator's own head, for it is an accumulated lore and science, built into maps, instruments and procedures for their use (Hutchins 1995). Something is also known about the traditional marine lore of a few Polynesian societies, where navigation is purely mental rather than using the external plotting and calculating devices of western navigation, but nevertheless also constitutes expert knowledge rather than everyday practice (Gladwin 1970, Lewis 1972). Naturally, psychologists know a large amount about human abilities to estimate distance and angle on the small scale, and have shown exactly how able we are to glance at a scene and then steer our way through it without vision (see, e.g., Lee and Thompson 1982). They have shown, for example, how the blind are also able to extrapolate from experience of a route to a short-cut from one spot to another (Landau *et al.* 1984), and a few have carried out experiments outside the lab (see, e.g., Baker 1989). Geographers have done much to elucidate for us the kinds of mental maps and other constructs urban-dwellers use to find their way around (see, e.g., Golledge 1995, Golledge *et al.* 1995). Still, I think it must be conceded that in many ways we know much less about navigation in our own species than amongst birds, bees and ants. Apart from the efforts of the geographers, there are simply relatively few studies of how humans actually find their way around real novel environments, or calculate angle and distance and current location in moving around on a scale larger than the psychological laboratory. One might have expected anthropologists to have had a keen interest in wayfinding amongst, especially, hunter-gatherer groups. But, on the whole, the information available is extremely disappointing. Work on Australian Aboriginal wayfinding, for example, reduces to a few notes by a seconded Indian policeman, some notes by David Nash, a paper by the explorer David Lewis, and the work reported below. The only work of any sophistication is that done on Eskimo groups (see MacDonald 1998). The reason that so little information exists is that wayfinding knowledge is mostly implicit and difficult to extract by explicit questioning:

> Inuit navigational skills are learned experientially rather than formally and it is perhaps for this reason that Inuit elders, invited by the uninitiated to talk about their wayfinding practices, never quite give a satisfactory account. Snowdrifts, wind directions and stars are all mentioned, but how these and other external markers translate into that comprehensive ability that enables Inuit to excel as wayfinders, seems to elude complete description.   (MacDonald 1998: 162)

And one reason why there is still so much to know is that, unlike many other animal species, human groups vary enormously in their navigational systems and abilities: navigation is quite largely a cultural matter, as shown not only in the history of European or Austronesian expansion, but also in the details of everyday life, as I hope to explain. Consequently one cannot talk of 'human navigation' in the same breath as one might talk of the navigation of the arctic tern (Waterman 1989: 15–16) or the desert ant (Gallistel 1990: 59ff.). Rather, varieties of human implicit navigation may exceed the range of types to be found across a wide range of animal species, as we shall see.

For obvious reasons, knowing where you are with respect to other places has a fundamental biological and cognitive importance. Even for species that are homeless, optimal foraging requires being able to get back to places earlier located. And for animals that have bases, being able to forage and then make a 'bee-line' home is clearly essential. Observations show that when a desert ant makes such a bee-line home, it heads off in the right direction, and then when it has traversed the estimated distance to base, circles around to pick up final landmark cues to guide it home (Collett and Zeil 1998: 26). There seem to be two modes of operation – a system that can calculate an approximate heading and distance to base from any novel location, and a second system for homing at the end of the trajectory. Following our own culturally developed systems of nautical navigation, we can distinguish these two kinds of cognitive operation as 'dead reckoning' vs. 'piloting', where dead reckoning involves estimation of position by calculating distance on each course, and piloting involves using observable landmarks to help one locate one's position on a mental or physical map, and thus to currently unobservable landmarks (Gallistel 1990: 4).

Dead reckoning is the computationally more intensive process, involving a procedure for calculating current position from estimates of distance and direction travelled from a previous known position, and is the process most animals use for long-distance navigation. There are four essential ingredients: places, distances, directions and time – time comes in as a factor both in estimates of distance through velocity, and in the use of many directional cues (e.g. a compass based on the sun must allow for its daily and seasonal variations). Dead reckoning is supplemented by piloting (especially, as with the desert ant, in locating the precise goal towards the end of a journey), and in turn involves headings calculated directly from landmarks, for example by lining them up on an approach towards a harbour, or triangulating with bearings from a number of visible landmarks. These processes have been the subject of much human conscious rumination and are explicitly formulated in the western marine navigation tradition – it is these explicit formulations that have effectively guided research on animal navigation (see, e.g., Gallistel 1990). Of these, dead reckoning is especially interesting, because it involves implicit computation of arithmetic functions: distance along each heading must be estimated by integrating velocity with respect to time, and vectors summed to give a current location. Gallistel (1990: 70–6) offers us a fully explicit computational model, arguing that accurate dead reckoning requires Cartesian rather than polar coordinates. He has gone on to argue that, since even animals with simple neural systems like the desert ant appear to instantiate such computational devices, a connectionist model of even such simple neural systems must be wrong since connectionist models cannot hold the values of variables constant just until they are needed (Gallistel 1996). Thus dead reckoning promises to be an important test area for theories of the fundamental nature of computation in organic systems.

The nature of the cognitive representations involved in navigation among the different species is not well understood at the current time. The fully trigonometric model outlined by Gallistel (1990) does not capture the systematic error patterns observable in animal wayfinding, which are better modelled in a succession of vector estimations (Müller and Wehner 1994). But regardless of that, the two input variables, estimations of angle and distance, are likely to involve multiple modalities. Angular estimations are based on various measures according to species, desert ants, for example, using the direction of polarized light and other measures of sun position, coupled with presumably in-built ephemeris tables (i.e. expectations of the sun's position across the day, allowing for season), while humans rely crucially on the vestibular system for measuring rotations. Distance estimations are probably largely based on optical

flow (measuring rate, yielding distance over time), kinaesthetic information (number of steps), and measures of effort (Etienne *et al.* 1998: 59).
Thus many different sources of information have to be combined, under
varying environmental conditions (like darkness), to yield a current estimation of homeward direction and distance.

6.1.2 *The fall from grace: why are we such bad wayfinders?*

Compared to other species, human *natural* abilities in the navigational
field can only be described as extremely poor – so impoverished that we
really need an explanation. Cultures have slowly attempted to recreate
culturally what we lack natively, developing especially in the west over
the last 500 years an elaborate structure of prosthetic ideas and devices
for working out where we are, culminating in GPS navigational aids
that at last let us rival the skills of migratory birds. In Chapter 7, I will
suggest that we can only understand this atrophy of native abilities in the
context of a theory about the co-evolution of the human genome and
culture.

Naturalists have been aware for a long time of the navigational feats of
animals and insects. But it is only in relatively recent years that we have
gained knowledge about *how* some of these feats are achieved. Many of
them rely on exotic senses that humans are presumed to lack entirely – the
sense of the earth's magnetic field, specialized sensors for polarized light,
sonar systems and so forth (see Waterman 1989, Hughes 1999). What we
have learnt is truly astonishing. Consider, for example, the moustache
bat's echo-location system: such a bat sends out a high frequency signal
(fundamental frequency 30 kHz, with four formants and most energy at
the second formant of 60 kHz) and compares the echo. From the speed
at which the echo is received, the bat determines the range to a target
object (at 2 metres distance the interval will be only 12 milliseconds),
from the range plus loudness it estimates the target's size, and from the
differential loudness in each ear it estimates the location with respect
to its own heading. From Doppler shifts (i.e. bunching or stretching of
frequencies in the echo) as small as 6 Hz, it can calculate the speed of
approach to a moving target. In short, it can paint an entire sound picture
of its spatial environment, distinguishing edible from inedible insects on
the fly. It does this in the left hemisphere of a brain the size of a peanut,
using neurons specialized to the harmonic frequencies of the echo and
the temporal delay between call and echo, with elaborate circuitry and
biomechanics to assure that the bat processes the echoes of its own calls

rather than one of its neighbours in the horde it normally flies amongst. To keep the echoes inside its acoustic 'fovea' despite the Doppler shifts, the bat exactly retunes its voice to compensate, with a precision way beyond any human voice control. Understanding all of this has taken 200 years of bat experiments since Spallanzani first blindfolded bats in 1794 (see Hughes 1999).

In this sort of way, different species paint mental pictures of their spatial environment using some pretty specialized sensory equipment – exotic senses include the ability to detect the polarization of light (as in bees), the earth's magnetic field (as in migratory birds) and weak electric fields (as in rays and sharks). Sometimes this gives them precise directional information. For example, some bird species are provided effectively with an inbuilt *inclination compass* which gives them not only a polar heading but also the latitude. This is like having a magnetized bar balanced midway on a universal joint – at the equator it will be horizontal, but as you approach each pole it will dip towards it, dipping more deeply the nearer you are. So you would know not only where the pole is (not actually *which* one incidentally), but roughly what latitude you were on. Ingenious experiments by Merkel, Wiltschko, Gwinner and others using artificial magnetic fields have shown that migratory birds like garden warblers have just such an inclination compass – the preference for the inclination compass over the polarity type possibly reflecting ancient adaptations to the switches in polarity between north and south pole that happen relatively frequently on geologic time scales (Hughes 1999: 137–48). Despite knowing all this for thirty years, we still have not managed to locate the relevant sense organ, the magnetoreceptor – its sensory basis remains an absolute mystery outside the fishes.

Other birds have an innate migratory response to the sidereal pole giving them effectively a polarity compass. For example, Emlen showed that birds in the northern hemisphere use the centre of apparent motion of the stars as a northerly fix. By rearing buntings in a planetarium where the stars appeared to circle around Betelgeuse in Orion instead of Polaris, Emlen could shift their migratory direction (see Hughes 1999: 136 for references). Again, because of the precession (circular motion) of the earth's axis over a cycle of 27,800 years, it makes excellent evolutionary sense that a bird would have an innate fix linked not to a specific star but to the celestial pole or centre of rotation. The most developed human cultural systems of navigation where there was no compass – those used by the great indigenous navigators of the Pacific – were also based on sidereal observations (Gladwin 1970).

Perhaps the most general directional fix is provided by the daily movements of the sun. Many arthropods, for example desert ants and honey bees, are equipped with polarized light detectors which allow them to use a solar compass even when they cannot see the sun – they need only a small patch of blue sky to detect the present location of the sun. The sun, however, is a potentially deceptive guide to fixed bearings – it moves roughly half a circle over our heads each day, but its course varies significantly with the seasons. At extreme latitudes, as at 70 degrees north in the Arctic, the sun both rises and sets near to north in May, and near to south in January (MacDonald 1998: 164). The azimuth of the sun (that is, the bearing on the horizontal plane made by dropping a vertical line from the celestial body to the horizon) does not progress regularly with time across the day, and the angle traversed in an hour also varies enormously with season and latitude. Thus using a solar compass involves a solar ephemeris – a look-up table that will give one where the sun should be with respect to a fixed point like north at any hour of any day in the year. It also involves a precise clock. Desert ants and honey bees calculate their location effectively using the equivalent of such a table (or systematic series of corrections) and a precise clock – they need to find tiny locations, and rough directions will not do. This has been shown experimentally by flying bees in an airplane at night between time zones – their first foraging flights will be based on where the sun should be according to their internal clocks. Traditional human wayfinding may well use a rough solar compass (see remarks on Guugu Yimithirr wayfinding in 4.1.2.1 above), but it is quite unlikely that any of these mathematical niceties (solar ephemeris and precise internal clock) are built into our nervous system in the way they are into that of the bees.

In trying to understand human navigation capacities it is interesting to have some comparative information about wayfinding abilities in other primates. The information is uneven in quality, and mixed in results. No primates other than humans appear to travel further than 10 km per day over ranges larger than 50 square kilometres (Tomasello and Call 1997: 28) – primates are thus relatively sedentary animals. Some species of Old World monkeys (e.g. Japanese macaques) clearly have the ability to forage using some kind of 'mental map', allowing them to take shortcuts and return to prior feeding areas. But New World squirrel monkeys fail on the simplest rat-maze task, and Tomasello and Call (1997: 33–4) suggest that differential abilities reflect different foraging strategies, some primate groups simply grazing along prior trails. When we turn to apes, the information is very poor. Perhaps the best evidence is the report by Boesch and Boesch (1984) that wild chimpanzees are able to return to find relatively rare stone anvils for cracking nuts, and often seem to go for the closest one. Early experiments by Tinkelpaugh (1928) suggest that chimpanzees may show the 'geometric' mapping system found in rats by Cheng and Gallistel (see Cheng and Spetch 1998), in which angular information in a room will be used as the primary clue, and shape/colour information ignored. Overall, there is no evidence in the primate order of the quite striking spatial abilities in other animals, and there is no evidence that the larger-brained species are any more resourceful navigators than smaller-brained monkeys (Tomasello and Call 1997: 38).

There are many other known animal navigation systems, built, for example, on exotic senses that can respond to faint chemical gradients or electrical currents. But humans clearly seem to have entirely missed out on this veritable bonanza of special-purpose biological navigation aids. And that is probably because, first, we derive from a primate line that displays no outstanding navigational abilities, and second, because we are an opportunistic species, moving too fast into different ecological niches, while retaining gene flow back to other populations. In any case, for whatever reason, human navigation is very obviously a matter of culture and technology, not a story of exotic directional senses and biological navigation modules.

6.1.3 Linguistic representations and human navigation

What might we learn about human navigation by looking at language? One answer might be that in language we can expect to find made fully explicit all the essential concepts that humans utilize in finding their way around. After all, consider von Frisch (1967) and the bees: honey-bees (*Apis mellifera*) make explicit their dead reckoning system through the way in which they communicate the location of a food source to their fellow bees – the direction of their famous waggle-dance indicates a (signed, $+/-$ or left/right) angle α with respect to the gravitational vertical which is identical to the horizontal (signed) angle β which holds between the current azimuth of the sun and the location of the food-source, while the tempo indicates distance (the straight section of the dance tempo increases with distance, while the rate of figure-of-eight repetitions decreases as distance increases – see Waterman 1989). Thus, although we might find out by other experimental means that bees seem to use a time-corrected solar compass, it would be hard to show by such means that this was the sole directional system necessary for their dead reckoning: but observing the communication shows that the crucial information needed by another bee to find the same location is just a solar bearing (signed with respect to its body direction or 'lubber-line') and a velocity representation of distance. If an animal as inarticulate as a bee can provide us crucial evidence in its communication system for the conceptual system it is using in navigation, what riches may lie in language for the understanding of human navigation!

However, there are a number of problems that make a straight extrapolation from language to navigational primitives actually hazardous. The problems here need to be rehearsed because there are a number of linguists (such as Jackendoff 1983: 95, Langacker 1987: 5) who hold that things are not so complicated: semantic representations just *are* conceptual representations in the central language of thought – so a spatial concept in language is just bound to be a concept in our spatial thinking. But there are many reasons to think that semantic representations form a distinct level of representation, which has a non-straightforward relation to non-linguistic representations (see Levinson 1997a for extended discussion). As noted in Chapter 2, we know that there are scores of distinct representations for space in the human mind: for each sensory input (from otoliths to finger tips) there are multiple systems (e.g. for the visual system: retinal, binocular, depth-assigned etc.). Similarly, for each motor output subsystem there are, for example, shoulder, wrist and finger coordinates. We simply do not know, or at least cannot a priori assume, which of these are accessible to linguistic concept formation, and whether the set that is available corresponds or even substantially overlaps with the set available to implicit navigation systems.

A second problem is that linguistic representations may be non-representative, rather specialized systems. For one thing, linguistic representations are designed for, or at least must be compatible with, communication requirements. Natural languages exhibit a range of context-specific interpretive features that presumably have no analogues in the 'language of thought': for example, linguistic utterances are massively ambiguous, and they incorporate devices like deixis and anaphora which ensure a disjunction between the way we speak and the way we think (thus I do not remember the content of the utterance "You seem to like it" as 'you seem to like it', but rather as 'Bill seems to like frozen yoghurt', otherwise quite distinct thoughts, like say 'Nick seems to like Mozart's Opus 32', may end up with the same memory trace or mental representation). Perhaps most relevant for this discussion, natural languages have relatively small vocabularies since they have to be learnable; hence lexical items are typically semantically general – they are generously broad cover-terms as it were. Hence a spatial preposition like English *on* covers a huge range of spatial relations, from cups on tables (object held by gravity on horizontal surface) to frescoes on ceilings (paint adhering to lower side of horizontal surface) to pictures on the wall (hanging on a vertical surface); and then of course there is an enormous further range of non-spatial uses as in 'on Tuesday', 'on the radio' etc. Although some (like Talmy 2000) have hoped to see a particular topological imagination behind such broad expansive generalities, the tendency for 'cover-terms' is probably mostly due to the learning constraints on lexical proliferation. These issues are further taken up in Chapter 7.

A final problem for those who hope to extrapolate from linguistic coding to *the* human spatial concepts – that is, the universal background of conceptual primitives used in everyday wayfinding, for example – is the simple fact of variation. Languages are at least partially cultural constructs, and this is especially obvious in the realm of lexical content. The semantic parameters underlying spatial vocabularies in different languages can simply vary fundamentally, as has been shown in Chapters 3 and 4.

The upshot must be that spatial language cannot a priori be assumed to provide, as it were, a direct porthole on the navigational mind. The thesis throughout this book has been that we will have to investigate independently spatial language on the one hand and spatial concepts used outside language on the other, and see if and how they are related – the relation, if any, is an empirical issue. Yet, as we have seen in Chapters 4 and 5, when we pursue this strategy of independently investigating linguistic and non-linguistic representations of space, what we find is that there is indeed a systematic relation between the two. This we have demonstrated by *exploiting* the very cultural and linguistic variation that makes the extrapolation from language to universal human spatial concepts impossible: we can try to establish *co-variation* between linguistic systems and non-linguistic systems of spatial thinking, including human wayfinding systems. This last is the focus here.

6.1.4 Dead reckoning abilities in relative vs. absolute communities

Can we show that there is any systematic correlation between different linguistic systems and human wayfinding abilities? At first blush it hardly seems likely, especially if one has been led by the linguistic analogy between say 'honey-bee navigation' and 'human navigation' to think in terms of a species-wide system of wayfinding. But given the findings in Chapter 5, where systematic cultural differences in spatial representation have been shown to exist, it no longer looks so implausible.

Speakers of languages where absolute coordinates are central turn out to be especially interesting in this regard. Imagine a language where you simply cannot say 'The boy is in front of the tree', or 'Take the first turning to the left, then the second right', because locutions like *in front of*, or *to the left* simply do not exist in the language. As we saw in Chapter 4, Guugu Yimithirr is such a language, and instead one must say in effect 'The boy is north of the tree', 'Take the first eastern turn' etc. Such a language requires instant access to such expressions and their current correct application. Clearly, to speak a language of this kind one must run constantly a dedicated background processor that will yield almost instantly and effortlessly an estimate of the relevant cardinal directions. Such a processor presumably does in software what many birds and beasts apparently do in hardware, namely take a range of sensory inputs (visual solar azimuth, wind pressure on the skin or hair, inertial measurement by otoliths and semicircular canals, observation of natural features like lichen growth and the orientation of termite mounds), compare them against stored information (like a solar ephemeris, or look-up table for azimuths at different times of the day in different seasons) and crank out an estimation of the direction of egocentric heading. How such a process works is at present mysterious: native exegesis probably only gives at best an imprecise glimpse – we saw a few such details in Chapter 4, such as conscious observation of the flight vectors of migratory birds, the directions of seasonal winds, alignment of sand dunes etc.[1]

Now one should note that to speak a language of this sort, knowing where, say, 'north' is at any given moment will not be sufficient for coding spatial arrangements or motions. It will also be essential to know the location of one's present position with respect to all other locations one may wish to refer to. Suppose I am located at some distance from location A, and I want to say that Bill left recently for A. In many of these languages with absolute coordinate systems it will be effectively required that one specify 'went north to A' or whatever is appropriate (thus Tzeltal has in effect a verb 'to north' or 'go downhill'). But clearly I can only give the requisite specification if I know where I am, and in particular the bearings from my current location to any other location I may want to refer to. In short I need to be constantly dead reckoning my current location on both a micro- and macro-scale, that is to say, calculating my current location in terms of the distance and direction travelled on each directed leg of a journey (see Figure 4.3 in Chapter 4). This leads to the following prediction: *speakers of absolute-coding languages should be better dead reckoners.*

To test this prediction my colleagues and I have carried out a set of informal pointing experiments. The method essentially (or rather ideally, because there are many practical constraints) consists of the following steps: (1) transport participants to unfamiliar places with restricted visibility; (2) ask each subject individually to point to a range of named familiar locations near and far;[2] (3) assess the accuracy of the pointings using a prismatic compass lined up along the pointing arm,[3] together with an estimate of the current location based on GPS or instrument-assisted dead reckoning and a plotting of the estimated directions on a survey map, with appropriate allowances for magnetic inclination; (4) assess the trends in a sample of individuals from a specific population using the special techniques of circular statistics (more below).

It is necessary to emphasize that these measurements have taken place in people's natural environments so that it has not been possible to fully standardize procedures – the ecologies already militate against that possibility, but in addition there are local sensitivities and social restrictions that have had to be observed. Table 6.1 summarizes the different sources and kinds of data.

6.1.4.1 Three 'absolute' communities[4]

Informal experiments were carried out by myself, Penelope Brown and Thomas Widlok in three communities where the languages make predominant use of absolute coordinates. Incidentally, in none of these communities was there any familiarity with maps.

a. **Among the Guugu Yimithirr speaking inhabitants of Hopevale, Cape York, Queensland** (Levinson 1992b; some data already presented in Chapter 4). The measurements were taken opportunistically, during expeditions taken for other purposes (e.g. to find cave-paintings or go fishing), so participants ($N = 11$) had no expectation that they were going to be tested. Using a four-wheel-drive vehicle, participants were taken to various locations up to about 100 km from base camp, usually on bush roads, sometimes followed by extensive walking on foot. At a single location, a subject was asked to point to a range of locations from 7 km to 350 km away. Current location was estimated using compass triangulations where possible,

Table 6.1. *Cross-cultural predictions: from language to dead-reckoning abilities*

Prediction group	Community	Investigator	Linguistic FORs	Local ecology	Travel to test	Test conditions
Absolute → Good dead reckoners	Guugu Yimithirr, Queensland, Australia	S. Levinson	Absolute	Bush, rain forest	Off-road, up to 100 km	Forest, visibility to 30 m
	Hai//om, Namibia	T. Widlok	Absolute, Intrinsic	Bush and desert	Off-road, up to 40 km	Visibility 20–40 m.
	Tenejapa, Mexico	P. Brown, S. Levinson	Absolute, Intrinsic	Sub-alpine fores open fields	2–15 km, foot trails	Inside windowless house
Relative → Poor dead reckoners	Dutch	E. Pederson, S. Levinson	Relative, Intrinsic	Urban, suburban forest	Road, then 5–10 km walk	Open forest
	British	R. Baker (1989)	Relative, Intrinsic	Road, forest	Road, then 2–4 km walk	Open forest
	Japanese	S. Kita	Relative, Intrinsic	Urban	Travel by underground	Urban

or dead reckoning by odometer and pedometer, plotted against the best survey maps available, and disregarding the generally unreliable place-names on the map. This country, although coastal, is very rough, requiring tortuous travel through light bush to heavy rainforest with visibility (except actually on the beach) very restricted, generally to, say, 20 to 30 metres.

b. **Among the Hai//om (Khoisan) Bushmen of the Namibian Kalahari** (Widlok 1994, 1996, 1997). Here measurements were taken after driving to some location along a bush road, and then walking some distance into the bush; a number of successive estimates were made along the way by ten participants. Current location in this case was more accurately divined using a Sony Pyxis GPS machine; the participants thought it self-evident that the experimenter was testing his machine against their knowledge, rather than the other way around. Maximum visibility in the bush was about 20 metres.

c. **Among the Tenejapan Tzeltal,** the slash-and-burn agricultural people in the Chiapas mountains of Mexico whose linguistic system was described in Chapter 4. The Tenejapans live within a restricted territory of about 25 km by 15 km. It proved difficult to find locations where participants had never been before, and in the end the following expedient was adopted: twelve participants who had walked 2–12 km to the site where the experimenters were staying were led as opportunity presented into a house without windows, and asked to point to a series of up to twenty locations at distances of 5 to 125 km. This deviation from the prior procedures had an interesting consequence to be noted below. As in all the groups, a prismatic compass was used to judge alignment of the arm, and measurements compared to survey maps. And again, as with the other groups, placenames on the available maps were unreliable and correct locations had to be estimated on other grounds.

The results can naturally be presented in different ways, but the most illuminating is to follow the methods employed for the study of animal direction estimation, and in particular the methods of so-called circular statistics.[5] Figure 6.1 (taken from Batschelet 1981: 32) illustrates the standard representation of estimates of direction by a sample of animals or participants. The conventions are the following: in the simplest case, the dots indicate the individual estimations of direction. A *mean vector* is constructed of direction a^o and length r: if all the estimates were in the correct home direction $r = 1$ (unit radius) and $a^o = 0$ (there is no divergence from the home arrow). The greater the spread of estimates,

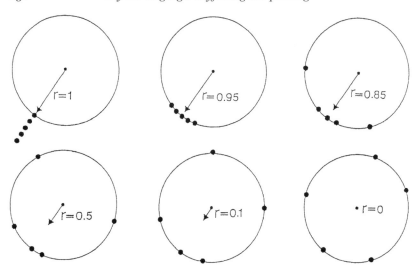

Figure 6.1. Measures of concentration in circular statistics: the mean vector length ranges from 0 to 1. It decreases as the concentration of the sample points around a mean direction diminishes (Batschelet 1981:32.)

the shorter the vector; the greater the angular errors, the larger the value of a^{o}, the mean error. Thus the mean vector length serves as a measure of concentration.

From the mean vector we may derive a measure of dispersion equivalent to the standard deviation in linear statistics, namely a *mean angular deviation* in degrees (Batschelet 1981: 34). The direction of the mean vector with respect to the homeward (or predicted) direction allows the computation of *the homeward component* (Batschelet 1981: 41). Confidence limits can be calculated in degrees (Batschelet 1981: Ch. 5) to allow us to decide whether there is a significant deviation of the mean estimates from the home direction (if so, the home direction lies outside the angular interval given by the confidence limits).

Figure 6.2 gives what is a typical sample of estimates of home direction by homing pigeons (data from Batschelet 1981: 12): they have been transported 66 km from home base and released and the compass direction of the fifteen vanishing points on the horizon recorded. The home direction in this and subsequent circular diagrams is represented by the long arrow pointing outside the circle, here at 265°. Note that the mean vector length is 0.9, representing a well concentrated cluster of estimates,

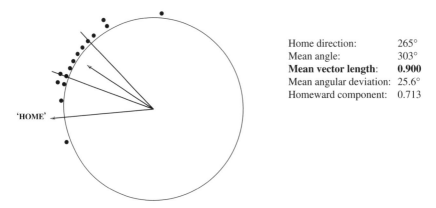

Figure 6.2. Homing pigeons: directions at vanishing point (after Batschelet 1981: 11f.)

and that the mean vector direction is 303°, and the component of the vector in the home direction is 0.713. The methods of circular statistics allow us to conclude that the homeward direction lies significantly outside the mean cluster of estimates, i.e. that the pigeons' estimates are systematically skewed to the north.[6]

Now compare a set of estimates taken from one of our human groups, in this case the Australian speakers of the language Guugu Yimithirr, as given in Figure 6.3. The procedure is somewhat different of course: the eleven participants were tested individually (transported actually to somewhat varying distances from real home base), they pointed from ground level with a maximum visibility of about 30 metres at the 'home direction', and the dots represent each of their initial estimates (rather than an estimate made when well under way after initial corrections as in the pigeon case). In addition to these extra difficulties, our human participants have been instructed to point not directly at their real home base (too trivial a task), but at the location of a place outside their territory (Laura) to which they rarely go, and which lies at a distance of 80 km (for comparison with the similar distance to that involved in the pigeons' task). Thus the 'home direction' here is a third location, distinct from the current location and actual base camp. Inspection will reveal a surprisingly accurate set of estimates: the mean vector length (representing concentration of the estimates) approximates to 1 (0.97), and the homeward component of the mean vector is 0.935. The home direction still, however, lies significantly outside the range expected (on

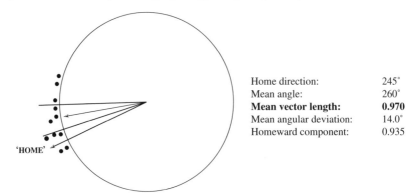

Home direction:	245°
Mean angle:	260°
Mean vector length:	**0.970**
Mean angular deviation:	14.0°
Homeward component:	0.935

Figure 6.3. Guugu Yimithirr speakers estimating the location of Laura at 80 km

95% confidence limits), indicating that again there is a slight systematic northerly bias.

The favourable comparison to pigeon navigational estimates is here used just to make the following rhetorical point.[7] To achieve this feat our Guugu Yimithirr participants are apparently using a dedicated cognitive process that constantly dead reckons current location within a mental map of other locations – as was said above, it achieves in software what pigeons apparently achieve partially in hardware (using magnetoreception, olfactory gradients, polarized light and no doubt other specialized sensory modules yet to be discovered).[8] Despite this, Guugu Yimithirr participants rarely reveal hesitation or doubt, nor are they ordinarily able to articulate their reasoning – the exceptions to this occurring in special circumstances, for example after fast vehicle travel on slowly curving roads, or after air travel (see Levinson 1992b).

To represent the rest of the data in a more compact way I will now slightly alter the conventions: I will summarize a hundred or more observations over each of the human samples by representing the mean value of a *set* of up to a score of estimations for each individual as a single dot on a circular diagram. Thus one dot may represent fifteen estimates by one individual, each estimation having so much deviation from the actual 'home' direction (the direction of the particular place named): the 'home' direction is now normalized to north on the diagram, and the angular distance of the dot from north indicates the mean deviation of the set of estimates from each of their 'home' directions. I now proceed to a second-order treatment of the group of individuals (so the mean vector represents a group mean of individual means), each individual

'HOME'

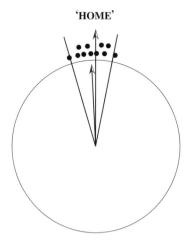

Mean angle:	−2.93°
Mean vector length:	0.954
Confidence interval:	+/−14°
Homeward component:	0.952

Figure 6.4. Guugu Yimithirr sample

participant being represented by a set of first-order estimates. I follow the methods outlined in Batschelet 1981: Ch. 10.

Figure 6.4 gives the results for our eleven Guugu Yimithirr participants, each making an average of fifteen estimations. The reader will note that the mean vector length and the homeward component of the mean vector remain essentially the same as in the smaller sample of first-order estimates represented in Figure 6.3. The concentration of estimates around the home direction is extremely high, and indeed there is no statistically reliable deviation from the home direction (that is to say we cannot be sure that the population mean is not exactly in the home direction).

Despite the stereotypical reports of the 'uncanny' sense of direction possessed by Australian Aboriginal peoples, there has only been one prior study (Lewis 1976, mentioned in Chapter 4; see also Lahiri 1965, Nash 1993). In that study Lewis collected thirty-four estimates of directions to named places (mostly at distances of about 300 km) while travelling by Jeep in the Western Desert. Although there were very different ecological conditions, with open vistas but vast distances, the estimates had a similar reliability. In our study the named locations were at distances from 7 to 350 km, mostly in the 50–100 km range. The ten worst estimates (average error 36 degrees) were to relatively local places, due to the general principle that the closer one is to a landmark the greater its change of angle with any change of one's position; they also coincided with particularly circuitous travel. Mode of travel made some difference, fast vehicle travel clearly interfering with accurate distance estimation, and travel by foot probably coinciding with the best distance estimation. The ten best estimates, as with Lewis' observations, were to places with historical symbolic value. I should record that all the participants were men.

We turn now to another hunter-gatherer group, the Hai//om people studied by Widlok (1996, 1997, 1999). Widlok collected data that can be represented in the same format, from ten individuals (seven male, three female) on a number of occasions when travelling with them by foot.[9] Individuals were tested at 15–40 km from base-camp. Each individual provided an average of nineteen estimations of named locations at a distance of 2–200 km. The Hai//om results are presented in Figure 6.5, from which it will be immediately evident that the accuracy of the estimates is essentially the same as in the Australian case. Statistical tests (Walraff Test, see Batschelet 1981: 124–8) show that there is no significant difference between the Australian and Hai//om samples.

As with Australian Aboriginal peoples, the Kalahari Bushmen are credited with superhuman orientation and tracking skills, an ideology fanned by South African forces in the Angolan war (Widlok 1996: 2–4). Nevertheless, and despite considerable attention to hunting and tracking skills in the ethnographic record, Widlok's work seems to be the first direct testing of dead reckoning skills. Widlok (1996) notes that there was some significant variation within his sample: judging by amount of average error, women were better estimators than men (with half the average error), and younger men better than older men. This is despite the fact that men, and especially older men, have greater hunting expertise in this society. Widlok notes that, as in the Guugu Yimithirr case, the methods employed by the Hai//om to estimate compass direction and the angles of distant locations are by no means self-evident: no attention was paid to the sun, and anyway tests were conducted around midday under partially overcast conditions (Widlok 1996: 7), the sites from which estimates were made were distant from paths, and so on. As in the Australian case, individuals were more confident about places of special ideological significance to them, for example places in their own named local territories.

'HOME'

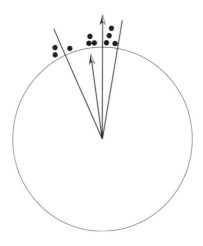

Mean angle:	−8.05°
Mean vector length:	0.931
Confidence interval:	+/−17°
Homeward component:	0.922

Figure 6.5. Hai//om sample

Our third population of speakers of a language with absolute rather than relative coordinates was the Tzeltal Mayan Indians of Tenejapa. As mentioned above, our testing method here deviated for practical reasons from the prior studies where participants were taken to unfamiliar locations. Instead, twelve individuals who had visited the investigators' base in the Majosik' paraje of Tenejapa for other reasons were taken inside a closed, windowless house and asked to point to twenty named locations. Participants came from 2 to 12 km away by foot; from outside the house, the location offers some restricted views along the local valley. They had no forewarning from other participants, as the tests were done over a period of two years as opportunity offered. The results are shown in Figure 6.6. One notes immediately that the estimates are closely clustered, with a mean vector length of 0.858; this is significantly less than in the two previous cases, but still shows a good consistent consensus about the directions of the named places. However, the main difference from the prior samples is that the estimations are significantly skewed, with the homeward component of the mean vector down to a value of 0.549,

'HOME'

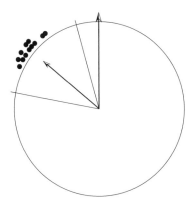

Mean angle: −50.17°
Mean vector length: 0.858
Mean angular deviation: 30.6°
Homeward component: 0.549

Figure 6.6. Tzeltal sample

and with the 'home' direction lying way outside the confidence interval (i.e. we can be reasonably sure that this is a systematic skewing, which would be repeated on further sampling).

The two important features of this set of estimates are the concentration of estimations on the one hand and the systematic skewing on the other. The concentration shows that participants are making consistent estimations; the deviation shows that some feature of the environment or the nature of the task is providing a false cue. The responsible feature in this case is almost certainly the orientation of the house in which the tests were conducted, which was on the diagonal to the linguistic axis system used by the Tenejapans. Their linguistic 'downhill' quadrant is centred on an angle 15 degrees or so west of north. The north-facing wall of the house is skewed about 30 degrees east from our north (i.e. a sighting to the middle of it has the value 030 N), and thus its face is skewed about 45 degrees east from the local 'north' or 'downhill'. If the participants had taken the wall to be facing 'downhill' (i.e. its longitudinal axis was taken as orthogonal to their 'downhill' or 'north'), their estimates should be systematically skewed by roughly the observed amount. This then is the likely explanation of the skewing.

The effect, though inadvertent, has a special interest: it seems to demonstrate that these participants are mediating their judgements by reference to the conceptual axes encoded in the language. Notice that no such reference is essential for these pointing tasks: if you ask me to point right now to the nearest bathroom in the building I am located in, I am unlikely to consult my (feeble) intuitions about where north is. In the same way when pointing to a range of locations, I might know their angular directions without reference to a mediating set of named quadrants or axes. In that case, individual estimations might be in error without the whole set being skewed. When the whole set is systematically skewed, the explanation would seem necessarily to be of the following kind: the angles between specific locations from the estimating location are preserved in some form of mental map, but the whole 'map' is misoriented by the observed angle of skew. But to say that a 'map' is skewed is to say that some overriding orientation cue has been misread – for example, animal experimenters artificially alter the perceived daylight to show that a time-corrected solar compass is being employed (as mentioned in section 6.1.2). Now linguistically expressed cardinal directions are in the Tenejapan, the Guugu Yimithirr and many other cases quadrant-like: each linguistic expression covers a 90-degree sweep of horizon. In the Tenejapan case (but not the Guugu Yimithirr) informants talk about the quadrants as anchored around the bisecting axes: the 'downhill' quadrant is bisected by *batz'il alan*, 'true downhill'. So if a Tenejapan says to himself 'This wall faces downhill (north)', this may be a true statement even if the wall is skewed; if he goes on to say to himself 'This wall is roughly orthogonal with true downhill' he will adopt a systematic skewing encouraged by the language: it is easy to take a linguistic cover-term as designating its prototype reference. Something of this kind seems to have happened here.

A few further remarks on the Tenejapan performance. The sample is statistically significantly different from the Hai//om and Guugu Yimithirr samples (by the Walraff test); nevertheless it clearly represents a population that think they know where they are by reference to the directions and distances of places around them (hence the systematicity of the skewing), and in that regard it is similar. From observations of many kinds of linguistic and non-linguistic behaviour I would have expected Tenejapans to be less good dead reckoners than the Guugu Yimithirr. After all, they are not hunter-gatherers, and orientation is not critical in their daily lives in the same way: their territory is crisscrossed by well-known trails that take one from one location to another, and, in their mountainous terrain, off-trail shortcuts are rarely practical.

Nevertheless, the skewing represented in this sample is almost certainly atypical, as evidence mentioned in section 6.2 attests. The one factor that makes orientation necessary in daily life despite these ecological factors is language, as already described, and Tenejapans do indeed know where they are, and even if their estimates of direction are not as accurate as the prior two groups, they are certainly good enough for linguistic purposes.

6.1.4.2 Two 'relative' communities

To compare these results against the performance of speakers of languages that use predominantly relative coordinates, Eric Pederson began to collect measurements (about six per subject) opportunistically during the forays of a Dutch wild-mushroom pickers' club. These participants (N = 5) were walking nose to ground as it were, and were 5–10 km from the car at the time they were questioned. We subsequently discovered that a large number of measurements (from 211 male and 234 female participants) had already been undertaken in England by Robin Baker (1989: 35–45) under admittedly rather different circumstances: participants were bussed to a wood, and led 2–4 km into the wood along a path with one major switchback; they were then asked to make just one estimation, namely of the direction of their starting point (in fact at about 1 km distance). I will use these two rather different samples as my baseline for the performance of relative-language speakers (Baker 1989 contains a great deal of further relevant information).

First, the Dutch participants were tested in circumstances approximating our prior absolute groups: they were off beaten paths, in woods with limited visibility, and they had been walking for some time, not expecting any test. In this kind of circumstance, they performed pretty badly, as is evident from Figure 6.7. The estimations are clearly distributed around the circle, and in fact they are the only sample to fail the V-test used in circular statistics to test for non-random behaviour. The dispersion of the mean estimates (represented by the dots) is reflected in a mean vector length of only 0.259 and the homeward component of the vector is not surprisingly very low at 0.222.

Although the sample of participants, and each participant's set of estimates, is low compared to our previous absolute groups, nevertheless one should note that in those other samples there are *no* participants who perform like the majority of these Dutch participants. From a dead reckoning point of view, these estimates show that these participants have constructed no clear representation of their current location in the mental map of their immediate environment or integrated that local

'HOME'

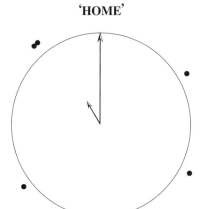

Mean angle: 329.14°
Mean vector length: 0.2585
Confidence interval: n/a
Homeward component: 0.222

Figure 6.7. Dutch sample

map into the larger world they know. If they find their way back to their starting point in the woods without too much difficulty, it is likely to be done as much by piloting (retracing a path) as by dead reckoning. This is surprising because this group of participants are particularly 'woodsy', spending most weekends and many evenings wandering in forests.

To counter the charge that the sample is too small to be revealing, let us consider the very large samples collected by Baker (1989) from British participants under the rubric of wayfinding experiments. Baker was interested to show that humans have faint magnetoreception; scholars who believe the contrary claim to have had a hard time replicating the non-random results (see Baker's 1989 introductory discussion for references). Thus these are the results that show the most systematic performance from Western participants to be found in the literature; for the same reason, I will select the male participants who performed considerably better than the female ones. Various points should be borne in mind: (a) the task is different from the previous tasks: participants were led through a wood for a short distance and only had to point back to their starting points about 1 km away; (b) consequently each dot

'HOME'

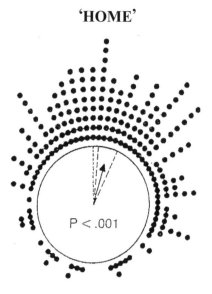

Mean angle:	15
Mean vector length:	0.55
Confidence interval:	+/− 10
Homeward component:	0.54

Figure 6.8. English male sample (from Baker 1989)

represents only one measurement, not a mean of up to twenty as before, and the whole analysis is first-order, not second-order as above. In other respects the data are comparable (e.g. participants were not expecting to be tested for orientation). The results for 211 male participants are shown in Figure 6.8.[10] They show a mean vector length of 0.55 (females 0.397), which is far lower than any of the absolute community samples (the lowest was the Tenejapan at 0.858); in other words, the estimates are quite dispersed, despite some concentration in the correct direction. The homeward component of the vector has a value of 0.54, which shows a tendency in the correct direction; and randomness can definitely be rejected by the V-test.

The essential thing to note is that on this very easy task – pointing to just one location at 1 km distance, left shortly before on a clearly defined path with not many turns – performance still comes no way near to that of our absolute dead reckoners. Only about half of the participants judge 'home' to be even in the correct 90-degree quadrant, and this failure cannot be ascribed to some misleading cue, as there is no systematic skewing.[11] Putting these direction estimates together with distance estimates, Baker (1989: 101–2) notes that the implication for these participants finding their return way to a 1000 metres distant 'home' or goal by a novel route are the following: 25% would arrive to within 407 metres, 25% would arrive no nearer than 969 metres, and 50% would navigate to within 717 metres of home – the evidence is of 'a weak and imprecise ability'. Thus this most favourable set of observations from speakers of a language with a relative coordinate system does not begin to approximate the systematic estimations we have obtained from the 'absolute' samples.[12]

6.1.4.3 Conclusions to dead reckoning experiments
These tests of dead reckoning skills by pointing seem to me the best kind of measure that one is likely to find (actual navigation back to 'home' allows serial correction, as observed for pigeons – and then it is hard to know what factors have actually come into play). What they unequivocally show is that dead reckoning abilities vary across human populations along cultural lines, thus rendering talk of a single uniform kind of basic human navigation suspect. The difference between, for example, the Guugu Yimithirr and Dutch samples suggests something more than a quantitative improvement by extensive practice: rather it suggests that Guugu Yimithirr speakers have in constant play a rather precise mental dead reckoning system, while Dutch or English speakers must attempt 'guesstimates' based on no systematic background navigation at all.

Overall it is clear that our 'absolute' language speakers are much better dead reckoners than our 'relative' language speakers. But we cannot be sure of course that the correlation with coordinate systems in language is either going to hold up worldwide, or that if it does there is any direct causal connection between dead reckoning abilities and language (or even if there is, which direction it lies in). Here it is worth pointing out that no simple ecological explanation of dead reckoning abilities is likely to succeed. The Queensland coastal country (inhabited by the Guugu Yimithirr speakers) with its rainforest and bush is a very different environment from the Kalahari dry forest and desert, and they again contrast of course with the mountain uplands of Chiapas where the Tenejapans have their territory. Some Guugu Yimithirr speakers live in urban environments without losing their dead reckoning skills. Equally gross cultural factors, like hunter-gather vs. agricultural economies, do not constitute the essential difference, since the Tenejapans are settled agriculturalists

Table 6.2. *Overall comparison of dead-reckoning experiments*

GROUP	Mean vector length	Mean angular deviation	Homeward component	V-test	Sample size	Estimations per subject
British, males (Baker 1989)	0.55	54±	0.54	<0.001	211	1
Dutch, woodsmen	0.2585	49±	0.22	3 failed; 3 <0.05	5	5–7
Tenejapan, Mayans	0.858	30±	0.55	<0.05	12	12–20
Hai//om, Kalahari	0.93	21±	0.92	<0.05	10	13–20
Guugu Yimithirr, Queensland	0.95	17±	0.95	<0.05	11	4–20

living in a densely populated and highly utilized environment. Finer-grained cultural factors may indeed be closely correlated with good dead reckoning skills: Lewis found Western Desert Aboriginals to be just as good as our coastal Queenslanders, and despite many cultural differences between these groups they both share a tremendous emotional attachment to specific locations in vast territories. One other cultural variable, namely the nature of gesture systems, does seem to co-vary with absolute frames of reference, and this is the subject of the second half of this chapter.

But the possible plurality of correlates with good dead reckoning abilities is beside the point. My argument has been the following. In order to speak a language that encodes angles on the horizontal in absolute co-ordinates, an individual will need to be constantly oriented (know where the local 'north' or 'south' is), and moreover will need to know where he or she is with respect to other places that may need to be referred to. The system can never go 'on holiday', since one never knows what experiences or directions one may need to talk about. Such languages, I have argued, *force* dead reckoning on a more or less constant basis. Speaking such a language is thus a *sufficient*, although not necessary, condition for being a good dead reckoner. At the very least, the needs of the linguistic output system are going to level out the kind of individual differences we are likely to find elsewhere. That is the hypothesis, and so far the data confirm it.

One final point underlines the linguistic or at least communicational nature of some of the information involved in dead reckoning skills. In all three absolute communities, participants sometimes confidently pointed to locations and then mentioned that they had never been there. But from many prior conversations in which other speakers had spoken of and pointed to such locations, our participants were confident that they knew where these locations were, even though now they were indicating the location from a quite different place! In short they had integrated these mentioned but never-seen places into a mental map, making estimations of both angle and distance of the kind necessary to support pointing to those places from a different place in the mental map. As far as I could tell in the Tzeltal and Guugu Yimithirr samples, participants were not markedly less accurate with what were for them virtual locations.[13] How such accurate information about distance and angle can be communicated is a puzzle to which I shall return in the next section.

6.2 GESTURE DURING SPEAKING: 'DEAD RECKONING' ON THE FLY

It turns out that there is another, less intrusive way to observe dead reckoning skills in 'absolute' speech-communities. In most cultures, most of the time, when people speak they gesture. A great deal of gesture seems to depict spatial arrangements. In 'absolute' speech communities there is an expectation that gestures should point accurately to the places referred to and depict the motions described in the correct orientation (the bearings need not necessarily be correct from the current location if, for example, they depict the protagonist's perspective in a story). This seems first to have been observed by John Haviland about fifteen years ago (but not published for a decade, see Haviland 1993, 1996). Many interesting properties of the gesture systems accompanying languages that prefer absolute spatial descriptions seem to follow from this basic property (Levinson 1996c compares the Tzeltal and Guugu Yimithirr systems in some detail, and see below). For example, gestures are large, with arms outstretched, allowing accurate sighting of the angles depicted. Unlike our gestures, they occur in all directions, for example behind the body. Directional gestures are often given while gazing in another direction, as if the speaker has immediate and automatic access to the bearings of anything he or she may want to refer to. Whereas in our gesture system the body figures prominently as an animator of actions, and a display of the left/right/front/back distinctions we are fond of, in systems associated with absolute coordinates it plays a different role especially with pointing actions: one can point through the body as if it were invisible. I will return to these features later. Incidentally, there is plenty of other evidence that gesture systems align closely with frame-of-reference specializations, so that, for example, those with an intrinsic frame of reference predominant gesture differently than those with all three frames available (Kita *et al.* 2001).

Observing gesture is, in a sense, a natural experiment of a similar kind to the pointing experiments mentioned in the prior section – the only substantial disadvantage being that the bearings of a recorded gesture on a screen can only be very roughly gauged. But on the basis of the more exact measurements from the pointing experiments we can be confident that these unreflective gestures have the same kind of accuracy. It is interesting then to note the speed of directional judgement required to keep up with the flow of speech, giving further evidence for the automaticity and background nature of the dead reckoning computations involved (recollect, the gestures may be from the point of view of protagonists who themselves are on the move). Here then is further evidence for dead reckoning abilities in everyday life, deeply connected to language and the process of speech production in 'absolute' speech communities.

In the sections that follow, some details are given about how gesture systems differ between absolute and relative speech communities. For the absolute systems, I will focus on the Tzeltal and Guugu Yimithirr cases, and contrast them to published work by David McNeill on American English gesture. However, the reader can find another such contrast between Arrernte and Dutch gestures carefully reported in work by de Ruiter and Wilkins (1998).

6.2.1 *The general picture from experiment and observation*

We have begun the intensive study of the gesture system of Tenejapans, in order to compare it to the extensive material that we have on spatial language and cognition in that community. I should mention at the outset that Tenejapans have a polite formal style in which gesture is strictly inhibited, so that gesture is only appropriate in certain social relationships, and naturally these kinds of interaction are the focus of the following remarks.

One place to start was to try and extend the rotation paradigm of experiments described in Chapter 5 above. The gesture version of the experiment ran as follows (in collaboration with Sotaro Kita). Participants watched a series of very short stimulus movies on a small LCD (battery powered) video display, inside a house with no windows. The stories were designed or selected to encode lateral motion. Participants were then rotated 180 degrees within the room, as in the experiments on conceptual coding, and asked to retell the story to a Tzeltal speaking interlocutor. Generally we used our native-speaker assistant as interlocutor, but because of the polite no-gesture style mentioned above, the interlocutor could not be kept constant, and in many cases my collaborator Penelope Brown acted as the recipient of the stories (being a familiar outsider, gestures were relatively uninhibited in her presence). Beyond the request to retell the story, nothing further was said about the purpose of the task: we were interested of course in seeing whether spontaneous gestures would preserve egocentric coordinates (i.e. utilize a relative frame of reference) or absolute coordinates. Coding a large amount of gesture is painstaking work, and at the present time not all the data have been analysed, but this we can report:

1. A Dutch comparison group systematically preserves body-centred relative coordinates.[14]

2. Some Tzeltal participants systematically preserve absolute coordinates – that is, if a motion is observed on the screen going from left to right, it is reported with a right to left gesture under rotation. This is a completely alien phenomenon from all we know about gesture accompanying languages that favour the relative frame of reference. All Tzeltal participants seem to systematically preserve absolute coordinates if absolute linguistic terminology is produced concurrently. Some Tzeltal participants produce consistent absolute gestures when retelling stimulus films shot in real three-dimensional space, while reverting to a relative frame of reference for two-dimensional cartoons – a result perhaps explicable in terms of the absence of real spatial information in the latter. Other participants produced gestures from the characters' perspective, a point of view that we believe can be directly related to the intrinsic frame of reference.

The picture from natural gesture use in narrative and conversation is actually rather clearer. John Haviland (1993, 1998) and (following him) myself have investigated Guugu Yimithirr gestures and found them to follow the same logic: a Guugu Yimithirr flick of the hand is, *ceteris paribus*, to be interpreted in a special way, namely as correctly oriented by cardinal direction. This can be shown by examining the detail of a narrative for which the historical and geographical setting can be verified: what we then find is a quite extraordinary mapping of exact directions between story and historical event.[15] The directions may be given from the location of narration, or they may be given from the point of view of protagonists and their locations at particular points in the story (Haviland 1993, 1996, 1998). Only some of these directional specifications are also given in speech: in many cases the gestures carry the communicational load. The practice is widespread and pervasive: a question about location may be answered with a gesture (sometimes without words), the interpretation of which may be complex, but always involves fixed absolute directions.

We have now repeated this exercise with Tzeltal speakers: we have narratives from over a dozen expert elders asked to retell various traditional stories and myths. Some of these myths concern the patron saint of Tenejapa, called Kajkanantik, and his travels. The films were shot at many different locations around the territory of Tenejapa, from house sites usually nestled deep in forest or surrounding vegetation. The compass directions were always recorded, and on this basis we can report that the tellers unerringly pointed to the locations referred to in the story, which sometimes lie far outside the territory or even beyond the direct acquaintance of the story-tellers. One can plot Kajkanantik's narrated movements on a map, checking the consistency of the gestures depicting the reported journey.

6.2.2 Distinctive properties of absolute gesture systems

Let me introduce the analytical category *'absolute gesture system'*, which lumps together the Tzeltal and Guugu Yimithirr systems in opposition to our own *'relative gesture systems'*, shared by most speakers of European languages, and members of many other speech communities too, like the Japanese.[16] We could define such systems in various ways. For example, we could definitionally relate them to languages where the predominant orientational frame of reference in language is absolute – i.e. where cardinal-direction-like fixed bearings are utilized in most linguistic descriptions that provide orientational information beyond the spatial structure of the described array itself. That is in fact the best, perhaps the only, sure predictor of where such systems are to be found. Still, in principle one might find a speech community that utilizes relative linguistic descriptions but absolute gestures in describing spatial arrays. So let us define 'absolute/relative gesture systems' in terms of *the coordinate systems used within the gestural depictions themselves*: we can use the rotational paradigm mentioned above to help us determine whether we have a relative or absolute system in any one case, or just observe the exact directions accompanying a range of natural speech events.[17] Note that in Chapter 2 it was shown that it makes perfect sense to talk about frames of reference in modalities other than language, and to ask about correlations of frame-of-reference specializations across modalities.

Now, it is a common enough finding that in spatial description in some languages alternative frames of reference will be available, and which one is actually employed will depend on properties of the task – e.g. the scale of the things to be described, what use the information is to be put to, and so on (see Tversky 1996). So in the same way one might want to talk about individual gestures utilizing particular coordinate systems, which might not be the common or normal ones: there may be variation due to individuals and contexts.[18] But when I talk of an 'absolute gesture system' what I have in mind is something more thorough-going:

a. Wherever an orientation-bound gestural depiction is discernible, an absolute (and not a relative) conceptual coordinate system is employed in at least the great majority of ordinary gestures, across a range of contexts, by most speakers of the community.
b. This absolute 'semantics', or its underlying cognitive style, is exploited by speakers and their recipients, and in that sense constitutes a genuine communicational or semiotic system. In short, absolute 'semantics' seems to pervade the production and interpretation of all the gestures in such a system – not just pointings, but depictions or 'iconic' gestures as well. Gestures that are not intended to be interpreted as mirroring the real orientation of things and events must then be made in a special way to declare that.

The thesis of this section is that this underlying 'semantics' of absolute gesture systems generates a set of more observable features that are associated with them. Compared to relative gesture systems, they seem to have a different morphology, have a special placement in reaching space, a different relation to gaze, and carry a greater communicative load. Not all these features are unique to absolute gesture systems – they may occur occasionally in relative gesture systems. But as a complex they seem distinctive of gesture systems based on fixed coordinates. A caveat is however in order. Gesture studies are in their infancy, there is little comparative material available, and quantitative patterns over large samples are nowhere to be found. The remarks below must be taken in the spirit of hypotheses, based on participant observation, large video corpora, but close analysis of only small samples of Tzeltal and Guugu Yimithirr gestures, compared to published results for English and Japanese gesture. I will state the generalizations boldly, and with hardly any illustration, for that alas would take another book.

Absolute gesture systems are fundamentally different, I shall claim, from our own relative systems. Nevertheless, a casual inspection may fail to reveal that. For example, in Australia white ranchers and doctors who have spent years in the company of Aboriginal people have failed to comprehend the system – this can be demonstrated from records of inter-ethnic conversations, where misunderstandings attributable directly to this source are rife.[19] Our first observations on Tzeltal absolute gestures were not made till 1990, although we had worked for years on Tzeltal verbal interaction. In short the differences are relatively subtle, easily overlooked, and reside as much in meaning as they do in form.

One additional preliminary point: the categories 'absolute/relative gesture systems' are analytical categories, not necessarily natural species.

It is one way to sort the cultural gestural systems of the world. There are other ways of course, utilizing orthogonal or partly overlapping criteria, for example: size of gesture space (the area around the body where most gestures occur), degree of communicative loading, number of emblems or quotable gestures, degree of flexibility of hand-shape etc. In some respects, the Tzeltal and Guugu Yimithirr gesture systems are fundamentally different – for example:

a. Tzeltal gestures are (as mentioned) inhibited or even totally suppressed in many social contexts, Guugu Yimithirr gestures are much freer (except in the context of in-laws).
b. Tzeltal hand-shapes are significantly different, the hand often taking a specific shape with fingers together and half bent.[20]
c. Tzeltal 'emblems' (quotable or conventional gestures) are of course distinctive: for example, the height of a cow is shown by holding the flat palm out at arm's length with thumb on top, but the height of a human by holding the index finger up – naturally there are no identical conventional gestures in Guugu Yimithirr.

Nevertheless, the point of this classificatory exercise in terms of underlying cognitive coordinate systems is to show that perhaps many shared details in these two otherwise disparate gesture systems can be attributed to this single psychological factor – an absolute frame of reference.

6.2.2.1 *The semiotics*

The first and foremost – indeed definitional – character of absolute gesture systems is of course their orientation. That this can systematically differ from relative systems of gesture is shown by the simple experiment mentioned above, in which participants describe a stimulus after being rotated. Without rotation, of course, the direction of absolute and relative gestures will be potentially identical. Outside of an experimental context Haviland (1993: 15–16) has shown how Guugu Yimithirr narrations of the same event when told by the same speaker at a different angle on another occasion will preserve the fixed bearings of the event in the gestural channel.

Even without rotation one can expect a difference: absolute gesturers expect their gestures to be inspected carefully for orientation, relative gesturers probably for the most part do not, so one may expect differences in systematicity. Schegloff, for example, has shown that North American gestures accompanying place specifications rarely make spatial sense at all:

If the place referred to is not visually accessible, then it appears that the point is not necessarily in a direction selected to be the 'actual direction' of the referent relative to the scene of the talk. For example ... different 'places' (which happen to be in different directions from the talk scene) are accompanied by points in the same direction, and two persons referring to the same place while talking together point in different directions.　　　　(Schegloff 1984: 280)

Our own examination of inter-ethnic interviews in Queensland shows that what Aboriginal people take to be directional gestures from their white counterparts are usually not so, but mere emphatic hand wavings. Haviland has put it another way: Guugu Yimithirr speakers can *lie* with their gestures, where we – except in limited demonstrative contexts – can hardly be said to do so.[21]

One point needs immediate clarification: we relative-speakers too point with some care for orientation when giving route-directions and the like. But the remarkable feature of these absolute systems is that all gestures, in any genre, are produced with the expectation that they will be inspected for the veracity of their orientational information. (This statement is correct even though some gestures are produced in a special way to indicate that they are *not* absolutely oriented.) A narrative relating events that took place half a century ago, a mythical journey, even a report of a dream come under the same scrutiny. In contrast, under these circumstances, we relative-gesturers will set up small virtual spaces in front of us, where some consistency but no veracity is expected.

The detailed semiotic systems that underlie the interpretation of absolute gestures lie outside the scope of this chapter, and in any case they have been ably explored by Haviland (1993, 1998, 2000). Suffice it to say that (a) not all gestures by those who produce absolute gestures necessarily belong to this kind – some seem to describe unoriented spaces, but in this case they are clearly demarcated by being located in a different part of the gesture space; (b) absolute gestures although correctly oriented may not be so oriented from the place of speaking, but rather be correctly oriented from the place (or origo) at which the protagonists in, say, a narrative currently find themselves; (c) complex switches of this reference point or origo may occur in a single sequence of gestures; (d) the location pointed at may have an indirect relation to the thing denoted – for example, Guugu Yimithirr speakers might refer with a pronoun to a long-dead protagonist by pointing to a distant place at which his descendants used to, but no longer, live (reflecting a very rich set of associations with places).

Incidentally, I have presumed that absolute vs. relative coordinates in gesture can be understood directly in terms of the distinctions already made in Chapter 2 about frames of reference in general. But what about intrinsic gestures – what do they look like and how does one recognize them? McNeill (1992) has proposed a distinction between character-perspective and observer-perspective, where a character-perspective involves an enactment, and an observer-perspective a depiction from a fixed outside viewpoint. Thus if I see a man run across my field of view towards the left, I could depict this by showing running motions as a pumping of arms (character-perspective) or in terms of a motion from right to left (observer-perspective). McNeill's observer-perspective is the relative frame of reference that we are familiar with, and tentatively we may identify the character-perspective with an intrinsic frame of reference, for it has the crucial property of not being oriented in a larger spatial coordinate system. McNeill notes blends between these, as when, for example, the speaker pumps his arms to indicate running, but nods or leans to the left to indicate the observed direction. In absolute systems one can find blends too: now the nod will indicate the actual direction, not necessarily the perceived direction, of motion.

6.2.2.2 *Gesture morphology in absolute vs. relative gesture systems*

Impressionistically, gestures with absolute vs. relative semiotics look really quite different in kind. In this section, I try to firm this intuition up by comparing samples of narrative. Although the observations here are based on limited analysis of data from just two cultures, Guugu Yimithirr-and Tzeltal-speaking communities, and thus must be considered tentative, everything I say here seems in accord with parallel work by other colleagues (see, e.g., Haviland 2000). One embarrassment is that we do not have much carefully coded data freely available for comparison from comparable natural contexts for the gesture systems in our own Western languages – the study of gesture is still an underdeveloped field.[22] I will therefore use as my main counterfoil the observations of gesture in experimental contexts by McNeill (1992). The following comments are based on a comparison of narratives in Tzeltal and Guugu Yimithirr on the one hand, and English on the other (Levinson 1996c), with supplementary evidence from Arrernte and Dutch speakers (de Ruiter and Wilkins 1998, Wilkins in press). This comparison does suggest systematic differences in the *morphology* of gestures in absolute vs. relative systems – that is, in the nature of the gesture space, the hand shapes involved, and

Table 6.3. *Gesture space: English (relative) vs. Guugu Yimithirr and Tzeltal (absolute)*

Gesture space	English all gestures		Guugu Yimithirr all gestures		Tzeltal all gestures	
Extreme periphery	25	(5%)	114	(50%)	86	(41%)
Periphery	187	(36%)	58	(26%)	70	(34%)
Centre	208	(40%)	36	(16%)	30	(14%)
Centre-centre	97	(19%)	19	(8%)	23	(11%)
Totals	**517**		**227**		**209**	

associated features of gaze and body position. I review some of these factors.

6.2.2.2.1 Absolute gestures are large and expansive. It is immediately evident that many of the pointings to places in both absolute cultures are made with fully extended arms, and thus lie naturally far away from the trunk. This contrasts with the data presented in McNeill 1992: 86–91 for American English speakers (said to be the same for speakers of other European languages), where the vast majority of gestures occur right in front of the trunk. A proper quantitative study would require a survey of a range of different genres, which has not yet been undertaken. But a rough calculation comparing statistics derived indirectly from McNeill's diagrams for American English gestures accompanying film-narrations with my own analysis of a seven-minute sample of Guugu Yimithirr historical narrative by one speaker, and a seven-minute sample of Tzeltal mythical narrative by one speaker, can be presented as in Table 6.3.[23]

There are some immediate and striking differences in Table 6.3 between the gesture space in the English data on the one hand and the Tzeltal and Guugu Yimithirr data on the other. But there are some obvious methodological problems, concerned with uncontrolled subject matter and other factors, which we should consider first. Unfortunately, there will be no easy way to control for genre across cultures – although one might hope to do so, for example by getting participants to retell the stories on wordless movies, such an activity builds in cultural presumptions of its own. The right way to do the comparison is simply to collect and process large amounts of data from daily natural interactions, a truly daunting enterprise because coding gesture is a deeply time-intensive operation involving many practical difficulties depending on camera angle and the like. Meanwhile, we must be content with little random samples that intuitively seem normal for the language and culture, and I proceed here on that basis.

Let us return to the facts in Table 6.3. Even for McNeill's category of deictics, that is pointing gestures that usually have some clear spatial reference, only 22% of American gestures lie in the 'extreme peripheral' area, that is, outside a square from the knees to the forehead.[24] In contrast, for all Guugu Yimithirr gestures taken together, 50% lie in this extreme peripheral area. Those Guugu Yimithirr gestures lying in the centre and centre-centre region (that is roughly in a square from the shoulders to the waist) tend to be there for highly motivated reasons: they are (1) associated with non-spatial gestures of a kind McNeill would call 'metaphorical' meanings (e.g. 'finished'), (2) with special conventions (e.g. counting on the fingers), (3) with reference to one's own body (e.g. in association with 'my heart was thumping'), (4) with reference to down-ward motion, (5) circumspect reference to taboo persons (e.g. the dead), (6) to mark a remark as a conversational aside. In contrast, this central area is where 60% of English gestures occur, mostly metaphoric and iconic gestures. The Tzeltal data pattern like the Guugu Yimithirr data: there is much greater use of the extreme periphery, and the centre loca-tions have many conversational asides, 'beats' or 'metaphorical' gestures, while the centre-centre location is almost exclusively filled by two-handed gestures that are either metaphorical or pointing vertically downwards.

In the two absolute-language communities, then, three-quarters of all gestures are at the periphery (extreme or less extreme), implying 'large' gestures with fully or partially extended arms. These large absolute gestures are not only found with pointing, but also with the depiction of absolute trajectories, where the extended arm may rotate 180 degrees around the shoulder, following, for example, a description of a motion event. Although pointings at full arm length no doubt do occasionally occur in our own familiar gesture systems (as in route directions), these extended trajectory gestures would, I think, be vanishingly rare in our own system.

Why should absolute gestures have this quality? One likely explana-tion is that they often carry fairly exact indications of direction, and the greater the line between shoulder and hand the more accurately the observer can judge the indicated angle. Consider, for example, the virtue of big analogue clocks in railway stations. Equally, the producer would be able (although, as remarked on below, this is not actually the norm) to sight along the arm to direct the trajectory accurately.[25] An-other likely explanation is that, because centre gestures are reserved for special effects (including non-spatial meanings) as mentioned, gestures

Table 6.4. *Dutch (relative) vs. Arrernte (absolute)*
gesture space

Gesture space	Dutch all gestures		Arrernte all gestures	
Extreme periphery	23	(29%)	55	(55%)
Periphery	34	(42%)	32	(32%)
Centre	12	(15%)	11	(11%)
Centre-Centre	11	(14%)	2	(2%)
Totals	**80**		**100**	

with fixed bearings should be clearly moved out of that space – i.e. into the periphery.[26]

Confirmation of these differences between systems comes from an independent study by de Ruiter and Wilkins 1998, Wilkins in press. They compared Dutch and Arrernte speakers who were more closely matched in genre than the comparisons just made. Both sets of participants (four from each community) were elderly local residents, filmed in their local settings talking about locations and events in the region in which they had spent most of their lives. In this context, they naturally pointed to local places. Using the same grid categorization of gesture space, the distribution was as shown in Table 6.4.

Both groups were engaged in a similar enterprise, describing local events and pointing places out to an interviewer, and this required clear deictic gestures. Still, the same difference that we saw above is found here too. The difference is best captured by another measure, namely gestures with fully extended arm vs. flexed arm (bent at the elbow): 57% of Arrernte gestures were fully (or near fully) extended, and only 11% of the Dutch gestures.

6.2.2.2.2 Involvement of both hands in depicting a single motion or direction. A partial consequence of these expansive gestures may be a tendency for gesture to be more evenly distributed across the dominant and non-dominant hands.[27] Those speaking European languages are known to favour gestures with the dominant hand (McNeill 1992: 329–32). Again, proper quantitative data is required here, but our test sample suggests that over 30% of Guugu Yimithirr gestures are performed with the left hand only, even by right-handed speakers. In contrast, some European samples show as little as 5% of gestures with the left hand only. Table 6.5

Table 6.5. *Right- vs. left-handed gestures by right-handed speakers in three languages*

	Right hand only	Left hand only	Both hands	Total
Guugu Yimithirr	58%	32%	10%	n = 172
Swedish	69%	5%	26%	n = 245
French	58%	12%	30%	n = 484

shows a comparison of the Guugu Yimithirr sample with a French and a Swedish sample studied by Marianne Gullberg (data by kind permission).

Caution is in order for such small samples, but these figures suggest that the left hand may be significantly more often in play in absolute right-handed gesturers than in relative gesturers.[28] But in addition to this quantitative evidence, there is also qualitative evidence for a differential involvement of the hands in relative vs. absolute gesture systems. One is a striking kind of gesture in which absolute gesturers will transfer a large trajectory started with one hand to be finished by the other, in accompaniment to a single intonational utterance, thus allowing, for example, a large sweep across the front of the trunk.[29] Given the preference for large gestures, this may simply be motivated by biomechanical constraints: a large 2-metre sweep by one hand across the body would require extreme twisting of the torso (see below). Another phenomenon, noted by David Wilkins for Arrernte gesturers, is the tendency to use whichever arm lies in the appropriate direction to be gestured: locations to the left side of the body are gestured at with the left hand, to the right with the right. In the Arrernte vs. Dutch study reported above, he found that Dutch participants made 17% of pointings contralaterally, but no Arrernte speakers made any such pointings across the body. In a further study of eight Arrernte children of increasing ages from 1;8 to 16 years, he found a statistically reliable increase of left-handed gestures over age – clearly Arrernte children have to learn this preference for the use of both hands, which is required by a cultural ban against contralateral pointing (Wilkins in press).

What may lie behind the dispreference for contralateral pointing in absolute gesture systems? One explanation here is that if the right hand were used to point to locations on the left side, it would (unless the trunk is twisted) end up across the body – thus failing to provide the clear silhouetted line between shoulder and hand that allows accurate direction to be judged. In my Guugu Yimithirr data there are clear pointings by the right hand to the left side, but they constitute about only 8%. of pointings, including on the one hand veiled references to taboo persons, and on the other the endpoints of large directional vectors begun on the far right. On the whole, then, the Arrernte pattern is repeated in the Guugu Yimithirr data. This pattern, if systematic, would predict that the use of the right hand would depend more on the contingencies of what one is talking about (and therefore the absolute locations referred to) than on any general favouring of the right hand.[30]

6.2.2.2.3 'Awkward' gestures towards the body and behind the body: 2D vs. 3D gesture systems. In our own gesture system an index finger would seldom point at the self to indicate other than self-reference. But in an absolute gesture system, where a pointing is used to establish a direction regardless of the body's position, this is not an exceptional occurrence: one way to point to locations at the rear is to point at a shoulder or to one's flank, or even through one's face as it were. Vectors that continue 'through the self' are indicated towards one's chest. This observation perhaps has some bearing on the 'disembodied' kind of spatial reckoning involved in an absolute system of coordinates: the self becomes as it were wholly transparent.

Also reasonably frequent are gestures to the rear of the frontal plane – such gestures may reach right behind the body and involve some trunkal torque. McNeill's (1992) study of (mostly) American gesture ignores this possibility, since the coding of gesture space is done in terms of extension in the frontal plane only, as if participants were scribbling on a blackboard – and quite rightly since there is little reason for us to gesture behind the body in our system: we generally rotate the depiction to suit our body position. American 'gesture space can be visualized as a shallow disk in front of the speaker...Adults usually perform gestures within this limited space' (McNeill 1992: 86). In contrast, Guugu Yimithirr or Tzeltal gesture space consists of a 2-metre sphere, with the front 180 degrees much more heavily used but the full 360 degrees being available.[31] It is the difference between an essentially two-dimensional and a fundamentally 3D system.

A speculative point is worth raising here. Relative spatial coordinates are fundamentally congruent with our visual experience, absolute spatial descriptions are not. Consider an array with cup to left of teapot on a table: cup is in left of visual field, it is "to the left" in English, but is, say, 'to the north' in Guugu Yimithirr. If we now go to the other side of the table, cup is "to the right" of teapot in English, and the cup is now in the right visual field. But in Guugu Yimithirr the cup remains stolidly north of the teapot, from whichever angle you look at it. Absolute descriptions can thus categorize mirror-image visual arrays (not to mention other visual incongruities) under the same description. Thus visual and spatial cognition are much more closely interconnectable by using relative co-ordinate systems: spatial memory can become visual memory, spatial calculations can be done in visual imagery. Now there is a long-standing strand of speculation that gesture in familiar languages may be hooked directly to visual imagery. If so, English gesture may inherit some of the properties of visual representations and mental imagery. Thus perhaps 'the shallow disk' characterization of relative-system gesture spaces is some kind of a direct reflex of Marr's 2.5D visual representation: a viewpoint-relative system with only partial depth information. The small disk size might even be relatable to Kosslyn's (1980) properties of mental imagery, where resolution dims towards the edges of the 'mental screen'. Absolute-gesture space on the other hand, being less closely hooked to vision and mental imagery, is freed from these constraints, and adopts a fully 3D representational system.

A telling detail has been noted by students of European gesture (e.g. Calbris 1990): where gestures behind the body occur, the index-finger point is transformed into a backwards pointing thumb over the shoulder, and the same has been noted for Japanese speakers using another relative system by S. Kita. This little opposition between the index finger and the thumb underlines the fundamental asymmetry in our kind of system between the front of the body and the back. In contrast, absolute systems of gesture do not typically change hand-shape character as they pass behind the frontal plane – these are fully 3D systems with the same hand-shapes behind as in front.[32]

6.2.2.2.4 Complex vectors indicated in a single gesture flow. Large, correctly oriented gestures allow the representation of complex planes and vectors. Absolute gesturers exploit this possibility, in at least three different ways:

a. A two-dimensional plane, represented by the flat hand, can be angled in three dimensions, to represent, for example, the exact angle of a mountain-side in its correct orientation, or a curled hand can be used to signify a particular eastern curved bank in the course of a river.
b. Some gestures have a kind of double articulation: they are oriented in one direction by the arm movement, but the hand is used to indicate

an independent angle.[33] For example, a boat drifting sideways blown by a south-east wind can be indicated by moving the arm aligned north-west with the hand held orthogonally.

c. Large sweeping gestures depicting motion or alignment allow detailed modulation to represent complex trajectories. Thus a single sweep of the hand from north to south may veer west midway to indicate the actual track of the motion. At their most complex, these are spectacular manutechnics, for example a single flowing gesture may indicate motion from the south turning now to the east and then returning along the same path to the west.

Many such gestures will encode features of the scene that are not represented in the accompanying speech, the analogue nature of the gesture channel here being used to maximal advantage.

6.2.2.2.5 Veracity of both path segments and overall 'map'. When giving route-directions in English in the street, I may well start by pointing in the correct direction for the first leg of the route, but soon I shall transfer the viewpoint to the body moving forward in transit – thus myself turning left and right from the position imagined on the route, with my trunk indicating the currently described direction of motion. As a result, it is quite unlikely that the gestures indicating later segments of the route will be in anything like the correct absolute direction from the place of speaking (see Kita 1998, in press a, for corroboration from another relative language).

Absolute gesturers will avoid this if they can: they aim to gesture each path segment in the correct direction, but in such a way that the end-point of the gestured map retains the correct angle from the place of speaking, or at least from a clear point of reference established in the description.[34] This no doubt corresponds to the different ways in which we and they use 'maps': if you ask a Dutch man to draw a local map he is likely to orient it according to the initial path, and to follow what Tolman called a 'strip map' that no longer preserves overall metric properties or directions; if you ask a Guugu Yimithirr or Tzeltal speaker they will draw the map so that it preserves the correct orientation with respect to the landscape, and they will attempt to preserve metric proportions and directions. We will return to what this says about cognitive maps below.

6.2.2.2.6 Gesture and gaze are independent, often disengaged, systems. David Wilkins has noted that, while, in our own cultural pointings, gaze in the appropriate direction usually precedes the gesture, in Arrernte the pointing is, especially in exposition, often not accompanied with gaze at all, but if so, the gaze may follow. I believe that both the Tzeltal and Guugu Yimithirr gesturers tend to follow the Arrernte pattern. Indeed, in both Guugu Yimithirr and Tzeltal it is notable that on large emphatic pointings the head is sometimes bowed right down, thus symbolically dissociating gaze and gesture. Thus it is quite normal to find large precise indications of direction made without any visual monitoring of the landscape or the arm; and this is so even when the gestures fall backwards behind the body – the full 3D gesture space can be used without any gaze in the indicated direction. Sometimes gaze will then be simultaneously directed at the recipient to check comprehension of the gesture. Where gaze does align with the direction gestured, it seems to carry specific discourse functions: to introduce new referents, to enact or embody the gaze direction of the participants in the narrative, to indicate where one would look to find the indicated referent if one was actually located at the narrative centre now established, and so on.

In contrast, when pointing to locations, relative-system gesturers are likely to look in the direction in which they are pointing, as shown by studies of route-directions (Kita 1998, in press a). There are no doubt exceptions, as in the conventionalized thumb-point over the shoulder to locations in the immediate vicinity (like the office next door) or to locations that have just been previously established, but by and large we look to ascertain where we should point. This difference between relative and absolute gesturers in the need to look at where they point would seem to be directly relatable to the differences in their underlying orientational systems. For, as we have seen, Tzeltal and Guugu Yimithirr speakers use languages that presuppose constant orientation on the part of their speakers – and the same goes for Arrernte speakers – and the speakers of all three languages can be shown to be constantly aware of their orientation with respect to the cardinal directions or other locations for miles around. In contrast, we have seen that Europeans have only very modest abilities to point accurately to where they have been. Thus it is likely that the European pattern of gaze-plus-pointing is a direct consequence of the fact that we need to visually search for the direction we have in mind, it not being given to us automatically by a constant background computation of head-direction as seems to occur amongst our absolutely oriented brethren. In absolute systems gaze is freed from this direction-finding role to be employed for other functions, as mentioned above, even for indicating direction by itself (gaze and head-tips may substitute for handed pointings, especially if the hands are otherwise occupied, e.g. carrying a child or weaving a net bag).

6.2.2.2.7 Body torque occurs only as demanded by the biomechanics. A closely related observation is that there appears to be a contrast in the degree to which the orientation of the trunk is involved in giving directional pointings in the two kinds of system. Absolute gesturers do not move their trunks simply in order to point behind them, although they may have to do so if the gesture involves a large arm movement or there are other biomechanical constraints. One may easily find examples where a speaker gestures in rapid succession to a series of points around him with the torso held rock-steady.

Relative gesturers may also restrict movement of the torso most of the time, but just for the reason that they appear to restrict gestures to the central part of the torso (as in McNeill's restricted 'shallow-disk' gesture space, mentioned above). However, when relative gesturers do wish to use deictic gestures in the correct directions, as when giving route-directions, they would appear to turn their trunks for other than biomechanical purposes: they wish to align their bodies, for example, with the direction in which a traveller would move in order that they can easily compute whether a next turn would be right or left (Kita 1998, in press a). Just as they use gaze to search out direction, they use body alignment to help construct a corporealized Kantian spatial description. Thus both body-alignment and gaze serve the purpose of aiding computation of direction for relative gesturers, while in the decorporealized orientational systems of the Guugu Yimithirr or Tzeltal sort, directional computation involves other faculties – the absence of body-alignment directly indicating the absence of a body-schema at the heart of such systems of spatial reckoning.

6.2.2.2.8 Iconic and absolute gestures can be fused even on diagonals. Many analyses of gesture take directional pointings to be distinct in type from depictions of shape, kind or manner of action, and the like. McNeill (1992), for example, distinguishes deictics from iconics along these lines, the typology presupposing limited possibilities of fusion between the types.[35] For example, although we may compound manner and direction of movement in a single gesture (as in a depiction of bouncing to the left), it seems unlikely that we would feel it incumbent on ourselves to preserve the *precise* angle of a fallen tree or a swerving truck – indeed the observer's viewpoint, McNeill has noted, is often replaced by an imagined participant viewpoint. The reason is perhaps that a relative system builds in a particular viewpoint, and there may be nothing privileged about a particular viewpoint: we might have approached the fallen tree from the other side. Thus there is a private, accidental feature to the information about viewpoint that makes it often of little communicational import.[36]

The nature of our relative gesture space is also a relevant factor here: we flatten out our 3D imaginings into 2D shallow disk or shield in front of our bodies where the bulk of our gestures occur. These two facts – the irrelevance of a particular viewpoint and the (more) 2D gesture space – conspire to create a 'virtual space' or scratch-pad aligned with our trunk. Perceptions and stimuli are likely to get rearranged to fit. Hence diagonals across our visual field, especially in the horizontal plane, seem likely to get reduced to parallels to our frontal plane.[37] The net effect may be that iconic gestures are likely to lose their relative orientation, especially if they do not fit the gesture space.

In contrast, absolute gesture systems with their 3D character allow a natural fusion of descriptive imagery and direction. For example, a Tzeltal gesture to where a church used to be uses the fingertip to gesture its demolition in a landslide from a specific direction. Mountain contours can be described in the correct alignment, cliff-falls sketched in their actual direction of fall, a fallen tree described in the alignment that it actually has, and so on. This makes it likely that 'iconic' gestures will be inspected for their full potential directional information: for example, when a yacht's sails are gestured with the palm upright as flapping into wind, this may be taken as an accurate depiction of the wind direction.

6.2.2.2.9 Conventionalizations along 'natural' lines. As Kendon (2000) has argued, gesture systems may well acquire conventional hand-shapes and entire complex motor sequences may come to have stable semiotics. At this point one might expect absolute systems of gesture to diverge from one another along the lines of their own cultural conventionalizations. And so they do. However, the systems that I have seen continue to share some properties even in this conventionalized sector of the system, for reasons that must have to do with natural associations. For gesture, like prosody, has an analogue basis, encouraging iconic associations.

Consider, for example, the association between the height of a pointing gesture and distance to the place indicated. As things get further away on a horizontal surface, they rise vertically in our visual field. This suggests a natural scale of distance for pointing gestures. However, a process of conventionalization is involved, because in both the Tenejapan and Guugu Yimithirr systems the hand may elevate way beyond the horizon and up into the sky in order to indicate really distant places. Moreover, if the places indicated are actually visible, the convention is not employed.[38] In both these societies people gesture as if the world were a deep bowl with themselves (or other reference point) deep down at the centre. Guugu Yimithirr 'distant location' gestures (pointing to the rim of the bowl as it were) rise to about 60 degrees maximally from the horizontal, as do Tzeltal ones; David Wilkins reports about 50 degrees maximal for Arrernte.[39]

Another kind of iconic association shared across absolute systems is between index-finger pointings for places, and flat-hand gestures for vectors and alignments. The index finger individuates, and by contrast the whole hand suggests a vector or a plane, in both the Guugu Yimithirr and Tzeltal systems. In other absolute systems like the Arrernte one (Wilkins 1999), where there are sets of conventionalized hand-shape distinctions (e.g. index plus little finger to indicate vector of motion) the index finger continues to be used to point to places. Thus the flat hand can be used to indicate oriented sides – these absolute 'side' gestures are precisely angled in three dimensions to capture the intended orientation (e.g. for a mountain slope that faces west and is 60 degrees to the horizontal).

There are many less obvious, iconic associations common to both Tzeltal and Guugu Yimithirr and other absolute systems (see Levinson 1996c, in press). One of these conflates time and space, through pointing at sun (or moon) position as an indication of time past or future. Again the analogue precision of this system is exploited to the full. To refer to remote times, at least in Tzeltal, the possibility exists of mapping time, a unilinear coordinate, on to the primary uphill-downhill coordinate, so that 'up' (southerly) events are in the future.

6.2.3 *Absolute gesture as an interactive system*

Gesture researchers are not agreed as to whether gesture is primarily a communicative system. Some scholars have put the emphasis on the internal psychological processes that gesture may subserve (McNeill 1992), for example in the facilitation of speech production (Morrel-Samuels and Krauss 1992), and point to the failure of gesture to systematically encode information (Krauss *et al.* 1991). Others champion what is perhaps the common-sense view that gesture is primarily motivated by communicative needs (Kendon 2000). The views are not necessarily inconsistent (as McNeill has tried to make clear in recent unpublished work): it is possible that gestures are designed so as to satisfy both internal needs and external customers. Still, the recent study of gesture in America or Northern Europe has certainly tended to undermine the view that gestures are primarily communicational in origin, function and intent (witness 'it is difficult to see how they could play an important role in communication', Krauss *et al.* 1991: 752). But from the perspective of the study of absolute gesture systems, where orientation and pointing are so predominant, the functions and motivations of gestures look fundamentally communicative in nature, whatever other functions they may have.

An absolute system of gestures lends itself to communicative uses for the following reasons. All absolute linguistic systems, i.e. systems of cardinal directions, are coarsely digital: they generally divide the horizontal into no more than four arcs, often 90-degree quadrants. But the sense of orientation on which they are parasitic is generally accurate to within 10 degrees of arc, as we have seen in the first half of this chapter. By supplementing the coarse lexical digital specification with a finer analogue system, they greatly increase the accuracy of the information conveyed, allowing detailed referential tracking by gesture (Levinson 1987a, b).

This provides ample reason for interlocutors to closely monitor speakers' gestures. That being the case, speakers can trade on it: they can gesture without the corresponding linguistic specification, saying something like 'he went' while gesturing 'north' (or rather a specific direction like 345 degrees in that quadrant). Once the availability of this second channel of communication is established, it offers further possibilities: in languages (like both Guugu Yimithirr and Tzeltal) where noun phrases can be freely omitted, one can associate places with protagonists and then by pointing establish who is doing what to whom (see Levinson 1987a), in a way reminiscent of the anaphoric system of American Sign Language. Thus we abruptly find ourselves in a quite different kind of communicational system, where information that could be in the verbal channel is systematically distributed across two quite different channels, gesture and language.[40]

Observers of our own kind of system have suggested, on the contrary, that 'Humans use two quite separate languages each with its own function' (Argyle and Trower 1979: 22), wherein 'the non-verbal channel is used for negotiating interpersonal attitudes while the verbal channel is used primarily for conveying information' (Argyle 1967: 49; both quoted in Beattie 1983: 5). However, it is easy to show that speakers of absolute languages utilize both channels to carry the very same kind of information (up to the limits of the medium): information conveyed originally through one channel is picked up and surfaces in the other. Thus a gestural specification of direction may be queried linguistically by the interlocutor, and a linguistic specification echoed by an interlocutor's gesture. The following interactional phenomena are all evidence of this close interrelationship between channels:

1. *evidence of gesture monitoring*, as when an interlocutor verbalizes a prior gestural specification of direction;
2. *use of gesture in place of words*, as when a speaker produces a gesture in the temporal space immediately after an incomplete linguistic string;
3. *the holding of gestures while seeking for agreement*, as when a speaker having specified a location by gesture holds his arm extended until recognition is signalled;
4. *gestural correction*, as when a prior gesture is queried by the interlocutor who makes a gesture in another direction as a candidate correction (often with the effect that both participants have their arms simultaneously extended).[41]

It may be that none of these are peculiar to absolute gesture systems – for example, Kendon (personal communication) reports feature (2) above for quotable gestures in Naples, Italy.[42] But the uniqueness of the interactional use of the gesture channel is not the point. The thesis here is that absolute gesture systems are in fact different in their underlying semiotics, and as a result encourage the kind of cross-channel spread of propositional information in a way that relative gesture systems cannot easily achieve.

6.2.4 Summary: absolute vs. relative gesture systems

In the sections above, I have tried to characterize what the Tzeltal and Guugu Yimithirr gesture systems have in common, and how these features may be motivated by the underlying absolute coordinate systems employed in language and cognition. Another complementary way to proceed would be to look at our own system, and try to explain why it has the features it does given the relative system of coordinates that underlies it. It is easy to see how such an account might go:

1. We create a virtual space in front of us, the 2D scratch-pad mentioned earlier. This reflects the importance to the relative system of the visual array – our gesture system is flat, as if it were re-projected directly from a retinotopic array (in such an array, the focal area is narrow – the

area behind us is blank of course, and depth in front is only indirectly inferred, unlike top and bottom and left and right which are real dimensions).

2. When forced to think outside this virtual space, for example because we want to point to real locations, we may start by gazing around to get our visual orientation. To reconstruct locations beyond our visual field, we try to imagine our body progressing in a strip-map (à la Tolman 1948), hence we orient our shoulders in the direction of virtual motion, making it easier to compute left and right turns, and from that the angle of travel; if we wish to describe landmarks met on such a route, we imagine the view from that location, and point and gaze at the virtual snapshot our visual memories make available (see Kita 1998).

From all this it follows that our gestures are mostly small and in front of us, that gestures behind us will normally be accompanied by a turning of the trunk, that pointings will be associated with gaze, and so on. In contrast, an absolute coordinate system is fundamentally detached from visual memory, and viewpoint information has to be thrown away in favour of cardinal direction information (hence our participants performing the 'animals task' under rotation, as described in Chapter 4, reconstruct a line of animals they saw heading left as now heading right in order to keep the cardinal orientation constant).

I have tentatively identified altogether ten putative features of absolute gesture systems, beyond their core semiotic defining properties, which are collectively distinctive compared to relative systems:

1. Gestures are large.
2. Two hands are more often involved.
3. The systems are full 3D systems, with gestures pointing through the 'transparent' body and behind it.
4. Complex sequences of exact vectors may be indicated in a single gesture.
5. Such gestures allow not only for correct fixed bearings but also by elevation for distances so that overall 'maps' remain correctly maintained.
6. Gaze can be released from orientational functions.
7. For the same reason, the trunk is relatively stable in such 'disembodied' systems of spatial reckoning.
8. Iconic and orientational information can be fused without idealization of direction.

9. There are detailed parallels in conventionalization across such systems.
10. Such systems play a demonstrable role in interactional communication, as measured by various further features (such as gestural correction).

Although all of these features can be explained (I have argued) by virtue of the underlying absolute semiotics, they are not all on a par.[43] For example, the interactive features (point 10) follow indirectly from the advantage that an analogue gestural system offers to a linguistically coarse cardinal-direction system, to which it is ultimately hooked. This analogue precision is then exploited, requiring careful monitoring by interlocutors. But systems of other kinds – especially perhaps systems with high numbers of conventional 'quotable gestures' or 'emblems' (like the Neapolitan system described by Kendon 1995, 2000, in press) – may also motivate close monitoring with many of the same interactive properties as outcome. So some (or more likely some aspects) of the properties in the above list may be due to heavy communicational loading, for which fixed coordinate systems provide only one possible motive. For example, the shape of the gesture space may be partially related to high-communication loading: thus, both Kendon's Neapolitans and Müller's (1998) Spanish gesturers use larger gestures in a higher frontal gestural area than English or German speakers, perhaps iconically related to the broadcast quality of these systems. But neither of these high-communication systems features the full 3D spaces of absolute gesturers. On the other hand, some of the features listed above are clearly specialized to the decorporealized spatial thinking lying behind absolute spatial systems: for example, the gestures through the 'transparent' body, the absence of the use of gaze and body torque to help with spatial computation, and the exploitation of complex spatial vectors. It will take a great deal more comparative gesture work before we are clear about all the causal factors here.

6.2.5 Deixis and absolute gestures

These ten properties of absolute gesture systems can be used to pre-emptively undermine a possible counter-argument to the thesis here being advanced. My argument is that absolute gestures are different in kind. The counter-argument is that they are simply one kind of gesture that we all use, but here writ large. In short, absolute gestures are just *deictic* demonstrative gestures, and the thing that makes them seem so different in absolute gesture cultures is that the world has been reconstrued as a giant invisible, but discernible, array of objects that can be pointed at, the world reduced to a virtual bowl. It is as if the extraordinary orientational system of absolute speakers makes available to them the kind of 'head-up display' that modern fighter pilots have projected onto their visors – invisible locations and objects are projected there, allowing instant access to an invisible world.

Thus when an absolute speaker points to such invisible locations, perhaps what we should compare such gestures to are the kind of gestures we ourselves would use to indicate, say, which of the visible mugs before me I have already drunk from. Such gestures preserve the correct direction, they are often made with fully extended arms, they have the same kind of fundamental communicational import, and they supplement the inadequate verbal specifications of proximal or distal deixis with more accurate analogue means. If necessary, they could be made by pointing behind ourselves, in which case we might use whichever hand was most conveniently placed, and if I point to the purple mug you might pick that up in speech and say 'Ah the purple mug', and so on and so forth. So is that all absolute gestures are, ordinary demonstrative gestures to an extraordinary projected invisible world?

The detailed semiotics of absolute and deictic demonstrative gestures do indeed have points of both similarity and contrast. For example, a detailed similarity is that it is possible to point demonstratively to an object that has an indirect relation to the thing referred to: for example, one can say, pointing at a newspaper, 'My great uncle used to own that' (intending the company that produces it) or one can remark, pointing at a just-deserted seat, 'He was very rude to me' (see Nunberg 1978).

However, a point of fundamental difference is of course that absolute pointings do not *require* any kind of deictic footing: 'north' does not have to be north of here, or north viewed from any protagonist's point of view (although it may often be so) – the reference point can be any object under the sun, and is quite normally an inanimate entity or another location.[44] Thus I can gesture 'north of that place' where that place is 100 miles from where we are speaking. Once again the central feature of absolute reckoning is its potential 'disembodiment'. Certain features of the local absolute coordinate system may show through in the structure of the virtual world gesturally indicated. This virtual world, as mentioned, is bowl shaped, like an upside-down planetarium projection, so that places far away are indicated by pointing higher up towards the rim. Unlike our virtual spaces, it is correctly oriented with respect to the actual world. But the Guugu Yimithirr linguistic system has a set of equal cardinal quadrants, while the Tenejapan system is based as mentioned on a cosmology of a tilted world. The distinctiveness of this Tenejapan system seems to show through in a tilted bowl: the rim is lower on the 'downhill' side, and places far away on the northern edges are indicated with lower gestures (at least by some speakers) than equidistant or even closer places on the 'uphill' side.[45] Thus again the overall character of the encompassing cosmology or allocentric 'mental map' shows through in a way that it probably does not in demonstrative deictic gestures.

Note incidentally that we now have an answer to a puzzle raised earlier in connection with the pointing experiments: How can one learn to point accurately to places one has never been to? This requires not only directional information but distance information too (otherwise one will not be able to point accurately to the same place from another location): the place has to be properly located on the mental map. Recollect von Frisch's (1967) honey-bees: when they do their communicative dance they signal both a polar coordinate and a distance to their fellows. Well, absolute gesture systems seem systematically to do this too (Levinson 1996c) – as we have seen, in both the Tzeltal and Guugu Yimithirr systems there is a systematic relation between the height one gestures and the distance indicated. Following the inverse Mercator projection, as it were, that maps the conceptual plane of the landscape onto a huge glass bowl surrounding the speaker: if locus A is further than B in the same direction, A will be above B on the wall of the bowl. This allows a speaker to point to anywhere in his world differentiating places not only by direction but also by distance. And this is the answer to the puzzle about how an observing listener could figure out from casual conversation where a place he has never been to must in fact lie.

Despite the exotic features of absolute gesture systems, there may nevertheless be some grain of truth in the attempt to see things in a universal light, by reducing the properties of exotic absolute gestures to the garden-variety demonstrative gestures of our own. But let us be clear about the fundamental differences I have sketched. Many of the features we have noted will not appear in our own deictic pointings to things in our visual field. We do not expect big hand movements indicating complex vectors, we do not expect pointing without gaze, we do not expect the fusion of iconic and orientational features that preserves diagonal angles on the horizontal, we do not expect the detailed parallels shared by

Tzeltal and Guugu Yimithirr in partial conventionalizations. Even if there is a germ of commonality out of which absolute gesture systems are constructed, in the hands of speakers of absolute languages these demonstrative-like features come to pervade the whole system.

For the comparative study of gesture, I have tried to establish a number of points:

a. Gesture systems differ cross-culturally.
b. They differ not only in, say, having a handful of 'emblems' or 'quotable gestures' that form a conventional inventory for a local community, but also in a number of fundamentals.
c. One of these fundamental differences is the quantity and quality of the communicational load taken by the gesture channel: for example, in absolute gesture systems truth-conditional information is happily conveyed in the gesture channel, and may then be picked up by an interlocutor in speech.
d. Another difference that follows is the care and consistency with which gestures are made and monitored – absolute gestures must add up to a consistent picture, and apparent inconsistencies will lead to inter-actional repair sequences just as verbal inconsistencies may do.
e. Absolute gesture systems end up using the body in different ways – arm movements are big, they use the whole 360-degree cylinder around the body instead of the small scratch-pad in front of the trunk as in English, and so on and so forth, as detailed above.

The function of systematic gestures in these absolute speech communities should now be obvious: linguistic specifications like 'north' are coarse, digital discriminations of direction; gestural specifications can be fine-tuned to the nearest 10 degrees or so, supplementing the coarse linguistic specifications. Moreover, gestural accuracy is important for learning how to dead reckon, upon which ultimately the coarser linguistic labelling depends. Gesture is part of the reason why children as young as four years old in Tenejapa have some grasp of the absolute system – without this ancillary semiotic channel it is hard to see how they could begin to master such abstract concepts as cardinal directions. Here it is useful to think of gesture as playing a role in a socially distributed system of spatial memory and computation (Hutchins 1995): recipients of gestural information can learn about locations, update their mental maps, or correct their interlocutors. We have seen how Guugu Yimithirr speakers can use this information to construct accurate mental maps of places they have never been to. And in Chapter 5 we saw how non-Aboriginal

Australians long resident in Alice Springs have come to partially acquire the mental habits of their Aboriginal interlocutors, not directly through Aboriginal languages (which they do not control) but probably through the gestures that accompany them.

It should be noted that this pattern of oppositions between relative and absolute systems is clearly just one way to look at gesture systems. Obviously, the typological split into absolute and relative gesture systems is not meant to be more than one way to cut the pie, and it is not likely to form any sensible cultural type: What do the Dutch and Japanese have in common, or the Tzeltal and the Guugu Yimithirr? Not much. But they do share a certain cognitive strategy with respect to coordinate systems for spatial reckoning, and a surprising number of properties of the gesture systems seem to follow from this cognitive specialization, which is in turn tied to the relevant language. So the point is this: it is a psychological style that is a crucial intervening variable between cultural forces and the physical comportment of the body. That is why a cognitive typology has some predictive power with respect to bodily use. Instead, we could do gestural butterfly collecting, and in that case we shall find plenty of differences between the Tzeltal and the Guugu Yimithirr. But that does not seem to me to be a useful direction to head in, and it is one that one hopes studies of gesture will avoid. In any case, for the student of spatial thinking, what makes gesture interesting is that it offers a glimpse, partially independent of language, into the spatial properties of thinking. What we see is an underlying congruence between linguistic representations and gestural ones, revealing a coherent but variable system of spatial reckoning.

I have mentioned that speakers of languages with relative spatial coordinates tend not to gesture accurate directions. But what happens when they describe the real world immediately around them? Schegloff (1984: 279) suggests that 'if the place referred to is visually accessible, then the point is in the direction of the referent'. My colleague S. Kita was curious about the veracity of gestures accompanying route directions in such speech communities. He has videotaped a score of route descriptions on a university campus in Tokyo, in Japanese, another language with a predominantly relative spatial coordinate system (Kita 1998, in press a). The majority of gestures (up to 70%, if one includes ambiguous ones) seem to be organized with respect to bodily coordinates, not absolute bearings, but in a campus setting quite a good proportion do reflect accurate pointings to the real locations. Most interestingly, speakers perform a quite elaborate bodily choreography, using gaze, torso orientation and different hands, suggesting that the body plays a kind of computational role in working out a route description from the information in memory. Quite typical is the following (abbreviated) sequence. A man is asked the way to the nearest subway station. Holding a bag in his right hand he turns to face a major road, pointing ahead of him: 'See that big road?' he says in effect. Now he shifts the bag from right hand to left and turns leftwards so that his trunk is angled as if going down that road, saying 'Go down the road'. Now he makes repeated gestures rightwards with his freed right hand: 'It's down an alley to the right' (this cueing of the linguistic terms 'left' and 'right' by the use of the relevant hand being a regular pattern). As we have already noted, relative-language speakers search visually for a local landmark in the first instance, and then point; second they align their heads and trunks in the imagined direction of travel and kinetically make the appropriate turns as if reliving the travel. Absolute-language speakers do not routinely do either of these two things – as mentioned, they do not need to look to point, and their body position tends to remain more or less steady regardless of the direction they are pointing in (Levinson 1996c). These kinds of difference suggest that a different kind of underlying spatial memory or 'mental map' is involved in relative vs. absolute communities, an issue to which we now turn.

6.3 DIFFERENT KINDS OF MENTAL MAPS

These observations about gesture systems are consistent with the following conjecture. Speakers of 'relative' languages may make primary use of what Tolman (1948) called *strip-maps*, consisting of (a) views of landmarks (hence the gaze associated with pointing), linked by (b) turns, which are encoded or primed or associated with kinaesthetic memory (hence the alignments of the body), and (c) paths (straight or constrained edges). Certainly, as one watches a route-describer twist and turn, one has the impression that the body is used computationally to recover or reconstruct the turns (Kita 1998). In fact just such a set of assumptions seems to be implicit in many of the recent models of human navigation based on experiments in 'artificial-reality' environments (see, e.g., Mallot 1996, who models human navigation in terms of directed arcs linking perspectival views of landmarks, thus dissolving even the integrity of places). On this account, our own navigational system (as opposed to that of, e.g., the Guugu Yimithirr) may often be *decidedly sub-rat*, Tolman (1948) having already fifty years ago elegantly showed that rats construct allocentric mental maps that allow creative short cuts. Beusmans (1996) reports that less than a third of Western participants running artificial-reality mazes seem to construct survey maps of the higher, rodent kind. So here is indeed a curiosity: the deprivation by culture of fitness-enhancing navigational skills in a big-brained ape who (in a different cultural setting) is perfectly capable of outperforming pigeons who are armed by evolution with advanced internal navigation aids!

Spelke and Tsivkin (2001: 72) evidently have had the same thought: 'even casual inspection suggests that one species is an exception to Gallistel's rule ["There is no creature so lowly that it does not know, at all times, where it is"]: *homo sapiens*'. They suggest that this failure must be compensated for by some special flexibility, and together with Herman they have carried out a series of experiments with infants testing the ability to find things again in a rectangular room after disorientation. They have made a spectacular finding: Western children up to two years (and in some conditions up to four) have a rat-like navigational system. Now rats have been shown by Gallistel and Cheng (see Gallistel 1990) to operate a navigational module (a closed system) which utilizes only geometrical information, and is impervious to additional visual or olfactory cues. They learn to find food by the angular qualities of a corner and not by, for example, the colour of a wall; they do not easily associate the location of the food with the coloured wall, which can be shown by moving both colour and reward together away from the geometrical corner the rat will look in. But children, on the other hand, just as they become competent speakers switch from the rat system to the multi-modal system, becoming open to associations between rewards and, for example, coloured walls. Spelke and Tsivkin suggest that language may play a special role in bridging ancient mammalian modules: we happily combine in language angular and other landmark information, as in 'to the left of the blue wall' (see also the speculations in Dennett 1991: 196). We are free to mix information from different systems, and we are even free to ignore the primacy of the allocentric geometric system that may come for free with mammalian genes. We are also free to vary, individually and culturally.

This explanation is still a little unsatisfactory in that it fails to explain why we relative-coordinate users would (or could afford to) throw away such an adaptive system as the rodent navigation module. But it can be enriched by the two following observations. The first observation only increases the puzzle. There is good reason to doubt that it is computationally possible to maintain a detailed survey map without a fixed-bearing system of the kind given by absolute coordinates. McNaughton *et al.* (1990) have pointed out the following simple point: if a survey map is constructed without absolute coordinates, each time one adds a landmark one must add the distances and angles to every other landmark, consequently the information expands roughly as the square of the number of landmarks.[46] Now it is true that there is a conceivable way around this computational abyss, namely to construct an artificial 'north' that is constructed out of the 'centre of gravity' as it were of the distribution of the landmarks (the demonstration is given by O'Keefe 1993), but this will not work in a constantly expanding area of exploration. The outcome is that extensive mental survey maps that maintain angles and metric distances between places seem to require absolute bearings like our north (then for each new landmark L you need only record the distance from L to some other locus A and the angle that A subtends from north at L). But knowing instinctively where north is requires extensive drill in orientation tracking, which is just what speaking a language with absolute spatial coordinates gives you. And since north is an entirely abstract artificial construct, equivalent to no single cue in the environment, it is not so clear that one would even invent it on one's own. And if one did, one would lose the communicational advantages given by following the local arbitrary convention (providing one is lucky enough to live in a speech-community that uses absolute coordinates). So speaking a language with absolute coordinates may directly facilitate mental-map construction, and speaking a language without such coordinates may indeed be a kind of cultural deprivation. There is, however, a significant cognitive overhead cost to absolute coordinate systems: your orientation and dead reckoning system must constantly tick in the background and never go on holiday.

The second observation may offer some explanation for the deprivation suffered by relative-coordinate users. As has been mentioned above, absolute and relative coordinate systems are not neutral as regards visual information. Relative-coordinate descriptions are fully congruent with visual memory. Thus given a snapshot of the breakfast table I can describe the (dis-)arrangement of jugs and coffee cups etc. on its surface; and vice-versa, from the description I could, in principle, remake the visual scene. But from a snapshot I cannot crank out an absolute description (unless 'north' is somehow inscribed upon the scene), and from the absolute description I cannot reconstruct just one privileged view so that I could remake the assemblage and take the same snapshot ('north' will not tell me what was at the front of the visual field) – absolute descriptions come without viewpoints. In a way, to think 'absolutely' one had better throw away visual memory: after all coffee-pot to left of cup becomes coffee-pot to right of cup from the other side of the table – but coffee-pot to north of cup remains constant regardless of the viewpoint.[47] If one opts for that (bee-like) system, one inherits its superior logical properties (e.g. transitivity of spatial relations without caveats), and one is encouraged to think in systematic metric maps that preserve angle and distance between landmarks in fixed bearings. If one opts instead to hook up spatial descriptions with egocentric visual viewpoints, one gets the bonus of recording directions partly in terms of systematically different views of landmarks (as in Mallot's 1996 'view-graphs'), but this road leads towards strip-maps and away from systematic metric 'survey' maps. In short: relative coordinate systems may favour 'piloting', navigation by constant reference to familiar landmarks, while absolute coordinate systems favour true 'dead reckoning' types of navigation. The two mindscapes may each have their own merits in different kinds of landscape.

How many distinct types of mental map are there, and how do they link up to the various distinctions between frames of reference made in Chapter 3 and elsewhere? Unfortunately, the conceptual distinctions relevant to mental maps have not been clearly worked out. But judging from explicit human cultural traditions of mapping, there are at least these importantly distinct kinds:

1. Strip-maps (one dimensional)
2. Unoriented survey maps (two dimensional)
3. Oriented survey maps (two dimensional with externally fixed coordinates)

Each of these connects landmarks, but in different ways – for example, Type 1 forms a directed graph with no branches, while Type 2 allows branches. Type 3 maps are distinctive in that, when you add a new landmark, the new landmark automatically inherits relationships with all other landmarks, but in Type 2 maps these new relationships may need laborious computation or real-world testing. The types also differ in frame-of-reference distinctions, but here one needs to distinguish the map itself from the relation between ego's location and the map. Just thinking in terms of the map itself (without ego in the picture as it were), Type 1 and 2 are orientation-free, Type 3 is orientation-bound. That means that no essential information is lost in the first two types if the map is rotated with regards to a larger framework (say longitude and latitude) – for these maps give us relative distances and angles between landmarks. Once we put ego's location into the map, the possibility arises of using ego's relative coordinates to orient the map – mentally, then, a map of Type 2 can be orientation-bound with respect to ego's coordinates (as can a map of Type 1, but because of its one-dimensionality, this will not transform its utility). Consider, for example, different mental maps of a complex building, say a giant international hotel. A cognitive strip-map will get me from my bedroom to the breakfast room, and another from my bedroom to the swimming pool. A survey map will tell me where the swimming pool is with respect to the breakfast room as well – it links up all the strips into an overall map. Now if I can orient the survey map with respect to my present location and orientation, I can even point at the swimming pool from wherever I am, thus allowing experimental short-cuts.

Interestingly, all three kinds can be found in the history of western cartography. Itineraries and maps based on them have come down to us copied from Roman times, and are evidently of the first type, being scrolls following major arterial roads (Dilke 1987). Medieval navigation charts, such as those covering the Mediterranean, were unoriented, and thus of Type 2: 'intended to be rotated, portolan charts have no top or bottom... there is no way of telling which, if any, of the four directions they were primarily intended to be viewed from' (Campbell 1987: 378). (Global medieval maps, more symbolic than practical, were mostly but not invariably oriented – hence the verb 'orient' – with east at the top.) Maps oriented by longitude and latitude, of Type 3, were of classical Greek invention, but effectively lost to the West till the translation of Ptolemy's *Geography* in 1407 (Woodward 1987).

However, other cultural traditions with explicit navigational systems suggest that there are other ways of thinking about movement through space. The three types of map above are *allocentric* – it takes an extra computation by piloting or dead reckoning to work out where ego is on the map, and to plot the course so far followed. The Micronesian indigenous navigation system in contrast appears to work in an essentially *egocentric* way: the navigator imagines the canoe to be fixed under the stars, and the world to be flowing past the canoe. Using star setting and rising points, he can then estimate his current position on a course by visualizing where (usually unseen) islands off to the side would now have arrived under specific star points. Mental maps of this sort would seem to consist of star-point headings (the course set from landfall to landfall) and a series of expected correspondences between times and landmark-to-star correspondences. Thus the navigator expects that the (often unseen) landmark will have moved from, say, close to the course heading at midnight to a position abeam of the boat at sunrise (see Hutchins 1995: 65–93). By maintaining an egocentric viewpoint, the navigator can integrate piloting information (from directly observed landmarks, including birds and special patterns of ocean swell) directly into the same format in which dead reckoning is done – thus avoiding the distinct methods of pilotage vs. dead reckoning in our tradition. Note that this Micronesian system uses absolute coordinates – star-setting points – and is thus like Type 3-oriented maps of our kind in this respect, but differs in using the observer's moving location as the origin of the coordinate system. This again shows the importance of distinguishing the *origin* of the coordinate system from the *type* of coordinate system (absolute, relative or intrinsic), a point made at length in Chapter 2.

The relation between these explicit navigation systems and implicit mental maps is unfortunately not clear, and a recent review notes that 'the principles of the organisation of the cognitive map are still obscure' (Save *et al.* 1998: 119). All we can show is that different animals act *as if* they utilized maps of different kinds (and as the Micronesian system shows us, there are quite distinct ways to compute similar or identical functions). Bees and desert ants clearly utilize computations that amount to an oriented survey map. Rats clearly utilize maps of both Type 1 and 2, with Type 2 survey maps allowing creative short-cuts. But there is no indication that rats have available absolute fixes that would allow the use of Type 3 maps. And there is no indication of such abilities anywhere in the primate order other than in human cultural systems.

There has been an active line of research in neuroscience on the brain bases for spatial thinking ever since the groundbreaking work by O'Keefe and Nadel (1978). Single neuron recording has isolated 'place cells' in the rat hippocampus which respond to specific locations defined at least in part by the geometrical properties of the test maze or box. Despite thirty years of experiment, it is still not entirely clear what external cues are involved (probably because rats also use uncontrolled odour and sound cues). The same technique has also revealed 'head direction' cells in the posterior parietal cortex which fire when the head is oriented in a specific direction with respect to a larger environment – the direction can be skewed by moving landmarks, suggesting a landmark plus inertial-reckoning (idiothetic) basis for computing direction (Sherry and Healy 1998). Since the hippocampus at least is a very conservative structure, and its relative size corresponds well to the navigational needs of different species, the overall picture is that mammalian neuroanatomy is geared to providing allocentric information about the organism's location and orientation with respect to landmarks – not with respect to fixed bearings. Now, interestingly, there is some evidence that the primarily spatial functions of the hippocampus in rats may have been invaded by other functions in the case of humans and other primates, where more general amnesia to 'declarative knowledge' follows from hippocampal damage (Squire 1992). Although the hippocampus is still implicated in human spatial memory (Maguire *et al.* 2000), it is possible that some loss of spatial abilities has been occasioned by the growth of new, more general memory functions for the hippocampus. It is just possible that this invasion of the 'spatial organ' by non-spatial functions accounts for the remarkable way in which spatial thinking seems to lie at the heart of much human reasoning (as reviewed in Chapter 3, section 3.2). In any case, in contrast to general allocentric memory for places, the capacity for fixed-bearing systems – the 'cognitive compass' innate in many arthropods and birds – seems to have no dedicated brain bases in humans, but rather seems to be reconstituted entirely from scratch by means of culture (by mechanical devices in Western cultures, and mental ones in the cultures favouring absolute frames of reference).

Returning now to the correlations we have found between dead reckoning skills and frames of reference in language, these clearly indicate different qualities of mental map. What kinds of errors of judgement lie behind the relatively poor estimates of spatial direction produced by Dutch or English participants? Such errors can lie either in bad estimates of angle, or bad estimates of distance, or both. For Western participants we have direct evidence on both counts. For example, fifteen residents of Cambridge (England) were asked by Moar and Bower (1983) to estimate angles from memory between local streets that form triangular arrangements – estimates systematically exaggerated angles towards 90 degrees, forming impossible triangles (with a mean excess of 45 degrees over the 180 maximum). The same study showed distance estimates also to be influenced by perspective or direction of travel, and thus to be internally inconsistent (see also Moar and Carleton 1982). Without good distance and angle estimates there is no possibility of constructing or maintaining a good mental map, and in fact the evidence seems to show that Western adults and children can build relatively good strip-maps, but fail to integrate them successfully into a survey map (Golledge *et al.* 1993). There is also evidence that Westerners build a special kind of strip-map, that is in certain respects logically deficient: instead of linking places or landmarks in a directed graph, it may link views (i.e. directionally dependent views of places). Such view-graphs cannot be reversed, and indeed Western participants seem worse at working out return trajectories (Gillner and Mallot 1997).[48] Western participants asked to draw route maps do not preserve metric angles (Tversky 1981, 1998), whereas Australian Aboriginals routinely draw maps in the sand when describing routes which do preserve fixed bearings precisely (Sutton 1998: 405–8, Wilkins 1997).[49]

In thinking about cognitive maps it is important not to lose sight of the fundamental computational function of maps, whether explicit cultural objects or implicit mental structures. The function of a map is *to make accessible the imperceptible by systematic relation to what can be perceived* (Gallistel 1990: 48). This is dramatically demonstrated by the Guugu Yimithirr ability to point to distant unseen places with the same surety that we point to places right before us. Our inability to do this demonstrates a fundamental cognitive difference.

6.4 SUMMARY AND CONCLUSIONS

Let me summarize. We began by noting that we cannot a priori assume any isomorphism between linguistic (semantic) representations and non-linguistic representations, for example of the kind that might be utilized in wayfinding. There are many reasons why these might be out of kilter. Thus the relationship between them is a matter for empirical investigation, which can be pursued by exploiting the cross-linguistic variation and seeing whether non-linguistic spatial representations do or do not co-vary in type with the linguistic ones.

In Chapter 5, a series of experiments were reported that suggest that there does in fact seem to be a tendency for at least some partial isomorphism in the kind of coordinate system employed in language and non-linguistic representations for memory and inference. Where languages are specialized in absolute or relative coordinate systems, non-linguistic representations follow suit. This is due not so much to Whorf's 'habitual thought' but to the systematic knock-on effects of a community-wide conceptual output system, namely a specific language, a point developed in the next chapter.

In this chapter we have gone on to see that speakers of languages with absolute coordinate systems turn out to be spectacular dead reckoners, at least as judged by pointing experiments. Correspondingly poor dead reckoning skills seem to be associated with speakers of languages using predominant relative coordinate systems. The explanation seems to be simply that languages of the former type effectively force a constant background dead reckoning system; this is the cognitive overhead for an otherwise highly superior linguistic and wayfinding system. It is hard to prove that language is the determinative factor; but an absolute system in language is probably a sufficient if not necessary condition for good dead reckoning skills.

In speech communities with languages favouring absolute coordinates, unreflective gesture provides a constant stream of confirmatory evidence for dead reckoning skills. In speech communities that prefer relative co-ordinate systems in language, gesture does not preserve fixed bearings. Instead, all the evidence from gesture points to egocentric strip-maps, in which kinaesthetic information about turns may play a direct role: the bodily coordinates named by 'left'/'right'/'front'/'back' systems seem reflected in the way the body is used as a computational aid in recovering route descriptions (Kita 1998). Finally, I have suggested that evolution may have left us (and perhaps the primates generally) with rather feeble native powers of orientation. Absolute ways of thinking, encouraged by language, gesture and culture, rebuild these powers artificially as it were. Obviously there are considerable advantages, especially in dead reckoning abilities, but there are also costs – ceaseless orienteering, and a decoupling of spatial memory from the view-centred systems of vision and motoric action. In contrast, a relative cognitive style offers the cognitive advantages of directly correlating spatial memory and the visual and motoric systems, and this may make for good piloting if bad dead reckoning. It also makes natural a whole way of organizing the cultural environment in egocentric coordinates, which has made possible many organizational foundations of complex societies, from traffic rules to writing systems, a point taken up in the final chapter.

Both wayfinding techniques and gesture appear at first sight to be excellent candidates for 'natural', acultural activities, largely determined by mammalian roots. But we have seen that this is not the case. An obvious general conclusion is that we must recognize that both 'human gesture' and 'human navigation' are not unitary phenomena, but are highly variable, partially cultural phenomena, like languages themselves, with which their properties seem to be intimately linked.

CHAPTER 7

Language and thought

7.1 TURTLES ALL THE WAY DOWN: MEMES AND MIND

Throughout this book, I have pursued the opposition between absolute and relative frames of reference, ranging through their underlying conceptual structure or internal 'logic', their linguistic expression, their use in non-linguistic memory and inference, and finally in gesture and wayfinding. We have noted that not all languages use both the relative and absolute frames, and when they are specialized in this way, the frames of reference run deep in the cognition of the speakers. There is a special point in following this twisting trail of evidence, and it is this: we may be able to learn something quite important about what, somewhat grandiosely, one might call the 'architecture of the mind' from cross-cultural observations of these sorts. An analogy may help: just like we can trace blood flow by injecting radioactive isotopes, or trace the course of an underground river system by dumping dye into a river before it goes underground, so by focussing on exotic semantic parameters and seeing where they turn up in 'inner space' – the range of internal representation systems – we can perhaps find out something important about our inner languages or representations and how they talk to one another.

In Chapter 1, I mentioned the strategy of research borrowed from Lucy (1992b), in which a linguistic difference in semantic type is first established, and then speakers of each type are pursued through a set of non-linguistic tasks, in the search for correlations between language and cognition. I can now review the progress I have made in the intervening chapters. In Chapters 2 and 3, I established the typology of frames of reference and showed how they could be brought into alignment across language and different aspects of cognition. In Chapters 4 and 5, I showed how the properties of the different frames of reference allow non-verbal tasks to reveal different patterns of mental coding under rotation, and I then used a range of rotation tasks to explore this coding through different aspects of non-verbal cognition, from recognition, to recall, to the transformation of observed motion to static path, and finally to transitive inference. The question was, if the language was predominantly absolute or, alternatively, relative, would the non-verbal performance follow suit? What we found is that, wherever we have the data (as in the full suite of experiments in Holland and Tenejapa), whatever dominant frame of reference we find in the language we also find echoed throughout every one of these other levels of non-verbal coding, as sketched in Figure 7.1. In Chapter 6, we looked at additional aspects of measurable behaviour – pointing and gesture – and again we found the same picture: speakers of a language in which the absolute frame of reference is dominant can accurately point at unseen places, and they do so routinely in conversation, while speakers of other languages do not appear to be able to do this.

The time has come to try to understand how this could be, and what its consequences are, that is, to place the findings in the context of the bigger picture, the relation between language and other cognitive faculties. In Chapter 2, I explored different kinds of conceptual distinction that have been proposed for different frames of reference across the senses and modalities. Very different kinds of system are going to be primary in, say, vision versus touch – the visual system is bound initially to a frame of reference akin to the relative frame of reference, while the haptic sense is more closely attuned to a 3D object-oriented reference system like the intrinsic frame of reference. Nevertheless, I came to the conclusion that these different systems can be largely brought into line, and the sensory systems must be able to build representations in different frames of reference. Otherwise we would not be able to visualize things that we feel in the dark, or recognize in the dark by touch things that we have seen in the light. But we noted that there are some distinct limitations to this inter-translatability across frames of reference. Specifically, it is not possible to transform a representation in a relative frame of reference into one in an absolute frame of reference, or vice-versa, without specific additional information (fixed-bearing information in the one direction, and viewer perspective in the other). This is ultimately the explanation for the divergence in cognitive style between absolute and relative thinkers I have been charting throughout this book. I will return to this point, but let me first assess where we are.

Before turning to the nature of non-linguistic cognitive representations of space, it may be useful to remind ourselves of the picture that emerged from Chapter 3 of the linguistic coding of spatial scenes. We have seen

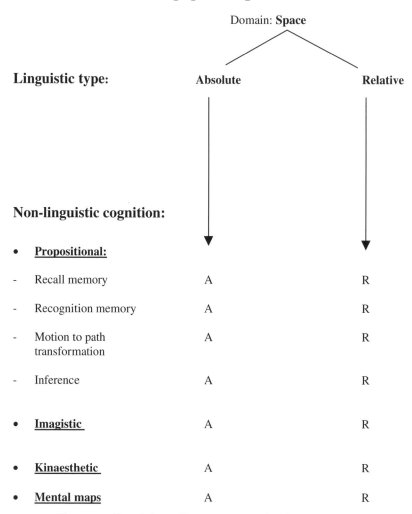

Figure 7.1. Correlations of language type and different aspects of
non-linguistic cognition

that, in addition to radial distance concepts as invoked in deictic discriminations, or topological concepts underlying a preposition like *at*, for the
frames of reference we need quite precise geometric representations. We
need, for example, to be able to specify orthogonal axes, the internal
geometry of objects, polar coordinate systems with angles of different
kinds, mappings of coordinate systems under rotation, translation or reflection, and so forth. Such precise geometry cannot be specified in the

topology-like representations that Talmy (1985, 2000) has argued underlie spatial semantics. But these properties could in principle be specified
in a propositional representation, that is some logic-like representation
of the kind normally presumed to form the basis for linguistic semantics.
A logic-like representation captures essential semantic properties like en-
tailment, contradiction, equivalence, converseness and so forth, which
form the basis for most of our semantic intuitions. Many linguists (like
those subscribing to cognitive linguistics) feel that linguistic representations involve an imagistic component (cf. Langacker 1987: 135–7), and
certainly the spatial semantic field, if any, ought to be a good candidate
for such representations. But there are severe difficulties here because we
need both precise geometry and semantic generality (over, e.g., metric
distances), and it is hard to see how imagistic schemata could deliver
both of these simultaneously. The upshot is that, for frame-of-reference
semantics, we seem to need at least a propositional representation, supplemented perhaps by a geometrical specification, as Jackendoff (1996)
has argued: the propositional representation can give us the logical inferences and the semantic generalities, while the geometrical specification
can give us axial and angular specifications.

Turning to the non-linguistic representations involved in human spatial thinking and performance, we saw in Chapter 2 that such representations must be multiple, and are probably numbered in the scores.
This is clear if one thinks even of a simple reaching gesture and counts
the different visual representation systems (from retinotopic to 2D to
3D), the different systems involved in calculating body orientation and
location (from vestibular, visual and other systems), and the different
kinetic systems involved in control of shoulder/arm, elbow, wrist and
finger movements. The kinds of representation that particularly concern
us here, however, are those involved in the abstract calculation of the spatial relation of one object to another, and those directly concerned in, or
required for, verbal and gestural communication about those locations.

We have found evidence for the same frame of reference being dominant in different uses of long-term memory – in recognition, constructive
recall and in logical inference about spatial relations. Arguably, just one
kind of representation is involved here, namely a single representation
of the spatial relations between things, capable of supporting logical
inference. This is perhaps not likely – consider, for example, the difference between recognizing the façade of a house versus drawing it from
memory. The representations involved in recognition may be much more
sketchy than those involved in recall, which is why we can recognize far

more than we can recall or reconstruct. The representations involved in inference may be somewhere in-between in specificity – inferring that the house across the street is taller than mine involves some kind of recall, but it can be sketchier than the information I would need to draw the facades. Let us concentrate on what kind of representation would be capable of supporting spatial inferences. This might be a *propositional* representation of some sort. For example, in the inference:

(1)   *The ball is to the left of the chair*
      The chair is to the left of the tree
      Ergo, the ball is to the left of the tree

a predicate-logic-like representation, together with an inference rule based on the transitivity of the relation *left of*, will be sufficient to capture the nature of the reasoning, as in:

(2)   *inference rule (meaning postulate):*
      $(\forall x)(\forall y)(\forall z) ((\text{Left-of}(x, y)\ \&\ \text{Left-of}(y, z)) \rightarrow \text{Left-of}(x, z))$
      inference:
      $(\exists x)(\exists y)\ (\text{Ball}(x)\ \&\ \text{Chair}(y)\ \&\ \text{Left-of}(x, y))$
      $(\exists y)(\exists z)\ (\text{Chair}(y)\ \&\ \text{Tree}(z)\ \&\ \text{Left-of}(y, z))$
      $(\exists x)(\exists z)\ (\text{Ball}(x)\ \&\ \text{Tree}(z)\ \&\ \text{Left-of}(x, z))$

However, Johnson-Laird (1996) argues forcefully that such representations, though adequate to the task of capturing spatial (and other) inferences, are unlikely to be involved in normal human reasoning about spatial representations. Instead, some more iconic spatial representation seems to be involved, a 'mental model', which would allow the above inference to be represented thus:

(3)   *Premise 1*   Ball   Chair
      Premise 2   Chair   Tree
      Conclusion   Ball   Tree

A mental model is not an image, for it is general or abstract over many such ball/chair/tree scenes, and in that respect it is close to the propositional representations representing linguistic meaning. So it is just the kind of representation that might be extracted from a linguistic utterance. But unlike propositional representations, in mental models the spatial axes are directly employed. Mental models, compared to propositional representations, have many desirable features: they match our intuitions, and indeed experimental data, about what constitute simple vs. complex spatial problems, they offer decision procedures where propositional representations do not, and they grade into inductive reasoning. And they explain the iconic power of diagrams, charts and maps in our everyday reasoning.

However, when we turn to navigational abilities and gesture, we are clearly into aspects of human performance where different kinds of representation are involved. The kinds of representation used in mental dead reckoning in humans (or indeed other animals) are not known, but, as mentioned in Chapter 6, such representations clearly involve multi-modal input from the sensory systems measuring rotation (largely the visual and vestibular systems) and measuring distance travelled (number of steps, mechanical effort, rate of optical flow). Such representations may be more analogue than digital, and in any case are unlikely to be in propositional format. As we saw, the nature of human mental maps may be very different in relative vs. absolute communities: strip-maps require only approximate distances, landmark views, and turns coded in bodily coordinates, while survey maps in fixed coordinates require the coding of exact metric angles and distances if they are to retain their economy and utility – the two kinds of representation may be plausibly assumed to be in rather different formats.

Less work has been done on the representations underlying gesture, but nevertheless there are some good ideas about the nature of gestural representation. Gestures are of various types, and in Chapter 6 I was concerned especially with so-called 'deictic' gestures (pointing to places or indications of direction), but 'iconic' gestures (which depict shapes and trajectories) are much the more frequent in, say, English narrations (McNeill 1992: 93). The underlying representational systems for these two different types have been assumed to be very different in kind: deictic gestures could be directly driven by reference to visible space, while iconic gestures might be driven by visual imagery. This may be an accurate picture for gesture in relative communities, where both kinds of representation would essentially be visual or imagistic information in a relative frame of reference. But it does not capture what we know about gesture in absolute communities, where directional pointings are quite normally to unseen, dead-reckoned places, and iconic representations are fused with absolute bearing information, so that, for example, a gesture indicating an angled mountain side will also indicate the correct cardinal orientation of the side. In this case, we are probably dealing with an abstract cognitive map in absolute coordinates which can be fused with imagistic information. Gesture is also of course closely tied to kinaesthetic representations (Kita 1993). Sometimes, as in the 'enactments' typical of children's gestures (McNeill 1992: Ch. 11), kinaesthetic information is what is depicted. But in all cases, gestures must themselves be directly driven by a kinaesthetic representation, governing the motions of the arm and hand. This kinaesthetic representation receives input, then, from visual, imagistic and dead reckoning systems.

We now have an inventory of the representation systems that seem to be involved in different aspects of spatial processing:

1. Propositional representations (possibly involving geometrical representations too), interfacing with language.
2. Geometrical representations, involved in axial and angular computations, for example in computing frame-of-reference information.
3. Mental models, or abstract spatial representations, translating easily to propositional representations and back.
4. Representations appropriate to a dead reckoning system, which may take inputs from many different representations, visual, kinaesthetic, geometric and especially cognitive maps.
5. Cognitive maps, which may themselves be hybrids of visual landmark representations and geometrical specifications.
6. Haptic-kinaesthetic representations, which interface with haptic input from touch, and gestural output in communication, this representation interfacing closely with mental maps, visual imagery and 3D object representations relevant to grasp or enactment.
7. Visual imagery, a 2D projection of 3D models, interfacing closely with actual visual representations.
8. Visual representations proper, which encompass a sequence of 2D representations, with added depth information (2.5D), processed upwards to reconstructed 3D representations.

In addition there are other representations that are tangential to the present theme, such as inertial information from the vestibular system yielding angular rotation measurements, or information from the otoliths in the inner ear indicating acceleration or vertical alignment.

The overall picture that emerges is thus a complex layering of spatial representation systems, driven initially by specific input/output systems (the senses, communication and action systems), but with many further internal layers of processing with their own internal representations. These representations themselves have restricted exchange relations with other representations, perhaps along the lines sketched in Figure 7.2.

Let me immediately deal with some likely objections to Figure 7.2. Of course, any 'blueprint for the mind' is laughably hubristic in our present

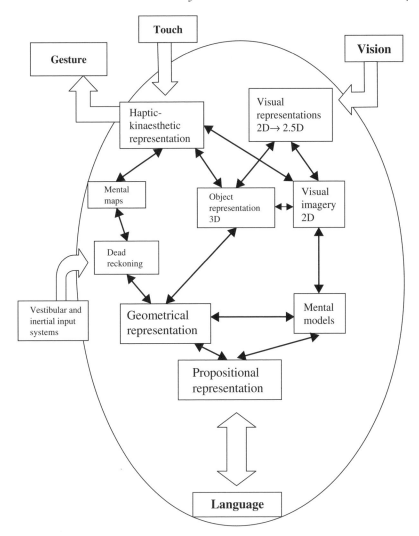

Figure 7.2. Some relations between spatial representation systems and their inputs and outputs

state of knowledge, but this should be interpreted just as a sketch of some basic spatial representation systems and their relations to one another (see Jackendoff 1996 for a similar exercise, which, however, underplays the different kinds of spatial representation).[1] Note that the relation between language and many other spatial representations is shown as quite indirect, perhaps in part reflecting the hemispherical specializations in the human brain, left for language, right for space. Some readers, linguists perhaps, may find such a diagram baroque. Why do we need to posit so many kinds of distinct levels of representation? The arguments for multiple representations are in fact precisely of the kind familiar to linguists, namely that certain representations seem required to support specific kinds of computation, and have to bridge across incommensurable representations – there is no direct mapping of vision onto language, and the inferences we can make in vision (e.g. of visual depth) have nothing to do with language, and vice-versa. In addition, there is indirect evidence in the form of selective brain damage for many of these levels of processing. Indeed, far from being too complex, such a diagram hugely oversimplifies the picture, isolating only major levels involved in central thought processes, and thus at least partially accessible to consciousness (see the references in Chapter 2 to other distinctions in the neuroscientific and cognitive science literature). Another kind of objection may be that such a model seems to proliferate 'mental modules' in areas where modularity theorists like Fodor have imagined one single, central representation in which general thinking takes place. But levels of representation do not map directly onto Fodorean modules – sometimes, as in syntax or phonology, we need multiple levels even within sub-components of an overall human ability. Modularity claims are additional claims about the 'encapsulation' of specific processes, and the evidence we have been accumulating is that frame-of-reference specialization in one level of representation can systematically influence those in others. Real Fodorean modularity may be confined to the input/output systems, that is, the interfaces between the senses or action systems and the representations essential in making those bridges to the outer world work. Yet another challenge might come from a connectionist perspective, where representations are demoted altogether. But nevertheless here too the functional properties of representations must be recaptured (see, e.g., Elman *et al.* 1996: 90–7).

If something like this picture is correct, then we can return to the central question. How far, through these inner representation systems, does the distinction between absolute and relative frames of reference percolate? That is, given that we have ascertained that a specific frame of reference is predominant in a language, how far into this world of inner languages does this preference penetrate? The answer appears to be, for the representations sketched, nearly all the way. Consider, for example, Tenejapan Tzeltal or Guugu Yimithirr speakers: recognition, recall, inference, all reflect the same absolute frame of reference found in their languages. Long-term memory thus codes for and preserves fixed bearing information. It probably does this in a range of slightly different formats, appropriate to fast recognition, slower and more complex recall, and careful spatial inference. Certainly propositional and geometrical representations, together with more abstract 'mental models', would need to be involved to account for the experimental data in Chapter 5.

But we can even find some evidence for the penetration of the absolute frame of reference in visual imagery – recollect, for example, from Chapter 4 that Guugu Yimithirr speakers describe recipes for action or recall dreams replete with fixed directions, while Tzeltal speakers can rebuild an assemblage of arbitrary complexity under rotation, building it as if it had been seen from the other side. The best account of this behaviour would seem to be that visual imagery is projected into an oriented mental space; just as we can hardly imagine our desks in the office without 'seeing' the telephone to the left and the computer to the right (or however it is disposed), thus interposing a point of view, so speakers of these languages when building a similar mental image seem to need to know which cardinal directions the major axes of the scene are aligned with, even in imaginary circumstances (see Emmorey 2001 for other data suggesting language-specific influences on mental imagery).

When we turn to the representations involved in wayfinding (as in Chapter 6), we find the same specialization of frame of reference in accord with the language. Absolute speakers need to know their 'heading' and their direction with respect to other locations in order to speak about the world – and they can only do this by running constant dead reckoning procedures in the background. These drive accurate mental maps – survey maps with fixed bearings – allowing speakers to point effortlessly, without looking, at unseen places they are describing. Relative speakers seem to use a quite different navigational mode, more akin to 'pilotage', with strip-maps constituted by landmarks, left/right turns and paths. Hence they cannot generally point accurately to unseen places. And when relative speakers gesture, their gestures preserve the right–left and towards–away axes of the stimulus or event described, not the actual bearings of events. Perhaps the most intriguing difference is that 'iconic' gestures, which depict such things as shape, in the case of relative speakers are viewer-based and in the case of absolute speakers are frequently locked into fixed coordinates. Visual imagery is here feeding gestural representation, and it comes plus or minus fixed bearings according to the language of the speaker. The kinaesthetic representations involved in absolute vs. relative gesture systems are also different – not only are fixed bearings preserved in the former, and not in the latter, but also there are many concomitant features associated with the motor patterns: absolute gestures are large, involving the full arm, are not guided necessarily by gaze, and constitute a much more fully fleshed semiotic system which can be read by interlocutors for rich analogue detail, as spelled out in Chapter 6.

Coming back to the analogy raised at the beginning of this section, if we pour blue (absolute) or red (relative) dye into our stream (language) as it dives underground, and run around the mountain to see where it comes out, the dye surfaces almost everywhere, having passed through the labyrinths of the mind. From the point of view of current thinking about how the mind works, this is quite extraordinary. The expectation is that, first, the inner streams are in many cases 'modular', and thus cannot run one into another, and second, that the modules come ready-built with the organism, and are not 'tunable' to a local cultural detail like the preferred frame of reference in a language. But this is not at all the picture that emerges from the studies in this book.

Trying to understand what is wrong with current models is the subject of the last section of this chapter. If the picture emerging from this book is correct, then we are a species lacking many wonderful modular endowments like echo-location or innate fixed-bearing dead reckoning systems, but with one spectacular specialization, namely language, which has come to play a dominant role in our psyche. Language has an interstitial status – it is a public, shared, cultural representation system at the same time that it is a private, internal representation system. And some choices made at the cultural, external, variable level come to ramify right through our inner representational systems. One major reason that frame-of-reference information ramifies right through in this way has already been given in Chapter 2. There we saw that absolute frames of reference and relative frames of reference are incommensurable – there is no automatic translation possible between them. From a proposition of the kind 'The knife is to the right of the fork' I cannot compute 'The knife is south of the fork' or vice-versa (see Figure 2.7). Once a language has opted for one of these frames of reference and not the other, all the systems that support language, from memory, to reasoning, to gesture, have to provide information in the same frame of reference. If I remember an array as 'The knife is right of the fork' but live in a community where no left/right terminology or computation is part of everyday life, I simply will not be able to describe it. For my memory will have failed to support the local description system, in, say, terms of north and south. The use of a language thus forces other systems to come into line in such a way that semantic parameters in the public language are supported by internal systems keeping track of all experience coded in the same parameters. That is why an absolute speaker can hardly fail to run a specific kind of dead reckoning system, constructing oriented survey maps. And, given this internal ramification, it is natural that such a speaker cannot avoid gesturing with respect to that same oriented map. Thus the need to output language coded in specific semantic parameters can force a deep-seated specialization of mind.

One could think about this absolute or relative specialization as a 'meme' – a cultural idea or construct that invades the organism and works its way into mind (Dawkins 1976, Dennett 1995, Sperber 1996). Dawkins' original idea was that memes flourish in so far as they are good at propagating themselves, a bit like a tune one cannot forget. The view that our minds are pervaded by culturally communicated ideas is a healthy antidote to the nativism that flourishes in cognitive science. But the sorts of examples that intrigued Dawkins – the idea of the wheel, an unforgettable tune – are not quite the right model for the phenomenon in question here, specializations in frame of reference. First, we normally do not have a choice between the systems – the linguistic traditions in our local communities have long ago opted for one system or the other. Secondly, these 'memes' penetrate so far because of the systemic ramifications required to support them – unlike an attractive tune, they impose a heavy burden of adaptation. We will explore these issues further below.

7.2 THE RELATION BETWEEN LINGUISTIC AND CONCEPTUAL CATEGORIES

It may seem that the facts adduced in Chapters 4, 5 and 6 point to such a close relation between the categories of language and the categories of thought that one might boldly equate them. There are indeed many theorists in the language sciences who argue that the semantics of language is directly equivalent to conceptual structure, or the central representations we think in. Cognitive linguists like Langacker (1987: 5) or Jackendoff (1983: 95) have made this equation, as have psychologists and philosophical psychologists (see, e.g., Fodor *et al.* 1975: 530). There are many attractions of this view – it is economic of levels of representation, and it gives language a central place as a window on the mind.

Indeed, for many proponents of this view, universals of human conceptual structure can be directly ascertained by looking at the semantics of
a natural language like English. For neo-Whorfians, on the other hand,
the view that humans think in semantic categories may be attractive
for quite different reasons. But, as I have argued elsewhere at length
(Levinson 1997b), this view is quite clearly mistaken. It is worth running
over some of this ground in the light of the findings detailed in this book,
in part because those findings inevitably raise the ghost of Whorf and
linguistic relativity, and it is essential in that connection to banish naïveté
about the relationship between language and thinking.

The correct position, I argue, is that linguistic representations cannot
be identical to the representations in which we do our central thinking,
and yet nevertheless they have to be in some respects similar, since the
'languages of thought' must, directly or indirectly, support linguistic distinctions (I use the phrase 'languages of thought' in the plural because,
as we have just seen, all the evidence points to a myriad of internal representations in which mental computations are run). I will first run over
a set of reasons why semantic representations cannot be identical to the
conceptual representations in which we memorize scenes or events and
in which we reason about them, and then turn to the issue of lexical
'decomposition' and its implications.

First, it is obvious that languages provide uneven lexical coverage of
conceptual domains. Some languages have only two or three colour
words – often one word 'grue' covering blue and green; some languages
like English subsume mother's kin and father's kin in terms like *uncle*
(father's brother, mother's brother, father's sister's husband, mother's
sister's husband etc.), but most do not; some languages have words or
constructions for the logical connectives like *and*, *if* , *or*, but many do not.
There is no implication that the natives cannot see blue, or do not know
the difference between a father's brother and a husband of a mother's
sister, or cannot reason logically. The problem is that vocabularies are,
to remain learnable, strictly finite, hence patchy in coverage and semantically general. Obviously, then, thought is richer than language, but
equally it may be impractical or even impossible to express exactly what
one thinks.

Second, pragmatics opens up a systematic gap between what one says
and what one thinks. One reason for the failure of Searle's (1969) Principle
of Expressibility (which holds that 'whatever can be meant can be said')
is that languages have not only a semantics but a pragmatics. Consider
first a language like Guugu Yimithirr which lacks a conditional – the
conditional 'If p, then q' is happily conveyed by saying in effect 'Perhaps

p, perhaps q', even though that locution also encompasses 'p or q'. Or take a language without tense and without temporal connectives like 'before' or 'after' such as Yucatec (Bohnemeyer 1998); there are nevertheless quite systematic ways in which one can implicate temporal succession, by saying, for example, 'José stopped reading. He ate'. Conversational implicature takes one a long way, and it is just as well, since finite vocabularies and constructions would otherwise leave one in the lurch. Now notice that it may not be possible to *say* exactly what you mean, however long-winded you want to be. A reason for this is that the more you say, the more you implicate that something untoward is intended. Suppose, for example, I say "Some of the books I own are missing" – this will give rise to a presumptive inference or generalized implicature that 'Not all of the books I own are missing' (Levinson 2000a). But suppose I wish to make this explicit and say "Some but not all of my books are missing" – now that implicates 'All of my books might well have been missing', and that may not express the right thought. In short, the more you say, the more you implicate, and so in principle it is not possible to express exactly the thought corresponding to what you say! Instead, languages exploit the contrary principle, call it the Principle of Ineffability, roughly 'What is taken to be meant always exceeds what is said'. Given this principle, the semantics of linguistic expressions can be underspecified, which in turn gives those expressions much wider uses, allowing further economies in the language system.

Third, deixis ensures that there is always a substantial gap between what we say and what we think. An expression like *Come tomorrow!* invites the addressee to come to the place where the speaker is speaking or is based on the day after the act of speaking. But of course it can be used on many different occasions, addressed by different speakers to different addressees at different places and times to express different thoughts. There is in fact a long-standing puzzle about what exactly constitutes the thought corresponding to an indexical expression, that is, the form of the proposition that is, for example, stored in memory. One might think (as Frege, Montague and others suggested) that one can just cash this out in objective terms, say, 'Steve invited Dan to come to Steve's home on 1 April' – but suppose Steve mistakenly thinks that tomorrow is 2 April, then this clearly fails to correspond to the speaker's thought. On the other hand, if we make the proposition correspond to the subjective thought ('Steve invited Dan to come to Steve's home on 2 April') and the speaker later learns that tomorrow is 1 April, he should then expect Dan to come on the day after tomorrow, and that seems unlikely. An alternative possibility is that Steve simply remembers a proposition of

(a)

(b)

Figure 7.3. Choosing frames of reference

the form 'I now invite you to come tomorrow to where I now am' plus a list of contextual parameters (e.g. 'now = 1 April'), but that would imply that the 'language of thought' itself has indexicals, which need to be cashed out at a yet deeper level, leading to an infinite regress. In fact, the puzzles of indexicals are not easily dissolved (see Levinson 1997b, Miller 1982). The point here is simply that the existence of deictic expressions clearly establishes a mismatch between what we say and what we think.

Fourth, the very process of speaking forces a linearization of thinking, a choice between parallel thoughts (Levelt 1989). If the scene on my desk in front of me has computer to the right of telephone, there is more than one way to describe it – I could say 'The telephone is to the left of the computer', or 'The computer is to the right of the telephone'. Language forces a linearization that may be quite alien to the way we think more generally. In addition, and most pertinently for this book, language forces the choice between perspectives or frames of reference. Consider Figure 7.3 (a). There are many ways in which we could describe the figure, for example:

1. "A line, so long, bisected by another line of the same length orthogonal to it"
2. "A horizontal line, so long, bisected by a vertical line of the same length"
3. "An upside-down T"

Now note that description (1) is also true of the variant figures in Figure 7.3 (b), but the other descriptions are now false. That is because, of course, the first description is in an intrinsic frame of reference, and so is orientation-free, while the other two are in the relative frame of reference, and so are orientation-bound. Both frames of reference are available to us, but we have to choose one only to encode in a clause of English.

So can we think in more than one frame of reference at once? I suspect that the answer depends on the temporal granularity of 'at once'. Introspection suggests that there is a kind of singularity of instantaneous perspective, as reflected in the mental switch in perceiving ambiguous figures like the Necker cube. And we rarely find distinct frames of reference used in language and the accompanying gesture. Still, the parallel availability of both frames of reference available to English or Dutch speakers can be shown in many ways – consider, for example, the experiments mentioned in Chapter 5 (section 5.6) where we found we could systematically induce a switch from intrinsic to relative frame of reference by increasing the memory load. Thus more than one frame of reference can be available in our cognition, but in language we must make a choice.

Fifth, the fundamental fact that spoken languages are public representations, while conceptual representations are private ones, will ensure that they will part company in systematic ways. Spoken languages have the corresponding properties: (a) they have small, learnable vocabularies of cultural origin, with language-specific distinctions; (b) because the lexemes and morphemes are limited, they have to do general duty, so are semantically general or underspecified; (c) because languages are broadcast in the vocal-auditory channel they must build in redundancy (e.g. cross-referencing plurality in noun, adjective and verb), they must minimize articulation time through the use of deixis and anaphora, and they must be quickly parsable within an auditory short-term memory buffer. Private 'languages of thought' have none of these constraints, and they cannot have anaphora or deixis without a potential infinite regress of layers of interpretation. If external languages have to meet external functional constraints (like learnability and elliptical redundancy for broadcast communication), internal representations have to meet quite different internal functions, such as ease of recall from memory, precision for motor control, and lack of ambiguity for inference.

The argument so far is that, on the one hand, not everything we think can be expressed, and thus semantic representations are at most a subset of conceptual representations, and, on the other hand, semantic representations have elements systematically absent from conceptual representations, like anaphora and indexicals. It follows that these two kinds of representation have as it were different vocabulary, and they may of course also have a different structure. One distinct possibility is that semantic representations are really quite remote in nature from conceptual representations, in that semantic representations may be indeterminate in form and content, or semantically general over distinct conceptual representations (Levinson 2000a: 256–9). Consequently, not only the Fodoreans and the cognitive linguists, but also the extreme Whorfians are wrong to suppose that we think in just the same *kind* of conceptual categories in which we speak. The main reasons for thinking otherwise have been economy arguments (Jackendoff 1983: 19), or arguments to the practical difficulty of making a distinction between linguistic meanings and more general conception (Langacker 1987: 155), or arguments about the nature of a central inner 'language' into which sensory information could be converted, allowing us to speak about what we see, feel and hear (Fodor 1983).

I have established, I hope, that any simple equation of semantics and conception is theoretically mistaken. However, there are very good reasons to think that semantic representations must be nevertheless rather close to conceptual representations. There is on the one hand the Fodorean argument that the 'language of thought' (that is, the propositional representation in which we do a lot of our reasoning) must have many of the same kinds of generative capacity that language has, with its associated recursive syntax, rules of inference etc. (Fodor 1983, Jackendoff 1983). In addition, the relative speed and apparent ease with which language is encoded and decoded suggests some kind of close parallelism with a propositional representation (Levelt 1989). The learnability of languages also suggests a close basis for semantic structures in conceptual ones (Pinker 1989). Further, any semantic distinction must clearly be supported by a corresponding conceptual distinction: if the language I speak forces the use of honorifics or cardinal directions, I must be able to compute levels of rank and fixed bearings in representations rich enough to make all the linguistic distinctions. Last but not least, there is the extended empirical demonstration in this book that such features as frame-of-reference specializations are shared across semantic representations and conceptual ones. All of this, and much else besides, points to the conclusion that semantic representations have some kind of partial isomorphism with, and (largely) one-to-many mappings to, conceptual representations of a propositional kind.

Let us now turn to the issue of the 'granularity' of semantic representations. One of the things that I have certainly established is that in the spatial domain, as in many others, there is significant semantic diversity across languages. Now consider the implications of semantic diversity for the position of the theorists (from Langacker to Fodor) who claim that there is no semantic representation distinct from general-purpose conceptual representations. At first sight, perhaps, they seem committed to rather strong Whorfianism, that is the position seems to entail that semantic diversity entails cognitive diversity. But there are two ways to escape that conclusion. One way out is to assume that every concept in every language is part of the universal mental endowment of all humans, from which individual languages only draw a tiny subset for their vocabulary. Another way out is to presume that our universal mental endowment is much more modest, but that it is nevertheless rich enough to offer a set of primitives from which all complex semantic concepts can be constructed. Those who eschew the 'lexical decomposition' of lexemes into semantic primitives go the first route, and those who embrace it take the second. But I want to carve a new route down the middle, so let us review the two positions.

Those who identify semantics with conceptual structure and subscribe to lexical decomposition, like Jackendoff (1983, 1992: 48ff.), can escape strong Whorfianism as follows. Despite the fact that different languages have expressions with quite different semantic content, these lexemes can be decomposed into universal semantic primes or atomic primitives. Since those primitives are also the primitives of conceptual structure, conceptual structure does not vary with the language. Linguistic diversity is merely a matter of complex packaging at a higher level, of universal conceptual primes at a lower level. As I have made clear, I do not believe that a simple conflation of semantics and conceptual structure is defensible, but still, if we assume some kind of partial isomorphism, decompositional theories would explain how it is possible to learn a language by building up complex cultural constructs from more elementary concepts. They also potentially offer insights into such notions as 'possible lexical item', as a compound constructable from existing concepts combined by restricted rules.

Lexical decomposition (or componential analysis) seems to be currently out of favour (see, e.g., Lyons 1995), and in general any advantage that accrues from analysing lexical meanings into component parts, of the kind '*man*' = *male (x) & adult (x) & human (x)*, can be exactly mimicked by a 'meaning postulate', or ad hoc inference rule, of the kind $\forall x$ *(man (x)* → *(male (x) & adult (x) & human (x)))*. Now those who want to hang on to the view that semantic representations just are identical to conceptual representations, but wish to avoid lexical decomposition, find themselves in the following quandary. Since different languages have lexemes with differing semantical content, and since – by assumption – lexemes map one-to-one onto unitary simplex conceptual representations, speakers of different languages must have, so it seems, different conceptual representations. If so, verbal vocabularies reveal mental vocabularies – and now we are into strong Whorfianism. To escape this dilemma, Fodor (1975, Fodor *et al.* 1975) adopts the peculiar position that every attainable human concept is already part of our innate mental endowment, not in the weak compositional sense that we might be able to construct the notions of deuterium or Deuteronomy, but in the strong sense that humans throughout history have always had just those concepts innately. Like Putnam (1988: 15) and Jackendoff (1992: 50), I take this to be an unintentional *reductio ad absurdum*.

But Fodor *et al.* (1975) had a good reason to reject decompositional theories, namely Miller's (1956) theory of recoding. The evidence is that our working (short-term) memories have very distinct limits – George Miller influentially held that this limit holds for items or 'chunks' of information regardless of their inner complexity, and that our computational memory or register could hold maximally around seven such chunks at a time (modern research suggests even less, around four such items, see Cowan 2001). That is why we 'chunk' long telephone numbers into three or four shorter sequences of numbers, why we combine long names into acronyms, and invent jargon to cover complex new concepts. In the light of all this, decomposition seems psychologically implausible – our working memory could hardly hold the semantic primes associated with a single word of any semantic complexity. Indeed, the existence of these processing limits suggests a powerful motivation for the development of a complex vocabulary. Natural languages provide each of us with a huge set of ready-made compound semantical notions that allow us to run our limited inferential engines over intricate detail. As Miller (1956:95) put it:

> The most customary kind of recoding that we do all the time is to translate into a verbal code... Our language is tremendously useful for repackaging material into a few chunks rich in information... The kind of recoding that people do seems to me to be the very lifeblood of the thought processes.

There is a way to have both the non-compositional cake and to eat it with compositional relish. We simply need to assume that there is a level

where that decomposition can and has taken place, and another level –
the level at which we habitually operate – where we cease to decompose.
The existence of a decompositional level is essential, it seems to me, if
we are to explain how we learn new words or construct new jargon. The
Fodorean nativist theory would in principle make it possible to learn
a new word that had absolutely no semantical connection to anything
else you knew – for example, it should be possible to learn the word
carburettor without knowing anything about petrol engines or motor cars,
for the concept would simply exist there in the recesses of the mind
waiting to be activated. This is clearly not how we learn words, and
a decompositonal theory is much more plausible. Secondly, the non-
decompositional theory makes no essential claims about the nature of
a possible concept – such concepts are simply provided innately and
it makes no sense to inquire why we have the notion *carburettor*, it is
just an empirical fact. In contrast, the decompositional theory offers the
prospect of a science of concepts, wherein the semantical primes can
be characterized, their rules of combination worked out, and thus the
generative capacity of the system delineated.

What we seek then is a theory that gives us *both* decompositional meanings of lexemes for learning purposes and unitary meanings for cognitive
processing. Such a theory can be constructed simply by mapping lexemes
onto unitary concepts at one level, the level of routine language processing, and these in turn onto a level where the unitary molar concepts are
broken down into formulae composed of atomic concepts. The generative capacity and the universals (if any) lie at the atomic level, while
all the advantages that accrue to us by virtue of thinking in high-level
'chunks' are reaped on the molar level. The psychological plausibility of
such a dual-level account is in fact supported by Miller's recoding theory.
In that theory, the sequence *fbiibmlseeec* becomes suddenly easy to recall
if one recodes it as the familiar acronyms FBI, IBM, LSE, EEC. This is
because in long-term memory these acronyms form strong conceptual
units, while sequences across them do not. In short, recoding uses the
strength of long-term memory associations as a way around the bottleneck of short-term memory with its limits of about four units or chunks
(see Cowan 2001 for references to modern work). Mnemonic techniques
rely on imposing structure on long lists, the structure being recoverable
from long-term memory. But such recoding does not imply lack of access
to the underlying detail – a telephone number recalled in chunks of three
can be reanalysed for its area code or other functional units. In short, recoding is a dual-level theory about mental processing. And this dual-level

analysis of the meanings of words is also noticeable in our daily life –
complex concepts packaged into single words like *condominium, intestate,
descendant* or *uncle* make it possible to reason quickly that we may inherit
a bonanza from the sale of Uncle George's condominium after he has
died intestate. But we may have to prove that we are indeed the nearest
descendants, and now we will have to care in detail about what exactly
constitutes these notions.

I shall assume that such a dual-level theory can be made to work. Now
let us consider what the implications are for the larger Whorfian questions about the relation between language and cognition. High-level
molar concepts, the sort of thing packaged in lexical meanings, differ
from language to language. This is the level at which we run much of
our normal thinking, and consequently, Whorfian effects of language
on cognition are to be expected. On the other hand, we are not the
prisoners of these high-level concepts, since they can be unpacked into
their component low-level concepts with relative ease when need arises.
Such low-level concepts, or some of them at least, are indeed candidates for universal concepts (although that of course does not require
that they are innately specified; it will be sufficient that they are likely to
emerge out of the interaction between the organism and common terrestrial experience). Thus such a dual-level theory allows us to consider
seriously the possibility of Whorfian effects of language on cognition
while simultaneously hanging on to the fundamental 'psychic unity of
mankind'. Incidentally, whatever the rhetoric, such a view should be perfectly acceptable to Fodor, who has never denied the facilitatory effects
of language on human thought as long as this could be thought of as due
to 'performance factors' like memory:[2]

I am not committed to asserting that an articulate organism has no cognitive
advantage over an inarticulate one. Nor ... is there any need to deny the Whorfian point that the kinds of concepts one has may be profoundly determined by
the character of the natural language one speaks.   (Fodor 1975: 85)

Whorf (1956), despite unclarities and overstatements in his writing,
seems to have held approximately just such a dual-layered view, certainly
distinguishing between universal perception and language-influenced
conception (see Lucy 1992a: 40–1). For example, in our domain, he
stated:

Probably the apprehension of space is given in substantially the same form by experience irrespective of language. The experiments of the Gestalt psychologists
with visual perception appear to establish this as a fact. But the CONCEPT

OF SPACE will vary somewhat from language to language, because, as an intellectual tool, it is so closely linked with the concomitant employment of other intellectual tools... (Whorf 1956: 158, emphasis in the original)

7.3 NEO-WHORFIANISM

The kind of theory emerging from this book can be assimilated to a number of neo-Whorfian perspectives to be outlined below. But it is not Whorfian in any strict sense. Whorf emphasized the role that obligatory grammatical categories may have on patterns of thinking – their background character, their obligatoriness and frequency have, in his words, 'a behavioral compulsiveness' (1956: 137–8). But the frames-of-reference distinctions are as much lexical as grammatical. Secondly, Whorf imagined the influence of language on thought to inhere in an entrainment of 'habitual thought', as if unreflective language use would set up inescapable categories and analogies (Lucy 1992a: 45ff.). This could be interpreted in a behaviourist fashion, although Whorf partially distanced himself from the behaviourism of the day (1956: 66).

But the argument in this book is based on no such thesis of insidious entrainment. The argument is an architectural one. Language is an output system. The output must meet the local semantic requirements. Consequently, the input to language production must code for the right distinctions. As a consequence of that, scenes must be memorized complete with the relevant features. In order to code for those features, subsidiary processes must run – for example, to code for fixed bearings, a mental 'compass' must compute directions. An indirect consequence of coding for particular features is that inference will be done over those features. And other output systems like gesture will reflect the same coding of features in memory. So, given the architecture of the system, once one puts serious semantic constraints on the output, the rest of the system will be forced to support, code and operate on those features. And so the imprint of language-specific categories will run deep in cognitive processes.

The argument of course is not specific to spatial concepts. It relies only on the output system (the local language) containing semantic distinctions that (a) require special conceptual codings at experience-time (i.e. the time at which events or scenes are memorized) which otherwise would not be made, (b) these codings not being recoverable by converting other more natural perceptual codings at speaking-time. There would seem to be a host of lexical and grammatical categories which have these properties. Consider, for example, languages with honorifics, like Japanese or Javanese, where virtually every sentence encodes the humble, neutral or exalted attitude of the speaker to the addressee, regardless of what they are talking about. Such languages force one to compute the proper attitude to one's addressee, according to the local system. Or consider the difference between English and languages like the Bantu or Papuan ones with up to six 'absolute' tenses. In Yélî Dnye you need to be specific about whether an event happened earlier today, yesterday or the day before, and you will need to keep track of the diurnal timing of events in memory if you are to use the tense system properly. Similarly there are languages that force the marking of plurality, like English, and languages that do not, like Yucatec. And it is demonstrable that the speakers of Yucatec remember things with less specificity about number than English speakers (Lucy 1992b). Clearly, any language that forces a language-specific coding of events will require its speakers to remember those relevant parameters at the time at which events are experienced. And the evidence, so far as it goes (see Lucy 1992b), is that if there is no such special necessity for coding such features they may not be recollected systematically. The implications for the interface between language and thought are fairly clear. Semantic parameters are not universal, that is not shared by all languages. And if a language lacks such a semantic parameter, there is a good chance that the speakers of it fail to think in terms of those parameters too – as shown, for example, by the fact that English or Dutch speakers do not code spatial scenes in absolute coordinates.

We have found it helpful to distinguish different possible kinds of 'Whorfian effects', that is, effects of linguistic coding patterns on thinking, according to the time-line of coding a scene in memory, speaking about it, and remembering it after it was coded in language, as sketched in Figure 7.4. From right to left in the diagram, the fact that thoughts have already been coded linguistically may of course affect the way they are recollected, categorized or used in inference. Such effects are uncontroversial – any search engine demonstrates the point, although it can be taken in controversial directions (as in Whorf's (1956: 135) analysis of *empty gasoline drums* suggesting 'null, inert, safe'). Clearly, exposure to specific languages also has effects on perception, as shown in the loss of our phonetic sensitivities to non-native speech sounds. In the case of sign language, native signers show enhanced sensitivities to facial expressions since these play a crucial role in sign languages, and are better at mental rotation than non-signers since signers typically produce signs from

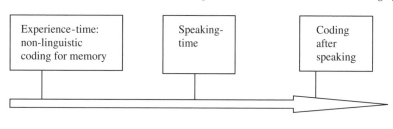

Figure 7.4. Distinct types of 'Whorfian effects'

an egocentric point of view while facing their interlocutors (Emmorey 2001). Next there are effects that are operative only or primarily at the moment of speaking: at the moment of linguistic coding, thoughts have to be regimented to fit the lexical, grammatical and linear structure of the particular language – 'thinking-for-speaking' in Slobin's (1996) memorable phrase. Again, such effects are uncontested in theories of speech production (Levelt 1989), although they may be much more far reaching than expected, as suggested by Slobin's work (see below). Finally, there is what we may call 'experiencing for speaking', where the argument is that events at the moment of experience must be coded in terms appropriate for later expression in the local language – all arguments here are controversial, including the ones in this book.

Recently, there has been a resurgence of interest in Whorfian ideas, with converging strands of thought from different quarters, from philosophy, from linguistic anthropology, comparative semantics, and from developmental psychology. These developments are worth reviewing briefly as a means of putting the facts presented in this book into perspective. First, in philosophy, there is far from universal agreement with Fodor's view that no natural language can exceed the computational power provided by an innate language of thought. Many philosophers, from Dennett to Carruthers to Gauker, hold that conscious propositional thinking just is in the relevant natural language, inheriting all the benefits of accumulated cultural representations. Dennett (1991: 210–20) further maintains that language, together with other cultural ideas, has entirely reworked the mind, giving us a serial computational device running on the parallel computational system of the brain. It is this serial device that constitutes our stream of consciousness. It follows that 'the details of a natural language – the vocabulary and grammar of English or Chinese or Spanish – constrain a brain in the manner of a high-level programming language' (Dennett 1991: 302).

A second strand of neo-Whorfian ideas has emerged in linguistic anthropology (see, e.g., Gumperz and Levinson 1996). Early important work on semantic universals – notably Berlin and Kay's 1969 work on colour terms – had suggested that universals, or more exactly typological constraints, may lie behind the apparent semantic diversity of languages. But nevertheless, linguistic difference, however constrained its basis, has been consistently shown to correlate with perceptual and cognitive difference. Thus, in a little noticed but important study, Kay and Kempton (1984) showed that colour terms bias perception in triad colour tasks, where judgements are required of similarity between three coloured chips equally distant in psychophysical measurement (see also Davidoff *et al.* 1999). And in the first sustained experimental work, Lucy (1992b) showed that the presence or absence of obligatory number marking in language has non-linguistic consequences. He compared speakers of English, which requires obligatory number marking in nouns (as in *There are birds in the garden*), to speakers of Yucatec, which does not require (and in the case of inanimates inhibits) number marking on nouns (saying in effect 'There be bird in the garden'). He found that English speakers duly describe pictures of inanimate objects with the correct number marking, and when tested on non-linguistic tasks also duly attend to number. Thus they judge the similarity of pictures taking number into account, and in recognition tasks notice changes in number. In contrast, Yucatec speakers do not describe number, and in non-linguistic tasks they systematically tend to ignore number in judgement and recognition tasks. These studies seem to establish 'experiencing-for-thinking', that is, coding for memory in non-linguistic tasks being influenced by language patterns. In recent work, Lucy and Gaskins (2001) have gone on to examine how this lack of number marking relates to other semantic properties of Yucatec nominals, which tend to encode material substance ('plastic', 'wood', 'maize' etc.) in contrast to English nominals, which tend to encode shape regardless of material ('bottle', 'plank', 'pancake' etc.). They find that in non-linguistic sorting tasks, Yucatec-speakers will sort by material, while English-speakers will sort by shape, although there is an interesting developmental divergence here in middle childhood. Such studies were the first to test the effects of language on cognition properly and directly, by independently examining language and non-linguistic cognition, and they have set the stage for other studies, including those reported in this volume.

The third strand of work converging in a neo-Whorfian direction is to be found within developmental psychology and the study of language acquisition (see Bowerman and Levinson 2001). Some of the most spectacular findings have concerned how infants acquire the sound-systems of their language. For example, it is now clear that infants within the first six months of life, long before they can say anything, have already retooled their acoustic systems to perceive the contrasts in the local language and downplay possible contrasts that are not significant in that language (Kuhl 1991). This is a very striking language-specific effect on the perceptual system, a kind of psycho-acoustic biasing of the system, and because it is so early in development, it suggests that the human organism may be innately equipped precisely to specialize in this way (a point picked up below).

Language-specific effects of local semantic contrasts have also been shown to be remarkably early. In a 'preferential looking task', in which infants are shown two scenes of which only one matches a description, infants will look longer at the scene that matches. This allows the researcher to investigate the comprehension of words even before the child produces them. Using this technique, Bowerman and Choi (2001) have shown that young infants are sensitive to the language-specific semantics of spatial terms in their language. Korean lumps together tight-fitting relations between figure and ground, but English distinguishes 'in' and 'on' cases of tight-fitting relations (as in a cassette slipping into its case vs. a Lego block stuck on top of another). Korean and English eighteen-month-old infants correctly attend only to the distinctions relevant to their language. Patterns in the earliest comprehension of these distinctions show that infants are already on divergent acquisition paths (Bowerman 1996). However, looking at non-linguistic implicit categorization, Choi *et al.* (in preparation) have recently shown that nine-month-old infants have equal facility to make English vs. Korean spatial distinctions, and it is only at the later eighteen-month stage that they are tuned into the local language-specific distinctions. In the same implicit categorization tasks, adults seem unable to adopt the pattern of the other culture. Thus, by the time we reach adulthood, just as we find alien language sounds hard to distinguish, so we apparently find it hard to adopt a conceptual categorization that cross-cuts those in our language.

The message of much recent acquisition work is that semantic and grammatical diversity is not a formidable obstacle for children learning language – the local parameters constitute a sort of local flavour or style that comes to be a resource (Slobin 2001). Thus, for example, the rich semantic texture of locative predicates in Tzeltal mentioned earlier (sections 3.6, 4.2.1) is echoed in other kinds of predicates, and Tzeltal children are rapidly cued to the semantic style of the language, learning verbs in large arrays as early as they learn nouns (Brown 1998, 2001), in contrast to English children who early learn a few 'light' verbs and massive numbers of nouns. Looking at older children, from four years on, it is noticeable how the increasing mastery of grammatical and semantic distinctions leads to a specific rhetorical style which makes full use of these parameters and downplays descriptive material that does not easily fit with these distinctions. For example, Romance languages code path or direction in motion verbs, which then exclude manner components in the same clause (Talmy 1983, 2000), and children's narratives fail to mention manner elements increasingly with age (Slobin 1996). It was the observation of these patterns that led Slobin to talk of 'thinking-for-speaking', a mindset involved in actually speaking a specific language, where events must be construed at the time of speaking to fit compactly within the grammatical and semantical resources of the language. Such styles are also visible in gesture, where speakers of languages with motion verbs of the Romance kind display less (and differently distributed) manner gestures (Özyürek and Kita 1999), indicating that 'thinking for speaking' also shapes mental imagery.

These developments suggest that the old picture of language acquisition needs considerable revision. In that old picture, language development primarily reflects underlying conceptual development, which must first make available the concepts to be labelled, as it were. In the new, emerging picture, language facilitates such cognitive development, by helping to construct complex concepts. There is a striking example from the spatial domain, as already mentioned in Chapter 6. Rats have been shown to employ strictly geometric criteria in recognizing places and finding their way around – it will not help to give them other kinds of clues like colour or patterns on walls, because they navigate by angular relations between landmarks (Gallistel 1990). Children of eighteen months to two years, who have yet to acquire significant spatial language, behave in a similar way (Hermer and Spelke 1994). The explanation is presumably that this geometric pattern of place recognition is an ancient mammalian 'module' or self-contained processing ability. When children acquire spatial language, they suddenly transcend these limitations, being able to associate, for example coloured walls with angular directions. Spelke and Tsivkin (2001) speculate that language may play a crucial role in building links across such ancient modular devices, and they give another telling example from the growth of mathematical ability, which again has a primitive modular basis. They conclude that Fodor may be fundamentally wrong about external language being unable to add computational power to our innate inner language of thought – the crucial role of language in cognition may be to build bridges across modular capacities, giving us cross-modal generalizations unavailable to our inarticulate cousins.

Acquisition evidence will be crucial in helping us arrive at a balanced view of the role that language plays in cognition, and in the next section we turn to what is known about the acquisition of frames of reference. But the point is here that all these strands of work, here briefly sampled, converge in painting a new picture of the role of language in cognition, as a fundamental facilitator of complex concepts and higher-level reasoning, and the very foundations for human cultural abilities.

7.4 THE ACQUISITION OF LINGUISTIC FRAMES OF REFERENCE BY CHILDREN

For many of the important issues addressed in this chapter (questions of the kind 'Are frames of reference universal?', 'Are they innate ideas?' and so on), one kind of evidence might in principle prove decisive – namely the study of how children acquire spatial and linguistic abilities. Although quite a lot is known about such developmental trends in our society, the studies often pursue different aspects of spatial knowledge using different methods from those employed here (but see, e.g., Acredolo 1988, Pick 1993, Johnston and Slobin 1979). In any case, when we turn to other, non-European, languages, the evidence is very thin on the ground. However, there have been a number of studies of developmental trends associated with the work reported in this book, and these are the focus of what follows.

On the view that evolution has endowed us with a rich stock of innate concepts, one might expect to be able to distinguish such 'natural' categories from 'unnatural' or constructed ones by looking at the time course of development. Thus Landau and Gleitman (1985) suggest that natural categories should display four properties: (a) they should be learnt early in development (before, say, age three); (b) in the course of learning, one should not be able to detect attempts to construe the relevant terms in other, but related, ways; (c) they should be universally coded in all languages in the 'core vocabulary'; (d) even under poor input conditions (as where the child has perceptual deficits), they should nevertheless be learnable.

By such criteria, there is no evidence that any of the frames of reference are 'natural' concepts. First, in European languages, the intrinsic frame of reference is clearly learned first, but such notions as intrinsic 'in front of' are not mastered in production before the child is nearly four years old (Johnston and Slobin 1979: 538), and intrinsic 'left/right' not fully mastered till eight, while relative 'front'/'back' comes into the child's production just before five, and relative 'left/right' must wait till as late as age eleven (Piaget 1928, Weissenborn and Stralka 1984). The pattern is then one of slow development right through middle childhood, not of instantaneous grasp of the expressions for pre-existing concepts. Second, children do clearly attempt to construe such notions in various ways, struggling to construct the adult pattern. Third, as we have seen, not all languages code all frames of reference. Fourth, it is evident that such notions as 'left' and 'right' in fact require quite extensive training – imperial Czarist armies being drilled, for example, with bunches of straw tied to the left foot!

Instead of the instantaneous accessibility of 'innate ideas' predicted by the nativist model, an alternative perspective on the development of frames of reference comes from the Piagetian tradition (Piaget and Inhelder 1956). Piaget is decidedly out of fashion due to his *tabula rasa* assumptions and his presumption of domain-general learning, but within the spatial domain his observations are still instructive (see Karmiloff-Smith 1992). He held that the child in a natural maturational sequence comes to construct increasingly complex spatial concepts through experience in the world. The child starts with the simplest topological notions and, from age four, slowly extracts the notion of an empty projective space, proceeding on to the axes and angles of Euclidean geometry in later childhood. On this view, development should directly reflect the complexity of the underlying geometry, the slow incremental mastery of it by the child, and thus display a universal developmental pattern. Specifically, topological concepts should come first, then at age four or so the intrinsic frame of reference, followed rather slowly by the relative frame of reference. Although infants have recently been shown to have implicit, perceptual understandings much earlier than Piaget predicted, Piaget's predictions on the development of conscious spatial concepts in European children have held up well, and generally conform with more recent data on the acquisition of European languages (see Brown and Levinson 2000 for references).

Following Piaget's views in this at least, the working assumption in most research on child development has been that language development is a process entirely dependent on the development of the underlying non-linguistic concepts. But, as we noted in section 7.3, there are new developments that suggest that language may actually induce conceptual development in a number of domains, including spatial cognition (see also Bowerman and Levinson 2001 for a survey). Such a view is more consistent with Vygotsky's (1986) views than with Piaget's. In fact, acquisition of frame-of-reference information provides some support for such a perspective. For example, in an extended longitudinal study of Tzeltal children's acquisition of frames of reference, Penelope Brown has found that, judging from children's language production, children begin to learn the linguistic expressions associated with the absolute frame of reference soon after two years old, with productive uses outside frozen expressions by age two and a half, with the most complex inflected forms by three and a half (see Brown and Levinson 2000 for a summary). Some topological notions are acquired over roughly the same period, but intriguingly the intrinsic system with use of inflected body parts (as described in Chapters 3 and 4) is produced considerably later, after four years of age (this despite the fact that the same possessive inflections, which might constitute part of the difficulty, are already evident in absolute vocabulary well before four).

Now this early acquisition of the expressions used in the absolute frame of reference is quite surprising. Consider for a moment what correct and productive use of such expressions entails. It requires a grasp of the geometry of orthogonal axes and quadrants bisected by them, and the notion of an abstract conceptual 'slope' of parallel directed arcs with fixed bearing at about 345 degrees N. If anything constitutes what Piaget had in mind as 'Euclidean thinking', the end-point of conceptual development in the spatial domain, this is it! But of course, although Tzeltal children have clearly identified these linguistic expressions as important targets for acquisition, it does not follow from their production of these forms that they understand these highly abstract, geometrical meanings. So what do they understand?

Let us backtrack a little to recollect the details of the system and its ecology of use. The Tzeltal absolute system is based on an 'uphill'/'downhill' trajectory, abstracted off an overall territorial slope down towards the north. The system also has subordinate uses based on local actual slopes, differently oriented. Now, children typically grow up in a compound of houses accommodating an extended family (often a couple, together with their sons and their wives), such a compound lying at some distance from the next across the fields or through the forest. The family's fields may be distributed across a valley. Within the compound, houses are arranged if possible around a flat open space, used for drying crops. A child growing up in this environment will hear many utterances of the kind 'Descend and get the bucket', meaning go across the compound to the northern house, or 'He's ascended', meaning he has gone by vehicle to the local market town to the south, and so forth. Some compounds will be nestled into local slopes at different angles, and here the same expressions may also mean 'Go downhillwards and get the bucket' etc.

To return to the question – does the child really understand the cardinal direction senses of these expressions? There is no doubt that very young children are using the absolute terminology with correct fixed bearings. For example, consider the following interaction (here in English gloss) over a toy truck on flat ground between Child A (three years, five months) and Child B (two years):

> Child A : 'It's gone to Jobel (local town), it's gone to Jobel.' (moving truck south)
> Child B: 'It has ascended going.'

Here the younger child B has supplied the correct cardinal direction term ('ascend' = go south). But in this and many other such cases, perhaps the child has simply learnt a collocational association between the name of the local town (Jobel) and the motion verb 'ascend'. How can we be sure that the abstract semantics has really been comprehended? The only way to be sure is to get the children into an experimental context, which could not successfully be done with children under four. Brown (2001) tested children from four to twelve using a director-matcher task of the kind mentioned in Chapter 4 (see also Pederson *et al.* 1998) – one child had to describe an array of toy animals to another, facing the same way but seated in front. The director described his or her array, and the matcher reconstructed it on the table, asking questions until he or she was satisfied the second array matched the one being described. In a Tzeltal context, this was an entirely novel task. The results show that children as young as four years old could comprehend the system – that is they were adequate matchers. However, only children from 5;8–7;8 and beyond proved to be fully reliable directors – able accurately to say such things as 'Put the cow facing acrossways (east-west) and a bit uphill (south) of the pig'. Overall, then, the absolute system is fully mastered in production only over an extended period from age two up to age seven and a half. But comprehension of the system is remarkably early, given its highly abstract character. Very similar results using slightly different methods have been obtained by de León (1994) for Tzotzil-speaking children from a nearby Mayan community, so there is good reason to believe that the general picture is reliable. The gradual incremental improvement in learning in this domain is much more in line with the kind of theory developed by Karmiloff-Smith (1992) than with more nativist accounts of the kind in Landau and Gleitman (1985).

Still, from a Piagetian point of view, conceptual understanding of this kind by children of four years old has a real precocity. This is the age at which European children have learnt the basics of the intrinsic frame of reference, and are just beginning on relative 'front'/'back' – 'left' and 'right' will lag far behind, with calculation of others' intrinsic 'left' and 'right' by eight, and relative 'left' and 'right' by eleven. In Tzeltal the intrinsic system seems to be, if anything, later acquired than the absolute system, despite the abstract geometrical properties of the latter. How can this be explained?

I believe that the explanation lies in the facilitative effect of language on cognition. It is clear to children that the absolute system is important in adult production, as shown by really early use of the terminology. Children then work hard to crack the code. The nativists argue that this simply cannot be done, and the miracle of acquisition argues that such complex notions must be innately pre-given as wholes. But it is a matter of fact that the Tzeltal child ends up with a culture-specific concept of the kind *alan* meaning 'quadrant centred on N 345 degrees'. We do not know exactly how this is done. But then we are equally unclear how the infant of six months can reshape acoustic space in line with the phonemes of its target language, when as yet it still has no access to the semantical contrasts of minimal pairs. But from the careful work of Brown (2001) and de León (1994) there are clues to how the acquisition of absolute vocabulary is achieved. First, there is perceptual support. For example, where a child lives in a compound on a local slope, the 'up'/'down' meanings of the terms may have direct perceptual reinforcement (recollect that the terms can be switched to the anchorage of the local slope). Secondly, the 'input' language allows a close correlation of local places – houses in compounds, fields around houses, relations to other compounds – with directional expressions. From this, more abstract directional meanings can slowly be induced. Thirdly, many aspects of culture and behaviour are consonant with this absolute interpretation of the terms, and give important non-linguistic clues to how the terms are to be interpreted. Consider, for example, the systematic patterns of gesture described in Chapter 6. If the child hears 'ascend' and sees associated directional pointings south again and again, the highly abstract concept of a fixed bearing may become quite literally visible. For these reasons, I believe that the nativist claims that such concepts are unlearnable in principle, and must be stashed in the mind in advance by evolution, are not well founded. The learnability puzzles arise, at least in good measure, from the under-described nature of the learning experience. They are also increased by the insistence on the 'psychic unity of mankind' – once we admit that different languages might induce subtly different cognitive styles, we see that every aspect of adult behaviour, as with gesture, may yield cues to the semantic parameters utilized in a local language (see Levinson 2001 for elaboration).

There are some additional studies of the acquisition of absolute systems. In an important study of the Balinese absolute system of directions, Wassmann and Dasen (1998) used the methods described in this book to investigate age-stratified samples of children. Balinese, like a lot of Austronesian languages, has a quasi-absolute system built on mountain–sea and transverse axes – the system has some characteristics of a landmark system, since as one moves around the island the orientation of the axes changes. The system is important in daily life and discourse. Wassmann and Dasen used the non-verbal tasks described in Chapter 4, and found that even their youngest children (age four) code for memory in absolute coordinates. Older children in fact show some greater variability as they come into contact with Indonesian and its relative system in school. This is the best experimental data to date on children's early use of absolute bearings in non-linguistic cognition.

We have some preliminary data from Aboriginal Australian languages that suggests a rather later acquisition of absolute systems than has been found in the highland Mayan communities or in Bali. De León (1996) reports on a cross-sectional sample of schoolchildren in Hopevale, where Guugu Yimithirr is spoken. Full Guugu Yimithirr is now rarely acquired by children, and a new reduced form of the language alternates with English. Nevertheless, about 50% of children could correctly use some aspects of the cardinal direction terminology, with systematic oppositions by age ten, and nearly all children used the associated 'up'/'down' terminology in at least a local landmark way by age seven. In the Alice Springs area where Arrernte is spoken and the language is still being more fully acquired by children, Wilkins (in press) reports relatively early absolute gestures, but also an explicit culture of instruction in the absolute system. For example, a local kind of 'blind man's bluff' is employed both as a game and in order to teach the system, in which something is hidden in the sand, and a child directed towards it using absolute and deictic expressions (e.g. 'It is shooting you in the chest, it's shooting you from the north'). It is clear from observation that children under eight are not expected to be able to master the cardinal direction system. Relatively late acquisition of systematic cardinal direction terms is also reported by Cablitz (2002) for Marquesan, where the full system does not seem to be mastered before age seven or eight. In all these cases, we are dealing with bilingual communities, where the indigenous language is under erosion, and this may explain the difference from the strikingly early acquisition of absolute systems in the Mayan and Balinese cases. On the other hand, full acquisition by age ten of an abstract absolute system would make it coeval in acquisition with the full relative system – both are complex geometrical coordinate systems.

To sum up, the acquisition data suggests that none of the three frames of reference comes ready-made as a 'natural' conceptual system. Instead, the evidence is that they take time to build, with the earliest frames of reference mastered by about age four. In European languages this earliest frame is the intrinsic system, but in Tzeltal or Tzotzil it is the absolute system. In general, it seems to be that the relative system is the last system fully acquired, and it is clear that this is because of difficulties with the transverse, 'left' and 'right' distinctions. Hertz (1960 [1909]) held that it is the very artificiality of the left/right distinction dividing a symmetrical body that gives it its cultural and symbolic importance. But the difficulties may also have to do with the complex ternary nature of the expressions in the relative frame of reference, and the ambiguities that arise from the use of the same terms in both the intrinsic and relative frames. In any case, the development of the frames of reference as explicit linguistic concepts clearly poses difficulties for the child, and this is not surprising given their geometrical complexity. What is then surprising is that the most abstract, 'unnatural' element in this domain, namely the naming of a fixed arbitrary bearing like 'north', can be learned by children between the ages of four and six. This is only possible, I argue, because the cognitive and linguistic environment conspires to induce accelerated learning of abstract geometrical and navigational concepts.

Table 7.1. *Proposed universals of frames of reference in language and associated cognition*

1. All coordinate systems used in naïve (everyday, non-expert) natural languages operate with polar coordinates, not Cartesian ones. Such coordinate systems are constructed from the primitives described in Chapter 3, namely points, arcs, anchors, transformations and labelled angles.

2. Locational and directional uses of frames of reference specify the location of a figure with respect to a ground, with the exception of some alignment and motion descriptions in the absolute frame of reference where no ground is specified.

3. All languages use at least one frame of reference.

4. No language uses more than three frames of reference.

5. The three possible frames of reference are absolute, relative and intrinsic. They are distinguished by logical (inferential) properties and rotational properties, for example:

    Intrinsic systems – do not support converseness or transitivity;

    Relative systems – support converseness and transitivity under preserved viewpoint;

    Absolute systems – support converseness and transitivity without exceptions.

6. All combinations of frames of reference are possible in a language, except that a relative frame of reference implies an intrinsic one.

7. All languages use an absolute frame of reference on the vertical dimension; most use an intrinsic one on the horizontal plane.

8. Individual sentences may combine information in different frames of reference, but not usually describing the same figure–ground relation.

9. There are limited subtypes of each frame of reference:

    (a) The relative frame of reference, where it is a complete system, involves a mapping of primary coordinates (based on a viewer) onto the ground, using one (or more) of the three transformations: reflection, translation, rotation.

    (b) The absolute frame of reference involves abstract fixed bearings, specifying an abstract 'slope' of parallel lines across the environment. Landmark (sub-absolute) systems do not have these properties, but there are intermediate zonal systems that do, but recalibrate the fixed bearings in different zones (e.g on the other side of an island, or when moving into a different riverine drainage basin).

    (c) The intrinsic frame of reference has variants according to the following parameters:

    – use or avoidance of the absolute vertical to establish an 'armature' of fixed facets;

    – use or avoidance of axial and geometric properties to assign labelled facets;

    – use or avoidance of functional criteria, including canonical orientation and orientation of humans using the object.

10. Frame of reference information is usually coded lexically or by grammatical construction, and only rarely by morphology.

11. The primary frames of reference used in language correlate with the primary frames of reference used in non-linguistic cognition, as in the non-verbal memory of spatial arrays or in spatial reasoning.

12. The primary frames of reference in language correlate with the primary frames of reference in gesture.

13. The primary frames of reference in language correlate with the types of wayfinding techniques and kinds of mental maps used by speakers of languages; for example, speakers of languages with primary relative frames of reference do not use fixed bearings systematically in wayfinding, and use primarily strip-maps, while speakers of absolute languages use fixed coordinates in wayfinding and oriented mental survey maps.

14. The acquisition of distinct frames of reference is not equally easy, with relative age of acquisition in the order: intrinsic or absolute before relative.

7.5 UNIVERSALS VS. CULTURAL SPECIALIZATIONS

One message from this book is this: languages vary in their semantical organization, but not indefinitely. On the one hand I have proposed a clear universal claim: there are at most three frames of reference upon which languages draw, each of which has precise characteristics that could have been otherwise – for example, they utilize polar rather than Cartesian coordinates. On the other hand, languages vary considerably in the selection they make from these frames of reference, and the ways in which they instantiate the selected frames of reference in both conceptual and linguistic structure – this selection and instantiation having systematic consequences for non-linguistic cognition.

In Table 7.1 universals in the domain of spatial frames of reference in language are formulated as explicitly as possible, and in the strongest way compatible with the very partial data that we have in hand. These must be taken only as grounded hypotheses to be tested in further work with additional languages and cultures.

There are in fact very few hypotheses about semantic universals that have any serious empirical, cross-linguistic backing. Amongst these, for example, there is controversial work within the theory of 'natural semantic metalanguage' (Goddard and Wierzbicka 1994), work on ethnobiology (Berlin 1992) and colour terms (see Levinson 2000b for a review). In that context, the quite detailed findings and hypotheses about universals in frames of reference are significant additions to what little we know. But the findings reported in this book also make the point – already clear from the work on colour terms – that universals in semantics are basically of the form of constraints on variants: choice from three *types* of frames of reference, and, from within each type, from various attested semantical variants. And just as it has been shown that different types of colour terminology can have effects on colour perception (Kay and Kempton 1984), so I have shown that choice of one of the variants as a primary frame of reference in language has cognitive consequences. In short, universals that allow variants (and few do not) are completely compatible with 'Whorfianism', understood as limited linguistic determinism.

Commenting on this (and his own) work, Heine (1997: 14) writes: 'What this means is there is both diversity and unity: The human species, irrespective of whether it is located in Siberia or the Kalahari Desert, has essentially the same pool of options for conceptualization.' Thus, he suggests, the results can be read as succour for both relativist and universalist. But this kind of bland conclusion is something we need to transcend. First, a model of universals just based on a lottery from an inventory of universals is very weak – it is effectively not open to refutation, as Kempson (1977: 97–9) pointed out (one just adds the next discovered variant to the universal stock). Second, it is easy to slip from 'the same pool of options' to 'the major patterns of human conceptualization are universal' (Heine 1997: 14), implying of course that we all think identically. But that, as we have seen, does not seem to be correct.

There is another possible kind of bland conclusion, namely that the patterns we have found illustrate interactions between universals of cognition and cultural or linguistic specificities, a blend or pabulum of mutual influences. Pinker (1994: 407) laments the prevalence of 'the mindless dichotomies of heredity-environment . . . the unhelpful bromides about inextricably intertwined interactions'. This does an injustice to interesting recent attempts to find structure in those interactions (Karmiloff-Smith 1992, Elman *et al.* 1996). Together with many in the cognitive sciences, Pinker hopes instead that a view of mind as a highly specialized, highly structured system of innate 'modules' will guarantee a single common structure in language and mind under the cloth of cultural and linguistic diversity. Again, I do not think this is the right picture – it is not *unity* we see under the variation, but a set of highly constrained types of system. There is nothing implausible about the presumption of a highly structured mind (although modularity of processing and innateness are quite unrelated issues – see Elman *et al.* 1996), but there is something radically wrong with the idea of unstructured environments incapable of causal efficacy (as in the views of Tooby and Cosmides 1992: 47). I think it is more profitable to formulate the issues differently, in terms of a systematic interaction between structure in the environment and structure in the mind. This I attempt in the next section.

7.6 INNATE IDEAS VS. CO-EVOLUTION AND BIASES: OR HOW WE LOST OUR MENTAL COMPASS

There is a widespread view in the cognitive sciences that in a recent review I have dubbed 'simple nativism' (Levinson 2000c). On this view, both the form (the syntax) and the content (the semantics) of language are essentially innate. Although both ideas go back at least to medieval thought, in recent times it is Chomsky of course who has influentially argued for the universality and innateness of linguistic form, and Fodor for the native nature of mental content. Putting them together (in a way that Chomsky, for example, has been careful to avoid) gives us the brash 'simple nativism' of Pinker (1994) or Tooby and Cosmides (1992). Of special relevance to the themes of this book is the idea that all semantic categories are universal and innate, directly projected from universal concepts:

Language has means for making reference to the objects, relations, properties, and events that populate our everyday world. It is possible to suppose that these linguistic categories and structures are more or less straightforward mappings from a pre-existing conceptual space, programmed into our biological nature: Humans invent words that label their concepts.   (Li and Gleitman 2002: 266)

On this view, then, language is simply the projection of native cognitive structure and categories, with the consequence that 'the grammars and lexicons of all languages are broadly similar' (Li and Gleitman 2002: 266), or 'from a Martian's eye perspective all humans speak a single language' (Pinker 1994: 237).

This view is simply ill-informed about the scope and depth of linguistic diversity, and it is worth reminding ourselves of some basic facts. Natural languages may or may not be in the vocal-auditory channel – they can be shifted to the visual-manual one, as in sign languages like American Sign Language. When they are broadcast in an acoustic medium, they may have as little as 11 or as many as 141 distinctive sounds or phonemes (Maddieson 1984). Languages may or may not have morphology – that is, inflection or derivation. Languages may or may not use constituent structure (as in the familiar tree-diagrams) to encode fundamental grammatical relations (Austin and Bresnan 1996). Thus they may or may not have widescale syntactic constraints on word or phrase order. Languages may or may not make use of such basic word class distinctions as adjective, adverb or even, arguably, noun and verb (Mithun 1999: 60–7). If they do, the kind of denotation assigned to each may be completely alien from an English point of view. Languages force quite different sets of conceptual distinctions in almost every sentence: some languages express aspect, others do not; some have seven tenses, some have none; some languages force marking of visibility or honorific status of each noun phrase in a sentence, others do not; and so on and so forth. Linguists talk so often about universals that non-linguists may be forgiven for thinking that they have a huge list of absolute universals in the bag (i.e. features that all languages share) – unfortunately they have hardly any that have been tested even against the 5%–10% of languages for which we have good descriptions. Instead the main outcomes of contemporary research are either highly abstract generalizations that are impractical to test against a reasonable sample of languages, or empirically grounded conditional tendencies of the kind 'If a language has property X, it probably has property Y'. There are no doubt rich linguistic universals yet to be found, but the fact is that large-scale comparative linguistics is in its infancy. Meanwhile, Whorf's (1956: 218) emphasis on the 'incredible degree of linguistic diversity of linguistic system over the globe' looks considerably better informed than the opinions of many contemporary thinkers.[3]

In short, from a biological point of view, the most fundamental fact about human communication is its variability. Humans constitute the only species with a communication system that varies systematically in *form and content* over populations. Nearly all other higher animals have rigid, innately prescribed communication systems (although oscine birds and sea mammals have slight dialectal differences in the form, not the content, of communication systems; see, e.g., Hauser 1997: 273–302). In that context, the variability of human communication is a central biological fact, not something that ought to be dismissed as random variation. As we have seen, 'simple nativists' hugely underestimate the differences in human languages, which are so substantial that very few universals of the kind 'All languages have property X' have ever actually been established. The idea that languages are uniform in design, with merely sound façades as it were, is not going to wash, given the deep and fundamental differences in syntax, morphology, phonology and semantics across the seven thousand-odd languages of the world. The arguments put forward for 'simple nativism' cannot thus be made in terms of established universals of language. Instead, the Chomskyan argument is that the type of hidden structure and complexity of language is of a kind that would be unlearnable without pre-existing knowledge. This is usually coupled with a claim that the environment offers only impoverished and degraded information, incapable of explaining structured contents of mind (Tooby and Cosmides 1992: 46–8). Thus the human mind carries with it all the essential structure in language, acquired either as an accidental by-product of evolution (in Chomsky's view) or as an ancient evolutionary adaptation (as in Pinker and Bloom 1992).

All the evidence in fact points to the need for a quite different kind of theory, a theory in which the variation in our communication system is taken as one of the central facts to be explained in an evolutionary theory. For it is quite clear that the species is adapted precisely to handle the variation. Consider the evidence, already mentioned, from the study of the sensitivity of babies to the sound systems of their language – they have already apparently warped their acoustic space to distinguish the vowels of their native language by age six months, and the consonant system a few months later (see Kuhl 1991, Werker and Tees 1984). Distances between sounds that are distinct but must be classed together as one phoneme are systematically shrunk as it were, and distances between neighbouring sounds belonging to distinct phonemes are correspondingly stretched. The speed of this transformation argues indeed for special innate machinery – and in fact it can be shown that monkeys have no corresponding ability (Kuhl 1991). But it is special innate machinery for *tuning in to the local variant system*, that is, it is machinery that presupposes deep potential variation (from 2 to 46 vowels, or 6 to 95 consonants, for example; see Maddieson 1984). The same kind of rapid specialization has recently been shown by Choi *et al.* (in preparation) and McDonough *et al.* (in press) in the early learning of spatial semantic distinctions by infants. It is quite clear then that the human species is specifically equipped to handle cultural variation.

Such a capacity requires a new kind of theory, in which the species has evolved in the context of fast-changing cultural traditions, which provide an essential part of the selective environment for the genome (Cavalli-Sforza and Feldman 1981, Boyd and Richerson 1985, Durham 1991). In such a co-evolutionary theory, both genome and culture are conceived of as vertically transmitted lines of self-replicating and modifying information, which interact with one another in systematic ways. Models for a similar kind of interaction can be found in the study of symbiosis and parasitism, where two gene lines become inextricably intertwined, as with the fig and its fertilizing fig-wasp, neither of which can survive without the other. In the case of gene-culture evolution, one strand of information relies on cultural transmission, which permits horizontal transmission (borrowing) and fast change. That speed of adaptation is what makes culture evolutionarily advantageous, and to make that possible the genome must support special learning strategies that permit variation within expected bounds (Levinson 2000c).

Co-evolutionary theory has been developed by anthropologists and geneticists in a number of slightly different ways (see Durham 1991 for review). Although it has not received much attention from psychologists, it offers a much better model for an evolutionary psychology than the 'simple nativism' such psychologists normally espouse, for above all it attempts to account for the adaptive role that culture has played in human evolution. A co-evolutionary psychology accepts that the mind is prestructured (although not necessarily in the way imagined in simple

nativism), but insists that the cultural environment is also densely pat-
terned and structured, in a manner precisely designed to induce cognitive
patterns in that mind. When we learn a new word, we learn it from the
environment, which in turn only supplies words that have stood the test
of learnability in other minds.

To grasp the kinds of feedback loop that in co-evolutionary theory
are proposed to hold between biology and culture, consider the extraordinary facts about natural sign languages. Principally, these occur in
communities where there is a strain of hereditary deafness – the recessive genes responsible produce a small number of deaf people, who in
turn learn and pass on a specific cultural tradition of manual signing to
one another. The cultural tradition depends on the genes that make it
adaptive, and sign language makes it possible for the deaf to live full social and reproductive lives, so maintaining a community of signers (Aoki
and Feldman 1991). The very possibility of sign languages demonstrates
the extraordinary flexibility of language as a bio-cultural manifestation.
There is no other species that can transfer its communication system out
of one modality, for example the vocal-auditory channel, into another,
the motor-visual channel, and humans can go one further, as with the
blind-deaf use of the motor-haptic channel.

A co-evolutionary account gives us another possible approach to
linguistic universals, leading away from the 'innate ideas' of 'simple
nativism'. Linguistic universals have been formulated either in highly
abstract generative terms, in which case they cannot be tested empirically with any degree of confidence, or they are formulated as superfi-
cial but testable generalizations. The second kind of universals are, as
Greenberg has noted, either trivial of the kind 'All languages have at
least one vowel', or they turn out, as a matter of fact, to be statistical
and conditional tendencies, always with exceptions. The best example
of semantic universals, namely colour terms, is of this latter kind. A
co-evolutionary account seems natural: the 'universal focal colours' of
Berlin and Kay are perceptual landmarks, which ensure that 'the pattern of errors in use and transmission of color terms will be biased like
a loaded die, so that over time the linguistic references will converge
to match the neurophysiological foci of perceptual experience' (Deacon
1997: 119–20). Treating colour terminologies as in a push-pull relationship between neurophysiological biases on the one hand and cultural
pressures on the other has a number of distinct advantages: first, exceptional foci, like Russian light vs. dark blue, or Yélî Dnye dark red, can
be accommodated; second, the number and type of colour words are

related to the technological complexity of society (Berlin and Kay 1969), and specifically to the possession of a paint or dye technology (Gage 1999, Levinson 2000b); third, the long, slow emergence of colour terminologies, sometimes along exceptional trajectories, can be explained as the fixation of perceptual biases in cultural tradition over time (Kay and Maffi 1999, Levinson 2000b).

Another signal advantage of such a co-evolutionary account of universals is that we can remain agnostic or even sceptical about the many highly detailed 'innate ideas' that have been proposed. Innate ideas depend on the possibility of extensive 'representational nativism', that is, on the supposition that somewhere in the cortex genes have actually coded for a specific representation. The problem is that no neuroscientist can imagine how that can be done on any scale – there are neither sufficient genes nor relevant structure in the cortex to give us anything like Fodorean mentalese. Instead, it is much more plausible that there are architectural biases in the system, in the sense that, for example, different brain areas are differentially connected to one another and to sensory input and motor output (see Elman *et al.* 1996). Such preferential connectivity can give us the biases, the attractors in design space, which seem adequate to account for the statistical character of most linguistic universals. In addition, because co-evolutionary theory locates the other half of the structure in the environment, it is possible that certain conceptual solutions make good ecological and adaptive sense in any terrestrial environment, giving us further universal tendencies.

If we now turn to spatial frames of reference, we can see that we may not need the apparatus of 'innate ideas' to explain the strong universals we have discovered. Take the strongest, that all languages use the absolute frame of reference in the vertical dimension. There are many sensory systems that tune into the perceived vertical – the otoliths in our ears for example respond directly to an ecological property, namely gravitational force. Such perceptual biases from architectural neuroanatomical constraints hooked to perception make it highly likely that languages will reflect an orientation basic to our stance; combine this with our terrestrial experience of the relevance of the vertical for action and communication, and we have sufficient account for the universality of the vertical dimension in linguistic expression (cf. Clark 1973). An inevitably available concept is not necessarily genetically coded as an 'innate idea', i.e. a precoded concept, entirely internal to the organism. It may rather emerge from the interaction between low-level percepts, ecological facts and functional needs.

What about the three frames of reference, absolute, relative and intrinsic, applied to the horizontal? As we have seen, these are abstract concepts, coordinate systems each built on different principles with different logical properties. They might seem to be good candidates for innate concepts of the kind Chomsky (1965: 28) dubbed 'substantive universals', where a selection is made from a fixed inventory. Moreover, as noted, the intrinsic and the relative frames have antecedents in sensory perception, for example in visual object recognition and the system of three orthogonal egocentric planes directly instantiated in the semicircular canals of the inner ear. Recent work in the brain sciences based on human lesions and imaging or monkey models suggests that absolute representations of place for long-term memory may be located in the hippocampus (Maguire *et al.* 2000), relative representations of locations in egocentric coordinates for short-term memory may be located in the parietal, and some aspects of intrinsic representations in the supplementary eye field of the frontal lobe (Burgess *et al.* 1999: 21–2 and passim). Thus the three frames of reference may correspond to quite different pathways of neural processing, even though they may conspire to give us a seamless overall sense of space. Similarly, the visual perceptual system may be responsible for the figure–ground asymmetry of spatial language, and motor systems may be the source of the use of polar coordinates rather than Cartesian ones. This body of constraints and biases grounded in the organism and its relation to the immediate physical world provides the strong universal base for frames of reference.

But what is against the treatment of frames of reference as 'innate ideas' is precisely that they seem to emerge from a complex interaction between perception, internal neuroanatomy, ecology and cultural tradition. A first point is that, if the frames were innately given as conceptual constructs, they should all be universal, equally accessible, acquired at the same ages, and acquired young. As we have seen, the acquisition data do not remotely support those predictions. A second point is that there is significant variation across languages and cultures. Not all frames are manifest in all languages, and perhaps equally important, within each frame, languages vary greatly in the way they instantiate the conceptual details (as detailed in Chapter 3). Corresponding to this, some frames seem hardly conceptually accessible to speakers of languages that do not use them, a fact hard to explain if they were all innate concepts. A third point is that the presence of universal computational procedures in perception or action does not constitute evidence for universal *concepts*. For example, the fact that we can throw or catch a ball is not evidence for innate ballistical concepts – the species had to wait for Galileo to formulate such systematic ballistical concepts. Piaget emphasized the same point by stressing that perceptual or sensori-motor knowledge far outstrips conceptual or 'representational' knowledge: an infant within months of birth shows evidence of perceptual appreciation of straight lines (and can soon crawl in a bee-line), but has no workable concept of a straight line open to introspection till four years or more of age (Piaget and Inhelder 1956: Ch. 6). Recent work on infant perception – showing that six-month-olds do indeed have ballistical expectations, for example – does nothing to undermine this basic distinction between what is available for perception and what is available for conscious conceptual manipulation, and therefore for language. In the current jargon we say that many kinds of computation and representation are 'modular' – that is, their inner workings are inaccessible to other mental processes. That is why we are still trying to work out exactly how we reach for and grasp a pencil, let alone how we catch a ball. Nevertheless, despite the barriers to a simple transfer of perceptual to conceptual knowledge, much of our conceptual system may perhaps come during maturation from slow percolation out of perceptual and motor abilities in ways suggested by Piaget's work. Here the theory of 'representational redescription' developed by Karmiloff-Smith (1992) may be usefully applied: conceptual development in childhood may consist largely of re-working lower-level representations so that they increasingly become available to consciousness and other domains of cognition, under environmental stimulus and demand.

The co-evolutionary perspective offers an essential framework for thinking about all of this. Frames of reference as instantiated in particular languages are complex conceptual constructs. The elements out of which such constructs are made are various. They may include 'innate ideas', but if so, at the atomic level discussed in section 7.2, involving, for example, the building blocks of axial geometry or the process of transitive inference. They surely also include low-level representations involved in motor-control and perception of the kind previously mentioned, which serve to give us information about our location in larger space, the relation of our bodies to objects around us, and the properties of objects that guide their recognition – these forming a basis for possible exploitation in absolute, relative and intrinsic coordinate systems in higher-level conception.

If neurophysiological systems offer attractors in one direction, cultures offer attractors in other directions (see Sperber 1996 for models here). A specific language consists of (or draws on) ancient cultural traditions transmitted and modified over generations, in response to the cultural, ecological and communicative needs of its many users. Choices about which frames of reference are systematically coded, and exactly how each is conceived, are fixed in the lexicon and grammar of the linguistic system. Although enormously malleable compared to the genetic line of transmission, from the point of view of the infant acquiring its first language it is a robust and intransigent system resistant to anything more than fleeting innovations. The system provided by cultural transmission must conform to learnability constraints, and thus will tend to utilize the elements in the strong universal base provided by biology. But it can transcend such elements in all sorts of ways, constructing culturally specific geometric analyses of objects in the intrinsic frame, culturally specific transformations of axes in the relative frame, or culturally specific fixed bearings in the absolute frame.

The end result is that frames of reference as we see them in language are bio-cultural hybrids, just as is language itself. The universal elements in this domain are constraints and biases. The cultural traditions work within the constraints and tend to bend to biases, but they can transcend them, and always construct specific instantiations of frames. The universal and the relative are deeply interlocked in any one linguistic system. Such a system has knock-on effects, as we have seen, in other aspects of cognition, and can induce a learned or 'artificial' modularity of the kind, for example, we have found in communities where the absolute frame of reference in language induces a corresponding dedicated mental process or module, namely the constantly running mental compass.

This brings us to the question raised in the title to this section: How did we lose our mental compass? Many other species have special hardware dedicated to orientation and dead reckoning (like the desert ant mentioned in Chapter 6). It may be that the hippocampus, which in rats seems to be the locus for some of these computations, has been invaded by other functions in humans. But it may also be that there is a penalty to the flexibility that is motivated by the co-evolution of culture and language – predominant coordinate systems in navigation are clearly not set in advance for humans. Certainly, human populations that rely predominantly on the relative frame of reference seem to be bereft of any developed sense of direction (as shown again in Chapter 6). This seems to be the penalty of letting language invade cognition. As mentioned earlier, in a series of interesting experiments, Herman, Spelke and collaborators have explored the developmental trend in simple location finding (Spelke and Tsivkin 2001). What they have found is that just as they acquire the relevant aspects of language, children are able to transcend the rat-like geometrical system of location finding, which seems to be modular in nature, and combine it with information from other sources, such as the colour, shape or pattern of landmarks. They suggest that, as we come to rely on language to transcend modular mental processes, so we also inherit the limitations – for example, the metric imprecision – of the linguistic medium.

In conclusion, despite the fact that so much current theory emphasizes the innate basis of linguistic and conceptual categories, the facts of linguistic and cognitive diversity point to an important role for constructivism in human cognition. Constructivism is entirely compatible with strong universals, innate biases and domain-specific learning (Karmiloff-Smith 1992), and it is required to explain how learning a language seems to play an important role in restructuring cognition. A language 'canalizes' the mental landscape, offering complex concepts that would otherwise be mostly out of the range of independent invention – complex concepts, like specific instantiations of frames of reference, that then come to dominate the internal coding of states of affairs and events. Language-specific concepts contribute fundamentally to the computational power of individual human minds, but also of course make possible the distributed computation across social groups that is such a specific feature of the species. This is what has allowed us to colonize every niche on the planet. Although offering fundamental adaptive advantages, these language-specific specializations may come at a price, for they may reduce sensitivities in other areas, as clearly demonstrated in our phonetic specialization – a similar conceptual 'tuning' may also occur, as suggested by the relative-speaker's lack of a mental compass. But the advantages are overwhelming: because the inheritance of our linguistic abilities is in part transferred to cultural traditions, those traditions can accumulate conceptual innovations contributed by myriads of individuals, making possible the richly variable texture, the constant change combined with continuity, and the dependence on community that are the foundations of the human mode of existence.

Notes

I THE INTELLECTUAL BACKGROUND: TWO MILLENNIA OF WESTERN
IDEAS ABOUT SPATIAL THINKING

1. For example, the visual information from an observed scene seems to be split into object-identification features sent to the inferior temporal cortex, while information about location of the object is sent to the posterior parietal cortex, the two streams being united again in the hippocampus (Kolb and Whishaw 1990: 653). Within the parietal cortex, many different subsystems seem to be geared to different reference points, some such subsystems relating the position of things observed to the position of the eyes, others to the position of the head, and so on, so that our conscious coherence of spatial experience is constructed from a vast division of labour between complex specialized neuropsychological systems (Colby 1999: 786).

2. It is true that in language, metric distance is rarely encoded in spatial descriptions, and thus the term 'coordinate system' may seem inflationary – but there are good reasons to think about such linguistic descriptions as a limiting case of the metrically specific coordinate systems used in perceptual and motor systems. The parallels between linguistic and non-linguistic representations are the subject of Chapter 2.

3. Seeing this is believing it, but see the report in Haviland 1993, and Chapter 6 below.

4. As Einstein (1954: xiii) put it, 'Now as to the concept of space, it seems that this was preceded by the psychologically simpler concept of place'. For much detail on this theme, see Casey 1997.

5. Compare A.N. Whitehead: 'In the first place, the presented locus is defined by some systematic relation to the human body' (quoted in Casey 1997: 210).

6. Critique can be found in the commentary to the BBS article by Landau and Jackendoff 1993, and in Brown 1994.

7. Cicero (*De Oratore*, II, lxxxvi, Loeb edition): '[P]ersons desiring to train this faculty of memory must select places and form mental images of the things they wish to remember and store those images in those places, so that the order of the places will preserve the order of the things, and the images of the things will denote the things themselves, and we shall employ the places and images respectively as a wax writing-tablet and the letters written on it'

(cited in Yates 1966: 2). In modern terms, the idea was to use the distinct 'what' and 'where' systems of spatial processing as an enhanced means of recall – the 'where' system giving us the overall frame and order of recall, and the 'what' system the specific memory in each slot in the frame. This long-standing memory tradition led in the seventeenth century to the search for natural, memorable and universal notations, and thus, amongst other things, to Leibniz's invention of the calculus (Yates 1966: 384).

2 FRAMES OF REFERENCE

1. Rock (1992) is here commenting on Asch and Witkin (1948), who built directly on the Gestalt notions. See also Rock 1990.
2. One kind of disagreement is voiced by Paillard 1991: 471: 'Spatial frame-works are incorporated in our perceptual and motor experiences. They are not however to be confused with the *system of coordinates* which abstractly represent them.' But this is terminological; for our purposes we wish precisely to abstract out the properties of frames of reference, so we can consider how they apply across different perceptual or conceptual systems. Another kind of terminological objection is that in semantics (as opposed to perception) strict metric values on coordinates play no role.
3. 'When places are individuated by their spatial relation to certain objects, a crucial part of what we need to know is what those objects are. As the term "frame of reference" is commonly used, these objects would be said to provide the "frame of reference"' (Brewer and Pears 1993: 25). It is true that in physics, e.g. in special relativity, a reference frame can be identified with the object to which the coordinate system is attached, but this is because we are assuming a uniformity of coordinate systems, and abstracting away from psychology.
4. I shall use the opposition 'Figure' vs. 'Ground' for the object to be located vs. the object with respect to which it is to be located, respectively, after Talmy 1983. This opposition is identical to that between Theme vs. Relatum, Referent vs. Relatum, Trajector vs. Landmark, and various other terminologies.
5. Brewer and Pears (1993) consider the role of coordinate systems but what they have to say only increases our puzzlement: 'Two events are represented as being in the same spatial position if and only if they are assigned the same co-ordinates. Specifying a frame of reference would have to do with specifying how co-ordinates are to be assigned to events in the world on the basis of their spatial relations to certain objects. These objects provide the frame of reference' (Brewer and Pears 1993: 26). This fails to recognize that two distinct systems of coordinates over the same objects can describe the same place, as in the two descriptions of Fig. 2.1, where the ball is both in front of the truck and to the left of it.
6. I have drawn on Levinson 1996b for parts of this section, with kind permission of the publisher.

7. There are many good sketches of parts of this intellectual terrain (see, e.g., Miller and Johnson-Laird 1976, Jammer 1954, O'Keefe and Nadel 1978), but none of it all.

8. Some notion of absolute space was already presupposed by Descartes' introduction of coordinate systems, as Einstein (1954: xiv) pointed out.

9. This was in part due to the British empiricists like Berkeley whose solipsism made egocentric relative space the basis for all our spatial ideas. See quotations and discussions in O'Keefe and Nadel 1978: 14–16.

10. Much behavioural experimentation on, e.g., rats in mazes, has led to classifications of behaviour parallel to the notions of frame of reference: O'Keefe and Nadel's 1978 classification, for example, is in terms of body-position responses (cf. egocentric frames of reference), cue responses (a kind of allocentric response to an environmental gradient) and place responses (involving allocentric mental maps). Work on infant behaviour similarly relates behavioural response types to frames of reference, usually egocentric vs. allocentric (or 'geographic' – see Pick 1988: 147ff.).

11. See also Brewer and Pears 1993: 29, who argue that allocentric behaviour can always be mimicked through egocentric computations: 'Perhaps language ... provides the only conclusive macroscopic evidence for genuine allocentricity.'

12. These distinctions seem rarely to be properly made in the literature on mental maps in humans. Students of animal behaviour, though, have noted that maps consisting of relative angles and distances between landmarks have quite different computational properties to maps with fixed bearings: in the former, but not the latter, each time landmarks are added to the map, the database increases exponentially (see, e.g., McNaughton *et al.* 1990). Despite that, most rat studies fail to distinguish these two kinds of allocentricity, relative and absolute.

13. Paillard (1991: 471ff.) has a broader notion of 'frames of reference' than most brain scientists (and closer to psychological ideas): he proposes that there are four such frames subserving visually guided action, all organized around the geocentric vertical: (1) a body frame, presuming upright posture for action; (2) an object frame, presumably similar to Marr's object-centred system; (3) a world frame, a Euclidean space inclusive of both body and object; and (4) a retinal frame, feeding the object and world frames. He even provides a rough neural 'wiring diagram' (p. 473).

14. The age at which this switch to the non-egocentric takes place seems highly task dependent (see Acredolo 1988 who gives sixteen months as an end-point; see also Pick 1993 for a route-finding task, where the process has hardly begun by sixteen months).

15. This leap from a perspective image, or worse a silhouette, is possible (he argued) only by assuming that objects can be analysed into geometrical volumes of a specific kind (generalized cones); hence 3D models must be of this kind, where principal axes are identified.

16. Others have suggested that what we store is a 2.5D image coupled with the ability to mentally rotate it (Tarr and Pinker 1989), thus giving our apparent ability to rotate mental images (Shepard and Metzler 1971) some evolutionary raison d'être. Yet others suggest that object-recognition is achieved via a set of 2.5D images from different orientations (Bülthoff 1991), while some (Rock *et al.* 1989) suggest we have none of these powers.

17. I am grateful to Eve Danziger for putting me in touch with this work; see Danziger 1994 for possible connections to linguistic distinctions.

18. As mentioned in Chapter 1, enantiomorphs are otherwise identical objects that differ in handedness, like a left shoe vs. a right shoe, or indeed a letter **d** vs. **b**.

19. As Kant (1991 [1768]) made clear, objects differing in handedness (enantiomorphs or incongruent counterparts in his terminology) cannot be distinguished in an object-centred (or intrinsic) frame of reference, but only in an external coordinate system. See Van Cleve and Frederick 1991, and, for the relevance to a Mayan language Tzeltal, Levinson and Brown 1994.

20. E.g. the Cube Comparisons Test can be solved by (1) rotation using viewer-centred coordinates, (2) rotation around an object-centred axis imaged with viewer-centred coordinates, (3) rotation of the perspective point around the object, (4) purely object-centred comparisons.

21. Cohen and Kubovy display deep confusion about frames of reference: they suggest (1993: 379) that one can have orientation-free representations of handedness information in an orientation-free frame of reference by utilizing the notion 'clockwise'. But as Kant (1991 [1768]) showed, and generations of philosophers since have agreed (see Van Cleve and Frederick 1991), the notion 'clockwise' presupposes an external orientation.

22. This view, shared by Miller and Johnson-Laird (1976: 404) and Svorou (1994: 23), would seem to be subtly different from Levelt's (1989), as discussed below.

23. The equation is hers; actually, her survey perspective in some cases (e.g. outside the context of maps) may also relate to a more abstract 'absolute' spatial framework where both viewer and landmarks are embedded in a larger frame of reference (see also Tversky and Taylor 1998, and Tversky 1996).

24. The conceptual system is abstract over different perceptual clues, as shown by the fact that astronauts can happily talk about "above and to the left", etc., where one perceptual clue for the vertical (namely gravity) is missing (Friederici and Levelt 1990). Levelt (1989: 154–5) concludes that the spatial representation itself does not determine the linguistic description: 'there is . . . substantial freedom in putting the perceived structure, which is spatially represented, into one or another propositional format'.

25. For example, there is no convincing explanation of the English deictic use of 'front', 'back', 'left', 'right': we talk of *the cat in front of the tree*, as if the tree was an interlocutor facing us, but when we say *The cat is to the left*

of the tree we do not (as, e.g., in some dialects of Tamil) mean the cat is to the tree's left, therefore to our right. The reason is that the facts have always been under-described, the requisite coordinate systems not being properly spelled out even in the most recent works. See Chapter 3 for more details.

26. Except in some places: thus in the Torres Straits, where the trade winds roar through westward, spatial descriptions can be in terms of 'leeward' and 'windward'. Or where the earth drops away in one direction, as on the edges of mountain ranges, gravity can be naturally imported into the horizontal plane (see Chapter 4).

27. The reader may feel that the notion of 'front' is different for chairs and persons (and so of course it is), and in particular that 'in front of me' is somehow more abstract than 'in front of the chair'. But notice that we could have said 'at my feet' or 'at the foot of the chair' – here 'foot' clearly means something different in each case, but shares the notion of an intrinsic part of the relatum object.

28. The importance of the distinction between binary and ternary spatial relators was pointed out by Herrmann 1990.

29. For example, the Australian language Guugu Yimithirr has (derived) lexemes meaning 'north side of', 'south side of', etc., which involve both the intrinsic (or at least topological) and absolute frames of reference in the interpretation of a single word. Less exotically, English *on* as in *the cup on the table* would seem to combine absolute (vertical) information with topological information (contact) with intrinsic information (supporting planar surface).

30. This point is important: some psychologists have been tempted to presume, because of the ambiguity of English *in front* etc., that frames of reference are imposed on language by a spatial interpretation, rather than being distinguished semantically (see, e.g., Carlson-Radvansky and Irwin 1993). But as we have seen, the semantic structure of *in front* is binary on an intrinsic interpretation, ternary on a relative one.

31. We know one way in which this tripartite typology may be incomplete: some languages use conventionalized landmark systems which in practice grade into absolute systems; however, there are some reasons for thinking that landmark systems and fixed-bearings systems are distinct conceptual types.

32. I am indebted to many discussions with colleagues (especially perhaps Balthasar Bickel, Eve Danziger, Eric Pederson, David Wilkins) over the details of this scheme, although they would not necessarily agree with this particular version.

33. People who use absolute systems to the exclusion of relative systems do not seem to think about any one direction as primary, with the others found by (anti-)clockwise rotation. This is not surprising, for as Kant (1991 [1768]) pointed out, that would be to smuggle in notions of left and right. See 4.1.1 below.

34. We tend to think of human prototypes as inevitably the source of such proto-type parts. But such anthropomorphism may be ethnocentric: e.g. in Mayan languages plant-parts figure in human-part description (see Laughlin 1975, Levinson 1994). In many languages a quadruped animal model clearly plays a central role, so that, e.g., 'back' labels the upper surface of an object, 'belly' the underneath, and 'head' the front (see Svorou 1994: 73ff., Heine 1997: 40ff.).

35. Thus Miller and Johnson-Laird 1976: 401, thinking of English-speakers: 'People tend to treat objects as six-sided. If an object has both an intrinsic top and bottom, and an intrinsic front and back, the remaining two sides are intrinsically left and right...' Incidentally, the possession of 'intrinsic left/right' is perhaps an indication that such systems are ultimately not exclusively object-centred (since left and right cannot be distinguished without an external frame of reference, e.g. a notion of clockwise rotation).

36. In the next chapter it will be explained that, when F and G are contiguous, we in fact find ourselves outside the domain of frames of reference and in the domain of 'topology'. This is because frames of reference are about directions, hence require coordinate systems, and all of this is otiose when F and G can be treated as coincident in space.

37. See the notion of intrinsic region in Miller and Johnson-Laird 1976. They suggest this may be linked to perceptual contiguity within 10 degrees of visual arc (1976: 91), but that this perceptual notion of region has a conceptual counterpart that combines perceptual and functional information about the region of social or physical interaction of one body with another (1976: 387–8).

38. That this is a matter of cultural construal rather than brute fact is shown by the fact that, e.g., in Chamus trees have intrinsic fronts, defined by the side in which they lean or have the biggest or most branches (Heine 1997: 13).

39. But some languages encode relative concepts based directly on visual occlusion or the absence of it, which do not have intrinsic counterparts (as S. Kita has pointed out to me).

40. As shown by its priority in acquisition (Johnston and Slobin 1979). On the other hand, some languages hardly utilize an intrinsic frame of reference at all (see Chapter 4).

41. This does not seem, once again, the right analysis for English 'left'/'right', since F and G need not be in the same plane at all (*The tree to the left of the rising moon*), and intuitively *To the left of the ball* does not ascribe a left-facet to the ball.

42. Although transitivity and converseness in relative descriptions hold only on the presumption that V is held constant.

43. Conversely, other languages like Tamil use it in more far-reaching ways.

44. Note that F may be a part of G, as in 'the bark on the left (side) of the tree'.

45. The vector style of analysis in O'Keefe 1996 uses no secondary coordinates for 'front' and 'back' – but such an analysis obscures the commonality

between the intrinsic and relative uses of such terms – namely that both involve the assignment of facets to the ground.

46. Environmental clues will not explain the fact that such heightened dead-reckoning abilities extend outside familiar territory. I presume that such people have been socialized to constantly compute direction as a background task, by inertial navigation with constant checks with visual information and other sensory information (e.g. sensing wind direction). But see Baker (1989) who believes in faint human magnetoreception. These issues are taken up especially in Chapter 6.

47. Note that none of these environmental bases can provide the cognitive basis of abstracted systems: once the community has fixed a direction, it remains in that direction regardless of fluctuations in local landfall, drainage, wind source, equinox etc., or even removal of the subject from the local environment. Thus the environmental sources of such systems may explain their origins, but do not generally explain how they are used, or how the cardinal directions are psychologically 'fixed'.

48. Due no doubt to the introduction of the compass in medieval times. Before then, maps typically had east at the top, hence our term 'orient oneself', showing that our use of polar coordinates is older than the compass. Indeed, the compass rose was derived from wind directions, somewhat like contemporary Eskimo systems (see Macdonald 1998: 181–2).

49. Warlpiri may be a case in point. Note that such a system may be based on a solar compass, but since solstitial variation makes it necessary to abstract an equinoctial bisection of the seasonal movement of the sun along the horizon, it is less confusing to fix the system by reference to the mentally constituted orthogonal to the path of the sun.

50. Guugu Yimithirr, described in Chapter 4, would be a case in point, since there are no elicitable associations of sequence or priority between cardinal directions.

51. The Wik Mungan system (another Aboriginal language of Cape York) was described by Peter Sutton in a presentation to the Australian Linguistics Institute, Sydney, June 1992.

52. There is an important exception: vectors of alignment or motion may be stated without reference to G, as in 'The western slope' or 'The geese fly north in summer'. These are, to my knowledge, the only kinds of natural language spatial descriptions that are not Leibnizian – that is, that do not specify spatial properties of orientation and direction by reference to other objects or landmarks. Most discussions of spatial language assume there are no such relations (e.g. Svorou 1994: 49 'all spatial relations are conceived of with reference to L(and)M(ark)s').

53. See, e.g., Lewis 1972: 62–80 for discussion of a range of indigenous Pacific star and wind compasses. Although, e.g., the Fijian wind compass is organized in three arcs of roughly 120 degrees, there is clearly a tendency towards orthogonals, with regular subdivisions leading up to 32 compass points. The same is noted for Eskimo wind compasses by Macdonald 1998: 181.

54. I am grateful to David Wilkins, and other colleagues, for helping me to systematize these observations.
55. The 'theory of mind' literature suggests that an essential element of human cognition involves the ability to take the perspective of the other – this is what makes teaching, communication and strategic competition possible.
56. See Van Cleve and Frederick 1991 for discussion of this Kantian point. For the cross-cultural implications, and a working out of the place of absolute systems in all this, see Levinson and Brown 1994, Danziger 1994.
57. The problem is discussed in Locke, *Essay on human understanding*, book II, ix, 8. The question was brought back into philosophical discussion by Gareth Evans, and many of the papers in Eilan *et al.* 1993 explicitly address Molyneux's question.
58. See, e.g., Ettlinger 1987: 174: 'language serves as a cross-modal bridge'.
59. The issue may be less clear than it at first seems; see Tye 1991: 5–9.
60. This possibility of getting from a relative representation to an intrinsic one may help to explain the apparent inconsistency between the argument here and my colleague Levelt's (1996) view that both these frames are linguistic only and generated from a third kind of spatial representation. Levelt found that whether subjects adopt a relative (the majority solution) or intrinsic (the minority choice) linguistic description of an array, they make linguistic ellipses that always presuppose a uniform underlying spatial frame of reference. He therefore suggests that frames of reference reside in the mapping from spatial representation to language rather than in the spatial representation itself. But his data are compatible with an analysis whereby the spatial representation is itself in a relative frame of reference, and the mapping is optionally to an intrinsic or relative description. In Chapter 5, I describe some experiments that suggest that, for similar Dutch subjects, the relative frame is indeed the default non-linguistic frame of reference. The mapping from relative to intrinsic is one of the two mappings in principle possible between frames of reference, as here described, whereas a mapping from intrinsic spatial representation to linguistic relative representation would be in principle impossible. This would seem to explain all the data that we currently have in hand.

3 LINGUISTIC DIVERSITY

1. Similarly, Talmy (1988: 175–7) suggests that adpositions or grammatical elements are shape-neutral and material-neutral, so there should not only be no adposition 'through-a-shape' but also no 'through-a-medium', but again Karuk obliges with another spatial morpheme meaning 'in through a solid'! The point is taken up below.
2. A number of languages though, like Thai and Yélî Dnye, use unrelated morphemes in location and motion questions ('Where' vs. 'Whence' or 'Whither').
3. Systematic collection of dimensional expressions in Yélî by myself, and in other languages by colleagues, followed methods developed by Christel Stolz

1996 (see also Annual report of Max Planck Institute for Psycholinguistics, 1996: 68–71).

4. This section partially repeats information earlier published in Levinson 1996a.

5. Piaget's work has been heavily criticized in the light of recent studies of infant cognition. Babies apparently know things Piaget has been thought to think they do not. However, the criticism often neglects the careful distinction he made between perceptual and cognitive or 'representational' faculties, the former being by his own account fully in place by twelve months.

6. Talmy (1983) himself reports that Atsugewi makes many such distinctions, so his insistence on the shape- and medium-neutrality of spatial morphemes is puzzling. Presumably, he intends the generalizations as mere statistical tendencies, but since languages of many different families make such distinctions (and often many of them), we can hardly consider them aberrant (and the statistical tendencies have been radically affected by the loss of languages under European colonization).

7. Note that the intrinsic reading is often forced by the definite article, which in turn constrains the preposition: therefore *at the front of the TV* rather than *in the front of the TV*, but either *at* or *in the front of the book*. There has been relatively little work on the way these collocations select interpretations, perhaps because things look messy – for example the definite article in *to the left of Bill* fails to resolve the ambiguity. Note too that in English choice between the two possessive constructions constrains interpretations: *in front of Bill* is ambiguously relative or intrinsic, but *at Bill's front* only allows the intrinsic reading.

8. This explains why the intrinsic system is learned earlier by children than the relative system. What happens in the case of absolute systems, also binary in character? They seem to be learnt just as early as intrinsic systems – see Brown and Levinson 2000.

9. In many cultures such a face-to-face stance is, as we aptly say, confrontational: thus Australian Aboriginals such as Guugu Yimithirr speakers or Tenejapan Mayans will prefer to talk side-by-side (or even, if deference is at issue, front to back).

10. How would one know? Suppose that the route to be described had a shape approximating a capital P without the final join between the loop and the upright. A relative description might go "Go straight ahead, turn right, then come back this way, then left", while a more natural intrinsic route description would go "Go straight, turn right, then straight, then right again". It will be harder to distinguish the two systems when the relative system is successively transposed or deictically shifted to each step of the journey, but then we would expect the ternary relations presupposed by locutions like "Take the alley to the left of the gas-station".

11. More directly, the midday zenith of the sun throughout the year – as indeed of all other heavenly bodies – always lies on a north-south axis: above the tropic of Cancer, the zenith is always due south; below the tropic of

Capricorn, always due north; and in the tropics it varies between north and south according to season. This astronomical constancy may be utilized by many species (Gallistel 1990: 46).

12. For this reason, among others, I doubt the generalization that cardinal direction terms are most frequently derived from the sun and body-part terms (Brown 1983; cf. Heine 1997) – the danger is that we recognize as true cardinal directions only those that look like our own.

13. Because in most English speaking communities, *north* is used on geographic scales, especially with reference to maps, its semantics for most speakers is fixed to grid-north (often 15 degrees or more divergent from magnetic north), and it has no clear range of reference like, for example, the 90-degree quadrant of Guugu Yimithirr *gungga-*. Lacking this clear angle of specification, and being variously in opposition with such nautical notions as north-east or even NNE etc., the semantics of the term *north* does not lend itself to ordinary parlance as a complete replacement for, say, the relative angles.

14. Blake (1994: 161) points out difficulties with the formulation of implicational hierarchies in case-marking. Nevertheless the following is a first approximation:

Locative > **Ablative** > **Allative** > **Perlative / Translative** > **Essives**
Location > Source   > Goal   > Path   > Ground properties

Here, the possession of 'essive' cases (e.g. those marking dimensionality of the ground object) implies cases higher up the scale. But a better way to conceive the situation is, as mentioned, in terms of fractionation out of conflation. Such differentiation is also diachronically counteracted by a well-attested tendency for both ablatives and allatives to lose their dynamic meaning and become locatives.

15. Landau and Jackendoff 1993 treat the complex prepositions in English as a finite list of fixed expressions, forming part of the closed class of English prepositions. But this is misleading: *on the top of* is part of a generative system of spatial expressions, including *on the very tippety top of* etc. See Quirk *et al.* 1991: 665–73 for criteria distinguishing complex prepositions like *in spite of* from freely constructable preposition + nominal sequences.

16. See Steinhauer 1991: 177–221 and Heeschen 1982: 81–110. R. van den Berg (1997) shows how complex the choice of 'up'/ 'down' motion verbs is in relation to cardinal directions, on the one hand, and non-straight-line, non-horizontal routes, on the other.

4 ABSOLUTE MINDS: GLIMPSES INTO TWO CULTURES

1. Acknowledgements. This part of the chapter draws on material published in more detail in Levinson 1997a, based on fieldwork conducted from July to September 1992 in Hopevale Aboriginal Community, Cape York Peninsula, Far North Queensland, Australia (I had spent an earlier period there in

1982). All the detailed acknowledgements made in that paper hold here too: John Haviland and Lourdes de León shared the early weeks of fieldwork and gave me many useful ideas about how to pursue the enquiries reported here; above all, I am grateful for the tolerance, interest and support from the community at large. But special thanks are due to Roger Hart, who helped me transcribe large amounts of Guugu Yimithirr text with exemplary patience, and to Dan Charlie and Walter Jack, who were instructive company on many bush trips, and to Jimmy Hart for crab and refuge at the beach. John Haviland's (1979a, 1993) earlier grammatical work on the language made all of this possible.

2. Guugu Yimithirr has terms for left-hand and right-hand, but these are only body-part terms (as mentioned in Chapter 3). Other body-part terms like 'nose' may be used in expressions glossing 'nose to north' etc. to indicate orientation of a body, but they play no other essential role in spatial description. The terms for 'up' and 'down' share some of the morphological properties of the cardinal directions, and can be thought of as belonging to the absolute system (and are in fact used locally as cardinal directions; see Haviland 1979a: 76). There are terms for 'inside', 'outside', 'underneath', 'in between' etc., together with locative, ablative and allative cases. But there is nothing remotely similar to our familiar 'left'/'right'/'front'/'back' system (see Haviland 1993).

3. In a workshop organized by Haviland and myself at the Linguistics Institute of Australia, Sydney, July 1992, the question of the distribution of such systems was addressed. It seems, from the information available, that most of the Australian languages make essential use of such systems with the exception of those in the Daly River area, where 'upriver', 'downriver' notions may take their place. Eva Schultze-Berndt (2000) of our research group has since investigated such a riverine system in Jaminjung, in the Timber Creek area of the Northern Territory. Guugu Yimithirr seems to be somewhat unusual in the extent to which so-called topological and intrinsic frame-of-reference concepts are replaced by absolute direction expressions. The GY system of directionals is, however, not particularly elaborate as Australian systems go; for example, there is a much more complex set of morphological derivatives of cardinal direction roots in Warlpiri (Laughren 1978) or Kayardild (Evans 1995). Incidentally, I am grateful to the participants at that workshop for sharing their ideas and encouraging the line of work here described, and for a subsequent correspondence with David Nash.

4. The information comes from an unpublished dictionary by Haviland (available in the archives of the Australian Institute for Aboriginal and Torres Straits Islander Studies, Canberra), where he gives *thalbaarr* as the alternate for *jibaarr*, and *nguwaar* as the alternate for *guwa*. Although I found informants able to confirm this, they had no explanation. See also the following note.

5. The significance of the *-rra* suffix on the north and south terms, as opposed to the zero suffix on the west and east terms, is now opaque. The zero suffix

on the latter might be interpreted as giving them some kind of conceptual priority, but there is no other evidence for this.

6. Many of these, but not all, are covered in Haviland 1993.

7. Of course, locative case plus placename may also suffice. It is the angular specification on the horizontal plane that requires use of cardinal directions.

8. I may add by way of background that Hopevale was established as a mission in a large reservation, which covered part of the original territory of GY speaking peoples before the Palmer River goldrush of 1872 shattered their world. From 1886 till 1967 the survivors from this and various other groups were collectively administered by Lutheran missionaries, who undermined many aspects of traditional culture; thereafter the township was organized by a slowly evolving independent management (Haviland 1985, Haviland and Haviland 1980, Haviland and Hart 1998), recently in a complex context of land-right claims. Today the community numbers about 1,500, but the pool of residents is in constant flux between this and other Queensland towns and reservations. As employment opportunities are low, most residents rely on social security payments, which, together with school, anchors most families to Hopevale centre, but dispersed settlement and pastoral and hunting pursuits remain the favoured way of life, now conducted with horses, guns, four-wheel-drive vehicles and outboard-powered dinghies to complement spear and woomera. Much traditional hunting and gathering knowledge persists, but most food comes from the central store. Overland communication was still at the time of fieldwork by dirt road, difficult in the wet season, but regular light airplane services were transforming travel.

9. The excellent grammatical and lexicographical work by Haviland describes the language largely as it was spoken by elderly speakers twenty years ago. It is still spoken that way, but by increasingly few people. There are extensive grammatical and lexical changes underway, in the direction, it seems, of simplification.

10. Work on acquisition of the language, and especially its spatial aspects, has been begun by Lourdes de León (1996).

11. Large parts of the corpus, filmed or tape-recorded by J.B. Haviland since 1971, by myself and Penelope Brown in 1982, and by myself again in 1992, are deposited in the Australian Institute for Aboriginal and Torres Straits Islander Studies, Canberra, or are held at the Max Planck Institute for Psycholinguistics, Nijmegen, The Netherlands.

12. Details of this 'kit' of elicitation techniques are available from the Language and Cognition Group, are P.O. BOX 310, Nijmegen, The Netherlands.

13. The tasks have various sources of inspiration, especially Clark and Wilkes-Gibbs (1986), Weissenborn (1984), von Stutterheim and Carroll (1993) and were developed in the Max Planck Cognitive Anthropology Group jointly, but with initial impetus by Lourdes de León (see de León 1991).

14. For example, *en route* to Cairns for a land-rights meeting, a group of men on a bus before dawn repeatedly gestured the boundaries of traditional territories held by various lineage groups, saying, e.g., "it run *yarrba*, this way", even

though the bus was passing through a very rough and circuitous stretch of road. Checks against my compass seemed to show general accuracy even under these conditions.

15. The ethnography of wayfinding is, with the exception of studies of oceanic navigation, extremely poor (see Levinson 1996a, 1996d for review). Amazingly, even studies of hunter-gatherers usually omit any systematic survey of navigational techniques (but see Widlok 1997). The importance of such data to the understanding of prehistory should hardly need to be stressed.

16. I have retained a conventional statistical presentation in Table 4.1 for comparison with Lewis' results in Table 4.2. But there is a sounder method for the statistical treatment of circular estimations (Batschelet 1981), and the data is reanalysed in this way in Chapter 6.

17. I obtained this bush lore from two men who had worked as stockmen on stations outside the reservation, and it may well be station lore rather than Aboriginal in origin (e.g. the star knowledge is suspect, given the lack of traditional names for constellations, but see Lewis 1976: 274).

18. This was the 'Pear Film' produced by the Berkeley project for the cross-linguistic study of discourse, and I thank Wallace Chafe for permission to use it and Jack Dubois for a copy and the associated instructions.

19. I now know that the place to look is in the study of animal cognition, and the study of pre-linguistic thinking in the human infant (see, e.g., Spelke and Tsivkin 2001).

20. I thank the administrator of the home, Mrs Thelma McIvor, for permission to use the rooms.

21. This idea I think I owe to John Haviland in conversation, and certainly thanks are due to him for the ideas for some of the probes here described. Nick Evans (1995) also raises the subject in connection with the use of another Australian language, Kayardild.

22. Mythical stories are oriented, but given their connection to the landscape that is hardly surprising. One historical story described in Levinson 1987b contains a sequence describing a fight in oriented fashion; there were no witnesses, and the protagonists either died or were transported to a penal settlement, so it is unlikely that the directions there – as opposed to the rest of the story – have historical veracity.

23. Fieldwork in Tenejapa on spatial themes was conducted jointly with Penelope Brown intensively from 1990 to 1995.

24. The main purpose of the delay (forced 30 seconds delay followed by another 15–30 seconds moving between stimulus and response) was to minimize the chances of the employment of a sub-vocal *linguistic* coding. Such a coding would require use of the auditory loop in short-term memory, which without rehearsal decays in c. 10 seconds (Baddeley 1990: 31, Potter 1990: 24). This is the system involved in, e.g., remembering a number just looked up in a telephone book when dialling. Any other vocal input such as conversation during such subvocal rehearsal will effectively mask this short-term memory, and in many applications of the tasks mentioned below short vocal interchanges took place between stimulus and response. Another effect of

such a delay is to flush the very brief 'iconic' visual memory buffer, which is thought to have a half-life of c. 10 seconds (Baddeley 1990: 31): such a visual image would encode a relative viewpoint (see Chapter 2), and might favour relative coding of arrays.

25. This experiment was designed by myself and improved by Bernadette Schmitt.

26. The design of this experiment is by Eric Pederson and Bernadette Schmitt, building on the earlier design by myself used in Hopevale and described above.

27. This task was devised and piloted by Eric Pederson, with the help of Bernadette Schmitt, and is thus affectionately known as 'Eric's maze'. It is a development of the maze task used in Hopevale and described above – a later improved version of the Hopevale task is known as 'Steve's maze' and is mentioned briefly in Chapter 5.

5 DIVERSITY IN MIND: METHODS AND RESULTS FROM A CROSS-LINGUISTIC SAMPLE

1. This chapter derives from an earlier working paper written by Laszlo Nagy and myself – it is now transformed to a point where Laszlo would scarcely recognize it, nevertheless I have absorbed many ideas and especially methodological points from him. Moreover he was responsible for the statistical treatment of the cross-linguistic sample – thus *sine qua non*. I record my gratitude to him.

2. There is some positive evidence against this interpretation in our sample. We have two Tamil populations, one urban and better educated, one rural and less educated – the former are predominantly relative coders in language and cognition, the latter predominantly absolute coders in language and cognition. But the urban relative coders are not markedly more consistent coders than the less-schooled rural population.

3. In particular, the results reported here for Arrernte were collected by David Wilkins, for Belhare by Balthasar Bickel, for Hai//om by Thomas Widlok, for Japanese by Kyoko Inoue, for Kgalagadi by Sabine Neumann, for Kilivila by Gunter Senft, for Longgu by Deborah Hill, for Tamil by Eric Pederson, for Totonac by Paulette Levy, for Tzeltal by Penelope Brown (in collaboration with Levinson), for Yucatec by Christel Stolz. My thanks to all these colleagues not only for collecting the relevant data, but for helping us to understand it in the context of the language and culture. Full publication of many of these results will be forthcoming in due course.

4. See Pederson *et al.* 1998, Hill 1997, Wilkins 1989, in press for the relevant linguistic data.

5. KRUSKAL-WALLIS one-way analysis of variance for 104 cases:

Group	Count	Rank sum
Abs	51	3822.500
Rel	53	1637.500

6. There would be another possible strategy, namely to follow the situation-specific strategy through pairs of matched linguistic and non-linguistic tasks. Senft (2001) attempts to do this in a reanalysis of the Kilivila data, using extended linguistic data.

7. The Dutch control group of forty subjects ranged in age between twenty-one and seventy-seven. One of these subjects reported difficulties distinguishing left and right, proved anomalous on the tasks, and is eliminated from the statistical procedures below.

8. See Neumann and Widlok 1996 for a careful comparison of the linguistic and animals task data in Hai//om and Kgalagadi. Incidentally, Widlok there classifies some Hai//om expressions as relative which in the terms of this book would be classified deictic – expressions like 'towards me'. As far as I can see, Hai//om is a language that solidly uses just an absolute or intrinsic frame of reference.

9. The Type I or α error denotes the unjustified acceptance of the alternate hypothesis. For example, one might infer from the sample that there *is* a difference between two groups, though in fact both groups belong to the same population. This error probability has to be controlled carefully if differences are hypothesized (like in the difference prediction).

10. Testing power refers to the 'ability to detect an existing effect' and is therefore the counterpart of the Type II or β error, the unwarranted rejection of the alternate hypothesis. Power issues are of special concern if no differences are expected (similarity prediction), but also in general, if effect and sample sizes are small. As α and β type errors are antagonistic, testing power can be increased by allowing a higher α type risk, for example p $=$ .10 instead of .05.

11. Wilkins' report is unpublished, and I am grateful for his permission to repeat the basic facts here.

12. Although below the 5% limit, this result is non-significant if controlled for multiple Type I errors.

13. I am able to add here cultures for which the linguistic tasks showed mixed relative and absolute coding strategies as conventional, specifically Kgalagadi (a Bantu speech community of Botswana), Kilivila (an Austronesian language of the Trobriand Islands, Papua New Guinea) and Yucatec (a Mayan language of Mexico).

14. The task referred to is the mirror-image discrimination task briefly described in Chapter 4 (see Figure 4.10). This task is expected to have a relation to spatial coding strategies, especially the use of the intrinsic coordinate system.

15. In the animals task, in a few communities significant proportions of subjects utilized the same fixed direction for all trials, regardless of stimulus direction – in effect regarding direction as irrelevant – and these subjects were then set aside. Incidentally, we treat these 'monodirectional' responses as symptoms of coding in the intrinsic frame of reference, where orientation of the overall spatial assemblage is irrelevant.

16. The samples tested were: Tamil (age: animals, direction; transitivity, away; marginal effect for across); Belhare (age: animals; schooling and 'play': both animals and transitivity); Hai//om (age: animals and transitivity); Japanese (age, schooling: transitivity); Kilivila (age: transitivity); Kgalagadi (age, schooling: animals); Totonac (schooling, conservatism (wearing traditional dress): animals); Tzeltal (age, schooling: both animals and transitivity); and Yucatec (age: animals).

17. They misunderstand the rat literature however, thinking that (a) rats use any available landmarks (see Gallistel 1990: Ch. 6 for compelling counter-evidence), (b) rat landmark use involves absolute coordinates (as far as we know they use orientation-free local cognitive maps – see O'Keefe 1993 for the theory). I take up some of these issues in Chapter 6 below.

18. For example, in the Eric's maze task, we had the following results for two groups in 'outdoors' settings:

	Relative-coders	Absolute-coders	Untypable	N
Kgalagadi	10	2	4	16
Kilivila	10	2	4	16

In the case of these 'mixed languages', linguistic use in a particular situation tends to match the corresponding non-verbal coding – for example, percentage choices of linguistic expressions in the different frames of reference are roughly equal to the distribution of non-verbal coding results for carefully matched tasks in Kgalagadi (see Neumann and Widlok 1996).

19. We have some direct evidence for the role of memory load in Dutch subjects' switching between intrinsic and relative frames of reference – higher load induces the switch to the relative frame of reference (see Levinson *et al.* 2002).

6 BEYOND LANGUAGE: FRAMES OF REFERENCE IN WAYFINDING AND POINTING

1. MacDonald 1998 gives similar information for Inuit wayfinding. A major clue to direction is the west-northwest alignment of snow-drifts, detailed knowledge about the movement of the sun (which at this latitude rises *and* sets near to north in May, and near to south in January), knowledge of stars and their movement, the flight directions of birds etc. There are special hazards in the Arctic – like finding that the ice you are on has broken free, or being caught in a blizzard – that require constant care and special techniques; yet it is still hard to obtain explicit descriptions of the implicit knowledge behind expert navigation.

2. The instructions are thus of the form 'Point to Laura!' where Laura is the name of a place familiar to the subject either through direct experience or by hearsay (a point taken up below). Considerable ethnographic effort has to be put into the selection of such a list of places to be named: familiarity with the place in the local community has to be assessed, the local understanding

of the actual location of the place so named must be established (e.g. a designation on a map may not correspond at all to the local naming practice, or the name of a large geographical feature (like a river or mountain range) may be construed as a particular locus on that feature, and so on). In the Guugu Yimithirr and Tzeltal case studies a fixed protocol of place names was then utilized, and the order was arranged in such a way that there was no systematic angular relation between successive names – in particular opposite ends of axes, or places in similar directions, or successions in a (anti-) clockwise direction were avoided, in the hope that each estimate would be relatively independent. A similar procedure was used by Widlok in the Hai//om study (1996: 4).

3. Where possible, we asked for a landmark (e.g. a tree) in the correct direction, so that more accurate sightings could be made.

4. I shall use this locution as a shorthand for the long-winded 'communities in which speakers of the primary language predominantly use absolute coordinates for spatial description' (and *mutatis mutandis* for 'relative communities').

5. For the uninitiated, circular statistics consists of a set of specialized techniques where the standard statistical measures (standard deviations, tests for significance, confidence intervals etc.) have all been fundamentally reconstructed to deal with the peculiarities of deviations around a circle. For example, 357 degrees and 003 degrees are only six degrees apart – requiring conversion of all degree measurements into sine/cosine specifications.

6. Incidentally, bees outshine pigeons as estimators of distant locations – their waggle dances indicate spot-on direction, and a mean vector length of 0.98! See Wehner 1983: 370.

7. The comparison is probably unfair because the pigeons may well have been hooded under transportation (although the source fails to specify). Also it is well known that even when disappearing on a distant horizon pigeon estimates tend to be systematically skewed by up to 60 degrees, with a smooth gradual correction taking place over many kilometres thereafter, perhaps as various sensory estimates of direction are integrated over time (Waterman 1989: 174–5, Schöne 1984: 109–10).

8. Actually virtually all these sensory specializations are still controversial; see Waterman 1989: 139, Schöne 1984: 108 for olfactory gradients, Gallistel 1990: 43 for doubts about magnetoreception (see also Schöne 1984: 191–4), Hughes 1999 for recent evidence in favour.

9. I thank Thomas Widlok for providing the raw data that made this analysis possible; his own reports should be read for the details and for his own analysis (Widlok 1994, 1996).

10. Some of the values here are our calculations from the tables provided in Baker 1989.

11. Incidentally, the same participants when asked to point to compass directions do significantly worse than when asked to point to their starting point: now the homeward component of the mean vector is 0.087, i.e. the mean error is about 90 degrees off target (Baker 1989: 91).

12. Baker reports some small but significant intra-sample variation, with, e.g., twenty-one-year-olds better than nine-year-olds, and males better than females in these walkabout experiments. But in judging compass direction when spun blindfolded, women appear better than men, and suburbanites better than orienteers (Baker 1989: 94–5).

13. As mentioned in Chapter 4 (see the data row 'from hypothetical locations' in Table 4.1), Guugu Yimithirr speakers were asked to imagine they were at some other location and then to point back to where they were currently standing, and additionally to other locations where they were not. Astonishingly, they were quite able to do this, with only the slightest increase in average error (from about 14 degrees mean error to about 19 degrees – see also Levinson 1992b, 1997a).

14. Similar experiments have been carried out by McCullough (1993) on North American English-speakers and Mandarin Chinese-speakers with the same result.

15. This exercise unfortunately does not lend itself to brevity or easy publication; see the unpublished papers by Levinson 1984/1986, Haviland 1986. Fragments of evidence are published in Haviland 1993, 1996, Levinson 1987a, Levinson 1996c.

16. This is not to suggest that Tzeltal and Guugu Yimithirr gestures do not also differ in fundamental ways. For example, Tenejapans consider reserved gesture-inhibited demeanour to be proper and polite, while Guugu Yimithirr speakers are – except with in-laws – casual and bodily relaxed, and so on and so forth. What is, however, rather remarkable is the extent to which they are nevertheless rather similar systems, despite incommensurable differences in language, culture and ecology – similarities that can be attributed entirely to their common absolute frame of reference.

17. Of course we should not mistake a behavioural test or symptom for the underlying object of study – a conceptual or cognitive fact, always approached indirectly. Any operational test will be coarse and subject to error. For example, any speaker utilizing a relative coordinate system but producing displays rotated for ease of comprehension (as by an aerobics leader who says 'left' and moves right while facing her acolytes) will mimic the behaviour of an absolute gesturer under rotation.

18. For example, when I direct someone down the road pointing in the correct direction, is this an absolute gesture? We have to be careful: not all allocentric, geographically based systems are absolute systems of coordinates; and pointings in the correct direction may even be driven by egocentric relative systems, where one turns the body to gesture in the real geographical direction but in such a way that descriptions in terms of 'left' and 'right' also make sense.

19. In 1982, together with Penelope Brown, I filmed such inter-ethnic interactions, and the records and final report on the project are deposited in the Australian Institute of Aboriginal and Torres Straits Islanders Studies, Canberra.

20. It is not at all improbable that this shape of the relaxed hand is due directly to the fact that Tenejapans are hoe-agriculturists whose waking hours are largely spent holding a wooden handle of a hoe or machete or axe in constant jarring contact with soil or wood.

21. Note that deictic gestures do generally carry truth-conditional content: *That one is mine* is true iff the indicated one is mine. We return below to the possible close connection between deictic and absolute gestures.

22. Most data about our Western systems come from introspection (e.g. Calbris 1990) or from experimental evidence of restricted type (e.g. the retelling of cartoons, as in McNeill 1992). Observations on natural data of different genres, as by Kendon (2000), are sadly very rare. Some psychological work of a quantitative kind, which cannot be easily exploited for other purposes, has been done in contexts like academic tutorials or news interviews (e.g. Beattie 1983). See McNeill (2000) for the state of the art.

23. All the speakers were seated in normal chairs; the Guugu Yimithirr and Tzeltal speakers were not filmed directly face-on, which makes the estimation of gesture location with respect to the trunk somewhat imprecise, but allows estimations of depth in front of the speaker. The data comes from Guugu Yimithirr film SCL 09/82 Hopevale V21 Bambi 1 00:14:24–21:22 and Tzeltal V49 00:11:58:18–19:03:11 (the former archived in AIATSIS, Canberra and both in MPI for Psycholinguistics, Nijmegen).

24. This is my own calculation from McNeill's (1992: 91) figure 3.2 (d).

25. In Australian societies, where reference to the dead is properly circumspect, one often finds small directional gestures made to identify dead persons by reference to their present kin or prior house site etc. (Haviland 1993: 32–3). The very modest, retracted nature of these gestures suggests that they are the exception to the rule. Likewise, Haviland (1993: 27–8) has noted that Guugu Yimithirr speakers may retain the inner gesture space for non-directional gestures, a sort of unoriented virtual space; this would provide another motive for making clear that intendedly directional gestures lie beyond it.

26. Incidentally, large gesture spaces are found associated not only with absolute gesture-systems. Thus McNeill (1992: 303–7) has noted that English-speaking children use a relatively very large gesture space, demonstrations often involving the entire body and its movement through space. Here the explanation though is of a different kind: space for young children, he suggests, is an actual medium in which actual actions can be mimicked, rather than the symbolic medium that adults come to use in their reduced gesture space.

27. This suggestion I owe to David Wilkins.

28. Some sources suggest that the Guugu Yimithirr pattern may not in fact be very different from European norms – Debra Stephens (1983) reports c. 52% right-handed, 26% left-handed and 22% double-handed gestures for a sample of eight right-handed American speakers (iconics and deictics

only, all areas of the gesture space). However, McNeill and Levy (1982) report over 80% right-handed unilateral gestures from right-handers, as do Wilkins and de Ruiter (in press).

29. A Guugu Yimithirr example occurs on the tape Hopevale 21 (Bambi 1) Timecode 16:14:02–16:19:05.

30. David McNeill comments here that this association of a hand with the correct absolute direction for the events depicted places an important constraint on the expressive power of these systems compared to a relative system. In a relative system a particular hand can be consistently associated with a particular discourse entity regardless of its (perhaps changing) location.

31. Full arm extension to the front is also normal in absolute gestures. This makes the exercise carried out in Table 6.3, using McNeill's 1992 grid for the categorization of gesture space, really rather inappropriate: straight ahead gestures may end up being categorized as 'centre-centre' where they really fall way outside McNeill's 'shallow disk'. The exercise was undertaken just to make the contrast between the different kinds of systems. To do this properly would require mapping gesture spaces in a 3D sphere or cylinder.

32. In both the Guugu Yimithirr and Tzeltal extracts studied, thumb-points over the shoulder do occur but much more often the index finger is used in just the way that we use it in front of us. The important point is that absolute gesturers use symmetrical systems of hand-shape for in front and behind the body: thus they *also* use thumb points in the frontal region, gesturing to one side or the other, and this intuitively would be as odd for us as pointing with the index finger over one's shoulder.

33. For example, in the Guugu Yimithirr extract, a westward gesture with the palm of the hand indicating north-side-of-creek, or in the Tzeltal extract, the arm indicating that a river lies off to the south-west from the point of speaking, while the hand indicates that it runs south-east.

34. It is actually quite hard to get extended route-directions from people who live in traditional communities – they would rather send a kid to show you! These statements are based in the case of Guugu Yimithirr on naturally occurring descriptions of unfamiliar locations, and in the case of Tzeltal on role-played route directions of a kind one might give to itinerant labourers, but in Tzotzil (a more widely used neighbouring language).

35. Since then, David McNeill tells me, he has changed his views, so that the categories 'iconic', 'deictic', 'beat' etc. are now considered a way of classifying *aspects* of gesture, allowing a single gesture to manifest more than one type (although 'metaphoric' may remain an exclusive category).

36. Where on the contrary the viewpoints are indeed restricted, e.g. when following a route-description, we may expect a different story. Similarly, if one taps recent visual memory, viewpoint information may be vividly remembered and conveyed.

37. This is actually a hypothesis, not a finding; the idea I owe to S. Kita.

38. David Wilkins' acute observation. See also Haviland 1993: 25–6.

39. Interestingly, for at least one participant studied in depth, the Tzeltal 'bowl' seems tilted, with a lower rim to the north, as one might expect given the absolute system built on the assumption of a tilted world.

40. McNeill (1992: 172) describes superficially similar phenomena in English where the gap in, e.g., "He gets her a drink and _ starts to play the piano" occurs with a gesture to the side associated with "him". The difference is that in English the interpretation of these gaps is normally syntactically determined, whereas in Guugu Yimithirr or Tzeltal the resolution is more normally pragmatic.

41. See, e.g., the diagram in Haviland 1993: 25.

42. See too Cassell *et al.* (1999) for some evidence about the cross-channel importance of gestural information in English.

43. I am grateful to Sue Duncan and Sotaro Kita for relevant points here.

44. Haviland (1993, 1998) has been keen to point out that many Guugu Yimithirr gestures are indeed from the point of view of speakers or protagonists, but the point remains that they need not be. Thus in a discussion of land rights, locations like creeks, springs and hills function as the reference points with respect to which other areas are located gesturally.

45. Incidentally, this is not a direct reflex of the geography. Thus film V49 was shot at Oxebwitz close to the northern boundary of Tenejapa, where the 'downhill' edge of the Tenejapan world is fringed by a mighty escarpment.

46. Strictly, what is at least essential is to triangulate the location of the new landmark L by reference to a minimum number of old ones A, B, C etc.; taking the angle subtended by AB from L will give us an arc of possible locations, which might lie either side of the line AB; so we will need another angle subtended by BC from L, the intersection of the two derived arcs giving us our location (see Gallistel 1990: 49–50). But now working out the angle from L to a new goal D, whose location has been triangulated ultimately but not proximately from A and B, is going to be non-trivial. Hence McNaughton *et al.* are probably effectively correct that such a mechanism is impractical. Note that this issue, whether allocentric maps use fixed bearings or not, is quite different from the issue about the relative advantages of allocentric vs. egocentric maps. Here, as Randy Gallistel pointed out to me in correspondence, egocentric maps are hopelessly computationally inefficient: for every time one changes one's location all the angles and distances to all landmarks change from an egocentric point of view. Hence organisms have no choice but to develop allocentric maps of one kind or another.

47. Randy Gallistel has in correspondence questioned this: he suggests that good dead reckoning may rely heavily on anticipating viewpoints. In fact, we have some evidence that our absolute Tenejapans have indeed impressive powers of mental rotation (see Levinson 1996b: 123–4). But my argument is that they are good at mental rotation because they construct at once a full 3D model of a scene, rather than hanging onto just one viewpoint. From a 3D model you can quickly project 2D viewpoints (mental images) from any direction. It is the favouring of the 2D image in memory

correlated with its advantage for relative descriptions (in terms of left/right and so on) that seems to me to be the possible source of the handicap experienced by relative strategists in the realm of survey maps and dead-reckoning abilities.

48. Although arthropods use fixed-bearing survey maps for long-range navigation, they use landmark-based piloting for the final stages. Here they too exhibit asymmetries of trips from A to B versus B to A, suggesting the use of view-graphs (Wehner 1983: 375).

49. Thus Tindale wrote (1974: 38–9) of Western Desert Aboriginal sand drawing: '[the line] is made along a line of movement in the correct compass direction'; see also Munn 1986: 58–88.

7 LANGUAGE AND THOUGHT

1. Jackendoff (1996) offers a single representational level he calls 'spatial representation', generalized from Marr's (1982) 3D model. This is hopeless as a general model of our spatial knowledge, since it is object-oriented, thus effectively only in an intrinsic frame of reference. We need viewpoint projections to capture the relative frame of reference, and oriented mental maps to capture the absolute frame – hence the more complex picture in Figure 7.2. See also Peterson *et al.* 1996: 558, who conclude that the evidence is against any single amodal spatial representation.

2. 'What then is being denied? Roughly, that one can learn a language whose expressive power is greater than that of a language that one already knows. Less roughly, that one can learn a language whose predicates express extensions not expressible by those of a previously available representational system . . . Now while this is all compatible with there being a computational advantage associated with knowing a natural language, it is *incompatible* with its advantage being, as it were, principled . . . all such computational advantages – all the facilitatory effects of language upon thought – will have to explained away by reference to "performance" parameters like memory, fixation of attention, etc.' (Fodor 1975: 86).

3. Pinker (1994: 237–8), for example, seems to claim that all languages have nouns vs. verbs, phrase structure, auxiliaries, tense, aspect, mood, inflection etc. In fact, not one of these features is unequivocally an absolute universal, i.e. a feature shared by all the languages of the world.

References

Acredolo, L. 1988, Infant mobility and spatial development, in J. Stiles-Davis, M. Kritchevsky and U. Bellugi (eds.), *Spatial cognition: Brain bases and development*, pp. 157–66. Hillsdale, NJ: Lawrence Erlbaum.

Ameka, F. and Levinson, S.C. in preparation, Positional verbs and locative predicates, Special issue of *Linguistics*.

Anderson, S. and Keenan, E. 1985, Deixis, in T. Shopen (ed.), *Language typology and syntactic description*, Vol. III: *Grammatical categories and the lexicon*, pp. 259–307. Cambridge: Cambridge University Press.

Aoki, K. and Feldman, M.W. 1991, Recessive hereditary deafness, assortative mating, and persistence of a sign language, *Theoretical Population Biology* 39(3): 358–72.

Argyle, M. 1967, *The psychology of interpersonal behaviour*, Harmondsworth: Penguin.

Argyle, M. and Trower, P. 1979, *Person to person: Ways of communicating*, London: Harper and Row.

Asch, S.E. and Witkin, H.A. 1948, Studies in space orientation II: Perception of the upright with displaced visual fields and with body tilted, *Journal of Experimental Psychology* 38: 455–77. [Reprinted in: *Journal of Experimental Psychology*, General, 1992, 121(4): 407–18.]

Austin, P. and Bresnan, J. 1996, Non-configurationality in Australian Aboriginal languages, *Natural Language and Linguistic Theory* 14(2): 215–68.

Baayen, H. and Danziger, E. (eds.) 1994, *Annual Report of the Max Planck Institute for Psycholinguistics 1993*, Nijmegen: Max Planck Institute for Psycholinguistics.

Baddeley, A. 1990, *Human memory: Theory and practice*, Needham Heights, MA: Allyn and Bacon.

Baker, R.R. 1989, *Human navigation and magnetoreception*, Manchester: University of Manchester Press.

Batschelet, E. 1981, *Circular statistics*, New York: Academic Press.

Beattie, G. 1983, *Talk: An analysis of speech and non-verbal behaviour in conversation*, Stony Stratford: Open University Press.

Berg, R. van den 1997, Spatial deixis in Muna (Sulawesi), in G. Senft (ed.), *Referring to space*, pp. 197–220. Oxford: Clarendon Press.

Berlin, B. 1968, *Tzeltal numeral classifiers*, Berkeley: University of California Press.

1992, *Ethnobiological classification: Principles of categorization of plants and animals in traditional societies*, Princeton, NJ: Princeton University Press.

Berlin, B. and Kay, P. 1969, *Basic color terms: Their universality and evolution*, Berkeley: University of California Press.

Berlin, B., Breedlove, D. and Raven, P. 1974, *Principles of Tzeltal plant classification*, New York: Academic Press.

Berthoz, A. 1991, Reference frames for the perception and control of movement, in J. Paillard (ed.), *Brain and space*, pp. 81–111. Oxford: Oxford Science Publications.

Beusmans, J. 1996, Two strategies for route learning in a driving simulator. Talk given at the 3rd Annual CBR Workshop on 'Mental Representations in Navigation'. Cambridge Basic Research, Cambridge, MA.

Bickel, B. 1997, Spatial operations in deixis, cognition, and culture: Where to orient oneself in Belhare, in J. Nuyts and E. Pederson (eds.), *Language and conceptualization*, pp. 46–83. Cambridge: Cambridge University Press.

Bierwisch, M. 1967, Some semantic universals of German adjectivals, *Foundations of Language* 3: 1–36.

Bierwisch, M. and Lang, E. 1989, Somewhat longer – much deeper – further and further. Epilogue to the Dimension Adjective Project, in M. Bierwisch and E. Lang (eds.), *Dimensional adjectives: Grammatical structure and conceptual interpretation*, pp. 471–514. Berlin: Springer.

Bisiach, E. and Luzzatti, C. 1978, Unilateral neglect of representational space, *Cortex* 14: 129–33.

Blake, B.J. 1994, *Case*, Cambridge: Cambridge University Press.

Bloom, P., Peterson, M., Nadel, L. and Garrett, M. (eds.) 1996, *Language and space*, Cambridge, MA: MIT Press.

Boesch, C. and Boesch, H. 1984, Possible causes of sex differences in the use of natural hammers by wild chimpanzees, *Journal of Human Evolution* 13: 415–40.

Bohnemeyer, J. 1998, Temporal reference from a radical pragmatics perspective. Why Yucatec doesn't need to express 'after' and 'before', *Cognitive Linguistics* 9(3): 239–82.

Bohnemeyer, J. and Stolz, C. in preparation, The expression of spatial reference in Yukatek Maya: A survey, in S.C. Levinson and D.P. Wilkins (eds.), *Grammars of space*.

Bourdieu, P. 1977, *Outline of a theory of practice*, Cambridge: Cambridge University Press.

Bowden, J. 1991, Grammaticalization of locatives in Oceanic languages. MA thesis, University of Auckland.

Bowerman, M. 1996, Learning how to structure space for language: A cross-linguistic perspective, in P. Bloom, M. Peterson, L. Nadel and M. Garrett (eds.), *Language and space*, pp. 385–436. Cambridge, MA: MIT Press.

2000, Where do children's word meanings come from? Rethinking the role of cognition in early semantic development, in L. Nucci, G. Saxe and

E. Turiel (eds.), *Culture, thought, and development*, pp. 199–230. Mahwah, NJ: Lawrence Erlbaum.

Bowerman, M. and Choi, S. 2001, Shaping meanings for language: Universal and language-specific in the acquisition of spatial semantic categories, in M. Bowerman and S. Levinson (eds.), *Language acquisition and conceptual development*, pp. 475–511. Cambridge: Cambridge University Press.

Bowerman, M. and Levinson, S.C. (eds.) 2001, *Language acquisition and conceptual development*, Cambridge: Cambridge University Press.

Bowerman, M., de León, L. and Choi, S. 1995, Verbs, particles and spatial semantics. Learning to talk about spatial actions in typologically different languages, in E.V. Clark (ed.), *Proceedings of the 27th Child Language Research Forum*, pp. 101–10. Stanford: CSLI.

Boyd, R. and Richerson, P.J. 1985, *Culture and the evolutionary process*, Chicago: The University of Chicago Press.

Brewer, B. and Pears, J. 1993, Frames of reference, in N. Eilan, R. McCarthy and B. Brewer (eds.), *Spatial representation: Problems in philosophy and psychology*, pp. 25–30. Oxford: Blackwell.

Brown, C.H. 1983, Where do cardinal direction terms come from? *Anthropological Linguistics* 25(2): 121–61.

Brown, P. 1994, The INs and ONs of Tzeltal locative expressions: The semantics of static descriptions of location, in J.B. Haviland and S.C. Levinson (eds.), *Space in Mayan languages*, Special issue of *Linguistics* 32(4/5): 743–90.

1998, Children's first verbs in Tzeltal: Evidence for an early verb category, *Linguistics* 36(4): 713–53.

2001, Learning to talk about motion UP and DOWN in Tzeltal: Is there a language-specific bias for verb learning, in M. Bowerman and S. Levinson (eds.), *Language acquisition and conceptual development*, pp. 512–43. Cambridge: Cambridge University Press.

Brown, P. and Levinson, S.C. 1993a, 'Uphill' and 'downhill' in Tzeltal, *Journal of Linguistic Anthropology* 3(1): 46–74.

1993b, Explorations in Mayan cognition. Working paper 24, Cognitive Anthropology Research Group, Max Planck Institute for Psycholinguistics, Nijmegen.

2000, Frames of spatial reference and their acquisition in Tenejapan Tzeltal, in L. Nucci, G. Saxe and E. Turiel (eds.), *Culture, thought, and development*, pp. 167–98. Mahwah, NJ: Lawrence Erlbaum.

in preparation, *Tilted worlds: The language and cognition of space in a Mayan community*.

Brown, P., Senft, G. and Wheeldon, L. (eds.) 1993, *Annual Report of the Max Planck Institute for Psycholinguistics 1992*. Nijmegen: Max Planck Institute for Psycholinguistics.

Brugman, C. 1983, The use of body-part terms as locatives in Chalcatongo Mixtec, *Survey of California and Other Indian Languages* 4: 235–90.

Brugman, C. and Macaulay, M. 1986, Interacting semantic systems: Mixtec expressions of location, *Proceedings of the Berkeley Linguistics Society Meeting* 12: 315–27.

Bühler, K. 1982 [1934], The deictic field of language and deictic words, in R.J. Jarvella and W. Klein (eds.), *Speech, place and action*, pp. 9–30. New York: Wiley.

Bülthoff, H.H. 1991, Shape from X: Psychophysics and computation, in M.S. Landy and J.A. Movshon (eds.), *Computational models of visual processing*, pp. 305–30. Cambridge, MA: MIT Press.

Burgess, N., Jeffery, K. and O'Keefe, J. 1999, *The hippocampal and parietal foundations of spatial cognition*, Oxford: Oxford University Press.

Cablitz, G.H. 2002, The acquisition of an absolute system: learning to talk about space in Marquesan (Oceanic, French Polynesia). In the *Proceedings of the 31st Child Language Research Forum, Stanford, 2002*, pp. 40–9. http://csli-publications.stanford.edu.

Calbris, G. 1990, *The semiotics of French gesture*, Bloomington: University of Indiana Press.

Campbell, A. 1987, Portolan charts from the late thirteenth century to 1500, in J.B. Harley and D. Woodward (eds.), *The history of cartography*, vol. 1, pp. 371–463. Chicago: The University of Chicago Press.

Campbell, J. 1993, The role of physical objects in spatial thinking. In N. Eilan, R. McCarthy and B. Brewer (eds.), *Spatial representation: Problems in philosophy and psychology*, pp. 65–95. Oxford: Blackwell.

Carlson-Radvansky, L.A. and Irwin, D.A. 1993, Frames of reference in vision and language: Where is above? *Cognition* 46: 223–44.

Casey, E. 1997, *The fate of place*, Berkeley: University of California Press.

Cassell, J., McNeill, D. and McCullough, K.-E. 1999, Speech-gesture mismatches: Evidence for one underlying representation of linguistic and non-linguistic information, *Pragmatics & Cognition* 7(1): 1–33.

Cassirer, E. 1923, *Das Erkenntnisproblem in der Philosophie und Wissenschaft der neueren Zeit*, Berlin: Cassirer.

Cavalli-Sforza, L.L. and Feldman, M.W. 1981, *Cultural transmission and evolution: A quantitative approach*, Monographs in population biology, 16. Princeton, NJ: Princeton University Press.

Cheng, K. and Spetch, M. 1998, Mechanisms of landmark use in mammals and birds, in S. Healy (ed.), *Spatial representation in animals*, pp. 1–17. Oxford: Oxford University Press.

Choi, S., McDonough, L., Mandler, J. and Bowerman, M. in preparation, Development of language-specific semantic categories of spatial relations: From prelinguistic to linguistic stage. Paper presented at the Workshop 'Finding the Words'. Stanford University, May 2000.

Chomsky, N. 1965, *Aspects of the theory of syntax*, Cambridge, MA: MIT Press.

Clark, H.H. 1973, Space, time, semantics, and the child, in T.E. Moore (ed.), *Cognitive development and the acquisition of language*, pp. 28–64. New York: Academic Press.

Clark, H.H. and Wilkes-Gibbs, D. 1986, Referring as a collaborative process, *Cognition* 22(1): 1–39.

Cohen, D. and Kubovy, M. 1993, Mental rotation, mental representation, and flat slopes, *Cognitive Psychology* 25: 351–82.

Colby, C. 1999, Spatial perception. Entry in *MIT Encyclopedia of the cognitive sciences*, pp. 784–7. Boston, MA: MIT Press.

Collett, T.S. and Zeil, J. 1998, Places and landmarks: An Arthropod perspective, in S. Healy (ed.), *Spatial representations in animals*, pp. 18–53. Oxford: Oxford University Press.

Cowan, N. 2001, The magical number 4 in short-term memory: A reconsideration of mental storage capacity, *Behavioral and Brain Sciences* 24(1): 87–114.

Danziger, E. 1994, Out of sight, out of mind: Person, perception and function in Mopan Maya spatial deixis, in J.B. Haviland and S.C. Levinson (eds.), *Space in Mayan languages*, Special issue of *Linguistics* 32(4): 885–907.

1996, Parts and their counter-parts: Social and spatial relationships in Mopan Maya, *The Journal of the Royal Anthropological Institute, inc. Man* 2(1): 67–82.

1999, Language, space and sociolect: Cognitive correlates of gendered speech in Mopan Maya, in C. Fuchs and S. Robert (eds.), *Language diversity and cognitive representations*, pp. 85–106. Amsterdam: Benjamins.

Danziger, E. and Pederson, E. 1998, Through the looking glass: Literacy, writing systems and mirror-image discrimination, *Written Language and Literacy* 1(2): 153–67.

Davidoff, J., Davies, I. and Robertson, D. 1999, Colour categories in a stone-age tribe, *Nature* 398: 203–4.

Dawkins, R. 1976, *The selfish gene*, Oxford: Oxford University Press.

Deacon, T. 1997, *The symbolic species: The co-evolution of language and the brain*, New York: Norton.

Dennett, D. 1991, *Consciousness explained*, Boston, MA: Little Brown.

1995, *Darwin's dangerous idea*, London: Penguin.

Dilke, O.A.W. 1987, Itineraries and geographical maps in the early and late Roman empires, in J.B. Harley and D. Woodward (eds.), *The history of cartography*, vol. 1, pp. 234–57. Chicago: The University of Chicago Press.

Duhem, P. 1985, *Medieval cosmology*, Chicago: The University of Chicago Press.

Durham, W. 1991, *Coevolution*, Stanford, CA: Stanford University Press.

Eilan, N. 1993, Molyneux's question and the idea of an external world, in N. Eilan, R. McCarthy and B. Brewer (eds.), *Spatial representation: Problems in philosophy and psychology*, pp. 236–55. Oxford: Blackwell.

Eilan, N., McCarthy, R. and Brewer, B. (eds.) 1993, *Spatial representation: Problems in philosophy and psychology*, Oxford: Blackwell.

Einstein, A. 1954, Foreword, in M. Jammer (ed.), *Concepts of space: The history of theories of space in physics*, Cambridge, MA: Harvard University Press.

Elman, J.L., Bates, E.A., Johnson, M.H., Karmiloff-Smith, A., Parisi, D. and Plunkett, K. 1996, *Rethinking innateness: A connectionist perspective on development*, Cambridge, MA: MIT Press.

Emmorey, K. 2001, *Language, cognition and the brain: Insights from sign language research*, Mahwah, NJ: Lawrence Erlbaum.

Etienne, A.S., Berlie, J., Georgakopoulos, J. and Maurer, R. 1998, Role of dead reckoning in navigation, in S. Healy (ed.), *Spatial representation in animals*, pp. 54–68. Oxford: Oxford University Press.

Ettlinger, G. 1987, Cross-model sensory integration, in R. Gregory (ed.), *The Oxford companion to the mind*, pp. 173–4. Oxford: Oxford University Press.

Evans, N. 1995, *A grammar of Kayardild*, Berlin: Mouton Grammar Library.

Fillmore, C. 1971, Towards a theory of deixis. Paper read at the Pacific Conference on Contrastive Linguistics and Language Universals, University of Hawaii.

1975, *Santa Cruz lectures on deixis*. Mimeo, Indiana University Linguistics Club.

1982, Towards a descriptive framework for spatial deixis, in R.J. Jarvella and W. Klein (eds.), *Speech, place and action: Studies in deixis and related topics*, pp. 31–59. New York: Wiley.

Fodor, J. 1975, *The language of thought*, New York: Crowell.

1983, *The modularity of mind*, Cambridge, MA: MIT Press.

Fodor, J.D., Fodor, J.A. and Garrett, M. 1975, The unreality of semantic representations, *Linguistic Inquiry* 4: 515–31.

Fortescue, M. 1988, Eskimo orientation systems, *Meddr Grønland: Man and Society* 11: 3–30.

Friederici, A. and Levelt, W.J.M. 1990, Spatial reference in weightlessness: Perceptual factors and mental representations, *Perception & Psychophysics* 47(3): 253–66.

Friedrich, P. 1971, *The Tarascan suffixes of locative space: Meaning and morphotactics*, Bloomington, IN: Indiana University Press.

Frisch, K. von 1967, *The dance language and orientation of bees*, Cambridge, MA: Harvard University Press.

Furby, C.E. and Furby, E.S. 1976, Garawa compass directions, *Talanya* 3: 1–13.

Gage, J. 1999, *Colour and meaning*, London: Thames and Hudson.

Galea, L.M. and Kimura, D. 1993, Sex differences in route-learning, *Personality and Individual Differences* 14: 53–65.

Gallistel, C.R. 1990, *The organization of learning*, Cambridge, MA: MIT Press.

1996, Insect navigation: The brain as symbol processing organ or knowledge and purpose as the mechanisms of habit. Talk given at the 3rd Annual CBR Workshop on 'Mental Representations in Navigation'. Cambridge, MA.

Gardner, H. 1985, *The mind's new science*, New York: Basic Books.

Geertz, C.C. 1972, Deep play: Notes on the Balinese cockfight, *Daedalus* 101: 1–37.

Gillner, S. and Mallot, H. 1997, Navigation and acquisition of spatial knowledge in a virtual maze. Technical Report 45, Max-Planck-Institut für biologische Kybernetik, Tübingen.

Gladwin, T. 1970, *East is a big bird: Navigation and logic on Puluwat Atoll*, Cambridge, MA: Harvard University Press.

Goddard, C. and Wierzbicka, A. 1994, *Semantic and lexical universals*, Amsterdam: Benjamins.

Golledge, R.G. 1995, Path selection and route preference in human navigation: A progress report, in A.U. Frank and W. Kuhn (eds.), *Spatial information theory*, pp. 207–22. Berlin: Springer.

Golledge, R.G., Dougherty, V. and Bell, S. 1995, Acquiring spatial knowledge – Survey versus route-based knowledge in unfamiliar environments, *Annals of the Association of American Geographers* 85(1): 134–58.

Golledge, R.G., Ruggles, A., Pellegrino, J. and Gale, N. 1993, Integrating route knowledge in an unfamiliar neighborhood: Along and across route experiments, *Journal of Environmental Psychology* 13: 293–307.

Goodenough, W.H. 1956, Componential analysis and the study of meaning, *Language* 32: 195–216.

Gregory, R.L. 1987, *Oxford companion to the mind*, Oxford: Oxford University Press.

Gumperz, J.J. and Levinson, S.C. (eds.) 1996, *Rethinking linguistic relativity*, Cambridge: Cambridge University Press.

Haiman, J. 1980, *Hua: A Papuan language of the Eastern Highlands, Papua New Guinea*, Amsterdam: Benjamins.

Hanks, W. 1990, *Referential practice: Language and lived space in a Maya community*, Chicago: The University of Chicago Press.

Harley, J.B. and Woodward, D. (eds.) 1987, *The history of cartography*, Vol. 1, Chicago: The University of Chicago Press.

Hatfield, G. 1990, *The natural and the normative: Theories of spatial perception from Kant to Helmholtz*, Cambridge, MA: MIT Press.

Hauser, M. 1997, *The evolution of communication*, Cambridge, MA: MIT Press.

Haviland, J.B. 1979a, Guugu Yimidhirr, in R.M.W. Dixon and B. Blake (eds.), *Handbook of Australian languages*, Vol. I, pp. 27–182. Canberra: Australian National University Press.

1979b, Guugu Yimidhirr brother-in-law language, *Language in Society* 8: 365–93.

1985, The evolution of a speech community: Guugu Yimidhirr at Hopevale, *Aboriginal History* 9(1/2): 170–204.

1986, Complex referential gestures. Unpublished MS.

1993, Anchoring, iconicity and orientation in Guugu Yimithirr pointing gestures, *Journal of Linguistic Anthropology* 3(1): 3–45.

1996, Projections, transpositions, and relativity, in J.J. Gumperz and S.C. Levinson (eds.), *Rethinking linguistic relativity*, pp. 269–323. Cambridge: Cambridge University Press.

1998, Guugu Yimithirr cardinal directions, *Ethos* 26(1): 7–24.

2000, Pointing, gesture spaces, and mental maps, in D. McNeill (ed.), *Language and gesture*, pp. 13–46. Cambridge: Cambridge University Press.

Haviland, J.B. and Hart, R. 1998, *Old man fog and the last Aborigines of Barrow Point*, Washington, DC: Smithsonian Institution Press.

Haviland, J.B. and Haviland, L. 1980, 'How much food will there be in Heaven?' Aborigines and Lutherans around Cooktown before 1900, *Aboriginal History* 4(1–2): 118–49.

References   355

Healy, S. (ed.) 1998, *Spatial representation in animals*, Oxford: Oxford University Press.
Heeschen, V. 1982, Some systems of spatial deixis in Papuan languages, in J. Weissenborn and W. Klein (eds.), *Here and there: Cross-linguistic studies on deixis and demonstration*, pp. 81–110. Amsterdam: Benjamins.
Heine, B. 1997, *Cognitive foundations of grammar*, Oxford: Oxford University Press.
Heine, B., Claudi, U. and Hünnemeyer, F. 1991, *Grammaticalization: A conceptual framework*, Chicago: The University of Chicago Press.
Hermer, L. and Spelke, E. 1994, A geometric process for spatial reorientation in young children, *Nature* 370: 57–9.
Herrmann, T. 1990, Vor, hinter, rechts und links: Das 6H-Modell, *Zeitschrift für Literatur und Linguistik* 78: 117–40.
Herskovits, A. 1986, *Language and spatial cognition: An interdisciplinary study of the prepositions in English*, Studies in natural language processing, Cambridge: Cambridge University Press.
Hertz, R. 1960 [1909], La prééminence de la main droite: Etude sur la polarité religieuse, in R. Needham and C. Needham (eds.), *'Death' and 'the right hand'*, pp. 89–113. London: Cohen and West.
Hill, C. 1982, Up/down, front/back, left/right: A contrastive study of Hausa and English, in J. Weissenborn and W. Klein (eds.), *Here and there: Cross-linguistic studies on deixis and demonstration*, pp. 11–42. Amsterdam: Benjamins.
Hill, D. 1994, Spatial configurations and evidential propositions. Working Paper No. 25, Cognitive Anthropology Research Group, Max Planck Institute, Nijmegen.
    1997, Finding your way in Longgu: geographical reference in a Solomons Islands language, in G. Senft (ed.), *Referring to space: Studies in Austronesian and Papuan languages*, pp. 101–26. Oxford: Clarendon Press.
Hockett, C.F. 1960, The origin of speech, *Scientific American* 203: 89–96.
Howard, I.P. 1987, Spatial coordination of the senses, in R.L. Gregory (ed.), *The Oxford companion to the mind*, pp. 727–32. Oxford: Oxford University Press.
Hughes, H.C. 1999, *Sensory exotica: A world beyond human experience*, Cambridge, MA: MIT Press.
Hunn, E. 1996, Columbia Plateau Indian place names: What can they teach us? *Journal of Linguistic Anthropology* 6(1): 3–26.
Hutchins, E. 1995, *Cognition in the wild*, Cambridge, MA: MIT Press.
Huttenlocher, J. 1968, Constructing spatial images: A strategy in reasoning, *Psychological Review* 75: 550–60.
Jackendoff, R. 1983, *Semantics and cognition*, Cambridge, MA: MIT Press.
    1991, Parts and boundaries, *Cognition* 41: 9–45.
    1992, *Languages of the mind: Essays on mental representation*, Cambridge, MA: MIT Press.
    1996, The architecture of the linguistic-spatial interface, in P. Bloom, M. Peterson, L. Nadel and M. Garrett (eds.), *Language and space*, pp. 1–30. Cambridge, MA: MIT Press.

Jacobson, S.A. 1984, Semantics and morphology of demonstratives in Central Yup'ik Eskimo, *Etudes/Inuit/Studies* 8: 185–92.

Jammer, M. 1954, *Concepts of space: The history of theories of space in physics*, Cambridge, MA: Harvard University Press.

Jarvella, R. and Klein, W. (eds.) 1982, *Speech, place and action: Studies in deixis and related topics*, New York: Wiley.

Jeannerod, M. 1997, *The cognitive neuroscience of action*, Oxford: Blackwell.

Johnson-Laird, P.N. 1983, *Mental models: Towards a cognitive science of language, inference, and consciousness*, Cambridge: Cambridge University Press.

    1996, Space to think, in P. Bloom, M. Peterson, L. Nadel and M. Garrett (eds.), *Language and space*, pp. 437–62. Cambridge, MA: MIT Press.

Johnston, J.R. and Slobin, D. 1979, The development of locative expressions in English, Italian, Serbo-Croatian and Turkish, *Journal of Child Language* 6: 529–45.

Just, M. and Carpenter, P. 1985, Cognitive coordinate systems: Accounts of mental rotation and individual differences in spatial ability, *Psychological Review* 92(2): 137–72.

Kahr, J. 1975, Adpositions and locationals: typology and diachronic development, *Working Papers on Language Universals* 19: 21–54. Stanford University.

Kant, E. 1991 [1768], Von dem ersten Grunde des Unterschiedes der Gegenden im Raume. [Translated as: 'On the first ground of the distinction of regions in space'.] In J. van Cleve and R.E. Frederick (eds.), *The philosophy of right and left: Incongruent counterparts and the nature of space*, pp. 27–34. Dordrecht: Kluwer.

Kari, J. 1989, Some principles of Alaskan Athabaskan toponymic knowledge, in M.R. Key and H. Hoenigswald (eds.), *General and Amerindian ethnolinguistics*, pp. 129–50. Berlin: Mouton.

Karmiloff-Smith, A. 1992, *Beyond modularity: A developmental perspective on cognitive science*, Cambridge, MA: MIT Press.

Kay, P. and Kempton, W. 1984, What is the Sapir-Whorf hypothesis? *American Anthropologist* 86: 65–79.

Kay, P. and Maffi, L. 1999, Color appearance and the emergence and evolution of basic color lexicons, *American Anthropologist* 101(4): 743–60.

Kempson, R. 1977, *Semantic theory*, Cambridge: Cambridge University Press.

Kendon, A. 1995, Gestures as illocutionary and discourse structure markers in Southern Italian conversation, *Journal of Pragmatics* 23: 247–79.

    2000, Language and gesture: Unity or duality?, in D. McNeill (ed.), *Language and gesture: Window into thought and action*, pp. 47–63. Cambridge: Cambridge University Press.

Kendon, A. and Versante, L. in press, Pointing by hand, in S. Kita (ed.), *Pointing: Where language, culture and cognition meet*, pp. 109–37. Mahwah, NJ: Lawrence Erlbaum.

Kenesei, I., Vago, R.M. and Fenyvesi, A. 1997, *Hungarian*, London: Routledge.

Kita, S. 1993, Language and thought interface: A study of spontaneous gestures and Japanese mimetics. Unpublished PhD dissertation, University of Chicago.

1998, Expressing a turn at an invisible location in route direction, in E. Hess-Lüttich, J. Müller and A. van Zoest (eds.), *Signs and space; Raum und Zeichen*, pp. 160–72. Tübingen: Gunter Narr.

in press a, Interplay of gaze, hand, torso orientation and language in pointing, in Kita in press b, pp. 307–28.

Kita, S. (ed.) in press b, *Pointing: Where language, culture and cognition meet*, Mahwah, NJ: Lawrence Erlbaum.

Kita, S., Danziger, E. and Stolz, C. 2001, Cultural specificity of spatial schemas, as manifested in spontaneous gestures, in M. Gattis (ed.), *Spatial schemas and abstract thought*, pp. 115–46. Cambridge, MA: MIT Press.

Klatsky, R. and Lederman, S. 1993, Spatial and non-spatial avenues to object recognition by the human haptic system, in N. Eilan, R. McCarthy and B. Brewer (eds.), *Spatial representation*, pp. 191–205. Oxford: Blackwell.

Kolb, B. and Whishaw, I. 1990, *Fundamentals of human neuropsychology*, New York: Freeman.

Kölver, U. 1984, Local prepositions and serial verb constructions in Thai, *Arbeiten des Kölner universalien Projekts* 56.

Kornfilt, J. 1997, *Turkish*, 'Croom Helm Descriptive Grammars', London: Routledge.

Kosslyn, S.M. 1980, *Image and mind*, Cambridge, MA: Harvard University Press.

Krauss, R.M., Morrel-Samuels, P. and Colasante, C. 1991, Do conversational hand gestures communicate? *Journal of Personality and Social Psychology* 61(5): 743–54.

Kuhl, P. 1991, Perception, cognition and the ontogenetic and phylogenetic emergence of human speech, in S.E. Brauth, W.S. Hall and R.J. Dooling (eds.), *Plasticity of development*, pp. 73–106. Cambridge, MA: MIT Press.

Lahiri, T.K. 1965, Tracking techniques of Australian Aborigines. MS, Australian Institute for Aboriginal Studies, Canberra.

Landau, B. and Gleitman, L. 1985, *Language and experience: Evidence from the blind child*, Cambridge, MA: Harvard University Press.

Landau, B. and Jackendoff, R. 1993, 'What' and 'where' in spatial language and spatial cognition, *Behavioural and Brain Sciences* 16: 217–38.

Landau, B., Spelke, E. and Gleitman, L. 1984, Spatial knowledge in a young blind child, *Cognition* 16(3): 225–60.

Lang, E. 1989, The semantics of dimensional designation of spatial objects, in M. Bierwisch and E. Lang (eds.), *Dimensional adjectives: Grammatical structure and conceptual interpretation*, pp. 263–417. Berlin: Springer.

1995, Basic dimension terms: A first look at universal features and typological variation. Fachbereich Allgemeine Sprachwissenschaft Working paper No. 1, Berlin.

Langacker, R.W. 1987, *Foundations of cognitive grammar*, Vol. I: *Theoretical perspectives*, Stanford, CA: Stanford University Press.

1991, *Foundations of cognitive grammar*, Vol. II: *Descriptive application*, Stanford, CA: Stanford University Press.

Langhorne, M.C. 1948, The effects of maze rotation on learning, *Journal of General Psychology* 38: 191–205.

Laughlin, R. 1975, *The great Tzotzil dictionary of San Lorenzo Zinacantán*, Washington, DC: Smithsonian.

Laughren, M. 1978, Directional terminology in Warlpiri, in Th. Le and M. McCausland (eds.), *Working papers in language and linguistics*, 8: 1–16. Launceston: Tasmanian College of Advanced Education.

Lee, D.N. and Thompson, J. 1982, Vision in action: The control of locomotion, in D. Ingle, M.A. Goodale and R.J.W. Mansfield (eds.), *Analysis of visual behavior*, pp. 411–36. Cambridge, MA: MIT Press.

Leech, G. 1969, *Towards a semantic description of English*, London: Longmans.

Leer, J. 1989, Directional systems in Athabaskan and Na-Dene, in E. Cook and K.D. Rice (eds.), *Trends in linguistics*, Vol. 15, pp. 575–622. Berlin: Mouton.

León, L. de 1991, Space games in Tzotzil: Creating a context for spatial reference. Working Paper No. 4, Cognitive Anthropology Research Group, Max Planck Institute, Nijmegen.

1993, Shape, geometry and location: The case of Tzotzil body part terms, in K. Beals *et al.* (eds.), *CLS 29: Papers from the parasession on conceptual representations*, pp. 77–90. Chicago: The University of Chicago Press.

1994, Exploration in the acquisition of location and trajectory in Tzotzil, in J.B. Haviland and S.C. Levinson (eds.), *Space in Mayan Languages*, Special issue of *Linguistics* 32(4/5): 857–84.

1996, The development of geocentric location in young speakers of Guugu Yimithirr. Working Paper No. 33, Cognitive Anthropology Research Group, Max Planck Institute, Nijmegen.

Levelt, W.J.M. 1984, Some perceptual limitations on talking about space, in A.J. van Doorn, W.A. van der Grind and J.J. Koenderink (eds.), *Limits in perception*, pp. 323–58. Utrecht: VNU Science Press.

1989, *Speaking: From intention to articulation*, Cambridge, MA: MIT Press.

1996, Perspective taking and ellipsis in spatial descriptions, in P. Bloom, M. Peterson, L. Nadel and M. Garrett (eds.), *Language and space*, pp. 77–108. Cambridge, MA: MIT Press.

Levine, S. and Carey, S. 1982, Up front: The acquisition of a concept and a word, *Journal of Child Language* 9: 645–57.

Levinson, S.C. 1983, *Pragmatics*, Cambridge: Cambridge University Press.

1984/1986, The semantics/pragmatics/kinesics of space in Guugu Yimidhirr. Talk given to the International Conference of the Sociology of Language, Plymouth, June 1984, and to the University of Bamberg psychology department, 1986.

1987a, Minimization and conversational inference, in M. Pappi and J. Verschueren (eds.), *The pragmatic perspective*, pp. 61–129. Amsterdam: Benjamins.

1987b, Pragmatics and the grammar of anaphora, *Journal of Linguistics* 23: 379–434.

1992a, Primer for the field investigation of spatial description and conception, *Pragmatics* 2(1): 5–47.

1992b, Language and cognition: The cognitive consequences of spatial descriptions in Guugu Yimithirr. Working Paper No. 13, Cognitive Anthropology Research Group, Max Planck Institute for Psycholinguistics, Nijmegen.

1994, Vision, shape and linguistic description: Tzeltal body-part terminology and object description, in J.B. Haviland and S.C. Levinson (eds.), *Space in Mayan Languages*, Special issue of *Linguistics* 32(4): 791–855.

1996a, Language and space, *Annual Review of Anthropology* 25: 353–82.

1996b, Frames of reference and Molyneux's question: Cross-linguistic evidence, in P. Bloom, M. Peterson, L. Nadel and M. Garrett (eds.), *Language and space*, pp. 109–69. Cambridge, MA: MIT Press.

1996c, The body in space: Cultural differences in the use of body-schema for spatial thinking and gesture. Working Paper No. 39, Cognitive Anthropology Research Group, Max Planck Institute, Nijmegen.

1996d, The role of language in everyday human navigation. Working Paper No. 38, Cognitive Anthropology Research Group, Max Planck Institute for Psycholinguistics, Nijmegen.

1997a, Language and cognition: The cognitive consequences of spatial description in Guugu Yimithirr, *Journal of Linguistic Anthropology* 7(1): 98–131.

1997b, From outer to inner space: Linguistic categories and non-linguistic thinking, in E. Pederson and J. Nuyts (eds.), *Language and conceptualization*, pp. 13–45. Cambridge: Cambridge University Press.

1999, H.P. Grice on location on Rossel Island, *Proceedings of the Berkeley Linguistics Society* 25: 210–24.

2000a, *Presumptive meanings*, Cambridge, MA: MIT Press.

2000b, Yélî Dnye and the theory of basic color terms, *Journal of Linguistic Anthropology* 10(1): 1–53.

2000c, Language as nature and language as art, in R. Hide, J. Mittelstrass and W. Singer (eds.), *Changing concepts of nature at the turn of the millennium*, pp. 257–87. Vatican City: Pontifical Academy of Science.

2001, Covariation between language and cognition, and its implications for language learning, in M. Bowerman and S. Levinson (eds.), *Language acquisition and conceptual development*, pp. 566–88. Cambridge: Cambridge University Press.

in press, The body in space: Cultural differences in the use of body-schema for spatial thinking and gesture, in G. Lewis and F. Sigaut (eds.), *Culture and the body*, Oxford: Oxford University Press.

Levinson, S.C. and Brown, P. 1994, Immanuel Kant among the Tenejapans: Anthropology as empirical philosophy, *Ethos* 22(1): 3–41.

Levinson, S.C. and Wilkins, D.P. in preparation, *Grammars of space*.

Levinson, S.C., Kita, S., Haun, D. and Rasch, B. 2002, Returning the tables: Language affects spatial reasoning, *Cognition* 84: 155–88.

Levy, P. 1994, La base verbal en Totonaco, in Carolyn J. MacKay and Veronica Vazquez (eds.), *Investigaciones linguisticas en mesoamerica*, Estudios sobre lenguas americanas 1, Mexico City: Seminario de Lenguas.

1999, From 'part' to 'shape': Incorporation in Totonac and the issue of classification by verbs, *International Journal of American Linguistics* 65(2): 127–75.

Lewis, D. 1972, *We, the navigators*, Canberra: ANU Press.

1976, Route finding by desert aborigines in Australia, *Journal of Navigation* 29: 21–38.

Li, P. and Gleitman, L. 1999, Language and spatial reasoning. MS, University of Pennsylvania.

2002, Turning the tables: Language and spatial reasoning, *Cognition* 83: 265–94.

Lucy, J. 1992a, *Language diversity and thought: A reformulation of the linguistic relativity hypothesis*, Cambridge: Cambridge University Press.

1992b, *Grammatical categories and cognition: A case study of the linguistic relativity hypothesis*, Cambridge: Cambridge University Press.

Lucy, J. and Gaskins, S. 2001, Grammatical categories and the development of classification preferences: a comparative approach, in M. Bowerman and S. Levinson (eds.), *Language acquisition and conceptual development*, pp. 257–83. Cambridge: Cambridge University Press.

Lyons, J. 1977, *Semantics*, Vols. I and II, Cambridge: Cambridge University Press.

1995, *Linguistic semantics: An introduction*, London and New York: Cambridge University Press.

MacDonald, J. 1998, *The arctic sky*, Toronto: Nunuavut Research Institute, Royal Ontario Museum.

MacLaury, R. 1989, Zapotec body-part locatives: Prototypes and metaphoric extensions, *International Journal of American Linguistics* 55(2): 119–54.

Maddieson, I. 1984, *Patterns of sounds*, Cambridge: Cambridge University Press.

Maguire, E., Gadian, D., Johnsrude, I., Good, C., Ashburner, J., Frackowiak, R. and Frith, C. 2000, Navigation-related structural change in the hippocampi of taxi drivers, *Proceedings of the National Academy of Sciences* 97(8): 4398–403.

Mallot, H.A. 1996, Action-perception learning: A scheme for learning cognitive maps from sequences of movements and views. Talk given at the 3rd Annual CBR Workshop on 'Mental Representations in Navigation'. Cambridge, MA: Cambridge Basic Research.

Marascuilo, L.A. and Serlin, R.C. 1988, *Statistical methods for the social and behavioral sciences*, New York: Freeman.

Marr, D. 1982, *Vision*, New York: Freeman.

McCarthy, R. 1993, Assembling routines and addressing representations: An alternative conceptualization of 'what' and 'where' in the human brain, in N. Eilan, R. McCarthy and B. Brewer (eds.), *Spatial representation: Problems in philosophy and psychology*, pp. 373–99. Oxford: Blackwell.

McCullough, K.-E. 1993, Spatial information and cohesion in the gesticulation of English and Chinese speakers. Paper presented to the American Psychological Society, Chicago.

McDonough, L., Choi, S. and Mandler, J. in press, Understanding spatial relations: Flexible infants, lexical adults. *Cognitive Psychology*.

McNaughton, B., Chen, L. and Markus, E. 1990, 'Dead reckoning', landmark learning and the sense of direction: A neurophysiological and computational hypothesis, *Journal of Cognitive Neuroscience* 3(2): 191–202.

McNeill, D. 1992, *Hand and mind: What gestures reveal about thought*, Chicago: The University of Chicago Press.

McNeill, D. (ed.) 2000, *Language and gesture: Window into thought and action*, Cambridge: Cambridge University Press.

McNeill, D. and Levy, E. 1982, Conceptual representations in language activity and gesture, in R. Jarvella and W. Klein (eds.), *Speech, place, and action*, pp. 271–95. Chichester: Wiley.

Meira, S. in preparation, Approaching space in Tiriyó grammar, in S.C. Levinson and D. Wilkins (in preparation), *Grammars of space*.

Meltzoff, A.N. 1993, Molyneux's babies: Cross-modal perception, imitation and the mind of the preverbal infant, in N. Eilan, R. McCarthy and B. Brewer (eds.), *Spatial representation*, pp. 219–35. Oxford: Blackwell.

Miller, G.A. 1956, The magical number seven, plus or minus two: Some limits on our capacity for processing information, *Psychological Review* 63(2): 81–97.

1982, Some problems in the theory of demonstrative reference, in R. Jarvella and W. Klein (eds.), *Speech, place and action*, pp. 61–72. New York: Wiley.

Miller, G.A. and Johnson-Laird, P.N. 1976, *Language and perception*, Cambridge, MA: Harvard University Press.

Mithun, M. 1999, *The languages of native North America*, Cambridge: Cambridge University Press.

Moar, I. and Bower, G. 1983, Inconsistency in spatial knowledge, *Memory & Cognition* 11(2): 107–13.

Moar, I. and Carleton, L.R. 1982, Memory for routes, *Quarterly Journal of Experimental Psychology* 34A: 381–94.

Morrel-Samuels, P. and Krauss, R. 1992, Word familiarity predicts temporal asychrony of hand gestures and speech, *Journal of Experimental Psychology: Learning, Memory and Cognition* 18(3): 615–22.

Müller, C. 1998, *Redebegleitende Gesten: Kulturgeschichte – Theorie Sprachvergleich*, Berlin: Arno Spitz Verlag.

Müller, M. and Wehner, R. 1994, The hidden spiral: Systematic search and path integration in desert ants, Cataglyphis fortis, *Journal of Comparative Physiology* A175: 525–30.

Munn, N. 1986, *Walbiri iconography*, Chicago: The University of Chicago Press.

Nash, D. 1993, Notes on way-finding in Australia's deserts by Warlpiri and their neighbours. Paper presented at the Conference on Spatial Representation, Max Planck Institute for Psycholinguistics, Nijmegen.

Needham, R. 1973, *Left and right*, Chicago: The University of Chicago Press.

Neumann, S. and Widlok, T. 1996, Rethinking some universals of spatial language using controlled comparison, in R. Dirven and M. Pütz (eds.), *The construal of space in language and thought*, pp. 345–72. Berlin: de Gruyter.

Norman, J. 1988, *Chinese*, Cambridge: Cambridge University Press.

Nunberg, G. 1978, The pragmatics of reference. PhD dissertation, University of New York.

O'Keefe, J. 1991, The hippocampal cognitive map and navigational strategies, in J. Paillard (ed.), *Brain and space*, pp. 273–95. Oxford: Oxford Science Publications.

1993, Kant and the sea-horse: An essay in the neurophilosophy of space, in N. Eilan, R. McCarthy and B. Brewer (eds.), *Spatial representation*, pp. 43–64. Oxford: Blackwell.

1996, The spatial preposition in English, Vector grammar, and the cognitive map theory, in P. Bloom, M. Peterson, L. Nadel and M. Garrett (eds.), *Language and space*, pp. 277–316. Cambridge, MA: MIT Press.

O'Keefe, J. and Nadel, L. 1978, *The hippocampus as a cognitive map*, Oxford: Clarendon Press.

Ozanne-Rivièrre, F. 1987, L'expression linguistique de l'espace: Quelques exemples oceaniens, *Cahiers du Lacito* 2: 129–55.

1997, Spatial reference in New Caledonian languages, in G. Senft (ed.), *Referring to space: Studies in Austronesian and Papuan languages*, pp. 83–100. Oxford: Clarendon Press.

Özyürek, A. and Kita, S. 1999, Expressing manner and path in English and Turkish: Differences in speech, gesture, and conceptualization, in M. Hahn and S.C. Stoness (eds.), *Proceedings of the twenty-first annual conference of the Cognitive Science Society*, pp. 507–12. Mahwah, NJ and London: Lawrence Erlbaum.

Paillard, J. (ed.) 1991, *Brain and space*, Oxford: Oxford Science Publications.

Pederson, E. 1993, Geographic and manipulable space in two Tamil linguistic systems, in A.U. Frank and I. Campari (eds.), *Spatial information theory*, pp. 294–311. Berlin: Springer.

1995, Language as context, language as means: Spatial cognition and habitual language use, *Cognitive Linguistics* 6(1): 33–62.

Pederson, E. and Roelofs, A. (eds.) 1995, *Max Planck Institute for Psycholinguistics annual report 1994*. Nijmegen: Max Planck Institute.

Pederson, E., Danziger, E., Wilkins, D., Levinson, S., Kita, S. and Senft, G. 1998, Semantic typology and spatial conceptualization, *Language* 74: 557–89.

Peterson, M., Nadel, L., Bloom, P. and Garrett, M. 1996, Space and language. In P. Bloom, M. Peterson, L. Nadel and M. Garrett (eds.), *Language and space*, pp. 553–77. Cambridge, MA: MIT Press.

Piaget, J. 1928, *Judgment and reasoning in the child*, London: Routledge.

Piaget, J. and Inhelder, B. 1956 [1948], *The child's conception of space*, London: Routledge and Kegan Paul.

Pick, H.L., Jr 1988, Perceptual aspects of spatial cognitive development, in J. Stiles-Davis, M. Kritchevsky and U. Bellugi (eds.), *Spatial cognition: Brain bases and development*, pp. 145–56. Hillsdale, NJ: Lawrence Erlbaum.

1993, Organization of spatial knowledge in children, in N. Eilan, R. McCarthy and B. Brewer (eds.), *Spatial representation*, pp. 31–42. Oxford: Blackwell.

Pinker, S. 1989, *Learnability and cognition: The acquisition of argument structure*, Cambridge, MA: Bradford/MIT Press.

1994, *The language instinct*, New York: Morrow.

Pinker, S. and Bloom, P. 1992, Natural language and natural selection, in J. H. Barkow, L. Cosmides and J. Tooby (eds.), *The adapted mind: Evolutionary psychology and the generation of culture*, pp. 451–94. New York: Oxford University Press.

Poincaré, H. 1946, *The foundations of science* (Trans. G.B. Halsted), Lancaster, PA: Science Press.

Potter, M. 1990, Remembering, in D.N. Osherson and E.S. Smith (eds.), *Thinking: An invitation to cognitive science*, Vol. III, pp. 3–32. Cambridge, MA: MIT Press.

Putnam, H. 1988, *Representation and reality*, Cambridge, MA: MIT Press.

Quirk, R., Greenbaum, S., Leech, G. and Svartvik, J. 1991, *A comprehensive grammar of the English language* (rev. edn), London: Longman.

Reichenbach, H. 1958, *The philosophy of space and time*, New York: Dover.

Renzi, E. de 1982, *Disorders of space exploration and cognition*, New York: Wiley.

Rock, I. 1990, The frame of reference, in I. Rock (ed.), *The legacy of Soloman Asch*, pp. 243–68. Hillsdale, NJ: Lawrence Erlbaum.

1992, Comment on Asch and Witkin's 'Studies in space orientation II', *Journal of Experimental Psychology: General* 121(4): 404–6.

Rock, I., Wheeler, D. and Tudor, L. 1989, Can we imagine how objects look from other viewpoints? *Cognitive Psychology* 21: 185–210.

Ruiter, J.P.A. de and Wilkins, D.P. 1998, The synchronization of gesture and speech in Dutch and Arrernte, in S. Santi, I. Guaïtella, C. Cavé and G. Konopczynski (eds.), *Oralité et gestualité: Communication multimodale, interaction*, pp. 603–7. Paris: L'Harmattan.

Save, E., Poucet, B. and Thinus-Blanc, C. 1998, Landmark use and the cognitive map in the rat, in S. Healy (ed.), *Spatial representation in animals*, pp. 119–32. Oxford: Oxford University Press.

Schegloff, E. 1984, On some gestures' relation to speech, in J. Atkinson and J. Heritage (eds.), *Structures of social action: Studies in conversation analysis*, pp. 266–96. Cambridge: Cambridge University Press.

Schöne, H. 1984, *Spatial orientation*, Princeton, NJ: Princeton University Press.

Schultze-Berndt, E. 2000, *Simple and complex verbs in Jaminjung* (Max Planck Institute Series, Doctoral Dissertations in Psycholinguistics), Nijmegen: Max Planck Institute.

in preparation, Sketch of Jaminjung grammar of space, in S.C. Levinson and D. Wilkins (in preparation), *Grammars of space*.

Searle, J. 1969, *Speech acts: An essay in the philosophy of language*, Cambridge: Cambridge University Press.

Senft, G. 1994a, Spatial reference in Kilivila: The Tinkertoy matching games – A case study, *Language and Linguistics in Melanesia* 25: 98–9.

1994b, Ein Vorschlag, wie man standardisiert Daten zum Thema 'Sprache, Kognition und Konzepte des Raumes' in verschiedenen Kulturen erheben kann, *Linguistische Berichte* 154: 413–29.

1995, Sprache, Kognition und Konzepte des Raumes in verschiedenen Kulturen, *Kognitionswissenschaft* 4: 166–70.

2001, Frames of spatial reference in Kilivila, *Studies in Language* 25(3): 521–55.

Senft, G. (ed.) 1997, *Referring to space: Studies in Austronesian and Papuan languages*, Oxford: Clarendon Press.

Senft, G. and Wilkins, D.P. 1994, A man, a tree, and forget about the pigs: Space games, spatial reference and an attempt to identify functional equivalents across languages. Talk given at the 19th LAUD Conference, Duisburg, March.

Senghas, A. 2000, Differences between first and second cohort signers in communicating orientation. Poster session at the 7th International Conference on Theoretical Issues in Sign Language Research, Amsterdam, 23–7 July.

Shephard, R. and Metzler, J. 1971, Mental rotation of three-dimensional objects, *Science* 171: 701–3.

Sherry, D. and Healy, S. 1998, Neural mechanisms of spatial representation, in S. Healy (ed.), *Spatial representation in animals*, pp. 133–58. Oxford: Oxford University Press.

Slobin, D.I. 1996, From 'thought and language' to 'thinking for speaking', in J. Gumperz and S. Levinson (eds.), *Rethinking linguistic relativity*, pp. 70–96. Cambridge: Cambridge University Press.

2001, Form-function relations: How do children find out what they are?, in M. Bowerman and S. Levinson (eds.), *Language acquisition and conceptual development*, pp. 406–49. Cambridge: Cambridge University Press.

Slobin, D.I. (ed.) 1985, *The crosslinguistic study of language acquisition*, Vol. II: *The data*, Hillsdale, NJ: Lawrence Erlbaum.

Sorabji, R. 1988, *Matter, space and motion: Theories in antiquity and their sequel*, London: Duckworth.

Spelke, E. and Tsivkin, S. 2001, Initial knowledge and conceptual change: Space and number, in M. Bowerman and S.C. Levinson (eds.), *Language acquisition and conceptual development*, pp. 70–97. Cambridge: Cambridge University Press.

Sperber, D. 1996, *Explaining culture: A naturalistic approach*, Oxford: Blackwell.

Squire, L.R. 1992, Declarative and nondeclarative memory – multiple brain systems supporting learning and memory, *Journal of Cognitive Neuroscience* 4(3): 232–43.

Staden, M. van 2000, Tidore: a linguistic description of a language of the North Moluccas. Unpublished PhD thesis, University of Leiden.

Stassen, L. 1997, *Intransitive predication* (Oxford studies in typology and linguistic theory), Oxford: Clarendon Press.

Stein, J.F. 1992, The representation of egocentric space in the posterior parietal cortex, *Behavioral and Brain Sciences* 15(4): 691–700.

Steinhauer, H. 1991, Demonstratives in the Blagar language of Dolap, in T. Dutton (ed.), *Papers in papuan linguistics*, Vol. I, pp. 177–221. Canberra: Pacific Linguistics A73.

Stephens, D. 1983, Hemispheric language dominance and gesture hand preference. Unpublished PhD dissertation, University of Chicago.

Stolz, C. 1996, Spatial dimensions and orientation of objects in Yucatec Maya. PhD dissertation, University of Bielefeld.

Stross, B. 1991, Classic Maya directional glyphs, *Journal of Linguistic Anthropology* 1(1): 97–114.

Stutterheim, C. von and Carroll, M. 1993, Raumkonzepte in Produktionsprozessen, *Kognitionswissenschaft* 3: 1–13.

Sutton, P. 1998, Aboriginal maps and plans, in D. Woodward and G.M. Lewis (eds.), *Cartography in the traditional African, American, Arctic, Australian and Pacific societies*, Vol. II(3), pp. 387–418. Chicago: The University of Chicago Press.

Svorou, S. 1994, *The grammar of space*, Amsterdam: Benjamins.

Takano, Y. 1989, Perception of rotated forms: A theory of information types, *Cognitive Psychology* 21: 1–59.

Talmy, L. 1983, How language structures space, in H. Pick and L. Acredolo (eds.), *Spatial orientation: Theory, research and application*, pp. 225–82. New York: Plenum Press.

1985, Lexicalization patterns: Semantic structure in lexical forms, in T. Shopen (ed.), *Language typology and syntactic description*, Vol. III: *Grammatical categories and the lexicon*, pp. 56–149. Cambridge: Cambridge University Press.

1988, Force dynamics in language and cognition, *Cognitive Science* 12: 49–100.

2000, *Toward a cognitive semantics*, Vols. I and II, Cambridge, MA: MIT Press.

Tarr, M. and Pinker, S. 1989, Mental rotation and orientation-dependence in shape recognition, *Cognitive Psychology* 21: 233–82.

Tindale, N. 1974, *Aboriginal tribes of Australia: Their terrain, environmental controls, distributions, limits and proper names*, Berkeley, CA: University of California Press.

Tinkelpaugh, O.L. 1928, An experimental study of representative factors in monkeys, *Journal of Comparative Psychology* 8: 197–236.

Tolman, E.C. 1948, Cognitive maps in rats and men, *The Psychological Review* 55(4): 109–45.

Tomasello, M. and Call, J. 1997, *Primate cognition*, New York: Oxford University Press.

Tooby, J. and Cosmides, L. 1992, The psychological foundations of culture, in J.H. Barkow, L. Cosmides and J. Tooby (eds.), *The adapted mind*, pp. 19–136. Oxford: Oxford University Press.

Tversky, B. 1981, Distortions in memory for maps, *Cognitive Psychology* 13: 407–33.
  1991, Spatial mental models, in G.H. Bower (ed.), *The psychology of learning and motivation: Advances in research and theory*, Vol. XXVII, pp. 109–45. New York: Academic Press.
  1996, Language and spatial cognition, *International Journal of Psychology* 31(3–4): 3010.
  1998, Three dimensions of spatial cognition, in M.A. Conway, S.E. Gathercole and C. Cornoldi (eds.), *Theories of memory*, pp. 259–76. Hove: Psychology Press.
Tversky, B. and Taylor, H.A. 1998, Acquiring spatial and temporal knowledge from language, in M.J. Egenhofer and R.G. Golledge (eds.), *Spatial and temporal reasoning in geographic information systems*, pp. 155–66. Oxford: Oxford University Press.
Tye, M. 1991, *The imagery debate: Representation and mind*, Cambridge, MA: MIT Press.
Ulltan, R. 1978, Some general characteristics of interrogative systems, in J. Greenberg (ed.), *Universals of human language*, Vol. IV, pp. 211–48. Stanford, CA: Stanford University Press.
Ungerer, F. and Schmid, H. 1996, *An introduction to cognitive linguistics*, London: Longman.
Ungerleider, L.G. and Mishkin, M. 1982, Two cortical visual systems, in D.J. Ingle, M.A. Goodale and R.J.W. Mansfield (eds.), *Analysis of visual behavior*, pp. 549–86. Cambridge, MA: MIT Press.
Van Cleve, J. and Frederick, R. 1991, *The philosophy of right and left*, Dordrecht: Kluwer.
Vandeloise, C. 1991, *Spatial prepositions: A case study from French*, Chicago: University of Chicago Press.
Vygotsky, L.S. 1986, *Thought and language* (rev. edn), Cambridge, MA: MIT Press.
Wassmann, J. and Dasen, P. 1998, Balinese spatial orientation: Some empirical evidence of moderate linguistic relativity, *Journal of the Royal Anthropological Institute (inc. MAN)* 4: 689–711.
Waterman, T.H. 1989, *Animal navigation*, Scientific American Library. Houndmills, UK: Palgrave MacMillan.
Wehner, R. 1983, Celestial and terrestrial navigation: Human strategies – insect strategies, in F. Huber and H. Markl (eds.), *Neuroethology and behavioral physiology*, pp. 366–81. Berlin: Springer.
Weissenborn, J. 1984, La genèse de la référence spatiale en langue maternelle et en langue seconde: Similarités et différences, in G. Extra and M. Mittner (eds.), *Studies in second language acquisition by adult immigrants, Proceedings of the ESF/AILA symposium*, pp. 262–72. Tilburg: Tilburg University.
Weissenborn, J. and Klein, W. (eds.) 1982, *Here and there: Cross-linguistic studies on deixis and demonstration*, Amsterdam: Benjamins.
Weissenborn, J. and Stralka, R. 1984, Das Verstehen von Missverständnissen: Eine ontogenetische Studie, *Zeitschrift für Literaturwissenschaft und Linguistik*, pp. 113–34.

Werker, J. and Tees, R. 1984, Cross language speech perception: Evidence for perceptual reorganization in the first year of life, *Infant Behavior and Development* 7: 49–63.

Whorf, B.L. 1956, *Language, thought and reality*, Cambridge, MA: MIT Press.

Widlok, T. 1994, The social relationships of changing Hai//om hunter/gatherers in Northern Namibia, 1990–1994. PhD dissertation, University of London.

1996, Topographical gossip and the indexicality of Hai//om environmental knowledge. Working Paper No. 37, Cognitive Anthropology Research Group, Max Planck Institute, Nijmegen.

1997, Orientation in the wild: the shared cognition of Hai//om Bushpeople, *Journal of the Royal Anthropological Institute* 3: 317–32.

1999, *Living in Mangetti*, Oxford: Oxford University Press.

Wilkins, D.P. 1989, Mparntwe Arrente (Aranda): Studies in the structure and semantics of grammar. PhD dissertation, The Australian National University, Canberra, Australia.

1997, Alternative representations of space: Arrernte narratives in sand and sign, in M. Biemans and J. v.d. Weijer (eds.), *Proceedings of the CLS Opening Academic Year '97-'98*, pp. 133–62. Nijmegen: Centre for Language Studies.

1999, Spatial deixis in Arrernte speech and gesture: On the analysis of a species of composite signal as used by a Central Australian Aboriginal group, in E. Andre, M. Poesio and H. Riser (eds.), *Proceedings of the Workshop on Deixis, Demonstration and Deictic Belief in Multimedia Contexts*, pp. 30–42. Utrecht: ESSLLI XI/FOLLI.

in press, Why pointing with the index finger is not a universal, in S. Kita (ed.), *Pointing: Where language, culture and cognition meet*, pp. 171–215. Mahwah, NJ: Lawrence Erlbaum.

Woodward, D. 1987, Medieval *Mappaemundi*, in J.B.Harley and D. Woodward (eds.), *The history of cartography*, Vol. I, pp. 286–370. Chicago: The University of Chicago Press.

Yates, F.A. 1966, *The art of memory*, Chicago: The University of Chicago Press.

Zee, E. van der 1996, Spatial knowledge and spatial language: A theoretical and empirical investigation (Ruimtelijke kennis en ruimtelijk taalgebruik: Een empirisch onderzoek). PhD dissertation, University of Utrecht.

Language index

Author index

MacLaury, R. 78
Maddieson, I. 317, 319
Maffi, L. 101
Maguire, E. 10, 277, 322
Mallot, H. 271, 274, 278
Marascuilo, L.A. 186
Markus, E. 273, 328
Marr, D. 29, 41, 55, 77, 155, 257, 347
McCarthy, R. 10, 333
McCullough, K.-E. 343, 346
McDonough, L. 319
McGregor, W. xxi
McIvor, T. 338
McNaughton, B. 273, 328, 346
McNeill, D. iii, xxii, 245, 251, 252, 253, 254, 256, 260, 262, 285, 286, 344, 345, 346
Meira, S. xxi, 73
Meltzoff, A.N. 56
Merkel, F.W. 221
Metzler, J. 17, 30, 329
Miller, G.A. xix, 10, 11, 12, 14, 27, 28, 31, 34, 35, 46, 72, 74, 76, 77, 84, 85, 294, 298, 299, 328, 329, 331
Mishkin, M. 10, 15, 115
Mithun, M. 63, 73, 107, 109, 317
Moar, I. 277
Molyneux, W. ix, 56, 57, 59, 333
Morrel-Samuels, P. 262, 263
Müller, C. 219, 266
Munn, N. 347

Nadel, L. 10, 12, 27, 28, 276, 328
Nagy, L. xxi, xxii, 339
Nash, D. xxi, 92, 217, 233, 336
Needham, R. 13
Neumann, S. xxi, 339, 340, 341
Newton, I. 6, 7, 8, 26, 27, 65
Norman, J. 101, 104
Nunberg, G. 267
Nuyts, J. iii

O'Keefe, J. 10, 12, 17, 27, 28, 47, 85, 273, 276, 328, 331, 341
Ozanne-Rivièrre, F. 90
Özyürek, A. xxi, 306

Paillard, J. 28, 327, 328
Pears, J. 24, 327, 328

Pederson, E. iii, xxi, xxii, 95, 150, 163, 171, 180, 181, 189, 190, 194, 310, 330, 339
Pellegrino, J. 277
Peterson, M. 347
Piaget, J. 11, 12, 29, 71, 83, 84, 94, 143, 308, 309, 323, 334
Pick, H.L. 10, 29, 31, 307, 328
Pinker, S. 14, 30, 296, 316, 317, 318, 329, 347
Poincaré, H. 6, 57
Potter, M. 338
Putnam, H. 298

Quirk, R. 335

Rasch, B. xxi, 157, 198, 199, 200, 341
Raven, P. 146
Reichenbach, H. 17
Renzi, E. de 1
Richerson, P.J. 319
Rock, I. 24, 327, 329
Roelofs, A. 57
Ruggles, A. 277
Ruiter, J.P. de 245, 251, 254, 255, 345

Sapir, E. 18
Save, E. 276
Schegloff, E. 249, 250, 270
Schmid, H. 13
Schmitt, B. xxi, xxii, 163, 339
Schöne, H. 216, 342
Schultze-Berndt, E. xxi, 68, 336
Searle, J. 292
Senft, G. iii, xxi, xxii, xxiii, 171, 339, 340
Senghas, A. xxi, 94
Serlin, R.C. 186
Shephard, R. 17, 30, 329
Sherry, D. 276
Simpson, J. xxi
Sinha, C. xxi
Sjoerdsma, E. xxiii
Slobin, D. xxii, 31, 72, 94, 133, 134, 145, 168, 303, 305, 306, 307, 308, 331, 336
Sonnenschein, A. xxi
Sorabji, R. 6, 7, 24
Spallanzani, L. 221
Spelke, E. 217, 272, 306, 324, 338
Sperber, D. 291, 323
Spetch, M. 223

Subject index